ANTIQUE GARDEN ORNAMENT

300 years of creativity: Artists, manufacturers & materials

John PS Davis

Antique Collectors' Club

© 1991 Antique Collectors' Club
World copyright reserved
First published 1991
Reprinted 1998

ISBN 1 85149 098 1

British Library Cataloguing-in-Publication Data
A catalogue record for this book is available from the British Library

Printed and published in England
on Consort Royal Era Satin from Donside Mill, Aberdeen, Scotland
by the Antique Collectors' Club Ltd., 5 Church Street, Woodbridge, Suffolk IP12 1DS

*Frontispiece. Life-size Triton fountain figure in Roche Abbey stone, by
Caius Gabriel Cibber, Chatsworth. (See Colour Plate 36 and page 125.)
Trustees of the Chatsworth Settlement*

THE ANTIQUE COLLECTORS' CLUB

The Antique Collectors' Club was formed in 1966 and quickly grew to a five figure membership spread throughout the world. It publishes the only independently run monthly antiques magazine, *Antique Collecting*, which caters for those collectors who are interested in widening their knowledge of antiques, both by greater awareness of quality and by discussion of the factors which influence the price that is likely to be asked. The Antique Collectors' Club pioneered the provision of information on prices for collectors and the magazine still leads in the provision of detailed articles on a variety of subjects.

It was in response to the enormous demand for information on 'what to pay' that the price guide series was introduced in 1968 with the first edition of *The Price Guide to Antique Furniture* (completely revised 1978 and 1989), a book which broke new ground by illustrating the more common types of antique furniture, the sort that collectors could buy in shops and at auctions rather than the rare museum pieces which had previously been used (and still to a large extent are used) to make up the limited amount of illustrations in books published by commercial publishers. Many other price guides have followed, all copiously illustrated, and greatly appreciated by collectors for the valuable information they contain, quite apart from prices. The Price Guide Series heralded the publication of many standard works of reference on art and antiques. *The Dictionary of British Art* (now in six volumes), *The Pictorial Dictionary of British 19th Century Furniture Design, Oak Furniture* and *Early English Clocks* were followed by many deeply researched reference works such as *The Directory of Gold and Silversmiths,* providing new information. Many of these books are now accepted as the standard work of reference on their subject.

The Antique Collectors' Club has widened its list to include books on gardens and architecture. All the Club's publications are available through bookshops world wide and a full catalogue of all these titles is available free of charge from the addresses below.

Club membership, open to all collectors, costs little. Members receive free of charge *Antique Collecting*, the Club's magazine (published ten times a year), which contains well-illustrated articles dealing with the practical aspects of collecting not normally dealt with by magazines. Prices, features of value, investment potential, fakes and forgeries are all given prominence in the magazine.

Among other facilities available to members are private buying and selling facilities and the opportunity to meet other collectors at their local antique collectors' clubs. There are over eighty in Britain and more than a dozen overseas. Members may also buy the Club's publications at special pre-publication prices.

As its motto implies, the Club is an organisation designed to help collectors get the most out of their hobby: it is informal and friendly and gives enormous enjoyment to all concerned.

For Collectors — By Collectors — About Collecting

ANTIQUE COLLECTORS' CLUB
5 Church Street, Woodbridge, Suffolk IP12 1DS, UK
Tel: 01394 385501 Fax: 01394 384434
—— or ——
Market Street Industrial Park, Wappingers' Falls, NY 12590, USA
Tel: 914 297 0003 Fax: 914 297 0068

For Denise

CONTENTS

COLOUR PLATES

ACKNOWLEDGEMENTS

I am enormously indebted to everyone who has helped me research, prepare, and write this, my first book.

First and foremost I must acknowledge the encouragement and help provided by my friends, and family, and in particular everyone at Fairbridge Road who pushed, prompted and when necessary plied me with nourishment to ensure that the completed manuscript did eventually reach the publisher. These include Richard and Charlie Wells, Dave Pead and, of course, my girl friend Denise.

To the many librarians and archivists all over the country who have responded to my numerous letters and prepared research prior to my visits, I am deeply indebted. I particularly wish to thank Miss Joan Sinar and Mr Andrew George at the Derbyshire Record Office; Laura Baseden and K H Rogers at the Wiltshire Record Office; J F J Colett White at the Bedfordshire Record Office; and F I Dunn at the Cheshire Record Office. Furthermore, without the help and assistance provided by the staff of the Victoria and Albert Museum Library, the British Architectural Library, the British Library and the Courtauld Institute, this book would never have been completed.

Several people and their publications have provided much help on specific subjects, and without their work this book would have been much shallower. They are my friend Pamela D Kingsbury, who was immensely helpful on the gardens and house created by Lord Burlington at Chiswick; Alison Kelly, the reigning expert on the Coade Manufactory, who kindly edited my draft; K J Birch, who advised on Bath stone; Sally Festing, the leading expert on the products of the Pulham Manufactory; John Kenworthy-Browne, who gave overall help on sculpture, particularly on Rysbrack's Seven Saxon Deities; John McKee, who gave enormous help on the Bagatelle bronze vases; John Powell, who advised on the Coalbrookdale Company; John F Smith, who helped with the history of Blashfield's Terracotta Manufactory; and Mark Higginson of the Derby Industrial Museum, who generously supplied information on the castings of Andrew Handyside's Britannia Foundry.

There are several publications that I have always had close to hand in preparing this book, and it would be improper for me not to mention them, for they have been the source of much information. These are: the late Rupert Gunnis' *Dictionary of British Sculptors 1660-1851,* still the foremost single reference book on British sculpture of the period; Francis Haskell and Nicholas Penny's outstanding book, *Taste and the Antique: The Lure of Classical Sculpture*; François Souchal's scholarly volumes, *French Sculptors of the 17th and 18th Centuries*; and Terry Friedman and Timothy Clifford's catalogue for the exhibition on John Cheere, *The Man at Hyde Park Corner, Sculpture by John Cheere 1709-1787.* Furthermore, I have frequently consulted numerous magazines. These include *The Builder, Art-Union, Art-Journal, Country Life, Apollo* and *The Burlington Magazine.*

I should also like to acknowledge the help and encouragement I received from the many institutions and their employees — particularly the secretaries, archivists, comptrollers and gardeners — who have provided me with a wealth of information and guided me around numerous gardens; in particular Edward Saunders at Melbourne Hall; Peter Day at Chatsworth; Eeyan Hartley at Castle Howard; Edward A Sibbick at Osborne House; Jane Anderson at Blair Atholl; Leslie Harris at Kedleston Hall; Marita Prendy. At the National Trust, I particularly wish to thank Anthony Mitchell; J P Haworth, Dr John M Maddison; Andrew Barber; Christopher Wall; Roger J H Whitworth; Christopher N Rowell; John McVerry; Susan Denyer. I am also grateful to the many families who have kindly allowed me to reproduce parts of their family papers. These include Her Majesty the Queen; the Trustees of the Chatsworth Settlement; the Howard family; the Earl of Radnor; Lord Lothian; Mr Whitbread; the Trustees of the Croome Estate; the Marquis of Northampton; Lord Scarsdale; Lady Lucas.

In the antiques and manufacturing trades I would like to thank Tim and Lindy Seago for my introduction to the publisher; Richard Crowther of T Crowther & Son for information supplied and for generous access to his family's collection of photographs; Miles D'Agar of Miles D'Agar and Nick Gifford-Mead Antiques for access to his library and for consistent support and encouragement. I am deeply indebted to Paul and Jimmy Crowther of H Crowther Ltd for their information on the manufacture of eighteenth century leadwork and its restoration, and to Yves Delachaux of GHM who was of great assistance on the history of French cast-iron garden ornaments.

I am grateful for access to Nigel Bartlett's library, and for his help with the different forms and types of marble. My thanks also go to James Rylands of Sotheby's, Billinghurst, and Jeremy Rex-Parker of Christie's for their help and advice. I must also acknowledge the truths I learnt from working with Peter Catling during my formative years.

I should also like to thank my publishers, John Steel and Diana Steel, for without them this book would never have been published. I am also indebted to Cherry Lewis who painstakingly edited the manuscript and transformed it into the present book.

Finally, for allowing me generous access to their gardens and for giving me permission to photograph and reproduce garden ornaments in them, I wish to thank Her Majesty the Queen, the National Trust, English Heritage, as well as the trustees and owners of numerous other gardens, both public and private. I am also indebted to Sotheby's, Christie's and Phillips for the photographs they have provided.

PREFACE

This book has filled every working hour for nearly three years. When I first took on the task of filling a gap that has always vexed me (no comprehensive book has been published on period garden ornament in Britain to date), I thought in my *naïvete* that I would be finished in a few months — how wrong I was. Having spent most of my working life with a well known antique dealer in garden ornaments, I believed that I knew almost all there was to know, and that everything I had learnt was the gospel truth. Again, how wrong I was.

There are many problems facing the collector of antique garden ornaments. But two stand out. The first, on deciding to buy a piece, is to satisfy oneself as to its age. When it is recognised that some dealers and auctioneers sell garden ornaments without actually specialising in the subject it can be seen that mistakes are easily made.

The second problem facing the collector who has taken the plunge and purchased a piece, is where to display it. Like many other forms of antique, the value of garden ornaments has seen rapid increases. Will the piece be safe in the garden? Could it be stolen? What damage could the weather do to it, and how will that affect its value? Would it be better in the house?

I hope these considerations do not put off the would-be collector of garden ornaments, for they have a charm far beyond their value and can so successfully complete a garden. If this book helps the would-be collector to a greater understanding of the subject in any way I will regard the time spent on it as time well spent.

In attempting to collate the various strands of material in a short volume covering three hundred years of garden ornament from the late seventeenth century to the present day, I have been constantly worried that I may have made some mistakes. Tracing the origins of any work of art has always been an imperfect science. There are countless pot-holes waiting to trip even the most wary student and, despite my best efforts, many pieces featured in this book still demand, in an attempt to ascertain their origins, a valued judgement.

I would be delighted to hear if anyone can throw further light on the origins or makers/artists of any of the subjects illustrated or mentioned here. One never stops learning and I would hope at some later point to build on the information in this work.

Finally, I should point out that this book does not cover such architectural features as garden houses, temples and bridges; it does cover in some detail many of the more important producers of garden ornament who have worked in Britain. A few European producers are also briefly mentioned, for many had agents in Britain. However, the book cannot be regarded as an authoritative guide to European manufacturers.

John P S Davis
London, 1991

"'There is nothing adds so much to the Beauty and Grandeur of Gardens, as fine Statues; and nothing more disagreeable than when wrongly plac'd; as *Neptune* on a Terrace-Walk...or *Pan,* the God of Sheep, in a large Basin, Canal, or Fountain. But to prevent such Absurdities, take the following Directions.

For open Lawns and Large Centres:
Mars, God of Battle, with the Goddess *Fame; Jupiter,* God of Thunder, with *Venus,* the Goddess of Love and Beauty; and the Graces *Aglaio, Thalia* and *Euphrosyne; Apollo,* God of Wisdom, with the nine Muses...*Minerva* and *Pallas,* Goddesses of Wisdom, with the seven Liberal Sciences; the three Destinies...*Demergorgon* and *Tellus,* Gods of the Earth...*Pytho,* Goddess of Eloquence; *Vesta,* Goddess of Chastity; *Voluptia,* Goddess of Pleasure; *Atlas,* King of *Mauritania,* a famous Astronomer; *Tysias,* the Inventor of Rhetorick; and *Hercules,* God of Labour.

For Woods and Groves:
Ceres and *Flora; Sylvanus,* God, and *Feronia,* Goddess of the Woods; *Actaeon,* a Hunter, whom *Diana* turn'd into a Hart, and was devoured by his own Dogs; *Eccho,* a Virgin rejected of her Lover, pined away in the Woods for Sorrow, where her Voice still remains...*Philomela,* a young Maid ravish'd by *Tereus*...afterwards transformed into a Nightingale...and lastly, Nuppææ Fairies of the Woods''

From *New Principles of Gardening,* by Batty Langley of Twickenham, 1728

INTRODUCTION

Man has never been able to negotiate little more than an uneasy truce with nature. No matter how sophisticated he thinks he has become, the forces of nature are ever ready to humble him with a display of awesome strength. Yet, inspite of this, the garden designer has persisted in his efforts to conquer nature and, through the device of sculptured gardens, has attempted to create a corner where nature is shaped by man and dominated by human representations.

The Greeks and Romans were the first in Europe to create large gardens where not only plants, trees and nature followed man's designs, but which were also adorned with marble and bronze effigies of gods and heroes. The contribution of these classical sources was to have far reaching effects on gardens throughout the western world. This influence is still clearly evident in many gardens today.

In Britain, the first concept of sculptured gardens was introduced during the Roman occupation, and one of the earliest, constructed at Flavian's Palace near Fishbourne in AD 75, featured a terrace linking the house to the garden. No original statues have been discovered on the site, but the presence of a central pedestal in the garden as well as several niches suggest that the garden was originally decorated with statuary.

With the departure of the Romans in the middle of the fifth century, such sophisticated symbols of man's subjugation of nature disappeared until England again felt the civilising influence of Italy, this time through the Renaissance. However, it was not until the sixteenth century that the ornamentation of gardens with decorative carved or cast works was introduced. One of the earliest of such gardens was at Nonsuch Palace in Surrey, and much of the inspiration appears to have come from Lord Lumley, the owner of the estate, who travelled in Renaissance Italy in the 1560s. Amongst the more influential gardens at this time were the Belvedere Gardens in Rome, whose statue court featured larger-than-life-size marble fountain figures symbolising the rivers Tiber and Nile, and the gardens surrounding the Villa di Castello, designed nearly a century before by Il Tribolo, which featured underground aqueducts as well as magnificent sculptured fountains.

The Italian Renaissance garden was designed to draw attention to the various sculptures and ornaments, which in turn were infused with symbolic meaning. At Nonsuch Palace the gardens were decorated with a variety of fountains and statues, probably imported by Lord Lumley, and celebrating Queen Elizabeth I and Virtue. Roy Strong in *The Renaissance Garden in England,* describes the design of the ornamental garden at Nonsuch as a 'moral tableau which the visitor is asked to read on more than one level'. Queen Elizabeth is the presiding goddess and the focal point of the garden's symbolism through the use of a number of sculptures of images associated with her, such as the pelican and the moon-goddess Diana.

By the early seventeenth century, the ornamentation of British gardens with statuary was being used to create a direct link between the house and garden. The garden no longer stood as a separate, individual work of art, but complemented and related aesthetically to the house.

At the same time there was a growing interest in the classical marble statues excavated in Italy. Lord Arundel in particular took a great interest in these, and bought a considerable number which he used to decorate his house and gardens at Arundel House. Other dignitaries soon followed suit. King James I obtained a number of bronze casts taken from some of the more renowned models in Italy, which he used to adorn his garden at St James's. This interest in garden statuary and ornament created a demand that was also satisfied by sculptors working in Britain.

An example of this growth is given by John Worlidge who, writing on the subject of statues in the garden in 1677, relates that 'In all places where there is a Summer and a Winter, and where your Gardens of pleasure are sometimes clothed with their verdant garments, and bespangled with variety of Flowers, and at other times wholly dismantled of all these; here to recompense the loss of past pleasures, and to buoy up their hopes of another Spring, many have placed in their gardens, Statues, and Figures of several Animals, and great variety of other curious pieces of Workmanship'. Worlidge goes on to state that 'This mode of adorning Gardens with curious Workmanship is now become *English'*. By the end of the seventeenth century the vogue for decorating gardens with fountains, statues and vases had become widespread. Writing in 1712, John James related that:

Statues and Vases contribute very much to the Embellishment and Magnificence of a Garden, and extremely advance the natural Beauties of it. They are made of several Forms, and different Materials; the richest are those of Cast-Brass, Lead gilt, and Marble; the ordinary Sort are of common Stone, or Stucco. Among Figures are distinguished Groups, which consist at least of two Figures together in the same Block; Figures Insulate or Detached, that is, those that you can go quite round; and Figures that are set in Niches, which are finish'd on the Fore-part only: There are likewise, Busts, Terms, Half-length Figures: Figures half as big as the Life, and those bigger than the Life, called *Colossal,* placed either on regular Pedestals, or such as are more slender, tapering and hollowed, or on flat Plinths; not to mention the Figures of Animals, which sometimes adorn Cascades; as do also Bass-Relievos, and Mask-heads.

These Figures represent all the several Deities, and illustrious Persons of Antiquity, which should be placed properly in Gardens, setting the River-Gods, as the *Naiades, Rivers* and *Tritons,* in the Middle of Fountains and Basons; and those of the Woods, as *Sylvanes, Faunes* and *Dryads,* in the Groves: Sacrifices, Bacchanals, and Childrens Sports, are likewise represented in Bass-Relievo, upon the Vases and Pedestals, which may be adorn'd with Festoons, Foliage, Mouldings and other Ornaments.

The usual Places of Figures and Vases are along the Palisades, in the Front, and upon the Sides of a Parterre; in the Niches and Sinkings of Hornbeam, or of Lattice-work made for that Purpose. In Groves, they are placed in the centre of a Star, or St. *Andrews* Cross; in the Spaces between the Walks of a Goose-foot, in the Middle of Halls and Cabinets, among the Trees and Arches of a Green Gallery, and at the Head of a Row of Trees, or Palisades, that stand free and detached. They are also put at the lower End of Walks and Vistas, to set them off the better; in Porticos and Arbors of Trellis-work; in Basons, Cascades, &c. In general, they do very well everywhere; and you can scarce have too many of them in a Garden.

John James' words come from the Frenchman Dezalier D'Argenville's book which he translated from the French in 1712. However, the reference is useful, for it reflects the growing interest in garden ornaments. By the 1730s the vogue for decorating gardens with fountains, statues, vases, etc, had become widespread, and 'numerous are the views of noblemen's and gentlemen's estates at this date, decorated with all manners of ornaments'.

To fill this increasing demand a considerable industry had been established. Artists and craftsmen were not only supplying garden ornaments, but were also carving and casting all manner of ornamental decoration for the facades and interiors of new or refashioned houses. The industry was heavily influenced by an influx of continental craftsmen, from the Low Countries in particular, no doubt encouraged by the coronation of William and Mary in 1689. Some of these continental craftsmen were far more talented than many of the native artists and they brought with them their own styles and techniques which were to set new standards for English artists to acquire and match.

In the first half of the eighteenth century the two most common materials used by these artists to create garden ornaments were stone and lead, and from these they were able to produce a vast repertoire of items. Some, such as the carved stone pieces, were produced to clients' specifications, and often necessitated the production of a drawing or small model in terracotta before work began. Patrons could also choose from a range of stock stone vases, some copied from 'antique' designs, whilst others were of a more contemporary nature often taken from designs supplied by the architect or garden designer employed by the patron in question. (These architects were to have a considerable influence on the production of garden ornaments, particularly vases.) Although a few one-off commissions were cast in lead, the majority of these lead ornaments were stock items reproduced for various clients in countless numbers. They were made from moulds of some of the popular subjects of the day, including not only antique subjects in Italy, such as the Venus de Medici and the Farnese Hercules, but also copies of more modern works, such as several of the statues in the gardens at Versailles. The *oeuvre* of these 'lead figure-makers' also included copies of famous works by artists working in England, such as the marble vases by Edward Pearce and Caius Gabriel Cibber at Hampton Court. Many of these statues reflected the changing fashions of the period, such as Arcadia, the mythical residence of Pan, the god of shepherds and shepherdesses. The eighteenth century fascination with Arcadia is clearly reflected in such statues, which changed from a classical-influenced style early on in the century, to the more contemporary models of later years.

The placing of garden statues during the eighteenth century is worthy of comment, for at least in the early years it appears to have been something of a haphazard affair. This phenomenon was commented on by several authors, foremost of which was Alexander Pope. His Fourth Epistle, published in 1731, satirises Lord Timon, an anonymous character (but reputedly Lord Chandos of Cannons fame), for his ill-conceived garden statuary:

> The suffering eye inverted nature sees,
> Trees cut to statues, statues thick as trees;
> With here a fountain, never to be played;
> And there a summer-house, that knows no shade;
> Here Amphitrite sails through myrtle bowers;
> There gladiators fight or die in flowers;
> Unwatered see the drooping sea-horse mourn,
> And swallows roost in Nilus' dusty urn.

Three years later James Ralph in *A Critical Review of the Publick Buildings, Statues and Ornaments in and about London and Westminster* would castigate most of the gentry for their inability both to choose and situate statues properly. There were, of course, exceptions to this, and by the middle of the eighteenth century matters had changed considerably. Much thought was given to the selection of the exact piece and its interrelation with the landscape, other figures, buildings and features to create a harmonic whole. Thus the positioning of these statues often had a deep symbolic meaning which, although less understandable today, would have been

An illustration by Thomas Rowlandson (1756-1827) captures the intense interest in statuary in late eighteenth century England

quite apparent to most educated people of the time. For example, a figure of Hercules placed at a junction of two paths, as at Blair Castle, would have represented the hero's choice between vice and virtue; whereas if a figure of Hercules wrestling with the giant Antaeus (son of Mother Earth) was placed on the borders of the garden with the countryside, this would represent the struggle between order and the wilderness of nature. The symbolic nature of such gardens encompassed a plethora of subjects, often associated with Greek and Roman mythology, but occasionally digressing into more contemporary themes. Liberty was an important feature of Lord Cobham's gardens at Stowe, whilst at Rousham the macabre spectre of death is represented; nevertheless, both these gardens also displayed the influence of classical mythology.

The garden ornaments produced in Britain during the eighteenth century also reflected the changing fashions of the period. Thus early figures are mainly baroque, whilst later ones tend to reflect other styles, rococo for example. By the end of the century there was a move towards a much lighter and more intricate style which was expounded by the architect Robert Adam. Changing styles of garden design also had a marked effect on the use of garden ornament. From the late seventeenth century through to the 1760s the design of gardens changed dramatically from the formal gardens laid out in the French and Dutch styles by Henry Wise to those of greater informality by Charles Bridgeman, a style which was further developed by William Kent. During this period, garden ornaments featured heavily in the landscape, but with the advent of Capability Brown's style of almost total 'naturalisation' in the mid-1760s, many of the otherwise formal gardens were replaced by gentle grass-covered gradients and naturally-grouped trees, in an artificially idyllic form of nature. Except as furnishings for temples, follies, and so on, statues and vases were rarely required for these new

Colour Plate 1. Portland stone figure of Inigo Jones at Chiswick House, London, before (left) and after (right) cleaning (see page 22)
ENGLISH HERITAGE

compositions, and many of those that had formed parts of earlier gardens were disposed of.

During the early years of the nineteenth century garden design was strongly influenced by the picturesque movement which advocated rustic landscapes dotted with ruined, neglected architectural features, in preference to the smooth sweeping lawns and clusters of trees laid out by Capability Brown. Formal features such as fountains and statues were very much out of place in this concept of contrived neglect in the garden. However, there were occasions when the odd garden statue or urn partially hidden within the landscape was acceptable, but the era of urns and statues at the end of avenues had truly passed. This phenomenon is reflected in the *oeuvre* of the leading sculptors of this period, for the vast majority of their works were intended for interior use only.

The Victorian era saw the destruction of the Georgian landscape garden. Elaborate flower gardens and terraces were introduced to numerous estates, often within the close environs of the house, and these were usually complemented by numerous statues, vases and fountains. This period also saw the growth of the middle class, now able to afford gardens around its own villas, and the resulting tens of thousands of new gardens were inevitably decorated with a variety of ornaments. Much of the statuary was based on the styles of earlier periods, but there were modern styles, too, such as the terracotta statuary produced by Blashfield and some of the Doulton works.

The nineteenth century also saw the growth of mass-produced garden ornaments, particularly in cast-iron and artificial stone. The manufacture of the latter had started seriously in the 1770s at the Coade works in Lambeth, but by the 1850s a variety of other formulae were being manufactured by such firms as Pulham, Blashfield, Doulton and Garnkirk, as were several cement based media such as that produced by Austin & Seeley. These mass-produced ornaments were generally far cheaper than any carved from marble or stone, or cast in metal.

Although cast-iron had been in production since the late eighteenth century, it was not used for garden ornaments, mainly because it was unfashionable. However, with the rapid developments of the Industrial Revolution it became more widely used and popular. At the Great Exhibition in 1851, a great variety of cast-iron ornaments was displayed, and several of the more notable foundries, such as André and the Coalbrookdale Company, received medals for their 'art castings'. Although at this point there were a number of manufactories producing artificial stone ornaments, there were far more iron foundries. However, garden ornaments were only a side line for these foundries, as can be seen in the Coalbrookdale Company's 1875 catalogue. This encompassed a wide range of stock manufactured goods, and while garden ornaments are listed in Section III, other illustrated sections covered: 'Registered Stove Grates; Hall Furniture in Iron; Ranges and Kitchens of all Descriptions; Gas Pillars of all kinds; Fence work of all kinds; Rain Water Goods; Pumps of all kinds; Furnaces; Pots; Boilers; Kettles; Holloware'. When one considers that almost every foundry in Britain was producing some form of garden ornament, it can be seen that the initial prejudices against cast-iron as a medium for garden ornament had, by this stage, been well and truly overcome.

If one looks at a mid-nineteenth century garden, such as Osborne on the Isle of Wight, the considerable influence the Industrial Revolution had on garden ornament can be seen. While eighteenth century gardens were predominantly decorated with stone and lead ornaments, the gardens at Osborne boast many examples of cement-based artificial stone and zinc pieces as well as a few bronzes. (Osborne is slightly unrepresentative of gardens of the time, as it was created by Prince Albert who was extremely well off.) Nevertheless, bronze has always been a particularly expensive medium to work in and the incidence of bronze ornaments to be found in gardens around Britain is low. The high cost of bronze is reflected in the statuary at Osborne, where the number of bronze pieces are heavily outnumbered by French and German zinc pieces, produced at a fraction of the cost to simulate bronze.

Another expensive medium is marble. During the eighteenth century only a very few pieces were carved for English gardens. Certainly some marble 'antiques' were imported from Italy and were used to decorate gardens, but these were few in number, and those that were used were rarely important works. During the nineteenth century some patrons, such as the 6th Duke of Devonshire, commissioned a number of marble copies of famous statues for their gardens. According to the Duke, in the *Handbook to Chatsworth and Hardwick,* 1844, his were carved from 'hard marble of the place [Carrara] that appears to defy the climate of the peak; and to resist all incipient vegetation on its surface'. One of the main disadvantages of white marble is that it does not stand up to the extremes of the English climate. This had been noted by John Evelyn in 1667, when he described the Arundel marbles as 'exceedingly impaired by the corrosive air of London'. Despite being carved from marble quarried from one of the peaks at Carrara, the surface of the Duke's statues have been heavily corroded.

The Apollo Belvedere at Castle Howard, Yorkshire, clearly shows the effects of time and the elements on lead figures
THE HON SIMON HOWARD

One of a set of four zinc figures by the Parisian foundry of Miroy Frères, in the private gardens of Osborne House, Isle of Wight
REPRODUCED BY GRACIOUS PERMISSION OF HER MAJESTY THE QUEEN

Our climate does not adversedly affect white marble garden ornament alone. Whilst some marbles, such as porphyry, Kilkenny, Istrian and Verona, are quite robust, they still suffer damage with time, and most other marbles are infinitely less durable. The durability of other media varies considerably, but none of the materials used for garden ornament is completely impervious to the weather, particularly ice and frost. Often worst affected are the stones not native to our climate, such as Vicenza stone. Cast-iron rusts, bronze oxidises, and many British stones lose much of their original surface. Eighteenth century lead statues are prone to collapse following expansion of their inner core and armature, while the socles of lead vases are prone to collapse as the result of metal fatigue and the weight they have to bear. The effects of the climate are of particular relevance to English garden ornament, and the varying durability of many of the materials used is mentioned in more detail in the following chapters.

Given that sculptured gardens were meant to celebrate man's ascendency over nature, it is ironic that the British climate should wreak such damage on the very ornaments that symbolise this aspiration. The dilemma facing owners of garden ornament are legion. The very nature of a statue or vase covered in lichen and

'Sentry boxes' at Anglesey Abbey, Cambridgeshire, cover marble busts during the coldest months
THE NATIONAL TRUST

moss is one of its most aesthetically pleasing aspects, yet on many materials this can cause untold damage. In an attempt to defer damage, many ornaments are sent to restorers to be cleaned, but this too can have catastrophic effects. When John Michael Rysbrack's eighteenth century statue of Inigo Jones was cleaned in 1987, there was considerable public outcry. Two photographs showing the statue prior to and after cleaning by high powered jets at pressures of up to forty pounds per square inch clearly show the appalling consequences of heavy-handed restoration (Colour Plate 1). Other institutions have taken to wrapping ornaments up, or placing them in 'sentry boxes' during the worst months, which I suppose is symbolic of twentieth century man's acceptance of nature's ascendancy.

CHAPTER ONE

LEAD
The late seventeenth century to 1800

The end of the 1600s saw the advent of the French-style garden in England. Modelled on the works of Louis XIV's gardener, André Le Nôtre, and exemplified by his work at Versailles and Vaux-le-Vicomte, a new fashion of garden design became popular. Grand parterres and avenues, complemented by numerous statues and vases to invoke classical settings and terminate views, were the order of the day. Prior to this, garden statuary although popular was rarely used, mainly because of the expense of commissioning a sculptor. With a marked increase not only in the size but also in the number of gardens, the consequent demand for statuary to decorate them rose considerably.

Lead ornaments were well suited to fill this new demand for several reasons: once the moulds for a model had been made, duplicates could be reproduced as frequently as required and were reasonably easy to cast, they were available more cheaply than bronze, stone or marble, and they were relatively unaffected by the weather. Furthermore, many models, such as figures standing on one leg, which were not feasible in stone without ungainly supports, could easily be cast in lead and reinforced with an iron armature. By the early years of the eighteenth century a considerable range of lead ornaments was available from which patrons could select particular models to adorn not only their fountains, groves and walks, but also the pediments and skylines of their houses.

The Making of a Lead Figure

To date I have as yet to discover a detailed account of how the eighteenth century lead figure makers cast their figures. However some contemporary information is available and this, combined with examination of the interior and exterior of existing works, points towards casts being produced along the following lines:

Given that the lead figure maker already had a model, shall we say a life-size stone statue, then the first process would have involved painting it with some form of releasing agent, such as oil. The statue would then have been carefully marked into sections, for with so many projecting parts it was necessary to make a number of moulds. Original models in less durable media such as plaster or clay would probably have been cut up to facilitate the mould-making process, rather than being marked. These divisions can be roughly segregated into areas such as hands, arms, legs, feet, head, torso (often in two pieces) etc, and would have been chiefly defined by the presence of 'under-workings'. Robert Dossie in *A Hand Maid to the Arts,* published in 1758, records: 'The art of properly dividing the molds [sic], in order to make them separate from the model, constitutes the greatest object of dexterity and skill in the art of casting; and does not admit of rules for the most advantageous conduct of it in every case'; and he continues:

The method of dividing the . . . molds [sic] can not be reduced, as I intimated, to any particular rules; but must depend in some degree on the skill of the operator, who may easily judge from the original subjects, by the means here suggested, what parts will come off together, and what require to be separated: the principle of the whole consists only in this, that where *under-*

workings as they are called, occur, that is, wherever a straight line drawn from the basis or insertion of any projection would be cut or crossed by any part of such projection, such part can not be taken off without a division: which must be made either in the place where the projection would cross the streight [sic] line; or, as that is frequently difficult, the whole projection must be separated from the main body and divided also length ways, into two parts...

Once the mould maker had identified these areas, the wet moulds could be applied.

As plaster (the material used for making moulds for plaster casts) was expensive, and in large masses took some time to dry thoroughly enough to bear the heat of molten lead, it appears that clay was the predominant material used for the moulds. Dossie stipulates that this clay had to be free of gravel and stones, and then mixed with a third or more of fine sand, or preferably sifted coal ashes to reduce cracking. For the large size moulds we are concerned with, the cohesive property of the clay was increased by combining a small quantity of flocks of cloth or 'fine cotton pluckt [sic] or cut till it is very short'.

Sections of this clay mixture must then have been pressed around each piece of the model statue and allowed to harden a little. For example, on the forearm of the model statue the still damp clay could be cut (using a thin sharp knife) around the wrist and elbow joint. Two further cuts running between the wrist and elbow joint across the top and bottom of the forearm would have allowed the mould maker to remove the complete forearm moulds. These would then have been allowed to dry further. Next, an interior core (or 'corps' as it was referred to) was modelled from clay. This would have been suspended (on wires or metal extending through the elbow and wrist ends) between the two halves of the mould to allow a gap of approximately ¼ inch or more between the inside of the mould and the corps. The two halves of the mould could then be bound together and the hole at one end plugged leaving a gap at the other end for the molten lead to be poured in.

Both mould and corps then had to be allowed to dry thoroughly for in Dossie's words 'It is extremely necessary to have the mould perfectly dry; otherwise the moisture, being rarefied, will make an explosion, that will blow the metal out of the mould, and endanger the operator, or at least crack the mould in such manner as to frustrate the operation'.

After the various component pieces of the statue had been cast, the moulds could be separated and the lead casts removed. The corps would then have been broken up inside the cast and removed together with the wires, leaving a hollow lead cast. How may casts could be obtained from one set of moulds is not clear, but certainly several. The situation is complicated, for it seems likely that the models from which the moulds were made would have been retained for the making of further sets of moulds. What is certain, however, is that a set of moulds exposed to the temperature fluctuations incurred during casting would have worn with time, and it seems likely that sometimes they were damaged when the casts were removed.

It is interesting to note that the number of figures cast from one set of moulds was seemingly important (as is suggested in a letter by the architect Captain William Winde to Lady Mary Bridgeman). Presumably the first few casts out of the moulds would have been of a better quality than later ones.

The next stage involved a blacksmith who would construct a sturdy wrought-iron armature around which the various components of the statue could be located. The hollow lead casts were then soldered together around, but not touching, the interior armature. To support the various parts of the figure in relation to the armature, plaster of Paris was poured into the lead casts. The plaster was often

combined with sand or refuse from the figure makers' yards, such as stone chippings, and broken tools such as files have been found embedded in the plaster of lead figures.

Now complete, the lead statue could be worked on and any solder lines or barbs removed. Details were chased up by hand using chisels, gravers and other instruments, while any fine details such as grapes or vine leaves could be attached using bronze nails.

The statue would then have been painted, either by an artist or the craftsman himself. The popular Arcardian and rustic subjects were usually painted to resemble a real person, as Richard Cumberland recounts in his satirical visit to Sir Theodore and Lady Thimble: 'But, how was I surprised to find, in place of Sir Theodore, a leaden statue on a pair of skates, painted in a blue and gold coat, with a red waistcoat, whose person, upon closer examination, I recollected to have been acquainted with some years ago, amongst the elegant group, which a certain celebrated artist exhibits to the amusement of stage-coaches and country waggons upon their entrance into town at Hyde-Park Corner'.[1]

The great majority of lead pieces, including items such as vases, antique and other figures, were painted white to resemble stone or marble, and traces of this paint still remain on many figures, such as the Hercules in Plate 1:4 and the vases in Plate 1:8. A number of other figures were originally gilded, such as the Gladiator mentioned by the younger Van Nost in a letter to Edward Dryden,[2] and the Sphinx in Plate 1:21. Other finishes were also used; for instance, brass on the four Stuart Kings at Glamis[3] and, in a similar vein, bronze for the Blackamoor at Hampton Court Palace. Some figures were oiled as well, presumably as a further protection from the elements and to give the enhancement of a glossy finish. Several references to this oiling survive. John Cheere, for example, describes in a letter to the 2nd Duke of Atholl how 'Once in two years it should be washed very clean and oyled over with Lindseed oyles'.[4]

Finally, each ornament, with the exception of vases, was leaded into a stone base. This involved locating the wrought-iron armature (which extended beneath the ornament) within a suitable hole (or holes) in the stone base (usually Portland), and securing it by pouring in lead. The technique used is unique to lead ornaments of this period and so often provides an accurate means of correctly identifying period works.

A great number of eighteenth century lead figures and vases survive today and are a testament to the untold numbers that were produced throughout the period. Many were swept away by the fashion in the late eighteenth century for landscaped gardens, whilst countless others were destroyed in later years. Statues at Stonyhurst Castle were even melted down to repair holes in the roof. Many others simply disintegrated, victims of the elements.

While vases are particularly prone to collapse because their socles weaken and become incapable of supporting both the considerable weight of the lead and any earth within, the main weakness of figures is in the method of construction. The presence of lime in the plaster corrodes the lead, while once water or damp penetrates the interior it becomes suspended in the plaster and sand mixture and soon rusts the iron armature (producing tell-tale rust stains on the stone base). This not only weakens the structure, see the figure of the Faun with Kid (Plate 1:6) which is now supported by an iron bar, but also causes expansion which literally tears the lead. The effects of this are clearly visible on the Gamekeeper in Plate 1:18, and beginning to show on the Mower in Plate 1:27, whilst what was an Apollo Belvedere at Castle Howard (Colour Plate 2), clearly shows the horrific consequences of neglecting a lead figure. The action of expansion has ripped the lead apart, and the soft plaster of Paris has been washed away to reveal the wrought-iron armature.

The Lead Figure Makers

The manufacture of lead ornaments from the late seventeenth to the late eighteenth century was almost entirely centred on the Hyde Park area of London, and in particular two streets, Portugal Row and Hyde Park Road. This area was described by James Ralph in 1734:

> There is nothing more remarkable, except the shops and yards of the *statuaries*; and sorry I am that they afford a judicious foreigner such flagrant opportunities to arraign and condemn our taste. Among a hundred statues you shall not see one even tolerable, either in design or execution; nay, even the copies of the antique are so monstrously wretched, that one can hardly guess at their originals.
>
> I will not lay the blame of this prostitution of so fine an art entirely on its professors; no, I rather attribute it to the ignorance and folly of the buyers, who, being resolved to have statues in their gardens at all events, first make a wrong choice, and then resolve to purchase their follies as cheap as possible: this puts the workmen in a wrong taste of designing, and hasty, and rude in finishing: hence excellency is never thought of, and the master, like the *Highwayman* in the *Beggar's Opera* is happy when he has turned his *lead* into *gold*.

Ralph's damning criticism continues and is reproduced here as it provides an interesting account of the prevailing tendency for the mass ornamentation of gardens with statues:

> I must confess, nothing is more amazing to me, than the ignorance of most of our gentry in the polite arts, and in statuary particularly; which is so flagrant, that, among the vast numbers of statues which are to be seen in the gardens of this nation, it is almost a miracle if you find one good one. Neither are we alone ignorant of the art itself, but even the use of it too; for there are as few statues well situated as chosen: and too many have reason to blush both for the figure itself, and the end it was designed to answer.
>
> Nothing can be more plain, than what is meant for decoration should be beautiful in itself, and placed with propriety too. What excuse then can be made for the wretched things which we see crowded on the eye, that shock, instead of affording entertainment?
>
> In the first place, therefore, a statue should be good in itself, in the next, it should be erected to advantage; and lastly, it should, in its own nature, be suited to the place. To complete an area, end a vista, adorn a fountain, or decorate a banqueting-house or alcove, is the just and natural use of statues: not to people a garden, and make a nuisance of what ought to be a beauty.
>
> Neither is every good statue adapted to every place: the equestrian statue of a hero would suit but ill with soothing falls of water, and all the softness of *Italian* luxury; neither would the river-gods become the hurry and pomp of a nobleman's courtyard. Common sense, one would imagine, would preserve us from absurdities like these; and yet there are so many proofs to the contrary, that we cannot be too severe in our censure, or take too much pains to bring about a reformation.[5]

Most of the lead figures produced during this period were never intended to be works of art, but simply impressive and comparatively cheap decorations for the garden. The poet William Shenstone expresses this view of lead figures in his *Unconnected Thoughts on Gardening,* when he says: 'Though they may not express the finer lines of an human body, yet they seem perfectly well calculated, on account of their duration to embellish landskips [sic], were they some degrees inferior to what we generally behold. A statue in a room challenges examination, and is to be examined critically as a statue. A statue in a garden is to be considered as one part of a scene or landskip: the minuter touches are no more essential to it than a good landskip painter would esteem them were he to represent a statue in his picture'.[6]

Certainly the quality of the lead figure makers' works range, for example, from the superb vase (Colour Plate 6) and River God (Plate 1:17 and Colour Plate 15) to a pitiful copy of the antique Spinario at Castle Howard which, as Ralph related, is indeed 'Monstrously wretched'.[7]

The Van Nost family

One of the earliest developers, and hence an important lead figure maker was John Van Nost (fl1677-1710), sometimes spelt Ost or Oast, who had two premises: one in the Haymarket (seemingly a house), the other, which he took over in 1699, on the Hyde Park Road, near the Queen's Mead Head.

On the Continent lead had been extensively used as a medium for garden ornaments (for example at Versailles) and it seems quite probable that Van Nost, being of Flemish origin,[8] gained much of his knowledge of lead manufacture prior

Colour Plate 3. Andromeda by the elder John Van Nost, lead, Melbourne Hall, Derbyshire. Although reversed, the figure bears a striking resemblance to the fresco by Carraci in the Farnese Palace, Rome. (See page 36)

LORD LOTHIAN

Colour Plate 4. Perseus by the elder John Van Nost, lead, Melbourne Hall, Derbyshire, the companion figure to Andromeda in Colour Plate 3. Unlike Carraci's rather wooden fresco figure, Van Nost has produced an elaborate and dramatic Perseus. (See page 36)

LORD LOTHIAN

to his arrival in England at the end of the seventeenth century. Van Nost was employed for some time by a leading sculptor, Arnold Quellin (1653-1686), and so must have been involved with one of Quellin's last commissions which was to supply four lead figures of the Stuart Kings to Glamis between 1685-86.[9] Quellin died in 1686, leaving his estate to his wife whom Van Nost married, thereby obtaining a number of Quellin's figures.[10]

Unfortunately very little information on Van Nost is known. He was soon involved in a flourishing lead figure business, but being a competent sculptor in his own right, like many of the lead figure makers, he was also carving chimney-pieces, tables and monuments as well as statues. According to the historian George Vertue (1684-1756) he employed Andries Carpentiere as an assistant, but he also had others including, for a short time, the sculptor William Palmer (1673-1739) as well as the carver Mr Holbert and the masons Hill and Smith. In August 1710 John Van Nost died. His will in the Greater London Record Office[11] reveals that he died a wealthy man, and is interesting in that it gives the name of his man servant, Thomas Manning, and the man who was to continue the business, his cousin, also called John Van Nost. On 17 April 1712, a sale was held of 'Mr Van Nost's Collection of Marble and Leaden Figures...' Fortunately the catalogue of

Colour Plate 5. A pair of amorini by the elder John Van Nost, lead, Melbourne Hall, Derbyshire. (See Plates 1:2 and 3 and pages 36 and 37)
LORD LOTHIAN

this survives,[12] and it provides the most comprehensive insight into Van Nost's work. Of the 140 lots listed, over ninety were lead ornaments such as vases, animals, fountains and figures, ranging in size from 'big as life' to 'small life', and included amongst others, the popular figures of shepherds and sheperdesses. There were also copies of 'antick' [sic] subjects, models taken from the work of 'John de Bellone' [sic] and figures of royalty such as William and Mary. The remaining lots comprised mainly chimney pieces and marble table tops, but also a number of Van Nost's own marble statues.

Regrettably much of Van Nost's leadwork has disappeared, although a considerable number of documented items remain at Melbourne Hall in Derbyshire, including the stupendous Vase of the Four Seasons (Colour Plate 6) and baroque figures of Andromeda and Perseus (Colour Plates 3 and 4), whilst other examples can be seen at Hampton Court Palace, Stonyhurst College and Cholmondeley Castle.

Plate 1:1. In his print 'The Analysis of Beauty', 1753, Hogarth shows a statuary yard, thought to be that of the figure maker John Cheere

The elder John Van Nost's business centred on Hyde Park was continued by his cousin, the younger John Van Nost (fl1710-1729). He appears to have taken over the business immediately.[13] Like his predecessor, Van Nost was a competent sculptor. Probably the best example of his work is the bronze equestrian figure of George I (Plate 3:16), now at the Barber Institute, Birmingham, another copy of which he made in lead for Stowe (Plate 3:17). Van Nost's output of lead statuary was substantial, supplying ornaments to, amongst others, Stowe, Cannons Ashby, Stonyhurst Castle, Castle Bromwich Hall, Wrest Park, Gough Park, Cannons and Moulsham Hall. His son, confusingly another John, also worked at the yard, and was apprenticed to Henry Scheemakers on 17 October 1726.[14] On 26 April 1729, the younger Van Nost died, and the business was taken over by his widow who, on 20 May 1731, advertised that there remained 'several extraordinary fine things belonging to the late famous sculptor Mr. John Nost, fine inlaid marble tables, marble chimney-pieces, figures'. She goes on to state that 'designing to go beyond seas, will dispose of them at reasonable rates at her house near Hyde Park'.[15]

By 1734 the business was being run by another Van Nost, Anthony (fl1734-1737). Business continued until late 1737, when the yard was taken over by John Cheere.

John Cheere

John Cheere (1709-1787) was to become the leading lead figure maker for the next fifty years, employing a large workforce.[16] His brother Henry (1703-1781), later to become Sir Henry Cheere, was one of the leading rococo sculptors of the period, and it seems likely that Henry was not only instrumental in obtaining the Van Nost family yard,[17] but also probably provided several lucrative commissions for his brother in later years.[18]

Several accounts of Cheere's yard survive. The anonymous author of *Leaves in a Manuscript Diary* recounts: 'I came out at the lodge and stepped into Mr Cheere's yard, which, on account of numberless figures in stone, lead and plaster you would swear was a country fair or market, made up of spruce squires, haymakers with rakes in their hands, shepherds and shepherdesses, bagpipers and pipers and fiddlers, Dutch skippers and English sailors enough to supply a first-rate man-of-war'.[19] Whilst John Thomas Smith in his *Streets of London* relates: 'The figures were cast in lead as large as life and frequently painted with an intention to resemble nature. They consisted of Punch, Harlequin, Columbine and other pantomimical characters; mowers whetting their scythes, haymakers resting on their rakes, gamekeepers in the act of shooting and Roman soldiers with forelocks, but above all that of an African, kneeling with a sundial on his head found the most extensive sale'.[20]

As well as these two descriptions, an engraving of a yard, thought to be Cheere's, is illustrated in William Hogarth's *The Analysis of Beauty* (Plate 1:1). Hogarth only refers to it as 'A Statuary's Yard'; though several of the figures illustrated, such as the Medici Venus (13), Belvedere Antinous (6), and Farnese Hercules (3 and 4) and the Apollo Belvedere (12), are known to have been stock Cheere figures, whilst the Sphinx (21) is strikingly similar to a lead example once at Buckland. Furthermore the figure marked 19 is working on a subject (supported by a block and tackle) which resembles the George II Cheere is known to have supplied to Jersey in the early 1750s[21]

Cheere's output was prolific; by 1751 he had taken over two other yards within the Hyde Park area, perhaps including those of Thomas Manning who had died a few years earlier. A great number of Cheere's documented ornaments survive today at Castle Hill, West Wycombe Park, Syon House, Blair Atholl, Glynde, Hampton Court Palace, Chiswick House, Somerset House, Stourhead, Jersey, Castle Howard, Keddleston Hall, Heaton Hall, and the Portuguese Royal Palace of Queluz. In addition, his works are thought or known to have been supplied to, amongst others, Compton Verney, Copped Hall, Painshill Park, Quenby Hall, Wilton, Wrest Park, Biel, Weald Hall, Bowood and Newhailes.

By the late 1770s the popularity of the formal garden had been replaced by the more fashionable sweeping landscapes, embodied in the works of Capability Brown (1716-1783). Consequently the demand for lead ornaments was dwindling. Cheere's production of lead garden figures seems to have slowed, and his business became more involved with the production of interior figures and busts in plaster, which he had been producing for many years at the same time as his leadwork. On Cheere's death in 1787, the manufacture of lead ornaments almost completely stopped and, according to John Thomas Smith, an auction was held of his stock. A number of his figures remained with dealers for several years, but the fashion for lead statuary had come to an end.

However, John Cheere and the Van Nosts were not the only lead figure makers, for several other sculptors in the Hyde Park area were also producing lead statuary.

Colour Plate 6. The Vase of the Four Seasons by the elder John Van Nost, lead, circa 1705, Melbourne Hall, Derbyshire. Height approx 96ins. (See pages 37 and 41)
LORD LOTHIAN

Andries Carpentiere

Probably the most important lead figure maker after Cheere and the Van Nosts was Andries Carpentiere (later called Andrew Carpenter) (1670s-1737), who first worked as principal assistant to the elder Van Nost. By 1708 Carpentiere, whom Vertue described as a 'gross, heavy man', had started his own business in Portugal Row (which led on to the Hyde Park Road). Like the elder Van Nost he was also a sculptor executing his own works as well as making many lead ornaments.

Some of his lead ornaments are similar to those of his employer, suggesting that he had access to at least a few of the Van Nosts' models. For example, the figure at Powis Castle of Fame riding on the back of Pegasus, which is signed by Carpentiere, is probably the same model as the Pegasus and Fame, for which the elder Nost received part payment from Sir Nicholas Shireburn in 1700.[22] The situation is decidedly unclear, but perhaps confirmation of Carpentiere's reproduction of several of the Van Nosts' figures can be found in the *Liste of Mr. Andrew Carpenter Figures* in the Castle Howard Archives.[23] This mentions several figures such as 'Cain & Abel' and 'Mercury' which were also stock Van Nost family models. Of course Carpentiere must also have modelled or carved his own works for reproduction in lead, but it does seem probable that he borrowed or perhaps purchased figures from the Van Nosts from which to make copies (some perhaps from the 1712 sale). If this was the case, then it may account for the

Colour Plate 7. Life-size group of Hercules and the Hydra, lead (the Hydra of local North Wales stone), Terrace Gardens, Powis Castle, Powys. (See Plate 1:4 and pages 41 and 42)

considerable confusion in attribution between Carpentiere's and the Van Nosts' ornaments. Carpentiere's work was substantial and included supplying ornaments to Stowe, Castle Howard, Wrest Park, Ditchley and Cannons. In 1737 he died leaving, no doubt, a gap in the market for John Cheere to see the advantages of moving into the production of lead ornaments.

Edward Hurst, Thomas Manning

Two less prolific Hyde Park sculptors were also making lead ornaments. Edward Hurst (fl1698-1718, with premises between 1699 and 1718), supplied figures of 'A Large Diana with a Buck' and 'A Shephard and Shepardis' to Charlecote Park.[24] The other, Thomas Manning (fl1710-1747) was the elder John Van Nost's man servant, and supplied a number of ornaments to Gough Park between 23 August and 17 November, 1720. These were a 'Neptune — £21, Mercury and Fame — £12 12s, 2 Boares — £8 8s, 2 large vases — £25'.[25] The only other known reference to Manning's work is a payment on 28 January 1743 in the Stourhead Archives for a 'River God, £18 15s',[26] and it seems reasonable to assume that this was also lead. Manning had several yards, including one which, according to Lethaby, was on the corner of White Horse Street (which joined on to the Hyde Park Road).[27]

Other lead figure makers

Although the most renowned lead figure makers had yards at Hyde Park, several other sculptors are also known to have used the compound. Richard Osgood (fl1691-?1728) supplied lead work to Chatsworth in the 1690s,[28] and according to the architect, Captain William Winde (fl1646-1722) in a letter to Lady Mary Bridgeman, Osgood, had 'the beste leaden figures' than those of 'Mr. Nostes, Mr. Lasones' and 'Mr. Varique', including an 'Extreordinary' model of 'An Adonis caste by Mr. Sibbert (deceased)'.[29] Presumably 'Mr. Sibbert' was Caius Gabriel Cibber (1630-1700) who had used lead for his figures of Faith, Hope and Charity on the exterior of the Danish Church in Wellclose Square. Of course many other sculptors sometimes also worked in lead, such as Peter Scheemakers (1691-1781) for his equestrian figure of William III at Hull, or Francis Bird (1667-1731) for the magnificent figures on the pediment of the Clarendon building in Oxford, but their use of it pales in comparison to the massive production of the principal Hyde Park lead figure makers.

Stylistic Sources

It is difficult to place the numerous models produced by the lead figure makers into separate periods, for many models, such as the Blackamoors in Plates 1:13 and 15, and the Samson and the Philistine in Colour Plate 8, were produced for many years, but they can be broadly separated into four groups: copies of antique sculpture, copies of Italian sculpture, copies of French sculpture and copies of English sculpture.

Antique sculpture

The popularity of lead copies of antique statues was primarily due to the increasing interest during the eighteenth century in the classical statues of Italy. During the seventeenth century few copies of these antique figures existed in England, but by the early 1700s a new enthusiasm for the classical works had developed. This was perhaps due primarily to the Grand Tour, an intrinsic part of an Englishman's education, which involved spending some time in Europe, and was incomplete without at least a short spell in Italy. Whilst there the English gentleman was introduced to the stupendous works of classical civilisation, and in particular architecture and sculpture. The popularity of these 'antique' sculptures was reflected and increased by contemporary publications on the subject, such as Montfaucon's *L'Antiquité Expliquée...* which was translated into English in 1721.

As the popularity of these figures rose, so the demand for lead copies to decorate the changing English garden increased. By the end of the lead figure makers' era, numerous models from the famous collections had been reproduced in lead. Examples are, from the Farnese collection: Hercules (Plate 1:7) and the Callipygean Venus; from the Belvedere collection: Antinous, Apollo, and Cleopatra; from the Medici collection: Apollo, the Lion, and Venus; from the Uffizi collection: the Wrestlers, the Dancing Faun, and the Crouching Venus; from the Borghese collection: the Gladiator and Silenus. Examples of other famous works in collections outside Italy were also popular such as the Diana de Versailles and the Faun with Kid in Plate 1:6. Less famous works of antique sculpture were also imported into England from the middle of the century, and the activities of Mathew Brettingham in this connection are briefly mentioned at the end of this chapter.

Italian sculpture
The reproduction in lead of works by Italian sculptors is an obvious continuation from antique sculpture, for whilst in Italy the Englishman was also able to admire the more recent works, particularly those of the already famous Giambologna (1529-1608). His models of Hercules overcoming Antaeus, the Rape of a Sabine, and Hercules and the Erymanthian Boar were reproduced. Most popular, however, were copies of his Mercury, and the Samson slaying a Philistine group (Colour Plate 8). Few other works were copied, though several figures, such as the Melbourne Hall amorini (Colour Plate 5 and Plates 1:2 and 3), were derived from Italian Renaissance sources.

French sculpture
A number of books illustrated prints of the statuary of Versailles, such as Simon Thomassin's *Recueil des Figures, Groupes, Thermes, Fontaines, Vases...dans le Château et Parc de Versailles,* 1694, and a number of the figure makers' models were taken from these works. Many of these are reversed copies, such as the figures of L'Aurore, La Terre and L'Europe at Avington Park and Hercule Tuant L'Hydre in Plate 1:5, and these must have been modelled from prints, such as those illustrated in Thomassin's publication. This is not always the case, however, for some lead copies, such as Giradon's Abduction of Proserpine and Regnaudin's Bacchus (Plate 1:16), are not reversed and were probably modelled from other sources — drawings or models, for example.

English sculpture
Most of the lead figure makers' models comprised contemporary English sculpture for this was readily available to them. Whilst they clearly took casts of their own works, they also took casts from the *oeuvre* of a few contemporary sculptors.

How they obtained casts of these contemporary works is of some interest. The lead figure makers were sculptors in their own right, and as such must have associated with other sculptors, including some of the more renowned of the day. Whether this association with other sculptors enabled lead figure makers to take casts of these sculptors' works is unclear. As they often had patrons in common they may have done so with the patron's but not the sculptor's consent. An example of this is Cheere's work at Chiswick House, the estate of Lord Burlington (1694-1753), for he reproduced copies in lead of the seats in Plate 2:40 and Colour Plate 27 and the Lions in Plate 2:39 and Colour Plate 26. Unfortunately it is not certain who executed the original works, but the fact that statuary as incidental as

Colour Plate 8. Larger-than-life lead group at Chatsworth of Giambologna's Samson slaying a Philistine, known during the eighteenth century as Cain and Abel, probably by Carpentiere, circa 1725, originally in the gardens at Chiswick House, London. (See page 43)

Colour Plate 9. Detail from Pieter Rysbrack's painting of Lord Burlington's estate at Chiswick, 1728. The pedestal of the Cain and Abel group shown in the painting is almost identical to that of the Samson and the Philistine group now at Chatsworth, Colour Plate 8

a seat and two flanking lions was reproduced suggests that in this case the casts were made with Burlington's consent, rather than the original sculptor's.

Lead Ornaments in English Gardens

One of the most interesting features of the lead garden statuary purchased by Thomas Coke for his Derbyshire estate of Melbourne Hall, is that several figures are directly derived from the famous frescoed gallery in the Farnese Palace, Rome by Annibale Carraci (1560-1609).

The elder Van Nost's statue of Andromeda (Colour Plate 3) at Melbourne is very similar to Carraci's painting which lies at the end of the gallery, but Van Nost's figure is reversed and more upright, perhaps for dramatic effect. However, Andromeda's companion figure, Perseus (Colour Plate 4), also supplied by the elder Van Nost, bears little resemblance to Carraci's painting except for the conventional helmet (petasus) and the head of Medusa. Instead of Carraci's plain depiction of a rather wooden figure, Van Nost produced an elaborately armoured and more dramatic, baroque Perseus.

Like the Andromeda, the four heavy Flemish style pairs of amorini depicting Eros and his brother Anteros fighting and later reconciling over a bunch of flowers, also derive closely from Carraci's scenes in the corners of the ceiling of the gallery (Plates 1:2 and 3 and Colour Plate 5). However, in this case the figures are not reversed. This is somewhat confusing, for like Andromeda, one might have expected the figures to have been modelled from engravings and hence reversed.

Colour Plate 10. Life-size figure of Faun with Kid by Carpentiere, Castle Howard, Yorkshire. Like many eighteenth century lead garden statues, this figure has slumped. (See Plate 1:6 and page 43)

THE HON SIMON HOWARD

The elder Van Nost is not known to have gone to Rome, so perhaps the four pairs of amorini were executed from a painting or sketch, whilst Andromeda was derived from a contemporary publication. Another plausible theory is that the idea and impetus for these amorini, and also Andromeda, came directly from Coke himself, for he is known to have spent time in Europe studying architecture.

It seems likely that the four groups of amorini were specially commissioned by Thomas Coke, for on 1 July 1699 Van Nost wrote to his patron: 'I have set up two models of boys but they were not to my mind, and having had some extraordinary reasons which called me out of town and which has been a great hindrance to my business; but I will now with all speed dispatch your boys with all care'.[30]

Van Nost was paid £42 for '4 pr of Boyes cast in mettall' in August 1706,[31] and this must surely refer to the four groups. It is interesting to note that other models of the pairs were produced in later years, for in the elder Van Nost's 1712 sale, lots 79 and 80 were respectively 'Two *Cupids* fighting, big as the life, lead... Two *Cupids* kissing ditto',[32] and it seems most probable that these, whose minimum sale price was £6 each, were taken from the same models as Coke's. They are a magnificent set of figures, and clearly show Van Nost's Flemish training as well as his ability to turn two dimensional drawings into fine sculpture.

The stupendous vase which stands in a clearing to the east of the gardens at Melbourne must be the grandest surviving example of the elder Van Nost's work. Raised on two steps and a stone pedestal, curiously not supplied by Van Nost,[33]

Plate 1:2. A set of four pairs of lead amorini made by the elder John Van Nost, circa 1706, the Parterre, Melbourne Hall. Height approx 32ins. (See Colour Plate 5)

LORD LOTHIAN

Plate 1:3. Details of the four corners of the Farnese Palace ceiling, showing Annibale Carraci's paintings of Eros quarrelling and later reconciling with his brother Anteros, the inspiration for Van Nost's four pairs at Melbourne

Colour Plate 11. Piper, lead, uncertain attribution, Terrace, Powis Castle, Powys

THE NATIONAL TRUST: PHOTO PHILIPPE PERDEREAU

Colour Plate 13. Rustic figure, lead, uncertain attribution, early eighteenth century, Terrace, Powis Castle, Powys

THE NATIONAL TRUST: PHOTO PHILIPPE PERDEREAU

Colour Plate 12. Group of rustic figures and a Piper, lead, uncertain attribution, early eighteenth century, Terrace, Powis Castle, Powys

THE NATIONAL TRUST: PHOTO PHILIPPE PERDEREAU

Colour Plate 14. Piper, lead, uncertain attribution, Nun Monkton Priory, Yorkshire. (See Plate 1:12 and pages 45-47)

MR AND MRS AKROYD

this important work, which stands over eight feet high, clearly shows the high standard of workmanship the eighteenth century lead founders were capable of producing (Colour Plate 6).

The socle, adorned with four monkeys, supports a bas-relief scene, in places nearly two inches in relief, of putti at play. Above this are four proud busts representing the four seasons united by garlands of flowers which surround more bas-relief scenes. The whole is surmounted by a rich basket of fruit. Its overall form is in keeping with designs popular at the turn of the century and reminiscent of, for example, both Cibber and Pearce's baroque marble finials executed for Hampton Court Palace in the 1690s.[34] In 1706 Van Nost was paid £100 for this vase,[35] a substantial sum even for this magnificent work, which suggests that it was specially modelled for the owner of Melbourne, Thomas Coke. However, it is interesting to note that the basket of fruit had been modelled by Van Nost a few years earlier, for it was used in combination with his two groups of children, of 1700, on the gate piers at Hampton Court. Only one further model of this vase survives today; originally at Painshill Park, it now stands in the quadrangle of Syon House. Unfortunately no definite information concerning the maker of the vase has come to light, although it seems likely to have been one of Cheere's works. Charles Hamilton, the owner of Painshill only started purchasing his estate around 1738,[36] by which time Carpentiere was dead and Cheere had taken over the Van Nost family yard, apparently complete with, amongst others, the elder Van Nost's mould for the vase. The details on the Painshill vase are of as fine quality as that at Melbourne, but it is an inferior copy in that much of the decoration on the upper part, such as the garlands and bas-relief scenes, have been omitted. Amongst several other minor variations, the Painshill vase is surmounted by a charming fox, not fruit, as is the case at Melbourne.

The powerful lead group at Powis Castle depicting Hercules battling with his second labour, Hydra, the many-headed monster (Plate 1:4 and Colour Plate 7), is based on a group executed for Versailles by the seventeenth century sculptor, Pierre Puget (1620-1694). However, since the Powis group is a reversed copy of the original at Versailles, the artist responsible must have worked from a print, such as the late seventeenth century publication by Simon Thomassin, *Recueil des Figures, Groupes, Thermes, Fontaines et Vases...dans le Château et Parc de Versailles,* which illustrates Puget's work (Plate 1:5).

Like the original, the Powis group was produced together with the Hydra, though in the Powis group the Hydra is carved of a local stone. This is odd, for the predominant stone used for eighteenth century garden sculpture was Portland, and it suggests that the Hydra was carved by a local sculptor using a stone he was familiar with and loosely working from an illustration of the original.

Other reversed lead models of Puget's Hercules, such as the dilapidated examples at Chatsworth and Goldney Hall, are free standing — without the Hydra.

Examination of the Hercules at Powis reveals traces of what was probably its original finish, white paint. It also clearly shows the beautiful patina of white, bright silvers and black which lead develops after years of exposure to the elements. The club seems to be a later replacement, for it is made of wood inset with iron-studs, while the other examples have, or had, leaden clubs.

No record of the purchase of this group, or the other lead figures at Powis, survives, but they were probably supplied in the first quarter of the eighteenth century. Andries Carpentiere's initials appear on the figure of Fame riding on the back of Pegasus at Powis,[37] and although this is not firm enough evidence to

Plate 1:4. Life-size group of Hercules and the Hydra, lead (the Hydra of local North Wales stone), probably dating from the early eighteenth century, Terrace Gardens, Powis Castle. (See Colour Plate 7)

THE NATIONAL TRUST

Plate 1:5. Detail from Thomassin's Recueil des Figures... *showing Hercule Tuant l'Hydre*

THOMAS HENEAGE ART BOOKS

attribute the Hercules group to him, it probably dates from his period of production. It is also worth remembering that lead figure makers were often employed by the same patron, such as Cheere and Carpentiere at Castle Howard, and Carpentiere and the Van Nost family at Stowe.

The impressive statue taken directly from Giambologna's marble group depicting Samson slaying a Philistine, was known as Cain and Abel in the eighteenth century. The original marble (now in the Victoria and Albert Museum), was executed in the early 1560s and given to the Duke of Buckingham by Charles I (to whom it had been presented by Phillip IV of Spain in 1623). For many years it stood in the grounds of York House until its removal to the hall of Buckingham House some time between 1703 and 1714.[38] The popularity of the statue during the late seventeenth century and the eighteenth century is best reflected by the large numbers of lead models produced for numerous country houses by makers such as the elder Van Nost and his family, Carpentiere and Cheere.

The earliest documented copy of this group was supplied to Chatsworth in 1691 for £50,[39] but unfortunately who produced the model is unknown. Perhaps it was Richard Osgood, for he must have had moulds of the figure as he is known to have supplied a copy to Lord Fauconberg's estate at Sutton Court in 1695,[40] and is also known to have supplied ornaments to Chatsworth.[41] Another possible source for this early Chatsworth Samson and the Philistine is the elder Van Nost, who is known to have supplied lead work to Chatsworth, and must have been acquainted with the owner of the marble original, the Duke of Buckingham, for he supplied statuary for the Duke's London house.[42]

Unfortunately, neither the Sutton Court nor the early Chatsworth models survive today. Curiously Carpentiere's models, two of which are mentioned within the list of figures he sent to Charles Howard, 3rd Earl of Carlisle (1669-1738), are recorded as being only six feet high.[43] However, this was probably a clerical error, for Bologna's group which stands over seven feet high (as do the surviving lead copies, allowing for some 'slumping') would have been well known to eighteenth century Londoners, and it seems improbable that Carpentiere would have modelled a reduced copy. No documented models of the elder Van Nost's copies have survived, although several, such as that at Harrowden Hall, have been attributed to him,[44] and he must have been producing copies for one is mentioned in the 1712 Sale Catalogue.[45]

An example of Cheere's cast survives in a private collection.

A lead copy of Giambologna's Samson and the Philistine still decorates the gardens at Chatsworth (Colour Plate 8) though it was probably originally in Lord Burlington's garden at Chiswick. A painting by Pieter Andreas Rysbrack (1690-1748) of the Chiswick gardens, circa 1728 (Colour Plate 9) depicts the group painted cream/white surmounting a pedestal of almost identical design to that of the Samson and the Philistine group now at Chatsworth, whilst the drawing of the 1691 Chatsworth group depicts it on a pedestal of much squarer form.[46] Certainly the possibility that the Chatsworth group was transferred to another pedestal cannot be ruled out. However, many of the Chiswick garden ornaments were moved to Chatsworth at the turn of the century and consequently it is highly probable that the group at Chatsworth was originally at Chiswick.

It is not definitely known which lead figure maker produced this statue for Lord Burlington, but the dating of Rysbrack's painting to 1728 would make it one of the early makers. To date, the only early lead figure maker known to have worked for Lord Burlington was Carpentiere, and according to an entry in Burlington's account book for 5 February 1721/22 Andries Carpentiere 'Recvd. seven pounds 10s for moving ye 3 figures of marble to Chiswick bronzing 3 heads'[47]; as such a tentative attribution to Carpentiere seems probable.

Both Andries Carpentiere and later John Cheere produced a number of lead figures for the Carlisle estate of Castle Howard, each supplying a copy of an 'antique' Faun. Cheere's bill is not dated, but lists a 'statue of a Dancing Faune, 6 foot, 1 inch, in lead on a Portland stone Plinth. . . £17 17s 0d,[48] and this almost certainly relates to the copy of the antique figure of a Dancing Faun,[49] which now lies beside its pedestal, broken at the ankles, in the centre of the Formal Garden.

Carpentiere's bill of 13 July 1723 lists 'ye Faunus',[50] whilst a footnote values it at £20, and this almost certainly relates to the other model of a faun at Castle Howard in the same garden but to the west (Plate 1:6 and Colour Plate 10). This, too, is a copy of another 'antique' statue known as the Faun with Kid, the original marble statue of which is now in the Prado, Madrid.[51]

Carpentiere's Faun with Kid, together with the other surviving lead model now at Chatsworth,[52] must have been modelled from a print because both are directly reversed copies of the original. The Castle Howard example has, however, suffered during its exposure to the elements over the last 260 years. It has been repaired at least once,[53] and can no longer support its own substantial weight, hence the necessity of an incongruous iron bar to prevent collapse.

The original larger-than-life-size marble figure of Hercules resting on his club was, between the mid-sixteenth and late eighteenth centuries, in the Farnese collection.[54] It is now in the National Museum, Naples. During the eighteenth century the so-called Farnese Hercules was one of the most admired antique

Plate 1:6. Life-size figure of Faun with Kid, lead, by Carpentiere, 1723, the Formal Garden, Castle Howard. (See Colour Plate 10)
THE HON SIMON HOWARD

Plate 1:7. Life-size figure of the Farnese Hercules, lead, by Carpentiere, 1723, Castle Howard
THE HON SIMON HOWARD

statues. It was illustrated in Montfaucon's *L'Antiquité Expliquée,* and Addison, in his *Remarks on several Parts of Italy, &c.,* relates that it was one of 'the Four finest Figures perhaps that are now extant'.[55] Its reproduction in lead by several of the leading lead figure makers is, therefore, not surprising.

Although the list of figures Lord Carlisle received from Andries Carpentiere does not mention a Farnese Hercules,[56] Carpentiere is known to have sold a model to Carlisle in 1723. His bill, dated 13 July, for this and three other figures relates: 'For the Hercules of Farnese...' a footnote valuing each, the Hercules at 'thirty guineas'.[57] This figure remains today on the approach to the Temple of the Four Winds at Castle Howard (Plate 1:7), raised on an imposing pedestal, perhaps designed by Nicholas Hawksmoor (1661-1736).[58]

The elder Van Nost is also known to have produced a model of this figure, but the whereabouts of any examples are unknown; two are listed in the 1712 sale catalogue, one being 'life size', the other 'small life'.[59] John Cheere also produced a Farnese Hercules, for he supplied one similar to Carpentiere's to James, 2nd Duke of Atholl (1690-1764) in the early 1740s;[60] another is illustrated in Hogarth's engraving of a statuary yard thought to be Cheere's (Plate 1:1 and page 31).

Several other models of the Farnese Hercules survive today, one at Quarry Park, Shrewsbury,[61] which varies from the Castle Howard and Blair Atholl examples in that the length of Hercules' club is a foot longer. Another Farnese Hercules stands in the grounds of Gloddaeth Hall.[62] Others are, or were, at Chirk Castle,[63] Elvaston Castle,[64] and in a private square off Ebury Street, London.

The pair of vases in Plate 1:8 are of particular relevance to English sculpture, because the bas-relief scenes on the friezes are taken from a pair of marble vases executed for Hampton Court Palace at the end of the seventeenth century by two prominent sculptors, Caius Gabriel Cibber and Edward Pearce (circa 1635-1695).

In his book on the works of Cibber,[65] Faber suggests that he may have cast models of these vases in lead. Cibber is known to have worked in the material, and it certainly seems plausible that he would have been able to take casts from both his and Pearce's originals. An alternative source is the elder John Van Nost, for at Hampton Court Palace in July 1701 he is recorded to have been paid for removing the vases, polishing their pedestals and cleaning them. Two months later he was paid £4 'For Polishing Severall parts of the two great Vauses att Hampton Court'.[66] So Van Nost certainly had access to both vases, and it seems reasonable to assume that while undertaking this work he, too, would have been in a position to take casts.

Whatever the case, the lead figure makers soon had casts of these two vases. At Wrest Park an exact copy of Cibber's vase formerly decorated the gardens,[67] whilst the bas-relief scenes from both vases were incorporated within many other vases. Of the two bas-relief scenes, Cibber's, which depicts a Bacchanalian procession, seems to have been the most popular, for it is found on several vases at Drayton House,[68] whilst further examples occur at Chatsworth,[69] Park Place,[70] and Anglesey Abbey (Plate 1:9) (this last example used to decorate the gardens at Drakelowe Hall). Interestingly, the sequence of scenes in Cibber's original is not the same on the Anglesey Abbey example, indicating that in this case the plaster piece mould must have been assembled incorrectly.

Pearce's relief of Amphitrite and the Nereids appears on vases at Park Place,[71] and Drayton House,[72] as well as on the example shown in Plate 1:8.

To attribute the pair at Wrest Park is difficult. The younger Van Nost is known to have supplied ornaments in the late 1720s,[73] but Carpentiere also worked at the estate,[74] and it may well be that he too had access to the moulds of Cibber's and Pearce's reliefs.

The set of four life-size figures on the Terrace at Powis Castle (Plate 1:10 and Colour Plates 11-13) are magnificent examples of the rustic statuary so popular during the first quarter of the eighteenth century. One of these, the Piper in Plate 1:10, is worth examining in more detail as it and the similar Pipers at Cannons Ashby (Plate 1:11) and Nun Monkton Priory (Plate 1:12 and Colour Plate 14) are basically identical, but, like a considerable number of lead garden statues, they have varying features. These variations can probably be explained by the necessity for moulds to be renewed as they became worn out and the likelihood that the original model, from which the moulds were taken, was made of clay and was modified from time to time.

A model made of clay, or parts of it, could be relatively easily remodelled to enable the variations, for example, in the number and size of the buttons on each figure and probably also the portrayal of the pockets in an open or closed form.

The varying pouches, hats and pipes were inevitably cast separately, as also was the footwear on the Nun Monkton Piper, which must surely have been taken from

Plate 1:8. Pair of vases, lead, of uncertain attribution, probably dating from the second quarter of the eighteenth century, flanking the Bowling Green House, Wrest Park. Height approx 60ins. Cibber's design, with its Bacchanalian procession, is on the left
ENGLISH HERITAGE

some other model, and incorporated into the figure when the various hollow cast lead component pieces were being assembled around the wrought iron armature. Those non-attached additions, such as tree trunks and sleeping hounds, would also have been cast separately and, as can be seen, helped to alter the characters still further. The poses of the arms of all three Pipers is more difficult to comment on, for although these variations would have been easily accomplished when the various parts of the figures were being assembled, it should be noted that all three figures have been restored, and also that the arms may well have slumped or bent during the two centuries they have been outside.

The flexibility of decoration of these statues must have contributed greatly to the *oeuvre* of each lead figure maker, and one can imagine that on occasion patrons were supplied with basically the same model modified to represent a variety of different subjects.

It seems plausible that all three figures originated from the Van Nost family workshops, or at least derived from a model known to have been produced by the

elder John Van Nost, for they can be broadly associated with the 'A Shepherd Piping, big as the Life, lead', or 'A Shepherd and Dog, big as the life, lead', which were respectively lots 31 and 69 in the posthumous 1712 sale. The figure at Cannons Ashby in Northamptonshire (Plate 1:11) seems to have been supplied by the younger John Van Nost, who wrote to Edward Dryden, the owner of the estate at that time, requesting payment for an outstanding bill in April 1713.[75] The figure on the terrace at Powis Castle (Plate 1:10) is of uncertain origin. It may have been supplied by one of the Van Nosts or Carpentiere (see pages 41-42). The source of the statue at Nun Monkton Priory (Plate 1:12), is less certain for it was supplied by an as yet unidentified lead figure maker, some time between 1723 and 1773.[76] It is unfortunate that these three figures are not better documented, for they might have been able to provide invaluable information concerning the frequency of remodelling and mould making during the eighteenth century.

All three figures have been restored, replaced on new slabs of Portland stone and repainted, that at Powis in white in imitation of marble; at Nun Monkton a beige-white in imitation of stone, whilst that at Cannons Ashby has been finished in a peculiar colour in an attempt to simulate lead, although that is most unlikely to have been its original finish.

Plate 1:10. Life-size figure of a Piper, lead, uncertain attribution, early eighteenth century, the Terrace, Powis Castle

THE NATIONAL TRUST

Plate 1:11. Life-size figure of a Piper, lead, probably by John Van Nost the younger, circa 1713, the Formal Gardens, Cannons Ashby

THE NATIONAL TRUST

Plate 1:12. Life-size figure of a Piper, lead, uncertain attribution, 1720s-1730s. Nun Monkton Priory. (See Colour Plate 14)

MR AND MRS AYKROYD

The accounts for work at Hampton Court Palace in the early years of the eighteenth century contain some important information relating to perhaps the most common statue produced by the Hyde Park lead figure makers, that of a kneeling life-size figure supporting a sundial. The accounts in September 1701 record payment to the elder John Van Nost for 'modelling a figure representing a Blackamoore Kneeling', and in December of the same year, for 'modelling a figure representing an Indian Slave Kneeling',[77] both of which were cast in hard metal and cost respectively £30 and £35. Van Nost received payment for erecting the Blackamoor in October 1701 and, in January the following year, a further payment of £1 15s 0d 'for makeing a journey to Hampton Ct, selfe and 2 men to sett up the Indian Slave'.[78] Whether these two were commissioned by William III as the first two parts of a set representing the four Continents, will probably never be known, since he died two months after the Indian was erected.

The popularity of these two kneeling sundial figures can be accounted for, to a certain extent, by their presence at Hampton Court, for other lords remodelling their gardens and wishing to emulate the current fashion (that is, the King's taste) would want and would have had copies made. This was to provide considerable business not only for the elder Van Nost and, no doubt, his family, but also for Carpentiere and John Cheere.

The earliest surviving example of these figures (the Hampton Court pair have since disappeared) can be seen at Melbourne Hall in Derbyshire which, unlike the other models, support salvers bearing small lead vases. They were purchased by

Plate 1:13. Life-size figure of a Blackamoor, lead, by John Cheere, 1741, the Forecourt, Okeover Hall
SIR PETER WALKER-OKEOVER, BT

Plate 1:14. Life-size figure of an Indian, lead, early eighteenth century, the Courtyard, Arley Hall
HON M L W FLOWER

Plate 1:15. Life-size figure of a Blackamoor, lead, attributed to Carpentiere, circa 1735, the South Front, Dunham Massey
THE NATIONAL TRUST

Thomas Coke, Vice-Chamberlain to Queen Anne and George I, who paid the elder Van Nost £30 for them in 1706.[79] Regrettably no reference as to how they were finished survives. Christopher Hussey mentions that their bodies were painted black, their eyes white and their sashes in bright colours,[80] but this could have been a later addition and perhaps, like the Blackamoor at Hampton Court, they were coloured in an imitation of bronze.[81]

Copies of these two figures were still being produced in the second quarter of the eighteenth century, some identical to the elder Van Nost's models, some with minor, some with major modifications. The Blackamoor John Cheere supplied to Okeover Hall in 1741 (Plate 1:13)[82] is, with the exception of the treatment of the hair, identical to that at Melbourne. Cheere's Blackamoor was simply cast with a bald head and the hair formed by chasing with a characteristic spiralling punch, whilst Van Nost's figure was actually cast with hair. The Indian at Arley Hall (Plate 1:14) is the same as the Melbourne model, but its provenance and maker remain unearthed.[83] The Blackamoor in the Courtyard of Dunham Massey (Plate 1:15) is strikingly different to that at Okeover, in particular in the positioning of the limbs. No conclusive evidence has come to light concerning the identity of the figure maker who supplied this, but it seems likely to have been Andries Carpentiere. A few miles from Dunham Massey is Bowden Church, for which in 1735 Carpentiere executed a monument to the 1st Earl of Warrington and his wife, paid for by their son and heir, the 2nd Earl, who rebuilt Dunham Massey in the 1730s. This certainly gives strength to the suggestion that the figure came from

Plate 1:16. Life-size figure of Bacchus, lead, uncertain attribution, early eighteenth century, the Formal Garden, Hardwick Hall
THE NATIONAL TRUST

Plate 1:17. Life-size figure of a River God, lead painted white, by John Cheere, circa 1750, the Grotto, Stourhead. (See Colour Plate 15)
THE NATIONAL TRUST

Carpentiere's hand, for lead figure makers frequently supplied both carved work as well as lead ornaments to the same estate. Unfortunately no trace has been found of any documented copies of a Blackamoor by Carpentiere. If the Dunham Massey figure is by him, the variations suggest that he modelled his own copy, rather than having access, at least in this case, to the Van Nost family moulds.

The lead figure makers were also producing models of a similar pose, but different subjects. John Cheere supplied a model of Father Time to Blair Atholl in 1743;[84] like the Blackamoor at Okeover, this Father Time has his right leg forward, but the feathered 'skirt' has been replaced with a loin cloth similar to that on the Indian at Arley. The head was also exchanged for that of a bearded old man and wings were attached. Another figure of Father Time, larger than the other copies and by an unknown maker, survives at St Paul's Walden Bury, but in this case the salver and dial are supported by one hand, while the other holds a time glass. The only other variation in terms of subject is a kneeling Hercules which used to stand in the gardens of Winton Castle, but it unfortunately disappeared in the 1950s. Although no illustrations of it have been traced, it is assumed that it had a head of Hercules, its groin draped with the pelt of the Nemean lion.

Like the great majority of eighteenth century lead figures, the figures' iron armature was leaded into a Portland stone base. Characteristic of these kneeling figures is the moulded form this takes, visible beneath the figures at Okeover and

Plate 1:18. Life-size figure of a Gamekeeper, lead, possibly by John Cheere, circa 1750, originally at Biel House and removed when the house was partially demolished
PRIVATE COLLECTION

Dunham Massey, whilst that at Arley is no doubt of a later date. However, it is interesting to note that the original models supplied to Hampton Court were both attached to black marble bases carved by the elder Van Nost. This may seem odd, for as a general aesthetic rule, lead and stone, and marble and bronze are regarded as good combinations. The curious combination of marble and lead is understandable at Hampton Court, for the Blackamoor, and no doubt also the Indian, were finished in an imitation of bronze.

The eighteenth century lead figure of Bacchus (or Autumn) in the gardens at Hardwick Hall (Plate 1:16) is directly based on a statue by the late seventeenth century French sculptor, Thomas Regnaudin (1622-1706). Regnaudin's original marble figure, executed for the gardens at Versailles between 1676 and 1687,[85] varies considerably from this English copy. The most notable differences are in the omission from the copy of a strap which runs vertically across the original figure's chest and a basket of fruit at the figure's right foot, as well as in the treatment of the drapery which in the copy only roughly follows the contours of the original. Although some of these variations can perhaps be accounted for by the considerable restoration this figure has undergone, including newly made legs and goblet,[86] and the replacement of the original Portland stone base with one·made of a Midlands stone, the statue is distinctly different from the Versailles original, and as such it cannot have been cast from any existing mould or pattern, but must have been modelled by a clearly talented artist working from a sketch or drawing. Unlike another eighteenth century lead copy of sculpture at Versailles illustrated earlier in this chapter (Plates 1:4 and 5), this model is not reversed, and so cannot have been modelled from a print.

As a result of the researches of Phillip Heath, the original location of this and the other five eighteenth century life-size lead figures at Hardwick Hall is now known. They were removed from Chatsworth in 1867, and so seem likely to have formed part of the early eighteenth century decorations to the Derbyshire estate. Although a number of lead figures are illustrated in Knyff's painting and Kip's engraving of the estate, neither the Bacchus nor the other five figures now at Hardwick, are clearly discernible in either.

Despite this, it seems reasonable to believe that the figure of Bacchus is an early work dating from around the turn of the century, probably cast by one of the many lead figure makers known to have supplied garden ornaments to the estate. These included, amongst others, Osgood, the elder John Van Nost, and Cibber. However, no further information as to the identity of the artist responsible can be ascertained, and although two Bacchus companion figures at Hardwick (representing Painting and Sculpture) are known to be models by the elder Van Nost,[87] there is no reason to assume that this Bacchus was also cast by him.

Henry Hoare's rustic grotto at Stourhead is adorned by two lead statues: one is a copy of the antique Cleopatra in the Vatican, slightly different copies of which survive in a private collection,[88] and West Wycombe,[89] the other is a wonderful figure of a River God resting on an urn and raising his hand (Plate 1:17 and Colour Plate 15), for which John Cheere received payment (together with a number of other figures) on 7 August 1751.[90]

The subject is taken from an engraving by Salvator Rosa of a scene from Virgil's *Aeneid* depicting the River Tiber and Aeneas.[91] Cheere's model of the Tiber is, however, in reverse and hence must have been modelled from a print.

Unlike the majority of Cheere's lead figures, this model appears to be unique in that no duplicate models have been traced. This is curious, for the figure is both exceptionally well modelled and not unappealing, and this suggests that it was specially commissioned by Hoare for his Aeneid-inspired gardens. The treatment of the figure is certainly reminiscent of the work of John Michael Rysbrack (1694-1770), and it is not surprising that the figure, prior to 1951, had been 'perversely and continuously attributed' to him.[92] Rysbrack executed several important works for Stourhead,[93] but although the River God bears some characteristics of his hand, no firm evidence to connect Rysbrack with Cheere's figure has come to light.

Whatever the case, Cheere was paid for this figure, and if it was he, not Rysbrack, who modelled the original, then this graceful figure must rank as one of his most outstanding works.

The lead figure of a gamekeeper in Plate 1:18 was the cause of some surprise to the writer of an article on Biel House: 'Pondering on the account of an agrarian murder in Ireland which he had just read in the papers, he suddenly raised his eyes and saw, as he thought, death staring him in the face. He remembers how he jumped behind the nearest tree, and, with a voice which he strove to render steady, called to the assassin to "put down that gun". He has not forgotten, either, his feeling of relief when he realised the situation, and was certain no one had seen him'.[94] Biel was partially demolished in the 1950s.[95]

Plate 1:19. Life-size group of the Abduction of Helen, lead, attributed to John Cheere, the French Garden, Wrest Park
ENGLISH HERITAGE

Plate 1:20. Life-size group of Diana and Endymion, lead, probably dating from John Cheere's period of production, mid- to late eighteenth century, the Jubilee Walk, Anglesey Abbey
THE NATIONAL TRUST

Painted with a green jacket, it is a superbly modelled figure, particular care having been taken in the details of the clothing. Unfortunately it is beginning to deteriorate and a rupture has appeared on the left leg. This has been caused by the rusting iron armature expanding and pushing the plaster core out, so ripping the lead. Happily its repair is in hand.

Precisely when this figure became popular is unclear, probably around Cheere's time, for it is almost certainly one of those figures mentioned in J T Smith's account of Cheere's yard as 'gamekeepers in the act of shooting'.[96] By the early 1750s Cheere had supplied a 'Statue of a Gamekeeper in the best manner and painted in proper colours' at a cost of £14 14s to the Duke of Atholl's garden at Blair Atholl.[97] This figure has since disappeared, despite Cheere's instructions concerning its unpacking and care: 'The Person that unpacks ye Game Keeper should take ye braces that hold it fast in ye Case of very carefully and once in two years it should be washd very clean & oiled over with Linseed Oile'.[98]

A further model of this figure is mentioned in E Brickdale's article 'The Use of Leadwork in Gardens',[99] but although illustrating the Sportsman (as it is referred to) and its companion figure, the Thief (a fox with a bird in its mouth), their location is not revealed.[100]

Four life-size lead groups depicting Venus and Adonis, Aeneas and Anchises, Diana and Endymion,[101] and the Abduction of Helen decorate the French garden at Wrest Park. They are all raised on pedestals of Portland stone, the design of which is in keeping with the nineteenth century style.

The purchase of these four groups by the owner of Wrest Park, at that time, the 2nd Earl de Grey, is recorded in a letter to his daughter in April 1846: 'The large groups of figures in the French garden are in lead and most beautiful works. They were brought to this country from Holland or Belgium, I believe by a man afterwards known as Ex-sherrif Parkins...I bought them off Brown, who was a good while before he could dispose of them...'.[102] The 2nd Earl de Grey rebuilt Wrest Park in the early 1830s,[103] and it seems probable that these four groups were purchased around that time. Two of the groups, Venus and Adonis, and Diana and Endymion, are known to have been stock John Cheere figures,[104] and as the production of lead statuary almost completely stopped at the time of Cheere's death, their purchase in the nineteenth century is curious. However, as has already been mentioned (page 31), a number of Cheere's figures were purchased by an anonymous dealer after his death, and it is likely that these four were amongst them. This anonymous dealer supplied a large number of Cheere's lead figures in 1812 to a private collection. A list of the twenty-one figures offered survives,[105] and of these sixteen are known to have been purchased. Another figure listed, of Shakespeare, was supplied to the Drury Lane Theatre, whilst the four remaining are all groups, and correspond exactly to the four in the French Garden at Wrest Park.

It would appear that the 2nd Earl de Grey was misinformed about the origins of these figures, which must have been part of Cheere's stock purchased after his death and, as the Earl adds in the letter referred to above, it must have been a long time before Brown 'could dispose of them'.

The Abduction of Helen (Plate 1:19) which is described in the 1812 list as 'The Rape of a Sabina by a Roman warrior, with the figure of her father on the ground', and priced at £100, is derived from a model by the French sculptor Phillipe Bertrand (1663-1724) depicting the abduction, or rape, of Helen. It is by no means a direct copy, and was perhaps modelled from a drawing or copy of Bertrand's work. Like a number of these life-size groups, it is attached to a lead-covered stone base, unlike single figures which are almost always attached directly to a Portland base.

The group of Diana and Endymion (Plate 1:20) now at Anglesey Abbey, originally adorned the gardens of Copped Hall, Essex, but no evidence concerning the date it was supplied or who made it has come to light.[106] It is the duplicate models of the group which survive at Wrest Park and the Royal Palace of Queluz, Portugal, which suggest that the Anglesey Abbey group may also have been supplied by John Cheere. The Wrest group is undoubtedly by Cheere and, as has been seen, was purchased, together with three other groups, by the 2nd Earl de Grey from an unknown dealer around the 1830s. The Queluz model is also by Cheere, but unfortunately his bill for the numerous figures he supplied in 1756 has not survived.[107]

The only further evidence to suggest Cheere's hand is again circumstantial. A *Country Life* article on Copped Hall illustrates the Diana and Endymion and two further lead figures, Diana and Apollo,[108] of which duplicate models by Cheere survive at Queluz. With this in mind, it seems probable that the Diana and Endymion from Copped Hall may also be by Cheere. Despite the fact that the group is signed and dated 'J. Cheere 1690', this is of no assistance; lead figures were very rarely signed, and with the exception of this group only one other dated lead figure is known, at Blair Atholl,[109] and that is not signed. But what makes the attribution quite wrong is the crudely worked lettering and the date of 1690, for Cheere was born in 1709! One can only assume that this inscription is a fake added at a later date.

The group of Diana and Endymion is another of the few examples of eighteenth century lead statuary supplied with a lead-covered stone base, as are the Queluz

Plate 1:21. One of a pair of Sphinxes, lead, attributed to John Cheere, circa 1770, flanking the Coronation Avenue, Anglesey Abbey. Width approx 62ins

THE NATIONAL TRUST

and Wrest models. As a general rule, only a few of the larger groups incorporate lead bases, and a feature of these is the chasing with various details, such as flowers, animals or figures.

From which estate the pair of lead sphinxes (Plate 1:21) now flanking the Coronation Avenue at Anglesey Abbey originated is unknown, but it is likely that they were cast by John Cheere, probably some time after 1760.

An earlier pair of the same basic design were used to decorate the gardens of Newhailes in East Lothian. Unfortunately these were stolen in 1949,[110] but they must have been those for which John Cheere was paid in November 1740.[111] However, the Newhailes sphinxes had one distinct difference from those at Anglesey Abbey; each was decorated with an elaborate head-dress, which swept down in a great curve on to the shoulders, giving the creature a very Egyptian look.

Sphinxes with these Egyptian-style head-dresses were popular in the first half of the eighteenth century, but by the 1760s they were becoming old-fashioned. Sphinxes continued to be a popular form of garden ornament but, with the advent

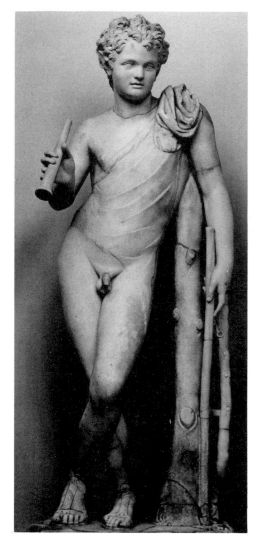 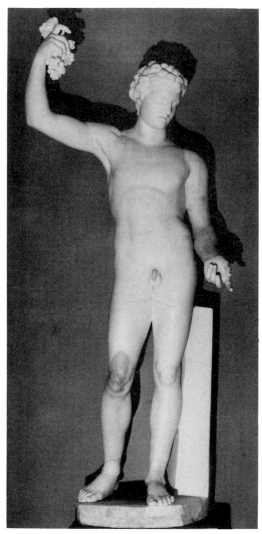

Plate 1:22. Satyr, Parian marble, antique, the Statue Gallery, Holkham Hall. Height approx 51ins. (See Colour Plate 16)

THE COKE ESTATE LTD

Plate 1:23. Satyr, Parian marble, Graeco-Roman, antique, the North Gallery, Petworth House. Height 67ins. (See Colour Plate 17)

THE NATIONAL TRUST

of the style popularised by the architect Robert Adam (1728-1792), a lighter, more delicate taste was to become the vogue. What is interesting about the pair once at Newhailes is that simply by removing the elaborate head-dress John Cheere created a strikingly different and more elegant model which was favoured by a number of noblemen and architects of the late 1760s and 1770s.

Of sphinxes without Egyptian head-dresses, probably the earliest pair flank the Lion Gateway to Syon House, which was designed by Robert Adam in the late 1760s. No bill exists, but John Cheere is known to have worked for the owner of the estate, the 1st Duke of Northumberland (1715-1786), and the Duke's account at Hoare's Bank records two payments to Cheere, one for £100 on 10 July 1767, and other for £70 two years later.[112] Another pair of sphinxes decorates the Dashwood estate at West Wycombe. They were formerly by the West Portico (built in 1771), but are now alongside the Temple of Diana. Again no bill has been unearthed, but John Cheere is known to have worked for the owner, Sir Francis Dashwood (1708-1781).[113]

At present two further sets are known, both of which comprise four sphinxes. One set adorned the bridge at Compton Verney and, as this was erected in the early 1770s, it too seems likely to have come from John Cheere.[114] The other set decorates the skyline of Somerset House in London. This was definitely supplied by John Cheere in 1778 at a cost of £31 each[115] but, although taken from the same mould, the sphinxes were modified by the addition of a garment extending from the harness on their backs to shroud their heads.

As three of these groups of sphinxes can be attributed to John Cheere, and two other groups are known to have been supplied by John Cheere, it is highly likely that those at Anglesey Abbey are also by this prolific lead figure maker. Like the others, the details of the hair and particularly the sphinxes' harnesses and saddle cloths are magnificent. Much of this was clearly chased by hand with punches and chisels to enhance the details. With a step ladder it is possible to examine this pair, and the presence of red ochre in a few of the less exposed crevices suggests that the sphinxes were originally gilded, for red ochre was a compound applied prior to gilding.

Models of this sphinx continued to be made and are still produced in a variety of media. In the late eighteenth century publication *Etchings of Coade's Artificial Stone Manufactory,* a slightly reduced version is illustrated, and this was copied by an unknown manufactory seemingly operating in the early years of the twentieth century in a cement-based artificial stone as well as in lead. Even smaller models were manufactured by the Wedgwood works in their Basalt or Egyptian Black Ware, for use as interior decoration.

One of the more interesting aspects of the lead statuary produced by John Cheere, is that from about 1760 his range of models started to include copies of antique marble statuary in England. The exact circumstances by which he obtained moulds or casts of these is still uncertain, but it seems probable that they were obtained from Mathew Brettingham (1725-1803). Brettingham, the eldest son of the architect Mathew Brettingham (1699-1769), spent several years in Rome in the middle of the century collecting antiques for the English gentry. His acquisitions included a number of marble statues which were supplied, amongst other country houses, to Holkham and Petworth. Brettingham is also known to have taken casts from some of these statues, and started producing plaster reproductions. However, as John Kenworthy-Browne points out,[116] it appears that Brettingham had difficulties selling them, and either the moulds or several of the casts passed into the hands of the foremost manufacturer of both lead and plaster statues, John Cheere.

Two examples of these statues are illustrated in Colour Plates 16 and 17, together with the corresponding original antique marble figures (Plates 1:22 and 23). Plate 1:22 shows the Parian marble figure of a Satyr purchased in Italy by Brettingham, either from Cardinal Alisano Albani (1692-1779), the renowned collector and dealer, or from Bartolomeo Cavaceppi (1716-1799), the leading restorer of antique marble statues in the latter half of the eighteenth century. It was supplied to the estate of Thomas Coke, 1st Earl of Leicester (1697-1759), at Holkham Hall, Norfolk, where it was described the following century by Adolph Michaelis thus:

STATUE OF A YOUTHFUL SATYR. The slim youth of graceful form, without a tail, leans with his left shoulder on a tree trunk near which the right arm hangs down easily. Beneath, on the trunk the remains of a crook (pedum) are visible, the crooked end lowest, and the remains of the tie by which the staff of the crook was tied to the trunk. Further to the front of the trunk, the bottom piece of the shaft of a spear must have rested in the arm of the Satyr. Both weapons are suitable to the character of the Satyr that haunts wood and field. A great part of the body is covered in a very thin tight-fitting nebris, the head of which is seen near the left shoulder; from which, besides, a little cloak falls down behind the trunk of the tree. The legs are crossed, left slightly bent and in front of right on which the body is supported. The feet are in sandals. Right arm lowered, but forearm raised; the hand may perhaps have always held the pipe. Restored by Westmacott: head, neck, three quarters of left arm, including the best part of the spear and pedum, half right forearm with the pipe. The remainder of the statue is antique, though broken in several places.[117]

The lead copy of this figure (Colour Plate 16) is a particularly interesting model. It clearly shows the superb quality of some of Cheere's lead casts, although the pipe in the right hand leaves much to be desired. The statue retains some signs of its original paint which suggests that it was finished in life-like colours and not in white, probably the commonest finish for copies of antique statuary. A further point of interest is the figure's base. Unusually, for an eighteenth century single lead figure, it is joined to a decorated and chased lead, not stone, base. As the edges of this have suffered considerable damage and been much restored, it seems probable that it was originally part of a larger group perhaps comprising other figures associated with the Satyr, such as woodland or mountain creatures.

Another example shows the antique Parian marble figure of a second Satyr, this time pouring wine, in the sculpture gallery at Petworth House in Sussex (Plate 1:23). This heavily restored statue was found in Italy by another Englishman, the painter and dealer in antique statues, Gavin Hamilton (1730-1797), and it is likely Brettingham would have been in a position to have a cast taken from the marble. Brettingham was an intimate friend of Hamilton, and acted as a receiver for Hamilton's acquisitions in Italy. Brettingham was also well acquainted with Charles Wyndham, 2nd Earl of Egremont (1710-1763), the owner of Petworth, for he is known to have been involved with assembling the collection of antique marbles which were displayed in a gallery designed by his (Brettingham's) father.[118]

Cheere's copy of the Petworth Satyr (Colour Plate 17), one of the models purchased after Cheere's death for a private collection in 1812, is as admirable as his copy of the Holkham model. The existence of a duplicate Satyr at Staunton Harold suggests the Petworth Satyr, together with a number of other lead figures on the facade, originated from Cheere's yard.

Eighteenth Century Arcadian and Haymaking Figures

During the eighteenth century masked balls or, *fête-champêtres,* set in Arcadian settings of country houses or in London's Ranelagh and Vauxhall pleasure gardens, were immensely popular. These were attended by fashionable society dressed as milkmaids, fruit and flower girls or in the costumes of the *commedia dell'arte.* Most popular of all, however, were the costumes of a shepherd or shepherdess. Numerous contemporary references to their popularity remain. *The Spectator* of 1711 recounts: 'There is not a girl in town but let her have her will in going to a masque and she shall dress as a shepherdess'.[119] This fascination with Arcadia was reflected in many art forms — for instance in porcelain figures and

Plate 1:24. A pair of three-quarter figures of a Shepherd and Shepherdess, lead, probably from one of the Van Nosts or Carpentiere's yard, early eighteenth century

Plate 1:25. Pair of life-size figures of a Shepherd and Shepherdess, lead, Edward Hurst, 1718, the Forecourt, Charlecote Park

Plate 1:26. Details from two anonymous paintings of the grounds of Wrest Park, circa 1720-21, showing the Arcadian and haymaking figures which used to surround the Pavilion

BEDFORDSHIRE RECORD OFFICE/LADY LUCAS

in the chimney-pieces by Sir Henry Cheere, but perhaps above all in lead statuary, of which numerous models were produced.

These Arcadian lead figures tend to reflect the clothing of the time, and the vast majority were painted to look life like. Examples of the more common type of lead shepherds and shepherdess models are shown in Colour Plate 18. These figures have been stripped of countless layers of paint to reveal the original colouring, and although they might be considered far too garish to place in a garden, today, it is

Colour Plate 15. Life-size figure of a River God, lead painted white, by John Cheere, the Grotto, Stourhead, Wiltshire. (See Plate 1:17 and page 52)

Plate 1:27. Life-size Mower whetting his scythe, lead, uncertain attribution, eighteenth century, the Formal Garden, Bicton Park

worth bearing in mind that the original colouring would probably have been even brighter. When one considers that the trappings of some of these models would have been gilt, we have a much better idea of just how decorative original works would have been. The proliferation of copies of these two rigidly posed models, suggests that they originated from Cheere's yard around the middle of the century.

Earlier shepherd and sheperdess models tend to be of a more relaxed or flamboyant nature, and at times incorporate classical dress, for Arcadia was the idealised pastoral setting of ancient Greece and Rome. This more expansive nature can be seen in the two early eighteenth century pairs. In the first (Plate 1:24) the Shepherdess clasping a lamb to her thigh is far less tightly posed than the

Plate 1:28. Haymaker, lead, probably third quarter of eighteenth century. Height approx 60ins
MILES D'AGAR ANTIQUES AND NICK GIFFORD-MEAD

Shepherdess in Colour Plate 18 and the Haymaker in Plate 1:28 and wears classical sandals on her feet. Her companion Shepherd is another variation of the figures illustrated in Plates 1:10, 11 and 12 and both probably originated from either the Carpentiere or Van Nost family yard.

The second early eighteenth century pair (Plate 1:25) appears to represent the only surviving examples of Edward Hurst's leadwork. These cost the owner of Charlecote Park £20 in 1718.[120] The Shepherdess, with her short skirt, sandals and laurel leaves in her hair, clearly owes much of her essence to antiquity. Other eighteenth century subjects which often appear with Arcadian Shepherds and

Colour Plate 16. Satyr by John Cheere, lead, after circa 1760. Height approx 51ins. The classical statue on which this figure is based is shown in Plate 1:22

SEAGO ANTIQUES

Colour Plate 17. Satyr by John Cheere, lead, late eighteenth century. Height approx 67ins. The classical statue on which this figure is based is shown in Plate 1:23

PRIVATE COLLECTION: PHOTO PETER GREENHALF

Shepherdesses, are Haymakers. Several examples of such statues (clearly peopling a garden as described on page 27) are discernible in the anonymous paintings of the Pavilion at Wrest Park c.1720-21 (Plate 1:26). Indeed, one of these figures still appears to have been popular during Cheere's era, for it can be associated with the 'mowers whetting their scythes', recorded by J T Smith[121] during a visit to the lead figure maker's yard. An extant example of what must be the same model illustrated at Wrest and manufactured by Cheere survives in the gardens at Bicton Park in Devon (Plate 1:27). Unfortunately this figure is beginning to split open at the stomach, and unless prompt action is taken it will soon disintegrate. Images of peasants making hay seem to have remained popular for much of the century, and the stiffly posed female figure of a Haymaker (Plate 1:28) is notably similar both in style and dress to the painted Shepherd and Shepherdess in Colour Plate 18.

Colour Plate 18. A pair of three-quarter-size figures of a Shepherd and Shepherdess, lead, attributed to the workshops of John Cheere, probably mid-eighteenth century. Height approx 56½ ins. (See pages 60 and 62)

MALLETT AT BOURDON HOUSE

Plate 2:1. Peter Scheemakers' Lion Attacking a Horse, Rousham, Oxfordshire. The difficulties in transporting a large block of stone for a statue such as this (the piece is approximately 67ins high) meant the sculptor had to execute the work from more than one block, and the joint can be seen in the illustration (left) between the lion's paw and the back quarters of the horse. (See Colour Plate 19)

C COTTRELL-DORMER

CHAPTER TWO
STONE
1680 - 1850

Stone is perhaps the oldest material which has been used for the ornamentation of British gardens. This is due to the ready availability of the material throughout the country, as well as the relatively early development of stone masons' skills prompted in turn by the development of building in that material. However very few early stone garden ornaments survive today. It was not until the last quarter of the seventeenth century that stone began to be used for garden ornaments in any quantity.

The number of sculptors and masons working in England in the late seventeenth century was considerable, but few were talented, and the majority of those that were had either trained abroad (particularly in the Low Countries), or were foreigners. By 1725 many more sculptors had been attracted to this country from the Low Countries, including some of Huguenot extraction. This influx of well-trained and talented artists was due partly to the inexperience of the native artists, and partly to a growing demand for good quality sculpture, a demand which stemmed from the development in taste acquired by many discerning patrons during the Grand Tour, when they had been introduced to the stupendous works of antiquity. Several of the foreign artists, such as Peter Scheemakers and John Michael Rysbrack, were to spend most of their working lives in England, and became leading sculptors.

During the eighteenth century the method of carving in stone varied considerably, depending on the nature of the subject, but the most common process, as far as many eminent sculptors of the day were concerned, was as follows:

Having been commissioned to execute a statue, for example, a contract would have been drawn up and the sculptor would have provided a clay model, or possibly drawing, from which to work. Once this had been approved by the patron, the sculptor would select a suitable block of stone in its 'green' state (a term used to denote a recently quarried limestone prior to hardening). Much of the laborious 'cutting' (as carving was often referred to) of the outline would have been entrusted to the sculptor's workforce, such as masons, carvers and apprentices, but as the figure began to take shape, he became more involved with the work, undertaking, especially on an important commission, much of the detail himself; all of this would have been done by hand using a hammer and chisels, and finally files and emery. It is difficult to explain the highly complex art of carving from the solid, but perhaps the best way of understanding the process is to visualise a subject lying in a bath of water, and slowly emerging inch by inch as the water is let out.

Eighteenth century sculptors were able to obtain blocks of stone large enough to execute life-size statues (say between six and seven feet in height), but when larger works were required, these were often carved from several separate blocks. This feature can be clearly seen on Peter Scheemakers' copy of the famous classical statue of a Lion Attacking a Horse at Rousham in Oxfordshire (Plate 2:1 and Colour Plate 19) which was carved from two main blocks, with several further additions. The joint line running vertically beside the lion's left paw is clearly visible. In view of this, one would perhaps expect eighteenth century stone vases

Colour Plate 19. Lion Attacking a Horse, Portland stone, Rousham, Oxfordshire. (See Plate 2:1 and page 67)
C COTTRELL-DORMER

less than six or seven feet in height to have been carved from the whole, but this is not the case. The majority of vases and finials were often carved by mason-sculptors, usually from several different blocks, a practice which continued into the nineteenth century.

The variety of types of stone used by eighteenth century sculptors was considerable. The majority of those working from London (which included many eminent artists) tended to carve their garden ornaments from Portland stone, for not only was the material well suited for carving, it was also robust, evenly coloured and readily available in the city. Amongst the many other types used were Ketton (quarried near Stamford), Tadcaster (Yorkshire) and Roche Abbey (near Doncaster). Due to the cost of transportation during the period, these provincially quarried stones were often used at estates within the environs of the quarries, and were frequently transformed into garden ornaments by provincial sculptors and masons, although eminent sculptors, such as Caius Gabriel Cibber, actually travelled to patrons' estates carving garden statues and ornaments from whatever suitable stone was available in the locality. Whilst there were obvious economic advantages in using those stones available in the locality of particular estates, it is

Colour Plate 20. Tiw, one of the seven Saxon Deities, Portland Stone, by J M Rysbrack, unsigned, formerly in the gardens at Stowe, now in the Herbaceous Garden, Anglesey Abbey, Cambridgeshire. (See Plate 2:6 and pages 75-80)
THE NATIONAL TRUST: PHOTO PETER GREENHALF

Colour Plate 21. Woden, one of the seven Saxon Deities, Portland stone, by J M Rysbrack, unsigned, formerly in the gardens at Stowe. (See Plate 2:7 and pages 75-80)
PHILLIPS SON & NEALE

worth remembering that these stones would also have been particularly fitting for their environment, a fact commented on by the architect Isaac Ware (?1707-1766) in his 1756 publication, *A Complete Body of Architecture:* 'All stones stand better, and serve for purposes of strength and beauty both, much more successfully upon on near the place where their quarries are, than elsewhere'. One further stone, which increased in popularity during the eighteenth century, was the limesone quarried from Bath, but whereas stones such as Ketton and Portland were used both for figurative and architectural forms, Bath stone tended to be used mainly for vases and sundial pedestals.

When one considers the large number of different stones which were quarried in England, it is hardly surprising that numerous problems arise when attempting to identify the stone used for a certain piece. This situation is further complicated

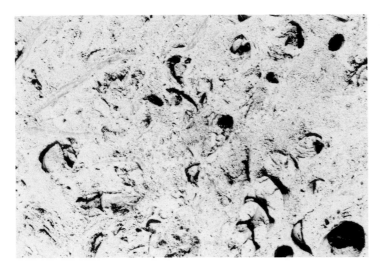

Plate 2:2. Details of two pieces of Portland stone showing the extreme variations in character. That on the left is obtained from the top of the quarry and is known as Roach, while that on the right, quarried from the bottom, is known as Base and is vastly more suited to carving in having little in the way of deposits in its make-up

by the varying ways stone garden ornaments weather. For example, a piece of Bath stone placed in a relatively dry environment will look completely different to a similar piece in a very damp area, for the surface of the latter will be covered with far more verdigris, moss and lichen. Furthermore, as stone is a natural material, the nature of one type of stone varies considerably from that of another. The main fluctuations in character often depend on where and at what height the block of stone in question was quarried, as can be seen in the details of two pieces of Portland stone in Plate 2:2. These are extreme examples, but the stone known as Roach (on the left) is obtained from the top of the quarry and is totally unsuitable for carving, while the stone on the right of the illustration, Base, has relatively little in the way of shells, cavities or calcite veins (known as 'snail creeps') and is vastly superior. The intermediary form of Portland, known as Whit, has deposits of shells and snail creeps in varying quantities, and it is this form of Portland stone which, together with Base, was used most extensively for garden sculpture and ornament during the eighteenth and nineteenth centuries.

The difficulties in identifying stone can be compounded by cement-based artificial stone pieces which can fool the novice, while foreign stones can also be the cause of much confusion, as they so often weather in, to us, a strange manner.

It is difficult to generalise about the use of stone for garden ornament. During the eighteenth century some of the most influential and discerning patrons, Lord Burlington and Viscount Cobham for example, employed leading sculptors to carve stone statuary for locations in their gardens. However, although both of them commissioned stone vases for decoration (often carved by mason-sculptors), they did not restrict their choice of garden ornaments to stone; both also used cheaper images made from lead. Other less discerning, or perhaps just less wealthy, patrons tended to decorate their gardens mainly with lead statuary, at times supplemented by stone vases, as was the case at Stourhead and Castle Hill, Devon. By the end of the eighteenth century, new, cheaper, man-made materials such as Coade stone were becoming popular, and by the middle of the nineteenth century a great variety of often far cheaper ornaments were available, such as pieces made from cast-iron and artificial stone. The demand for stone ornaments began to dwindle and by the end of the nineteenth century the output of such works in this country was on a very much smaller scale than it had been in the previous century. Of course, stone continued to be worked by masons and sculptors, and

Plate 2:3. Detail of a Portland stone sundial pedestal and its step, Anglesey Abbey, Cambridgeshire. The 'snail creeps', which feature strongly in poor quality Whit, are clearly visible on the uncarved step, while the top of the sundial, in a finer quality Whit, is virtually clear of deposits

THE NATIONAL TRUST

a great variety of ornaments were still made, some no doubt using the recently invented pointing machines. New developments in transportation during the nineteenth century meant greater flexibility for both sculptor and patron; thus John Thomas was able to carve his Portland stone fountain centrepiece in London and have it sent by rail to Castle Howard in Yorkshire (Plate 2:55 and Colour Plate 31).

There is little doubt as to the aesthetic suitability of stone in a British garden, for weathered stone ornaments blend so well with our flora, but the durability of the material is another matter and, again, varies considerably from stone to stone. No natural stone is capable of resisting the elements, and although many may appear to be in a relatively good condition, the effects of even one hundred years' exposure on something as robust as Portland will have worn a substantial part of the original detail away. Less durable stones will have suffered far worse.

This chapter looks first at the nature of Portland stone and illustrates many of the ornaments in this medium which stood or still stand in the famous eighteenth century gardens created by Viscount Cobham at Stowe and Lord Burlington at Chiswick House, London. Other eighteenth century Portland stone decorations are also discussed, and the use of this stone in the nineteenth century is illustrated in the enormous fountain at Castle Howard. The nature of Bath stone is examined and eighteenth and nineteenth century ornaments in the medium illustrated. Examples of eighteenth century ornaments in other stones and illustrations of admirable nineteenth century limestone copies of vases by James Gibbs (1682-1754) at Melton Constable, conclude this chapter.

Portland Stone

Portland stone is a limestone of a bright white colour which, when wet, changes to an off-white or grey. The easiest way to identify it is by its characteristic deposits. At times these are fossilised shells, but far more frequently they are short, often swirling lines or snail creeps. These deposits occur in varying quantities, as can be seen in the two examples illustrated in Plate 2:2 and in the detail of the step and socle of an eighteenth century sundial at Anglesey Abbey (Plate 2:3). The heavy snail creeps in the centre foreground are typical of lesser quality Whit, whilst the actual sundial is carved from a far finer quality Whit, with little in the way of deposits.

During the eighteenth century Portland was the stone most commonly used by London sculptors and masons carving ornaments for patrons' gardens. There were several reasons for this, of which the most important was the fact that the stone

Colour Plate 22. Calydonian Boar, Portland stone, attributed to Scheemakers, circa 1740, formerly in the gardens at Chiswick House, now at Chatsworth. Height approx 47 ½ ins. (See pages 89-91)

Colour Plate 23. Wolf, Portland stone, attributed to Scheemakers, circa 1740, formerly in the gardens of Chiswick House, now at Chatsworth, Derbyshire. (See pages 89-91)

Colour Plate 24. Lion, Portland stone, the Exedra, Chiswick House, London. (See Plate 2:37 and pages 91-94)

is finely textured and thus well suited to carving. Other reasons included the uniform and appealing colour, its robust nature and the relative ease with which it could be transported by sea from the quarries at Portland on the south coast to London.

These quarries were visited and briefly mentioned by Dr Pococke in the middle of the century:

> The workers in the quarry pay a shilling a ton for all the stone they take out of it. A cube of about two feet eight inches makes a ton. The king has retained to himself a small quantity of land, which has been worked for many public buildings, as for St. Paul's, Westminster Bridge, &c., and this is called the King's Quarry, but the greater part of it is worn out. The other quarries are mostly on the north side. In the two or three first strata, four or five feet each in thickness, the stone rises small. The good stone is in a stratum below these above twelve feet thick, . . . It is this good vein about the north-west corner where they find most petrified shells; the cockle, and oyster, and turben, are most common . . . The stones which have the cockle and oyster shell, being close and compact, are fit for forreign use [sic]; . . . The way of drawing it down is by fixing it on a low carriage, to which they chain a large stone, which drags behind on the ground, and they have two horses attended by a man

Colour Plate 25. Lioness, Portland stone, the Exedra, Chiswick House, London. (See Plate 2:38 and pages 91-94). As can be seen only too clearly here, statuary in public places is liable to vandalism

ENGLISH HERITAGE: PHOTO PETER GREENHALF

Plate 2:4. Half-statue of Sunna, Portland stone, by J M Rysbrack, unsigned, circa 1730, formerly in the gardens at Stowe, present whereabouts unknown. Height approx 39ins.

Rysbrack's interpretation of Verstegan's illustration is extremely vivid, with a wonderful realism in the deity's burning hair, though it is repeated with less effect on the burning wheel which he clasps as a symbol of his daily course through the heavens. As illustrated by Verstegan, the statue is carved as a half-figure

T CROWTHER & SONS LTD

fixed behind the cart, who, when he makes a signal, stand as firm as they can to resist the motion; but when they come to a rapid descent they are dragg'd after the cart, sometimes on their hams.[1]

Portland stone is one of the most suitable stones for use in the ornamentation of English gardens. It is not a very porous stone and although, like others, it will accumulate lichen and moss, it does not do so to the same extent as, for example, Bath stone. Its ability to withstand the ravages of our climate is clearly illustrated by, to choose from numerous examples, the seven Saxon Deities carved by John Michael Rysbrack for Stowe (Plates 2:4-10), which remain remarkably sharp considering they have been outside for 250 years. Although clearly of great durability, Portland is not completely weather proof; ornaments that have been subjected to the weather for many years will have lost a thin surface layer of stone leaving a shallowly pitted surface, with any deposits present standing in relief, for they are harder than the rest of the stone.

Portland stone ornaments at Stowe

During the eighteenth century the magnificent gardens of Stowe in Buckinghamshire were probably the most visited and influential in the country. Illustrated here are a number of the garden's Portland stone statues which are interesting, not only because they provide a comparison between two of England's most prominent sculptors, Peter Scheemakers and John Michael Rysbrack, but also because their location within the gardens reflects the symbolism which was so important during the eighteenth century. These statues, together with temples and landscaping, express contemporary beliefs as well as, to a certain extent, political events, and in this respect the gardens came to be regarded as a form of 'political' landscape.

The immensely wealthy soldier Sir Richard Temple, later Viscount Cobham (1675-1749), who succeeded to the estate in 1697, was a great patriot in the Whig mould. This is reflected in the garden statuary which, by 1731, included an equestrian lead figure of George I by the younger John Van Nost (see page 149), and stone statues by Rysbrack of Queen Caroline and George II, all celebrating the Glorious Revolution of 1688 and the succession of the House of Hanover over the Stuart despots. Around a garden building, designed by the architect James Gibbs, there were eight stone busts by Rysbrack: Elizabeth I, Shakespeare, Bacon, Milton, Hampden, Locke, William III and Newton (Plates 2:18-25), all personifying the greatness of England and the virtues of liberty. Amongst the many other ornaments were seven particularly curious and certainly unique stone statues, again by Rysbrack, of Saxon Deities who were thought to have given their names to the English days of the week (Plates 2:4-10 and Colour Plates 20 and 21).

Although Cobham's patriotism, or celebration of the English nation, is apparent in the statues of the queen, the two kings and the busts, the symbolism in the Saxon Deities is less apparent. During the seventeenth and eighteenth centuries, there was considerable interest in Anglo-Saxon history and it was to this age that many of the scholars of the day turned to interpret current affairs — at times with scant regard for historical fact. Thus comparisons were drawn between the ancient northern European tradition of democracy, believed to have been first introduced by the Jutish leader Hengist in the fifth century, to justify the end of the Divine Right of Kings and the Glorious Revolution.

As Cobham was a staunch Parliamentarian, and Parliament was thought to have descended from Hengist's *witan* (parliament or meeting), it is thus understandable that Cobham, wishing to symbolise within his garden his Saxon forebears, had the seven deities carved. As John Kenworthy-Browne in his authoritative article, 'Rysbrack's Saxon Deities', relates, they were 'robust symbols of traditional freedom'.[2]

Each of the statues was modelled directly from illustrations in a book on the German origins of the English nation, first published in 1605 by Richard Verstegan and entitled *A Restitution of Decayed Intelligence in Antiquities*. Verstegan's

Colour Plate 26. The Lion and Lioness flanking the entrance to the circular temple at Anglesey Abbey. These lead figures are attributed to John Cheere who copied them from the Lion and Lioness in Colour Plates 24 and 25. (See Plate 2:39 and page 94)

Plate 2:5. Mona, Portland stone, by J M Rysbrack, unsigned, circa 1730, formerly in the gardens at Stowe. Height approx 70ins.

Although unprepossessing, this elfin statue has some interesting points. Mr Kenworthy-Browne points out that the runic inscription on the base is incorrect, for it describes the figure as masculine, though it is obviously a woman, as described by Verstegan. Clearly this is a grammatical error. The curious hood with its protruding ears is most bizarre, but is a mellowed version of Verstegan's illustration, whose style is echoed in the curling shoes. The finest feature is the disc showing the face of the moon

CROWTHER OF SYON LODGE LTD

Plate 2:6. Tiw, Portland stone, by J M Rysbrack, unsigned, circa 1730, formerly in the gardens at Stowe, now in the Herbaceous Garden, Anglesey Abbey. Height approx 62ins. (See Colour Plate 20).

Father of the German race, Tiw held a sceptre in his right hand as a symbol of his status. The bald head, beard and air of enlightened benevolence give this statue its charm, and it was for this reason that the piece was, for many years, believed to represent Father Time

THE NATIONAL TRUST

illustrations are not accompanied by the Anglo-Saxon runic inscriptions which are found on the bases of Rysbrack's statues of Mona, Tiw, Woden, Thuner, Friga and Seatern (a runic inscription does not appear on Sunna, but as Verstegan shows the deity as a half figure on an ornate pedestal (Plate 2:4) it seems likely that the rune was featured on the now lost pedestal). However, as Mr Kenworthy-Browne suggests, it may be that Rysbrack consulted his friend Vertue as to what form these should take. Vertue was one of the founder members of the Society of Antiquaries and, as other members such as Humphrey Wanley (1672-1726) had done much work on the subject, Vertue, or at least one of the society's members, would have been in a position to advise Rysbrack as to what form each figure's rune should take.

Plate 2:7. Woden, Portland stone, by J M Rysbrack, unsigned, circa 1730, formerly in the gardens at Stowe. Height approx 77ins. (See Colour Plate 21).

The sword (broken) and crown show Woden to be the warrior prince, albeit a little portly for one 'fam'd for martial Deeds'. His armour is well carved, particularly on the joint plates of the right arm, although it is clearly anachronistic. The statue is attached to the cap of a Bath stone pedestal, probably contemporary. It is unusually rough and unfinished by eighteenth century standards but would have been very much in keeping with the statue's setting at Stowe in a sylvan temple

PHILLIPS, SON & NEALE

Plate 2:8. Thuner, Portland stone, by J M Rysbrack, unsigned, circa 1730, formerly in the gardens at Stowe. Height approx 67ins.

Rysbrack has given Thuner, the most powerful of the Saxon Deities, a bold and magnificent air of grandeur by raising and extending a pose that would otherwise be foreshortened by the figure's seated position. The left shoulder is lifted and the leg has been lowered below the platform of his throne. This foot has, in fact, been stretched beyond the compass of the statue, and is in itself a sign of quality, to be compared with the Calydonian Boar, attributed to Scheemakers, in Colour Plate 22.

PHILLIPS, SON & NEALE

Plate 2:9. Friga, Portland stone, by J M Rysbrack, unsigned, circa 1730, formerly in the gardens at Stowe. Height 79ins.

Rysbrack has somewhat marred the hermaphoroditic aspects of the deity, creating a rather inexpressive subject with little of the movement or subtlety found in most of the other Saxon Deities. It is therefore not surprising that when the seven were dispersed at sale in 1922, this figure failed to attract a bidder. Both the box and sword she once held have broken, revealing the remains of rusting iron bars

PRIVATE COLLECTION: PHOTOGRAPH JOHN KENWORTHY-BROWNE/RICHARD DEAN

Plate 2:10. Seatern, Portland stone, by J M Rysbrack, unsigned, circa 1730, formerly in the gardens at Stowe. Height approx 66 ½ ins.

The only deity not a genuine German god, but from his attributes — the wheel, the basket of flowers and the fish — he appears to be a god of fertility or the seasons, probably derived from the Roman Saturn or Greek Chronos. The left arm, which in Verstegan's illustration holds the wheel aloft, has been modified by Rysbrack (as have many of the features of all the Saxon Deities), so that the wheel is held closer to the body. In this case Rysbrack's attempts to produce a less vulnerable representation have been unsuccessful, for much of the left arm and wheel have broken. Interestingly, the presence of dowels shows that in the past the statue has been repaired; fortunately copper dowels were used which cause far less damage than iron

The statues must have been completed by 1731, probably slightly earlier, for they are featured in a poem by a cousin of Cobham, Gilbert West, written that year. This somewhat florid account clearly sets forth the whole ideology behind the Saxon Deities:

> Forsaking now the Covert of the Maze,
> Along the broader Walk's more open Space
> Pass we to where a sylvan Temple spreads
> Around the Saxon Gods, its hallow'd Shades.
>
> Hail! Gods of our renown'd Fore-Fathers, hail!
> Ador'd Protectors once of England's Weal.
> Gods, of a Nation, valiant, wise and free,
> Who conquer'd to establish Liberty!
> To whose auspicious Care Britannia owes
> Those Laws, on which she stands, by which she rose.
> Still may your Sons that noble Plan pursue,
> Of equal Government prescrib'd by you.
> Nor e'er indignant may you blush to see,
> The Shame of our corrupted Progeny!
>
> First radiant Sunna shews his beaming Head,
> Mona to Him, and scepter'd Tiw succeed;
> Tiw, ancient Monarch of remotest Fame,
> Who led from Babel's Tow'rs the German Name.
> And Warlike Woden, fam'd for martial Deeds,
> From whom great Brunswick's noble Line proceeds.
> Dread Thuner see! on his Imperial Seat,
> With awful Majesty, and kingly State
> Reclin'd! At his Command black Thunders roll,
> And Storms, and fiery Tempests shake the Pole.
> With various Emblems next fair Friga charms,
> Array'd in female Stole and manly Arms,
> Expressive Image of that Double Soul,
> Prolifick Spirit that informs the Whole;
> Whose Genial Power throughout exerts its Sway,
> And Earth, and Sea, and Air, its Laws obey.
> Last of the Circle hoary Seatern stands;
> Instructive Emblems fill his mystick Hands.
> In this a Wheel's revolving Orb declares
> The never-ending Round of rolling Years,
> That holds a Vessel fill'd with fading Flowers
> And Fruits collected by the ripening Hours.
> Be warn'd from hence, ye Fair ones! to improve
> The transitory Minutes made for Love,
> E're yet th'inexorable Hands of Time
> Robs of its bloomy Sweets your lively Prime.[3]

The Seven Deities is a magnificent set of statues, full of the movement and vitality characteristic of Rysbrack's hand. By 1744 they had been removed from their 'sylvan temple' (this circular grove is clearly visible in Sarah Bridgeman's plan of Stowe, 1739), in a triangular wooded area just to the north-west of the house (Plate 2:11), to the new Gothic Temple, which they surrounded. This temple was dedicated 'To the Liberty of our Ancestors', and its interior was decorated with

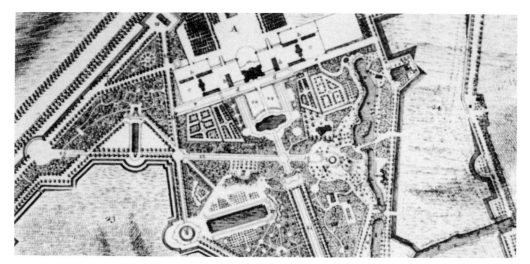

Plate 2:11. Detail of Sarah Bridgeman's 1739 plan of the gardens at Stowe. The original location of Rysbrack's Saxon Deities can be seen within the triangular area (top left) to the north-west of the house. The Great Cross Walk slanting across the south of the house terminates in the east with the circular Temple of Ancient Virtue and the Elysian Fields. Continuing the line of this walk, across the river and slightly south, the hemicycle outline of the Temple of British Worthies is discernible. The Temple of Modern Virtue stood to the north of the Temple of Ancient Virtue

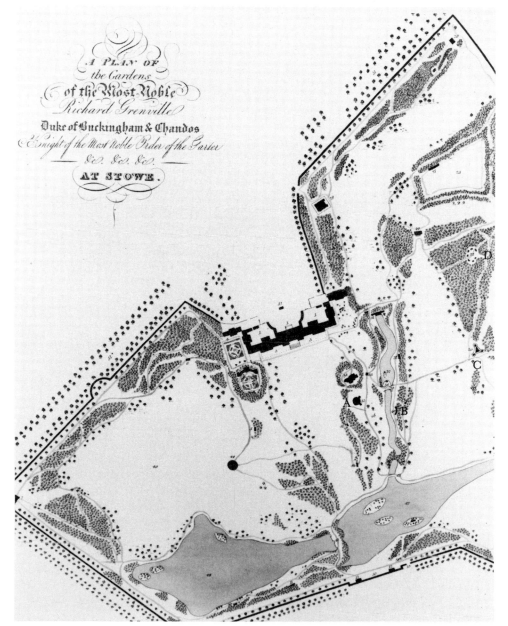

Plate 2:12. Detail of the gardens at Stowe, from an 1827 Map by William James Smith, published in J Seeley's Stowe: A Description of the House and Gardens.

To the south of the house is the circular Temple of Ancient Virtue (A). East of this, across the river Styx (by this date known as the Alder) is the Temple of British Worthies (B). North-east of this can be seen the triangular outline of the Gothic Temple (C). The walk leading north from the temple, through the wood, was known as the Gothic Walk, and off this to the left was the later oval site of the Saxon Deities (D)

armorials tracing Cobham's ancestry back to the Saxon Earls of Leicester. By 1777 they had been moved again to another grove off the Gothic Walk, to the north of the Gothic Temple (visible in Plate 2:12), where they were to remain until they were dispersed at sale in October 1922. Rather fittingly, the altar around which the deities were placed was replaced sometime after 1829 by one of rough-hewn limestone removed from a barrow near Thornborough in Buckinghamshire.

As we have seen, by 1731 Cobham's garden was adorned with many statues, symbolic of the greatness and liberty of England. Political events were soon to accentuate this symbolism. For some years Cobham had been unhappy with the politics of the 'prime' minister, Sir Robert Walpole (1676-1745), and like a number of Whigs he sensed Walpole did not have the best interests of the country at heart. As Denys Sutton writes, Cobham felt Walpole 'had encouraged corruption, supported Hanover to the detriment of the national interest and paid insufficient attention to French and Spanish interference with British trade. He took particular exception to the Government's support of the directors of the South Sea Company'.[4] In April 1733, Cobham, together with a number of other influential Lords, including Burlington, Bathurst and Chesterfield, had gone into opposition over the Excise Bill which they detested not only because of the proposed increase in taxation, but also because it was widely seen to endanger the liberties of the British people. After much anger from both the public and Parliament, Walpole was forced to withdraw the Bill. However, the crisis had created an anti-Walpole party within the Whigs called the 'Patriots' or 'Young Patriots' whose motto was 'Liberty'. Stowe became a centre of political activity, and the symbolism of liberty in the gardens (as opposed to the corruption and repression personified in the 'prime' minister) became more obvious.

The gardens to the south-east of the house were remodelled in the latter half of the 1730s and became known as the Elysian Fields (in Greek mythology the dwelling place of the blessed after death). This area, as George Clarke has written, was created by William Kent (?1685-1748), assisted no doubt by Cobham and his friends, and inspired by the writings of Addison and others,[5] and it was here that Cobham's political aspirations were to be fully expressed.

The Great Cross Walk, which is clearly visible in Sarah Bridgeman's 1739 plan (Plate 2:11) slanting across the south of the house, ended in the east with the circular Temple of Ancient Virtue, within which were four Portland stone statues: Homer, Socrates, Lycurgus and Epaminondas, respectively the greatest Greek poet, philosopher, lawgiver and general (Plates 2:13-16). These were carved by Peter Scheemakers (whose signature is discernible towards the bottom of the tree stump to Homer's right) to whom payment is recorded in Lord Cobham's account book on 13 December 1737: 'To Mr Scheemakers a Statuary for 4 Portland Statues £120'.[6]

Latin inscriptions praising the achievements of the four Greek Worthies appear above each statue; free English translations (taken from Seeley's 1817 description of the gardens) are given here in each case. On the inside of the temple, above each door, are further Latin inscriptions, reinforcing the theme of Ancient Virtue.

Over the entrance: 'To be dear to our country, to deserve well of the public, to be honoured, reverenced, loved is glorious; but to be dreaded and hated, is odious, detestable, weak, ruinous'.

Over the exit: 'Cultivate justice and benevolence, which in an eminent manner is due to relations and to friends, but in the highest degree to our country; this path leads to the mansions of the blessed, and to this assembly of those who are now no more'.

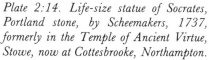

2:13

Plate 2:13. Life-size statue of Homer, Portland stone, signed Peter Scheemakers, 1737, formerly in the Temple of Ancient Virtue, Stowe, now at Cottesbrooke, Northampton.

'The first and greatest of Poets; the herald of virtue; the giver of immortality; who, by his divine genius known to all nations, incites all, nobly to dare, and to suffer firmly'
JOHN MACDONALD-BUCHANAN

Plate 2:14. Life-size statue of Socrates, Portland stone, by Scheemakers, 1737, formerly in the Temple of Ancient Virtue, Stowe, now at Cottesbrooke, Northampton.

'Who innocent in the midst of a most corrupted people; the encourager of the good; a worshipper of the one God; from useless speculations, and vain disputes, restored Philosophy to the duties of life, and the benefit of Society. The wisest of men'
JOHN MACDONALD-BUCHANAN

2:14

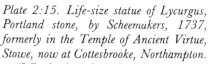

2:15

Plate 2:15. Life-size statue of Lycurgus, Portland stone, by Scheemakers, 1737, formerly in the Temple of Ancient Virtue, Stowe, now at Cottesbrooke, Northampton.

'Who having planned with consummate wisdom, a system of laws firmly secured against every encroachment of corruption; and having, by the expulsion of riches, banished luxury, avarice, and intemperance; established in the state for many ages, perfect liberty, and inviolable purity of manners. The Father of his Country'
JOHN MACDONALD-BUCHANAN

Plate 2:16. Life-size statue of Epaminondas, Portland stone, by Scheemakers, 1737, formerly in the Temple of Ancient Virtue, Stowe, now at Cottesbrooke, Northampton.

'By whose valour, prudence and modesty, the Theban commonwealth gained liberty and empire, military discipline, civil and domestic policy; all which, by losing him, she lost'
JOHN MACDONALD-BUCHANAN

2:16

Plate 2:17. The view from the Temple of Ancient Virtue across the River Alder to the Temple of British Worthies
STOWE SCHOOL

2:18

2:19

2:20

2.21

Plate 2:18. Queen Elizabeth 'who confounded the projects, and destroy'd the power that threatened to oppress the liberties of Europe; took off the yoke of ecclesiastical tyranny; restor'd religion from the corruptions of popery; and by a wise, a moderate and a popular government, gave wealth, security, and respect to England'

Plate 2:19. William Shakespeare 'whose excellent genius opened to him the whole art of man, all the mines of fancy, all the stores of nature; and gave him power beyond all other writers, to move, astonish, and delight mankind'

Plate 2:20. Sir Francis Bacon, Lord Verulam 'who, by the strength and light of superior genius, rejecting vain speculation, and fallacious theory, taught to pursue truth, and improve philosophy by the certain method of experiment'

Plate 2:21. John Milton 'whose sublime and unbounded genius equal'd a subject that carried him beyond the limits of the world'

Facing this Temple, and across the River Alder, known at the time as the River Styx (in Greek mythology the river across which Charon ferried the souls of the dead), stands another temple, that of the British Worthies (Plate 2:17). In the centre of this stone monument is a pyramid within which is a niche which used to contain a bust of Hermes, the God who carried the souls of heroes to the Elysian Fields, thus allegorically connecting the greatness of Britain with the golden age of Ancient Greece. The hemicycle outline designed by Kent consists of sixteen connected pediment niches within which are stone busts of gallant countrymen, heroes, patriots and wits. Eight of these busts, as has already been mentioned, are by Rysbrack (Plates 2:18-25), whilst Rysbrack probably also carved a ninth — that of Inigo Jones (Plate 2:26); all of the subjects are appropriately haughty and heroic. The remaining seven busts were no doubt executed in the mid- to late 1730s and, having little of the vitality found in those by Rysbrack, are almost certainly by Scheemakers; they represent Alexander Pope, Sir Thomas Gresham, King Alfred, Edward Prince of Wales, Sir Walter Raleigh, Sir Francis Drake, and Sir John Barnard (Plates 2:27-33). The seven Scheemakers busts can be seen to refer to aspects of the Patriots' opposition to Walpole's method of government, such as that of Edward, Prince of Wales, a discreet reference to George II's brother, Frederick, Prince of Wales, who had quarrelled with the King and to

2:22

2:23

Plate 2:22. John Hampden 'who, with great spirit and consummate abilities, begun a noble opposition to an arbitrary court, in the defence of the liberties of his country; supported them in parliament, and died for them in the field'

Plate 2:23. John Locke 'who, best of all Philosophers, understood the powers of the human mind, the nature, end, and bounds of civil government; and with equal courage and sagacity, refuted the slavish system of usurp'd authority over the rights, the consciences, or the reason of mankind'

2:24

2.25

Plate 2:24. King William III 'who, by his virtue and constancy, having saved his country from a foreign master; by a bold and generous enterprise, preserv'd the liberty and religion of Great Britain'

Plate 2:25. Sir Isaac Newton 'whom the God of nature made to comprehend his work (and from simple principles, to discover the laws never known before, and to explain the appearance never understood, of this stupendous universe)'

2:26

2:27

Plate 2:26. Ignatius Jones 'who, to adorn his country, introduc'd and rival'd the Greek and Roman architecture'

Plate 2:27. Alexander Pope. 'Who uniting the Correctness of Judgement to the Fire of Genius, by the Melody & Power of his Numbers, gave Sweetness to Sense, and Grace to Philosophy. He employ'd the pointed Brilliancy of Wit to chastise the Vices, and the Eloquence of Poetry to exalt the Virtues of human Nature, and being without a rival in his own Age, imitated & translated, with a Spirit equal to the Originals, the best Poets of Antiquity'

2:28

2:30

2:32

Plate 2:28. Sir Thomas Gresham 'who by the honourable profession of a merchant, having enrich'd himself and his country; for carrying on the commerce of the world, built the Royal Exchange'

Plate 2:29. King Alfred 'the mildest, justest, most beneficent of kings; who drove out the Danes, secured the seas, protected learning, establish'd juries, crush'd corruption, guarded liberty, and was the founder of the English constitution'

Plate 2:30. Edward Prince of Wales 'the terror of Europe, the delight of England, who preserv'd unaltered in the height of glory, and fortune, his natural gentleness and modesty'

Plate 2:31. Sir Walter Raleigh 'a valiant soldier, and an able statesman; who endeavouring to rouse the spirit of his master, for the honour of his country, against the ambition of Spain, fell a sacrifice to the influence of that court; whose arms he had vanquish'd, and whose designs he opposed'

Plate 2:32. Sir Francis Drake 'who, through many perils, was the first of Britons that ventured to sail round the Globe; and carried into unknown Seas and Nations the knowledge and glory of the English name'

Plate 2:33. Sir John Barnard 'who distinguish'd himself in Parliament by an active & firm Opposition to the pernicious and iniquitous Practice of Stockjobbing: at the same Time exerting his . . . Abilities to increase the Strength of his Country, by reducing the Interest of the National Debt; which he proposed to the House of Commons in the year 1737, and, with the Assistance of the Government, carried into Effect in the year 1750; on Terms of Equal Justice to Particulars & to the State; notwithstanding all the Impediments which private interests could oppose to Publick Spirit'

2:29

2:31

2:33

The sixteen illustrations of the J M Rysbrack (Plates 2:18-26) and Scheemakers (Plates 2:27-33) busts in the Temple of British Worthies reproduced by kind permission of Stowe School

Plate 2:34. The Temple of Modern Virtue at Stowe. An engraving in George Bickham's The Beauties of Stowe, *1750. The outline of the headless statue of the 'prime' minister, Walpole, can be seen on the left*

STOWE SCHOOL

whom the Patriots looked as the next ruler and openly supported.[7] The sixteen busts in the Temple of British Worthies (Plates 2:18-33) appear here with the inscription found above each statue.

Another temple, that of Modern Virtue, stood close to the Temple of Ancient Virtue. This ruined building was meant to contrast the decadence of Walpole's Britain with the inherent greatness of the British spirit, represented in the rest of the gardens and in particular in the Temples of British Worthies and Ancient Virtue. The Temple of Modern Virtue does not survive today, but from an engraving by George Bickham in *The Beauties of Stowe,* 1750 (Plate 2:34) and the contemporary accounts of the garden, it is clear that the deliberately ruinous heap of stones and the headless statue of the 'prime' minister within it, was a scathing attack on Walpole and everything he stood for.

The very different styles of the two great sculptors is clearly apparent in the statues at Stowe. The stiff formality found in Scheemakers' busts is quite distinct from Rysbrack's animated treatment. This is repeated in the figures made by the two sculptors, though, in this instance, some consideration concerning the differing commissions should be taken into account. Rysbrack's was clearly for more robust figures, whilst solemn classicism was of the essence concerning Scheemakers' work. What is strange is that Scheemakers' Greek Worthies were not carved from marble, for they were placed within the covered Temple of Ancient Virtue. Of course, marble was a much more expensive medium, but is it possible Cobham first intended them to be placed outside, like the seven Saxon Deities.

The great durability of Portland stone in our climate is again well illustrated by the statues formerly at Stowe. Scheemakers' four Greek Worthies were carved around the same time as Rysbrack's Saxon Deities, but have been outside for a mere sixty years, yet they are in a comparable condition to Rysbrack's statues, which, as has been mentioned, have been outside for over 250 years. Certainly a thin surface layer has in parts worn away on Rysbrack's figures, revealing

Plate 2:35. John Donowell's 'A View of the Gardens of the Earl of Burlington at Chiswick; taken from the Top of the Flight of Steps leading to ye Grand Gallery in ye Back Front'.

The Boar and the Wolf (Colour Plates 22 and 23) can be seen flanked by the two large finials on the parapet. The vista terminates in the Exedra, within which the Lions (Plates 2:37 and 38 and Colour Plates 24 and 25) and the seats (Plate 2:40 and Colour Plate 27) can just be made out. Also seen are the vases one of which is illustrated in Colour Plate 32

ENGLISH HERITAGE

calcareous lumps, and some of the more exposed parts, such as Woden's toes and sword (probably made of lead reinforced with an iron or bronze bar) have broken off, but they retain great definition.

Portland stone ornaments at Chiswick House

The Portland stone copy of the famous 'antique' Wild or Calydonian Boar, in the Uffizi, Florence, and its similarly posed companion figure of a Wolf, were supplied for the gardens of Lord Burlington's Villa at Chiswick sometime between 1736 and 1742 (Colour Plates 22 and 23). They are conspicuous by their absence from John Rocque's 'Plan du Jardin & Vue des Maisons de Chiswick...', 1736, but discernible respectively in George Lambert's 1742 paintings of Chiswick: 'The View from the Cascade Terrace or Bridge' and 'The View from the North Front looking East'. Eleven years later they are still to be seen in John Donowell's 'A View of the Garden of the Earl of Burlington at Chiswick; taken from The top of the Flight of Steps leading to ye Grand Gallery in ye Back Front' of 1753. As in Lambert's views, they are positioned looking down to the Exedra (Plate 2:35).

There is no proof as to who made these figures, but they are likely to have been carved by one of England's most eminent eighteenth century sculptors, Peter Scheemakers, an attribution based on a number of points.

The Boar and Wolf were supplied to Chiswick during William Kent's alterations in the late 1730s or early 1740s. Kent's connection with Scheemakers requires far more research, but it is enough at present to say that Scheemakers executed a number of works from Kent's designs and, of more relevance, for gardens landscaped by Kent. For example, Scheemakers supplied Portland stone copies of two antique statues, the Dying Gladiator (Plate 2:36) and the Lion Attacking a Horse (Plate 2:1), for the gardens at Rousham in Oxfordshire, which Kent remodelled a few years after Chiswick.

Plate 2:36.
Scheemakers'copy of the
Dying Gladiator at
Rousham. It is by no
means an accomplished
work and bears little
resemblance to the antique
marble figure now in the
Capitoline Museum. The
joint line across the
statue's cranium is clearly
visible

C. COTTRELL-DORMER

When Scheemakers returned from his studies in Italy, in 1730, he brought with him a number of his own clay models of 'antique' statues. Vertue saw eighteen or twenty of these, but those he mentions did not include a Calydonian Boar. However, in a sale of Scheemakers' collection of models, marbles and pictures of 10 and 11 March 1756, lot 56 on the first day was a marble *'Chalcedonian* Boar', and on the following day lot 22 was a model of 'The *Chalcedonian* Boar, by *Delvaux'.*[8] Laurent Delvaux (1696-1778) was Scheemakers' old partner (see Chapter 5) but had left England for good in 1733. Furthermore, in Scheemakers' retirement sale of 6 June 1771, lots 85 and 89 comprised a number of items including respectively 'a boar' and 'a wolf'.[9]

Given that Scheemakers supplied garden statuary for several of Kent's gardens and that he definitely had at least two models of the Calydonian Boar, as well as a figure of a Wolf, confirmation of Scheemakers' hand can be found in Daniel Defoe's account of the gardens at Chiswick in 1742, written within at most six years of the beasts' erection. He writes 'at the ends next the house [the north front] are two fine wolves in stone, cut by Mr Scheemaker'.[10] Defoe's referring to the two pieces as 'wolves' would appear to be a mistake (they are similar in pose), in view of the visual evidence of Lambert's paintings of 1742 which indisputably depicts a Boar and a Wolf.

There are similarities in construction between the Boar and Wolf and Scheemakers' Dying Gladiator at Rousham (Plate 2:36) which, although not substantial enough to further prove Scheemakers' hand, provides an interesting reflection on the economics of carving stone garden statuary during the period. Each of the three statues has been 'cut' from one block of stone, while the bases

Plate 2:37. Lion, Portland stone, circa 1738, the Exedra, Chiswick House. Height approx 33ins. (See Colour Plate 24)
ENGLISH HERITAGE

Plate 2:38. Lioness, Portland stone, circa 1738, the Exedra, Chiswick House. Height approx 33ins. (See Colour Plate 25)
ENGLISH HERITAGE

Plate 2:39. The lead Lion and Lioness attributed to John Cheere, flanking the entrance to the circular temple at Anglesey Abbey in Cambridgeshire. No information as to which estate these were originally supplied has come to light, but it seems probable that Lord Fairhaven obtained them some time after 1935 from the retailer and manufacturer J P White in Bedford, for the lioness is situated on a strikingly similar pedestal to that illustrated in White's catalogue of that date. (See Colour Plate 26)
THE NATIONAL TRUST

have then been extended by additional blocks to match the proportion of the figures to the size of their pedestals, thus wasting as little stone as possible. However, for some reason, the top of the Boar's head and the cranium of the Dying Gladiator have each been carved from separate pieces — indeed the line of fracture which occurs on the Boar's head includes most of both ears. It is tempting to suppose that these two pieces were made from blocks of stone which were just too small for the sculpture being carved. Perhaps there was a fault in the Portland stone itself, though this sort of crack is not in the nature of the medium, and one is left speculating why both the Dying Gladiator and Boar were executed in such a manner; this practice is never found on marble statues and is distinctly unprofessional for a sculptor of Scheemakers' class.

Both the Boar and the Wolf were removed to Chatsworth sometime between 1912 (when they were referred to in *The Architect & Contract Reporter* as being a Bear and a Boar) and 1928 when Chiswick House was sold. They now decorate the approach to the north entrance to Chatsworth.

The couchant statues of a Lion and a Lioness (Plates 2:37 and 38 and Colour Plates 24 and 25) which still flank the Exedra at Chiswick House had probably been completed by 1738 for, on 10 November of that year, William Kent wrote to Lord Burlington that 'the Piedestals for Lyons [were] ready to put up...'[11] In the light of this it seems reasonable to assume that they were erected on their pedestals late that, or early the following, year. The lions were the last addition

Plate 2:40. One of twelve stone seats. Portland stone, probably from a design by Lord Burlington, circa 1737, Chatsworth, Derbyshire. Height approx 18ins. (See Colour Plate 27)

to the prospect, for they are conspicuous by their absence from Kent's drawing of the otherwise completed Exedra (Plate 2:41).

Unfortunately, despite numerous contemporary accounts of the gardens at Chiswick, the identity of the artist who carved the two lions is still to be discovered. As we have seen, describing the gardens in 1742, Daniel Defoe simply mentions that 'At the ends next the House, are two fine wolves in stone, cut by Mr. Scheemaker; at the farther end are two large lions';[12] but this account does not imply that Peter Scheemakers also carved the lions. The Reverend Daniel Lysons, in *The Environs of London* is more specific; he relates that 'The lions and other beasts are the work of Scheemakers'.[13] However, this is not firm enough evidence to attribute the Lions to Scheemakers. Comparison of the Lions to other garden statuary by Scheemakers, such as the Dying Gladiator (Plate 2:36), Lion Attacking a Horse at Rousham (Plate 2:1 and Colour Plate 19),[14] and the Boar and the Wolf (Colour Plates 22 and 23), reveals discrepancies in the style and treatment, in particular in the detailing of the statues' bases. Furthermore, the very quality of the stone in which the Lions, in particular the Lioness, are carved is poor — the Lioness was executed from a Portland block with abundant cavities, calcite veining and shells. Scheemakers' other garden statues are carved from relatively unflawed Portland of a superior quality.

A further reason to doubt Lysons' account is his implication that all the 'beasts' in the garden were carved by Scheemakers, but this was not the case, for John Michael Rysbrack is known to have supplied a figure of a Goat in the late 1740s.[15] Furthermore, it is curious that, although earlier accounts mention Scheemakers' hand in the 'two Wolves', they make no direct reference to Scheemakers' involvement in the Lions, thus again questioning the authenticity of Lysons' account, which was, after all, written over fifty years after the Lions had been erected.

Another sculptor whose name has been put forward is that of Giovanni Battista Guelfi (fl 1715-1734), whom Burlington is thought to have brought back with him on his return from the Grand Tour in 1715. According to Vertue '. . . Guelphi [sic] was much employed for many years by Ld. Burlington in his house in London & made many statues for his Villa at Chiswick, being much continually almost employed for him several years. . .'[16] However, Guelfi also seems an unlikely candidate, for he returned to Italy in 1734, some four years prior to Kent's reference to the erection of the Lions' pedestals; if Guelfi had executed them, they must have been located elsewhere, and only moved to the Exedra during Kent's extensive alterations in the mid-1730s.

It is a shame that the identity of the sculptor responsible has not been established

Plate 2:41. Drawing by William Kent of the Exedra at Chiswick, showing eight of the twelve Portland stone seats removed to Chatsworth in the late nineteenth or early twentieth century. As the Lions (Plates 2:37 and 38) are not shown, the drawing (which is typical Kent, with dogs chasing across the foreground) must date to some time prior to November 1738. Other ornaments of interest are the two vases, probably designed by Lord Burlington (Plates 2:62 and 63)

Plate 2:42. One of six lead seats at Castle Hill, Devon, probably cast by John Cheere from moulds of the Portland stone seats once at Chiswick and now at Chatsworth. Height approx 18ins

Colour Plate 27. One of twelve Portland stone seats, probably from a design by Lord Burlington, formerly in the grounds of Chiswick House, now at Chatsworth, Derbyshire
TRUSTEES OF THE CHATSWORTH SETTLEMENT: PHOTO PETER GREENHALF

yet, for these magnificent beasts, with their distinct air of pathos, were extensively copied in lead by John Cheere during the latter half of the eighteenth century. This would perhaps suggest that Cheere was the original artist who carved them but, as all the documented copies which have been traced to date were not produced until after 1760, this is considered most unlikely. Extant Cheere copies, which are full size, can be seen at Quenby Hall, Castle Hill, West Wycombe and Heaton Hall, supplied respectively some time after 1759,[17] around 1770,[18] around 1770[19] and in 1774.[20] A further pair, of uncertain provenance, flank the entrance to the circular temple at Anglesey Abbey (Plate 2:39 and Colour Plate 26) which, bearing in mind the preceding information, are almost certainly by John Cheere.

Cheere was also to produce reduced copies of these Lions in plaster for use as interior decoration; a Lion survives at Stourhead,[21] while a gilded pair survives at Burton Constable,[22] and two gilt pairs surmount the door entablatures of the Colonnade Room at Wilton House.[23] The Lions were also to prove popular subjects with a number of eighteenth century porcelain manufactories, for reduced-size models were produced both at Bow and Plymouth.[24]

The twelve identical stone seats that today adorn the Beech Walk at Chatsworth (Plate 2:40 and Colour Plate 27) originally decorated the Exedra within the grounds of Chiswick House. Writing in 1845, Thomas Faulkner in *The History and Antiquities of Brentford, Ealing and Chiswick* described them *in situ* as 'on the turf, twelve antique stone seats, ornamented with drapery and festoons...used by the

Colour Plate 28. One of a pair of Portland stone Sphinxes, attributed to Guelfi, in the gardens of Chiswick House, London. (See Plate 2:45 and page 100)

ENGLISH HERITAGE. PHOTO PETER GREENHALF

Colour Plate 29. Lead Sphinx, circa 1748, at Chiswick House, London. A copy of the Portland stone models attributed to Guelfi (Colour Plate 28), this was supplied by the lead figure maker John Cheere. (See page 100)

ENGLISH HERITAGE: PHOTO PETER GREENHALF

95

Roman senators in the forum; they were brought from Rome by the Earl of Burlington. These are doubtless the identical seats upon which the senators were reposing in majestic gravity and awful silence, when Brennus entered Rome'.[25] However, Faulkner's romantic description cannot be true, for the seats are carved from Portland stone.

In John Rocque's 'A Plan and Elevation of the House and Gardens at Chiswick', 1736, the outline of the Exedra is clearly visible, but the seats are not depicted. They must have been supplied soon afterwards, for eight are clearly visible in William Kent's drawing (Plate 2:41), which by the omission of the Lions must date prior to late 1738 (see pages 91-93). They were probably carved by a stone mason rather than a sculptor, not because they are poorly carved, for this is not so, but because they are of a simple architectural nature, and it seems unlikely that Burlington would have gone to the expense of commissioning a sculptor when a mason-sculptor or carver would have been quite capable, and no doubt cheaper. Although William Kent laid out much of the gardens, including the Exedra, it is apparent that most of the vases were made after designs by Burlington (see pages 117-118) and it seems likely, therefore, that seats were also carved from one of Burlington's designs, incorporating some of the ornaments found on the pair of vases in the Exedra (Plates 2:62 and 63 and Colour Plates 33 and 34).

The seats were removed to Chatsworth at the end of the nineteenth or early twentieth century and are good examples of the durability of Portland stone. Considering that they have been exposed to the elements for over two and a half centuries in a particularly damp position (on the ground and backing on to a hedge) they are, with the exception of a few chips and an inevitable covering of lichen and moss, in remarkable condition.

Six lead copies of these seats (Plate 2:42) were produced for the gardens of Castle Hill in Devon, where they remain today. They are extraordinary subjects to have copied in lead, indeed Lawrence Weaver described them as 'a good example of how not to make a garden seat'.[26] However, as purely decorative items, without any practical use, they are quite charming and decidedly unusual.

There seems very little doubt that the two marble Sphinxes owned by the Ashmolean Museum and formerly on loan to the Botanic Garden at Oxford (Plates 2:43 and 44) were the originals on which the pair of Portland stone Sphinxes now in the garden behind Chiswick House were based (one of which is illustrated in Plate 2:45 and Colour Plate 28). However, the two marble Sphinxes are much shorter in length than those at Chiswick, and differ predominantly in that their backs are not partially covered by the ornate trappings that could broadly be described as saddle cloths. Sphinxes decorated with saddle cloths were particularly popular from the late seventeenth century through to the late eighteenth century, and seem to have been inspired by J Houzeau and L Lerambert's magnificent marble pair which are adorned by bronze cupids and were supplied to Versailles in 1668.[27]

In an attempt to attribute the Sphinxes at Chiswick, it is first necessary to mention the history and age of the two Sphinxes belonging to the Ashmolean Museum. These, together with a mass of other marble pieces, were given to Oxford University's Ashmolean Museum in 1755 by Henrietta-Louisa, Countess Dowager of Pomfret, who had purchased them from the 2nd Earl of Pomfret a few years earlier. Her gift formerly comprised part of the magnificent Arundel Collection of marbles, assembled in the seventeenth century by Thomas Howard, Earl of Arundel and Surrey, which, at its height, was said to have numbered over four hundred busts, statues and inscribed stones, excluding sarcophagi and the

Plate 2:43. Sphinx, Parian marble, late Roman period. Height approx 45 ¼ ins

THE ASHMOLEAN MUSEUM, OXFORD

Plate 2:44. Sphinx, marble, probably by Guelfi, 1710. Height approx 43 ½ ins

THE ASHMOLEAN MUSEUM, OXFORD

Plate 2:45. One of a pair of sphinxes, Portland stone, attributed to Guelfi, circa 1725, Chiswick House. Height approx 37ins. (See Colour Plates 28 and 29)

ENGLISH HERITAGE

Colour Plate 30. A Palladian term, Portland stone, early eighteenth century, formerly in the grounds of Chiswick House, and now at Chatsworth, Derbyshire
TRUSTEES OF THE CHATSWORTH SETTLEMENT: PHOTO PETER GREENHALF

like. It was slowly dispersed later in the century, the final major part being sold in 1691 to Sir William Fermor (grandfather of the 2nd Earl of Pomfret), who removed them to Easton Neston in Northamptonshire, where they remained until purchased by the Countess Dowager.[28]

As the two Ashmolean Sphinxes are carved very differently, and as they are not a pair (for example, both have their tails curling up and around to the right), there has been some controversy as to their authenticity. Indeed twenty years ago they were both thought to be 'modern' fakes and were removed from the Ashmolean to the harsh environment of an outdoor setting. However, it is now thought that the Sphinx in Plate 2:43 is a genuine antique and of Roman origin, whilst the more sophisticated carved Sphinx in Plate 2:44 is thought to be 'modern'.[29] Unfortunately no inventory of the items in the Arundel Collection survives so it is not known whether the 'modern' copy was ever part of the Collection. However, when John Loverday described his visit to Easton Neston in May 1731, he mentions 'the Sphynges',[30] so the 'modern' figure must have been in existence by that date. It could be that the Sphinx was purchased with the antique model by the Earl of Arundel, perhaps in the belief that it, too, was an antique, or alternatively the Earl, or his heirs, had a companion figure carved by one of the seventeenth century sculptors who worked on the restoration of the collection.[31] A third more plausible possibility is that it was carved for the 1st Earl of Pomfret whilst he was having his marbles restored.

The sculptor who restored Pomfret's marbles is known to have been the Italian Giovanni Battista Guelfi, of whom the most important contemporary description is given by Vertue. This account is of great relevance not only to the marble Sphinxes, but also to the stone pair at Chiswick:

'Signor...Guelphi. Statuary, some time wrought under Cavalier Rosconi. Statuary of great reputation at Rome. From thence Lord Burlington encouraged or brought him to England. He was some time at Ld. Pomfrets...Eston...Northampt. imployd. repairing the Antique Statues. Arundel Collect. Afterwards Guelphi was much employed for many years by Ld. Burlington in his house in London & made many statues for his Villa at Chiswick, being much continually almost employed for him several years. Also several Busts. He ... much commended him to the Nobility for an excellent Sculptor, procurd him many works to that of the Monument to Sec. Craggs Westmint Abbey. He left England 1734 after residing near 20 years. Went to Bologna a man of slow speech, much opinionated, and as an Italian thought no body could be equal to himself in skill in this Country. Yet all his works seem to the judicious very often defective, wanting spirit and grace. Its thought that Ld. Burlington parted with him very willingly'.[32]

Colour Plate 31. The Victorian sculptor John Thomas' monumental Portland stone fountain at Castle Howard, Yorkshire. The enormous larger-than-life figures were transported by train to Yorkshire where the fountain was operated by a steam engine. (See Plate 2:55 and pages 112-114)

THE HON SIMON HOWARD

Colour Plate 32. One of the twenty-seven Bath stone vases in the gardens of Chiswick House, London, probably from a design by Lord Burlington. (See Plates 2:35 and 61 and page 118)

ENGLISH HERITAGE: PHOTO PETER GREENHALF

Vertue's penultimate sentence is of particular interest, for the 'modern' Sphinx is by no means an accomplished work. Guelfi was a sculptor of some ability, but his work on the restoration of the Easton Neston marbles was unquestionably poor. Indeed Adolf Michaelis states that their restoration 'could not easily have been entrusted to more unfortunate hands. Great as has been the blundering perpetrated in all quarters of the shape of so-called "restorations", yet hardly ever have any antiques been so shamefully tampered with as in the tasteless additions made by this shallow botcher'.[33] The combination of the style and quality of carving found in the 'modern' marble Sphinx, together with the manner in which Michaelis describes Guelfi's work, does indicate a tentative attribution to this opinionated Italian sculptor.

There is no doubt that Guelfi must have been well aware of the two Sphinxes at Easton Neston, for he was, as Vertue states 'some time at Ld. Pomfrets'. As Vertue goes on to state that 'afterwards' he was employed by Burlington, this leads us to the stone Sphinxes at Chiswick. A pair of these saddle-clothed models are clearly illustrated surmounting gate piers at Chiswick in a painting circa 1728 attributed to Pieter Andreas Rysbrack of the south front (Plate 2:46) which coincides with the time Guelfi is known to have been in England. It thus seems likely that if Guelfi had executed Sphinxes for Burlington he would have based them on the model at the estate where he had just finished working, especially if it was he who had carved the 'modern' marble Sphinx, which, it should be noted, is carved in a similar manner to the stone pair in the gardens behind Chiswick House.

Today the gate piers illustrated in Rysbrack's painting form an entrance way to Green Park in Piccadilly,[34] and although they are still surmounted by saddle-clothed Sphinxes, these are made of lead, a medium Guelfi is not known to have used. However, it seems that these lead Sphinxes were replacements for the stone ones, which were transferred to the gardens behind Chiswick House. The exact date of their removal to this position was probably the late 1740s, for an entry in Burlington's account book records a payment to John Cheere in February 1748 for 'a sphynx in Lead'[35] (Colour Plate 29). It therefore seems reasonable to assume that the stone pair was transferred around this date. Both the pair of stone Sphinxes and the lead Sphinx referred to above are clearly visible in John

Donowell's 'A View of the Back Front of the House' (Plate 2:47). All three of these remain at Chiswick today as depicted by Donowell.

Lead models of these Sphinxes still seem to have been popular forms of garden ornament later in the eighteenth century, though the exact date at which they started being produced is unclear. Possibly the first model was that supplied by John Cheere and recorded in Burlington's account book, and thus it is likely Cheere took his mould from one of the stone Sphinxes. If this was the case, it seems reasonable to assume that pairs of these lead Sphinxes, such as the two pairs at Castle Hill (one of which is illustrated in Plate 2:48), those at Temple Newsam, Hopetoun House and Saltram and, of course, those now at Piccadilly, can be attributed to this prolific lead figure maker.

Colour Plate 33. One of a pair of vases and pedestals, Bath stone, probably from a design by Lord Burlington, the Exedra, Chiswick House. (See also Plate 2:62 and page 118)
ENGLISH HERITAGE: PHOTO PETER GREENHALF

Colour Plate 34. One of a pair of vases and pedestals, Bath stone, probably from a design by Lord Burlington, Exedra, Chiswick House. (See also Plate 2:63 and page 118)
ENGLISH HERITAGE: PHOTO PETER GREENHALF

Other Portland stone figures

The famous Medici Lions have over the years proved themselves to be the most popular lions for garden ornament. Great numbers of models were produced in a whole range of media, for example in marble for the gardens at Chatsworth, in lead for Stowe, in artificial stone for Osborne House, while great numbers of cast-iron models were produced by continental foundries.

Where the original antique marble lion, with its right foot on a sphere, was unearthed is unknown, but by 1598, together with a 'modern' companion carved by Flaminio Vacca, it flanked the steps leading to the gardens of the Villa Medici in Rome. The two Lions are frequently described as 'antique' statues, but thanks to Francis Haskell and Nicholas Penny's authoritative book on the most popular antique statues, this misnomer is being slowly rectified.[36] The statues were greatly admired during later years, but it is interesting to note that during the eighteenth century, Vacca's companion figure was the more admired of the two.

Colour Plate 35. Life-size figure representing Summer, Ketton stone, by Cibber, Belvoir Castle, Leicestershire. (See Plate 2:69 and pages 124 and 125)

THE DUKE OF RUTLAND

Plate 2:49. Copy of the sixteenth century Medici Lion, Portland stone, by Joseph Wilton, 1759, on a pedestal (also Portland stone) designed by Robert Adam, Kedleston Hall, Derbyshire. Width approx 77ins

LORD SCARSDALE

This preference for the sixteenth century Lion seems to have been shared by Joseph Wilton (1722-1803), who spent three years in Rome studying famous antique statues. When he returned to England in 1755 he no doubt brought back with him a number of models and marbles, for in later years he was to execute a number of copies of famous antique statues, including many of those in Rome. These presumably included a copy of the antique Lion's companion figure, for he carved one for Sir Nathaniel Curzon's gardens at Kedleston Hall (Plate 2:49).

The statue which remains today in the gardens to the south-west of the house is in remarkable condition. It is a fine piece of carving, over six feet wide, and is executed from a single piece of Portland stone. Whilst lead, iron and artificial stone copies could be produced without supports, most marble and stone copies (including the originals now in the Loggia dei Lanzi, Florence) and Wilton's figure were executed with conspicuous, yet essential, reinforcements of the legs, for the nature of the pose made it vulnerable to damage.

The Kedleston Archives record a payment to Joseph Wilton of fifty guineas in 1759, but whether this included the pedestal is unknown. However, the statue was placed on its pedestal, which is also made of Portland stone, by Samuel Wyatt (1731-1807), and was taken from an unexecuted design by Robert Adam. Adam's drawing survives in the Archives at Kedleston.[37]

Like the great majority of garden pedestals produced during the eighteenth century, rather than being carved from one piece of stone, it is carved in sections. In this case the die (central section, or 'dye', as it was referred to in the eighteenth century), is carved from four pieces, the vertical joint lines separating the wider side panel from the end panels being clearly visible just within the water-leaf moulding. For obvious structural purposes this method is reversed on both the cap and base. Thus the cap (sometimes called the cornice) is formed of four sections, two of which cover the sides of the pedestal, overlapping the joints on the die. These two sections, however, are not wide enough to cover the die completely, so two short sections are inserted into the resultant gap above the ends of the die. One frequently finds variations on this, whereby the die is composed of many smaller sections, or alternatively the cap is carved from only two or, at times, one block.

The popularity in Britain in the late eighteenth and nineteenth centuries of copies of the so called Dog of Alcibiades[38] is due partly to several antique pairs in Italy, such as those in the Uffizi, but mainly to a particularly fine antique model (with its head turned to its left) which was purchased by H Constantine Jennings (1721-1819) sometime between 1748 and 1756 and brought to England.[39] Some idea of the quality of this antique statue can be gauged by the fact that Horace Walpole reckoned it to be one of the five chief statues (antique) of animals and, when Jennings was obliged to auction it in 1778, Mr Duncombe paid the stupendous sum of one thousand guineas for it.[40]

Charles Duncombe removed the statue to his Yorkshire estate of Duncombe Park, where it remains today. He was a member of the Society of Dilettanti which was formed in 1734 by a number of notable collectors[41] to promote interest in the antiquities of ancient Greece and Rome. In 1743 Horace Walpole wrote that 'the Dilettanti, [was] a club for which the nominal qualification is having been in Italy, and the real one, having been drunk',[42] but this is over-damning, for under the Society's guidance much work and several subsequent excellent publications were produced on these antiquities.

In 1765 this distinguished, if drunken, Society whose members freely socialised, was joined by William Weddell.

Weddell's estate of Newby Hall in Yorkshire was refurbished by Robert Adam (1728-1792) between 1767-1783[43] to house his magnificent collection of 'antique marbles'. Amongst Adam's alterations was the addition of a porch, outside which was placed a Portland stone copy of Charles Duncombe's dog with another, reversed, forming a pair like those in the Uffizi. Regrettably the sculptor responsible for these two beasts remains unknown, but as Weddell must have been familiar with Duncombe's dog, not only through the publicity surrounding its sale, but also through the Society and his neighbour-member, one may speculate that the artist carved the copy looking to its left from the Duncombe original. Robert Adam also seems to have been an admirer of this dog, for in the sale of his property on 21 May 1818, lot 78 was 'A very fine large cast from Alcibiades dog...'[44]

Weddell died in 1792 and the estate passed to the 3rd Lord Grantham, who,

Colour Plate 36. Life-size fountain figure of a Triton, probably Roche Abbey stone, by Cibber, circa 1690, at Chatsworth, Derbyshire. (See page 125)

forty-one years later, inherited the estate of Wrest Park in Bedfordshire. Lord Grantham (then the 3rd Earl de Grey) rebuilt Wrest in the following years and by 1846[45] these two dogs had been removed to piers flanking the steps from the terrace to the garden of the newly built house, where they remain today.

Illustrated here is the reversed model (Plate 2:50) which, like its pair, is well carved, in remarkably good condition and is a good example of the calcite deposits found in Portland stone. Most of the stone is relatively unblemished, but the heavy 'veining' to the right of the statue's base and the snail creeps inside the dog's left shoulder clearly show the varying nature of this medium.

The Dog of Alcibiades was a much-copied subject; a marble copy stands in the grounds of Hever Castle in Kent, whilst Bertel Thorvaldsen incorporated a modified hound in his group the Shepherd Boy.

One artificial stone manufactory, probably that of Austin & Seeley, which is known to have been producing models, must have found the Dog of Alcibiades a particularly lucrative model, for pairs (in a cement-based medium very similar to

Colour Plate 37. One of a pair of sandstone finials, possibly carved by Daniel Harvey, Castle Howard, Yorkshire. (See Plate 2:75 and pages 126-127)

THE HON SIMON HOWARD

that used by Austin & Seeley) remain at Basildon Park (Plate 2:51), Bicton, Osborne, Chatsworth, Carlton Towers and Shrublands Park, to name but a few locations.

Plate 2:50. One of a pair of the Dog of Alcibiades, Portland stone, circa 1780, the Terrace, Wrest Park, Bedfordshire. Height approx 46ins.

This is a reversed copy of the Dog of Alcibiades from the antique marble at Duncombe Park, Yorkshire

ENGLISH HERITAGE

Plate 2:51. A pair of mid- to late nineteenth century cement-based artificial stone dogs at Basildon Park, Bedfordshire, copied from the antique Dog of Alcibiades, probably manufactured by Austin & Seeley

THE NATIONAL TRUST

The terminal or term figure is distinct from the architectural caryatid in that it is a free-standing ornament. The classical origin of these statues, which were found in many eighteenth century gardens, was described in 1767 by the architect Isaac Ware:

The Termini, or as we commonly call them in English, Terms, are so nearly allied to the Persian or Caryatic order, that it is a wonder those who gave that important name to those statues or figures, did not continue it also to these.

The origin of these figures is very plain: there were places where the possessions of one person or family ended, and those of another began; these points of ground were the terms or boundaries, of one or other possession, and it was very proper they should be marked in some manner, that they might be always known and regularly determined.

Nothing was a more natural cause of quarrel than the dispute about the term of the possession: the ancients who erected everything into a deity, and created imaginary beings of this denomination for their several purposes, were not long without a god of land-marks. This god they called Terminus, and as his office was to prevent disputes between neighbours and friends, they placed an image of him upon every one of these points or spots of land, where the estate or property of one person bordered upon that of another. The name of the god became familiar to the statue, and these were called Termini.

This was the origin of this piece of architecture; a mark was necessary, they placed the statue of their god as this mark, and called first him, then his statue, the protector of land-marks; there he stood always to watch them, and they made his statue without feet, that he might not be able to change place.

This was the origin of the Term or Terminus, which to this day is the statue of a human figure, or, if the reader choose, a heathen god, whose head and upper part only have that resemblance, the legs being supposed inclosed in a kind of scabbard.

For uniformity, as there were no legs, they took off the arms; and some retain this figure to this day.

It is a frequent ornament in gardens, some place them also in decorated rooms, to support vases, or other elegant works; but its proper situation is at the boundary of lands. We have given the representation of one, placed as a mark of boundaries of four counties and dressed him in four forms, as symbolical of their produce. This may stand as an instance of the manner in which the Terminus may be used with elegance and propriety.

By this deduction of the origin of the Terminus, we find that it is properly a mixed figure; in the lower part serving as the Persian or Caryatic orders in the place of a column, and decorated at the top with the head of a man, woman, satyr, faun or other device.[46]

Broadly speaking terms produced during the eighteenth century (which were predominantly carved from Portland stone) can be separated into two groups: those which are more figurative, such as the pair flanking the entrance to the Rose Garden at Anglesey Abbey which are carved with arms, their 'scabbards' or shafts half covered with fleeces, and those with shafts, sometimes plain, but more commonly decorated on the front (at chest height) with acanthus leaves, surmounted by a bust allegorical of, for example, one of the seasons, or an ancient god or worthy (Colour Plate 30).

During the eighteenth century garden statues were usually bought either from lead figure makers or were commissioned from sculptors; terms, however, were

Plate 2:52. Three of six terms, Portland stone, by Sefferin Alken, 1759, the Formal Garden, Longford Castle, Wiltshire. Height approx 78ins.

From left to right: Old Faunus, Young Faunus, Pan; the other three are Mercury (Plate 2:53), Bacchus and Antinous

THE EARL OF RADNOR

often produced by the less talented sculptor-masons, whose artistic abilities would suffice for the architectural work involved, such as decorative mouldings, capitals of columns and keystones. Of course, the most eminent of sculptors were also used to produce terms, such as the pair at Rousham in Oxfordshire by Peter Scheemakers.

One of the better examples of a sculptor-mason's work is seen in the six terms which remain today in the gardens of Longford Castle. These are notable in that each is executed from a single block of stone carved by Sefferin Alken (fl1744-1783) to whom payment is recorded on 2 January 1759. The ledger in the Longford Muniment Room reads: '. . . for six stone Terms at £8 8s 0d each', whilst the Portland stone from which they are carved came from a certain Mr Devall and cost £3 3s per term; in total quite a substantial price considering that the lead copy of the famous antique Farnese Flora which John Cheere supplied at the same time cost only £8 8s.

The style of these six figures, three of which are shown in Plate 2:52, is notably Palladian. They are similar to terms illustrated in Ware's book, and very much in keeping with earlier examples, such as those which are visible in Jean Rigaud's 1733 view of the 'South Front of Lord Burlington's Villa at Chiswick', and other examples such as those which used to stand outside the Orangery at Stowe.[47] The merging of the bust and the shaft or scabbard is successfully resolved by a neckline in the form of a ribbon, while the front of the shaft is decorated with bold acanthus leaves which are visible, if marred by heavy lichen, on another of Alken's terms at Longford, Mercury (Plate 2:53).

Terms were still a popular form of garden ornament during the Regency, when many were produced in Coade stone (see Plate 4:14).

110

Plate 2:53. Detail of Mercury at Longford Castle, and an illustration from Isaac Ware's A Complete Body of Architecture *showing, centre, a Palladian term marking the 'boundaries of four counties'. The front view on the right shows the merging of the bust and shaft with a ribbon neckline as seen in the figure of Mercury*

THE EARL OF RADNOR

The architect James Gibbs in *A Book of Architecture* illustrates a great variety of 'draughts' (designs) for vases and finials, amongst which are 'Three designs for Vases done for the Right Honourable the Earl of Oxford [see Plate 2:80]. There are two vases well executed in Portland Stone according to the middle Draught, which are set upon two large peers on each side of the principal walk in the gardens at Wimpole in Cambridgeshire'.[48]

These last two vases, in fact finials, together with a third are now on piers surrounding the courtyard of Wimpole Hall (Plate 2:54), and seem very likely to have been carved by Andries Carpentiere. Dr Friedman in his book *James Gibbs* relates that at Wimpole 'Gibbs was paid 10 guineas for drawings, and Andrew Carpenter, whom he subsequently employed at Ditchley and Amersham, carved twelve vases at £7 each and twenty-four baskets at £1 10s 0d, for which he received a total of £85 10s 0d during 1719-20'.[49] Furthermore, a drawing by 'Mr. Gibbs & executed by Mr. Carpenter',[50] of the finials at Wimpole survives in the Bodleian Library, Oxford. However, whether the £7 refers to these finials is not clear, for they are of magnificent quality, with nearly five inches in relief on the heads, and one wonders if even in the early eighteenth century such finials would have cost so little.

Although Portland stone was to a great extent usurped during the nineteenth century by new media, such as artificial stone and cast-iron, it was still used to produce large-scale fountains for many country houses. The gardens laid out by William Burn (1789-1870) for Thomas Coke, 2nd Earl of Leicester (1822-1909), at Holkham Hall, contain one of these, carved by Charles R Smith (1798-1888)

and portraying St George Slaying the Dragon, whilst W A Nesfield (1793-1881) in his alterations to Witley Court included a now damaged fountain representing Andromeda and Perseus by a certain Mr Forsyth.[51]

Another example of these fountains forms the centrepiece of the South Garden at Castle Howard, laid out by Nesfield in, as one of his letters mentions 'a stability of character in accordance with that splendid fellow Vanbrugh'.[52] This magnificent fountain was commissioned by the 7th Earl of Carlisle (1814-1879) who, after some debate about it being cast in metal, decided in 1851 that John Thomas (1813-1862) should execute the figures in Portland stone.[53] However, Atlas's huge orb was cast in metal, for obvious reasons of weight. John Thomas seems to have found monumental fountains a popular subject, for at the 1851 Great Exhibition he exhibited amongst others a 'Model of fountain comprising shells and marine plants surrounded by four Tritons, and surmounted with a group of Acis and Galatea'.[54] Perhaps as a result of this exhibit, Nesfield recommended the sculptor to the 7th Earl. In comparison with Thomas' model, illustrated in the Exhibition's official catalogue, the fountain at Castle Howard is more 'classical' (Plate 2:55 and Colour Plate 31) and, as at Witley, Nesfield may have been involved with the design. The pose of the Tritons certainly bears some similarities to a figure by Battista Lorenzi (see Plate 4:42), whilst the statue of Atlas kneeling, is perhaps derived from an antique statue.

Thomas received £1,118 10s 5d for the fountain figures which, being more than life size, were carved from several blocks (joint lines are visible just below each of the Tritons' breasts and across the waist of Atlas); this sum did not include the main bowl, side shells, pedestal and border which were carved by local masons.

Plate 2:55. Larger-than-life fountain of Atlas and four Tritons, Portland stone, by John Thomas and other masons, 1853, Castle Howard, Yorkshire. (See Colour Plate 31)
THE HON SIMON HOWARD

By 1853 the fountain had been erected and in a letter to Lord Carlisle of 30 October of that year, Thomas, clearly pleased with the final result, writes:

> Last Wedy (the apparatus for the fountains having been reported all ready) I was urgently requested to run down to Castle Howard with Mr. Easton [responsible for the fittings and plumbing] to make experiments with the jets whiles Ladies Carlisle, Elizabeth, & Mary &c were present & after various trials & criticisms I am proud to state that we arrived at a most satisfactory result not only as to individual form but to general effect, so much so that the Committee of Ladies considered that matters could not be improved — Lady Carlisle particularly wished me to give your Lordship a line which I do with great pleasure because the whole affair exceeded my expectations — the supply of water is so ample that we were able to introduce in addition to the principals 8 subordinate jets in the shells which materially conduce to the richness and action of the whole and as to the display on the Large Basin (the ground pool) there are 9 jets which in effect are as successful as those of Atlas thus [the letter is finished with a drawing].[55]

Thomas' reference to the principal jets refers to those which, in the summer months, issue forth from the top of the orb and each of the Tritons' conches. Clearly the water pressure Mr Easton had made available was more than sufficient for these five, hence the extra flow into the eight shells and a further nine peripheral jets in the basin.

In the days before water mains this was a considerable achievement bearing in mind the pressure had to be supplied either via reducing pipes from a large reservoir at some height above the fountain, or by an expensive and sophisticated pumping machine. At Castle Howard a large steam engine was used, but for less wealthy nineteenth century patrons with smaller fountains, gravity was still commonly used. Writing in 1823,[56] the architect and landscape gardener, John Buonarotti Papworth (1775-1847) gave advice on the technical specifications necessary for fountains. His table (shown below) gives ideal figures (for reservoirs within five hundred feet of the fountain) but does not take into consideration such factors as air and bends in the piping.

Height of reservoir (Feet)	Diameter of conducting pipes	Diameter of aperture or ajutage	Height of the jet (Ft.D)
5	1¾ inch	¼ inch	4: 91
10	2 "	½ "	9: 68
20	2½ "	½ "	18: 82
30	3¼ "	⅝ "	27: 48
40	4½ "	¾ "	35: 74
50	5 "	¾ "	43: 65
60	6 "	1 "	51: 24
80	7 "	1¼ "	65: 64
100	8 "	1½ "	79: 12

The great resistance of Portland stone to the ravages of climate are again well illustrated here for, being a fountain, it is particularly vulnerable but has suffered negligibly. It is interesting to note that the scallop shells around the fountain have lead liners, a precaution against damage, for Portland, when saturated with water is, during winter months, susceptible to the ravages of frost and ice.

Bath Stone

During the eighteenth century great numbers of garden vases were carved from Bath Stone. This is a limestone of a yellow colour (caused by the presence of ferric-oxide) which weathers down to an evenly pitted surface, and, being more porous than Portland stone, for example, is generally more susceptible to moss. A good example of this is given by comparing the Portland stone statue in Plate 2:7 with the Bath stone block on which it stands. Apart from its colour and texture, Bath stone is frequently, though not always, identifiable by the presence of crystalline veins, which run in comparatively straight lines through the stone (Plate 2:56).

Bath stone was quarried from a number of sites in the area around Bath, of which the most prominent, during the eighteenth century, were those run by Ralph Allen (1694-1764) a self-made man who, having made his fortune as the Bath Postmaster, became a leading member of Bath society. He constructed a substantial seat for himself at Prior Park, just outside Bath, where he entertained friends, amongst whom may be mentioned Pope and Pitt. He had two quarries in the hills above Bath, an open one at Hampton Down and a subterranean one at Coombe Down. To lower the cost of the stone he set up a system of carriageways to facilitate its transportation to his masons' yard on the banks of the Avon. This proved a considerable success and by the mid-1730s, he was able to sell blocks of stone at 7s 6d per ton, some 2s 6d cheaper than it had been earlier. In comparison with Portland stone, Bath stone was much cheaper; indeed the stone for each term carved by Alken for Longford Castle cost three guineas (see Plates 2:52 and 53), and each of these cannot have been carved from a block weighing more than one ton.

Allen's Yard was described by Daniel Defoe as follows:

> The stone-yard of this great, because good, man, who may be styled the Genius of Bath, is on the banks of the Avon. In it is wrought the freestone dug from the quarries in Coombe Down, which is another part of Odin's Down, purchased by him. He has likewise a wharf to embark the same stone in unwrought blocks, which are brought down from the quarry by an admirable tramway that runs upon a frame of timber of about a mile and a half in length, placed partly upon walls and partly upon the ground, like the waggon-ways belonging to the collieries in the North of England. Two horses draw one of these machines, generally loaded with two or three tones [sic] of stone, over the most easy part of the descent, but afterwards its own velocity carries it down the rest, and with so much precipitation that the man who guides it is sometimes obliged to lock every wheel to stop it, which he can do with great ease by means of bolts applied to the front wheels and levers to the back wheels. The freestone can be carried by the Avon into Bristol, whence it may be transported to any part of England, and the new works of St. Bartholomews Hospital in London, as well as the Exchange of Bristol, are built with stone from Mr Allen's quarry.[57]

The stone was, of course, extensively used for the buildings of Bath, but in the early years of the eighteenth century its use, at least in London, met with some opposition. The architect John Wood (1704-1754), in *An Essay towards a Description of Bath* wrote:

> The Introduction of the Free Stone into London met with great Opposition; some of the Opponents maliciously comparing it to Cheshire Cheese, liable to breed Maggots that would soon Devour it; and the late Mr. Colen Campbell, as Architect, together with the late Messeurs Hawksmoor and James, as Clerks of the Works of Greenwich Hospital, were so prejudiced against it, that at a Publick Meeting of the Governors of that Building at Salters Hill, in the Spring of the Year 1728, they Represented it as a Material unable to bear any Weight, of a Coarse Texture, bad Colour, and almost as Dear as Portland Stone for a Publick Work in or near London.[58]

However, such prejudice was overcome, and the stone was soon being used extensively for garden vases which were sent all over the country. Bath stone was used predominantly for vases and architectural work, rather than statues, because it was both coarser and cheaper than finer quality stones. The vases were usually carved in the vicinity of the quarries when the stone was still green, but were also made by London sculptor-masons such as W Atkinson, whose posthumous sale of 2 April 1767 included 'a large and magnificent vase in bath stone'.[59] Of the sculptor-masons operating from the Bath area during the eighteenth century, the two most prolific of these appear to have been the Greenway (after which Greenway Lane in Bath is named) and Parsons families, both of which had yards outside Bath in Claverton Street, near Widcombe.

Unfortunately no examples of works by the Greenway family have been traced, but John Wood relates that: 'Thomas Greenway, after Building a House in Saint John's Court so profuse in Ornament as to tempt the King to Bath to make part

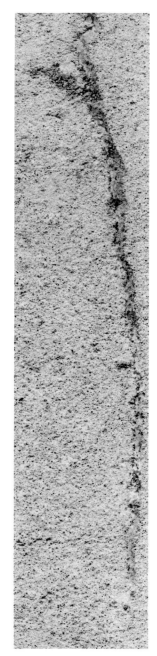

Plate 2:56. Close-up of a piece of Bath stone, showing the evenly-pitted surface and characteristic crystalline veins

Plate 2:57. An illustration from John Vardy's Some Designs of Mr Inigo Jones and Mr Wm Kent, *showing Kent's design for 'Two Vases with Pedestals for Mr. Pope'*
GREGG INTERNATIONAL

Plate 2:58. Single vase and pedestal, Bath stone, the vase taken from a design by William Kent, circa 1765, Longford Castle, Wiltshire. Height approx 15 feet including pedestal
THE EARL OF RADNOR

of it his Palace, particularly applied himself to small Ornaments in Free Stone, such as Crests, Vases, Fruits &c. and several that served their Apprenticeships to him pursued the Business, till they brought it to such a Perfection as to Merit publick Encouragement, and render their Works a rising Branch of the Trade of Bath'.[60]

Wood goes on to relate that 'Ornaments of a larger Kind, such as Chimney Pieces, Door Cases, Window Cases, Pedestals, Peers, Obelisks, Ballustrades and the like are commonly made by the same Artificers, and sent abroad to a great Distance from Bath; to which if we add the Exportation of our Free Stone in Rough Blocks, the whole together will make no inconsiderable Part of the Trade of the City'.[61]

An undated drawing, brought to the author's attention by Dr Friedman, illustrates several ornaments by Joseph Greenway and bears the inscription: 'Joseph Greenway Carver at the Cold-Bath, in Bath Executes the above Designs or any other Ornamental Work in Bath Stone which may be sent Safe to any part of Europe. NB. He will wait on Gentlemen and Ladies at their Lodgings with Variety of Draughts.' These designs include a sundial and several vases, one of which was probably designed by Lord Burlington (Plate 2:61) and one which was from a design by William Kent. This last, together with another, are illustrated in John Vardy's *Some Designs of Mr Inigo Jones and Mr Wm Kent* (Plate 2:57), in which they are described as 'Two Vases with Pedestals for Mr Pope'.[62] Quite a number of Bath stone vases of this design were produced and one of the most impressive, standing on its pedestal at least fifteen feet high, adorns one of the vistas at Longford Castle (Plate 2:58); unfortunately the name of the artist responsible remains unknown, but it may have come from Thomas Parsons.

Other members of the Greenway family were William, Benjamin and Daniel, of whom the last two are known to have worked at the Bristol Exchange in the mid-1740s.

Of the Parsons family more is known. Thomas Parsons' son, Robert, was born in 1718 and followed in the family business as a mason-carver. Although known today primarily for his Bath stone vases, Robert Parsons, who was also a Baptist minister, produced a variety of other works as is clearly apparent from an advertisement in the *Bath Journal* of 11 June 1753:

> Whereas a Report has prevailed, that R. PARSONS, MASON and CARVER, at the Bridge-Foot, Bath, has declined working in Marble; this will satisfy his Friends that such a Report is not true, that he continues to work Chimney Pieces, Monuments &c. in various sorts of Marble, as Italian, Irish and English: Together with his other Business of making Bath-Stone Ornaments, and fine chimines [sic], in a beautiful Stone, he has for that purpose, as usual; great Variety to be seen at his Yards, between the Bridge and Gibbs' Mill, leading to Claverton-Down. He executes Orders, by letter, as punctual as Personal, both in Neatness of Work and Price'.[63]

Although most of Robert's vases were executed from designs by famous artists or designers, it is apparent from the sketchbook of his son, Thomas (1744-1813), that he also carved a few from is own designs (one is illustrated in Plate 2:64a). This sketchbook,[64] which illustrated over 150 designs, provides some fascinating information, for it names the artists from whom many of the designs were taken, for example: Gainsborough, Wedgwood and Bentley, Gibbs, Cipriani, William Kent, Chambers, G Romano, Mrs Coade, Ware, Wyatt, Adam, Thomas Baldwin and Lord Burlington. The sketchbook seems to have been compiled over a period, but the inclusion of designs from Mrs Coade suggests that it dates from towards the end of the eighteenth century.

Robert Parsons is known to have supplied several garden vases to Longford Castle in Wiltshire. The account book records payment in January 1759 to 'Mr. Parsons for two vases from Bath packing cases &c. £6 18s 0d'.[65] This probably refers to the vase in Plate 2:59 and its pair (whose design in Thomas' sketchbook is shown in Plate 2:64o), rather than another set of four Bath stone vases, almost certainly also by Parsons, which adorn the same gardens.

Parsons is known to have worked at another Wiltshire estate, the magnificent gardens created at Stourhead, south of Bath, by Henry Hoare II (1705-1785). He received £110 between 1745 and 1751,[66] and in view of this it seems reasonable to assume that the Bath stone vase by the Temple of Flora at Stourhead (Plate 2:60) was supplied by Parsons. Certainly the design features in Thomas' sketchbook (Plate 2:64c) in which it is described as 'Antique'. The source of this design comes from Bernard de Montfaucon's popular *L'Antiquité Expliquée et Représentée en Figures*, published in 1719.[67]

Thomas Parsons' reference to four of the designs being 'Burlington' (Plates 2:64e-h) is particularly interesting. The sketchbook does, to a great extent, correctly acknowledge the respective designers responsible for particular designs,

and in the light of this it is probable that these four vases were from designs by Lord Burlington, who was, after all, not only an extremely wealthy patron, but also an active architect. Of these four designs, that in Plate 2:64e is perhaps the most interesting. Twenty-seven of these vases, which probably date from the mid-1730s, remain in the gardens of Chiswick House (Plate 2:35 and Colour Plate 32), while others were used to decorate other gardens created at the same time, such as the four at Rousham in Oxfordshire, one of which by the Praeneste (designed by William Kent) is illustrated in Plate 2:61. Like those at Chiswick, the Rousham pairs were constructed from several pieces of Bath stone. The socle, the lower body of the vase with its foliate decoration, the plain undecorated section forming the main body of the vase, and the upper part, with its band of Vitruvian scroll below Greek key decoration rising to an acanthus decorated stem, are each carved from individual pieces. The design was to remain popular with architects such as Mathew Brettingham for many years after both Kent and Burlington had died, for Brettingham seems likely to have placed the four similar vases at Blickling Hall, and possibly also those at Audley End.

Two further designs for vases illustrated in Thomas Parsons' sketchbook (Plates 2:64i and j) are listed as for 'ye late Earl of Egremont' (Charles Wyndam, 2nd Earl of Egremont), one of which, presumably made by Parsons, stands on an island in the lake at Petworth.[68] Unfortunately, it is not known from whose designs these vases were copied, but as pairs of these were incorporated within the Exedra at Chiswick (Plate 2:41), where they remain today (Plates ?:62 and 63 and Colour Plates 33 and 34), one may assume that the original design was either by William Kent or Lord Burlington. In the knowledge that many other garden vases at Chiswick are from designs by Burlington, it is quite likely that these two are also by him. Certainly Burlington was enthusiastic about the design in Plate 2:62 for as well as the pair in the Exedra, by 1742 at least a further five decorated the gardens to the west of the house.[69]

Robert Parsons is also known to have supplied vases to Moulsham Hall and Castle Hill,[70] whilst in his capacity as a mason he is known to have supplied 'rockified stone' and 'fossiles of different sorts' for the Grotto at Oatlands Park.[71] On his death in 1790 his son, Thomas, who had followed in his father's footsteps as both a carver and minister, carried on the business, but for precisely how long is unclear. In 1805 the Bath Directory lists him as a grocer in Claverton Street, but on his death in 1813, his obituary in the *Bath and Cheltenham Gazette* included these words: 'It has seldom fallen to the lot of any journalist to record the decease of an individual so deeply lamented, or so universally beloved. Few men possessed a more extensive acquaintance, and fewer still combined such rare qualifications. His knowledge of the Arts and Sciences was general; and, in the departments of Sculpture, Drawing, Chemistry and Astronomy, he certainly excelled'.[72] This

Plate 2:60. Single vase, Bath stone, after an antique design in Montfaucon's L'Antiquité Expliquée..., mid-eighteenth century, the Temple of Flora, Stourhead, Wiltshire. Height approx 54ins

THE NATIONAL TRUST

Plate 2:61. One of a pair of vases, Bath stone, probably from a design by Lord Burlington, the Praeneste, Rousham, Oxfordshire. A similar vase at Chiswick House can be seen in Colour Plate 32

C COTTRELL-DORMER

Plate 2:62. One of a pair of vases and pedestals, Bath stone, probably from a design by Lord Burlington, circa 1735, the Exedra, Chiswick House. Height approx 50½ins. (See Colour Plate 33)

ENGLISH HERITAGE

Plate 2:63. One of a pair of vases and pedestals, Bath stone, probably from a design by Lord Burlington, circa 1735, the Exedra, Chiswick House. Height approx 70ins. (See Colour Plate 34)

ENGLISH HERITAGE

Plate 2:64a. Robert Parsons

Plate 2:64b. Mrs Coade

Plate 2:64c. Antique

Plate 2:64d. James Gibbs

Plate 2:64e. Lord Burlington

Plate 2:64f. Lord Burlington

Plate 2:64g. Lord Burlington

Plate 2:64h. Lord Burlington

Plate 2:64i. For the late Earl of Egremont probably by Lord Burlington

120

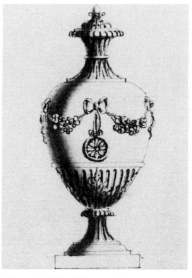

Plate 2:64j. For the late Earl of Egremont probably by Lord Burlington

Plate 2:64k. Thomas Parsons

Plate 2:64l. Thomas Parsons

Plate 2:64m. Robert Adam

Plate 2:64n. Robert Adam

Plate 2:64o. Not noted

Plate 2:64. A selection of the designs illustrated in Thomas Parsons' A Collection of Vases, Terms... Parsons noted in his sketchbook the names of the artists from whom many of the designs were taken, and these are noted under the individual designs

certainly suggests that he carried on carving to the end. Plate 2:64a-o illustrates a few of the designs in his sketchbook, some of which have already been mentioned.

A nineteenth century pair of Bath stone finials after a design by the architect James Gibbs adorns the Italian Gardens of Belton House in Lincolnshire (Plate 2:65). Like those in Portland stone at Wimpole Hall (Plate 2:54) these have been slightly modified from the original design; in this case swags of fruit have replaced linen swags. This particular form of decoration — garlands or swags hanging from the body of the vase — was popular with Gibbs and occurs on many of his other designs for vases (Plate 2:66).

Plate 2:65. One of a pair of finials, Bath stone, after a design by James Gibbs, probably nineteenth century, the Italian Gardens, Belton House, Lincolnshire. Height approx 72ins

THE NATIONAL TRUST

Plate 2:66. James Gibbs' designs for finials, reprinted in R Charles' The Compiler, 1879. Compare the left finial in the centre row with that in Plate 2:65

122

Other Stone

As we have seen, of all stone used for garden statuary, Portland was the one most commonly used. However, like all stones, its weight made it expensive to transport and one frequently finds that in locations some distance from Portland local stones of varying qualities were used.

A good example of this can be seen in a number of garden statues carved by the late seventeenth century sculptor Caius Gabriel Cibber who, according to one of his letters, would endeavour to serve any nobleman in freestone,[73] and who was employed by a number of landowners in the north of England.

In 1680, the 9th Earl of Rutland drew up a contract with Cibber, to provide statues for his estate Belvoir Castle outside Grantham. According to this contract, dated 28 January, Cibber was to carve seven statues of Ketton stone, at a cost of £35 each. Models for each statue were to be shown before work commenced. Four of the statues were commissioned to: 'Resemble the fower seasons of the yere and two others shall resemble the senses of smelling and tasting, and the last shall resemble Juno with proper additions to the statues aforesid'. Whilst the work was going on both Cibber's and his two assistants' board and lodging was to be paid for by the Earl, as was the transportation of the stone, which came from the famous Ketton stone quarries some twenty miles away, near Stamford.[74]

Plate 2:67. Enlarged detail of a piece of Ketton stone showing the 'petrified cod's roe' texture

Ketton stone is a relatively unflawed limestone, best known today for its use in the building of many of the colleges at Cambridge. The texture of the stone (Plate 2:67) may be described as 'petrified cod's roe', for it consists of closely packed spherical nodules. It is a light honey colour, but does vary and in more exposed parts is a cream-white. Being relatively unporous it is not so prone to collect lichen or moss, and it is remarkably durable — a fact clearly illustrated in the seven statues by Cibber at Belvoir which have withstood three hundred years' exposure to the elements remarkably well.

Cibber's statues formerly stood on one of the terraces at Belvoir, but are now to be found, in a somewhat haphazard fashion, in another part of the garden (Plates 2:68-74). All are suitably represented with their 'proper additions': Spring

2:68

2:69

2:70

2:71

Plate 2:68. Life-size statue representing Spring, Ketton stone, by Cibber, circa 1680, Belvoir Castle, Leicestershire
THE DUKE OF RUTLAND

Plate 2:69. Life-size statue representing Summer, Ketton stone, by Cibber, circa 1680, Belvoir Castle, Leicestershire. (See Colour Plate 35)
THE DUKE OF RUTLAND

Plate 2:70. Life-size statue representing Autumn, Ketton stone, by Cibber, circa 1680, Belvoir Castle, Leicestershire
THE DUKE OF RUTLAND

Plate 2:71. Life-size statue representing Winter, Ketton stone, by Cibber, circa 1680, Belvoir Castle, Leicestershire
THE DUKE OF RUTLAND

holding a wreath of flowers and standing by a flower pot; Summer (Colour Plate 35) with a sheaf of corn, his sickle now missing; Autumn with a bunch of grapes, leaning on a stump entwined with vines; Winter bearded, heavily clothed and warming his hands on a firepan; Juno with a peacock (sacred to her in antiquity) at her feet. Taste and Smell are represented with Renaissance symbols, whereby Taste has an ape at her feet and holds a basket of fruit, whilst Smell, who could easily be mistaken for a companion of Diana the huntress, is shown with a dog at her side.

Cibber's treatment of these statues' drapery is strange in that the folds run very much at cross purposes to the pose and consequent movement of the statues. Once noticed, this can detract from their charm, though it is, in fact, characteristic of some of Cibber's work; the drapery of the four statues he carved a year later for

2:72

2:73

2:74

Plate 2:72. Life-size statue representing Juno, Ketton stone, by Cibber, circa 1680, Belvoir Castle, Leicestershire
THE DUKE OF RUTLAND

Plate 2:73. Life-size statue representing Taste, Ketton stone, by Cibber, circa 1680, Belvoir Castle, Leicestershire
THE DUKE OF RUTLAND

Plate 2:74. Life-size statue representing Smell, Ketton stone, by Cibber, circa 1680, Belvoir Castle, Leicestershire
THE DUKE OF RUTLAND

the parapet of Trinity College, Cambridge, is treated in a similar way. Although awkward, Cibber's carving ability, which is maintained on each of the statue's pedestals, is unquestionable; of particular note is that beneath Summer (Plate 2:69) which bears the arms of the Earl's wife Katherine Noel, and the high-relief Medusa heads beneath Taste (Plate 2:73).

In the mid-1680s, Cibber was employed by Lord Kingston to carve statuary for his Nottinghamshire estate, Thoresby Hall. However, here he was carving in Portland stone, for the only surviving piece of Cibber's work from Thoresby Hall (the house was burnt down in 1745), is a Sphinx — now in a private collection.

After working at Thoresby, Cibber was subsequently employed at Chatsworth by the 4th Earl of Devonshire. Here he executed a number of works, including several garden ornaments, such as the pair of Sphinxes, which survive today, but his most stupendous work is the figure of Triton (Colour Plate 36). This figure, which clearly shows Cibber's abilities as a sculptor, and the two Sphinxes were carved, from a local stone, probably Roche Abbey stone. Again, considering these statues have been outside since 1690, one has evidence of the stone's durability.

Plate 2:75. A pair of finials, sandstone, from a local quarry within the estate grounds, early eighteenth century, Castle Howard, Yorkshire. Height of vase approx 72ins; height of pedestal approx 56ins. (See Colour Plate 37)

THE HON SIMON HOWARD

Plate 2:76. Life-size statue of a Nymph, French sandstone, copy of a marble statue by René Frémin, early eighteenth century, St. Paul's Walden Bury, Hertfordshire

THE HON LADY BOWES LYON

A pair of finials in the West Gardens of Castle Howard are particularly strange in their construction. Each comprises four sections, two parts for the body, one part each for the socle and the cap. Whereas the body of most finials and vases is joined horizontally, in this case the joint is vertical, the resultant line being discernible to the right of the swag of flowers on the finial in the foreground in Plate 2:75 (see also Colour Plate 37).

As Portland and Bath stone were expensive to transport to the north of England before the invention of the railway, these finials, like many of the stone garden ornaments at Castle Howard, such as the pedestal beneath Carpentiere's Hercules (Plate 1:7), are carved from a local sandstone of a sombre brown colour. It is not known who carved them but they probably date from the first quarter of the eighteenth century when Castle Howard was being built; this can perhaps be substantiated by the gadrooned moulding beneath the basket of fruit at the top of each vase and the frostwork plaques on their pedestals, both of which were popular forms of ornamentation in the early 1700s.

Of the many sculptor-masons employed at Castle Howard, several are known to have supplied vases. John Elsworth and his partner William Smith (both fl 1703-1715) carved vases for the Mulberry Garden in 1715;[75] Samuel Carpenter (1660-1713), whose best work at the estate is the wonderful Satyr Gate and its baskets of fruit, supplied two stone vases in 1706;[76] while William Skutt (fl 1719-1722) carved pedestals and vases for the Bowling Green in 1719.[77] However, the pair in Plate 2:75 could have been carved by Daniel Harvey (1683-1733) as one of his bills, dated 29 June 1721, states: 'Finished the Vase in ye avenue — £1...Carved Frost work on tow Piedestals — £2... Carved 2 Members as an addition to two Vases — £0 5s'.[78] This bill also includes a total of '£12 10s, for gilding and colouring two vases in ye green and one more in ye avenue'.

Harvey worked extensively at Castle Howard (although not permanently) between 1709 and 1726 carving not only vases, but also statues and other works of a more architectural nature, such as all the capitals on the Temple of Four Winds, to the east of the building.

In the gardens of St Paul's Walden Bury, raised on a pedestal stands a life-size stone statue of a Huntress playing with a dog (Plate 2:76). Although it could be mistaken for a statue of Diana, for it has several of the attributes of the deity — the bow, the quiver and the hound, this cannot be the case, for this figure does not bear the crescent moon (Diana was worshipped as a moon goddess) above her brow. The statue is, in fact, a French sandstone copy of a marble nymph, or companion of Diana, carved by the French sculptor René Frémin (1672-1722). The original marble statue was commissioned, together with nine companions, from separate artists by Louis XIV (1638-1715) for his gardens at Marly.

It seems likely that the elderly King originally intended the ten nymphs to accompany a marble copy of the famous antique Diana de Versailles (known in eighteenth century France as Diana de Ephesus after the deity's famous temple in the ancient Greek city of that name), also commissioned in the same year for Marly from another sculptor G Coustou (1677-1746). Of the ten nymphs commissioned in 1710, only eight appear to have been executed, and not all those arrived at Marly; one by J L Lemoyne (1665-1755) depicting a nymph with a dog and a spear (another of Diana's attributes), was not completed until 1724, and was placed in the gardens at La Muette. Frémin's statue does not feature in any eighteenth century Marly inventories and so was, no doubt, somewhere else. After the French Revolution, the gardens at Marly were destroyed and with the passing of time the nymphs which had found their way there were dispersed around the world. Frémin's is now on display at the Louvre.[79]

The sandstone copy of Frémin's statue at St Paul's Walden Bury, one of the most elegantly posed of the 1710 nymphs, is neither signed nor dated and, as its provenance is unclear, it is not possible to put an exact date on it. Quite a number of replicas of the original marble are known, one definitely by Frémin in terracotta,[80] and others by anonymous artists.[81] As the sandstone statue is not signed, it may be it was carved by one of Frémin's assistants, and if so would date from the eighteenth century. This dating seems probable, for the quality of the carving, although not as fine as that found on the marble statue, is magnificent, and it is a tragedy that this figure has suffered so much damage as well as the ravages of climate.

The varying textures of this weathered statue are worthy of comment. If one was uncertain whether the statue was cut from stone, as is possible at a first glance, it could easily be mistaken for one made from a cement-based artificial stone, even

2:77

2:78

2:79

Plate 2:77. One of a pair of finials, limestone, after a design by James Gibbs, circa 1850, the Formal Garden, Melton Constable, Norfolk. Height approx 72ins

Plate 2:78. One of a pair of finials, limestone, after a design by James Gibbs, circa 1850, the Formal Garden, Melton Constable, Norfolk. Height approx 84ins

Plate 2:79. One of a pair of finials, limestone, after a design by James Gibbs, circa 1850, the Formal Garden, Melton Constable, Norfolk. Height approx 72ins

though the subject, with its extended limbs and considerable undercutting, would have been difficult to produce in this medium. More exposed parts are heavily pitted, whilst the protected parts, such as Diana's thighs, are remarkably smooth; the combination of these two features is a characteristic found on many cement-based artificial stone ornaments which have been outside for many years. Another feature found on many weathered or damaged cement-based artificial stone ornaments is the presence of exposed reinforcing slate or metal bars. Several metal bars protrude from this statue, but they are, in fact, the remains of past restorations, and those bars which one would expect to find on a cement-based artificial stone statue, such as within the dog's right fore leg, are, of course, not present. The use of foreign stone for garden ornament in the United Kingdom has caused countless incorrect identifications, and this problem is further complicated by the variety of cement-based artificial stones which were produced. Some manufactories, mainly continental, went to great lengths to make their ornaments resemble natural stone; indeed, it has been known for lines of crystals to be laid within the mould to give the effect of veining found on natural stone. Collectors are strongly advised to proceed with the utmost caution.

Limestone pairs of all three of the designs in Gibbs' *A Book of Architecture* survive in the forlorn and forgotten gardens of Melton Constable in Norfolk (Plates 2:77-80). Tragically all of the estate records have disappeared,[82] so perhaps the

Plate 2:80. James Gibb's designs for the Earl of Oxford, reprinted in R Charles' The Compiler, 1879, on which the three designs in Plates 2:77, 78 and 79 are based

sculptor responsible will never be known. These six finials adorn piers interspersed between the balustrade surrounding the Formal Garden, and as this was only laid out between 1845 and 1850,[83] and the balustrade and finials are all carved from the same limestone and both are in a similar condition, it is highly likely that the finials must date from this period. As is clearly visible from the illustrations, the Melton Constable finials are in a bad state of decay, though they have only been exposed to the elements for a mere 130 years. The limestone from which they are carved is decidedly less durable than the three Portland stone finials at Wimpole (Plate 2:54) which have been outside for nearly twice as long.

There certainly seems to have been a revival in the popularity of Gibbs' designs during the nineteenth century, and many were reprinted during the period in such books as R Charles *The Compiler* which included the three pairs of Melton Constable finials (Plate 2:80).

Plate 3:1. Chateau de Bagatelle, the terrace, a photograph taken prior to the extensions made between 1860 and 1864. A bronze Cupid vase (Plate 3:10) can be seen in the right foreground. The 4th Marquis of Hertford is at the end of the terrace with a female companion
CHRISTIE'S SOUTH KENSINGTON

CHAPTER THREE

BRONZE

1700 to the early twentieth century

The use of bronze for garden ornament in Britain has always been limited. Although in the latter years of the nineteenth century it was used more frequently, in eighteenth century gardens such as Stowe, Chiswick and Rousham bronze was not used at all. The main reasons for the infrequent use of bronze were economic: not only was the metal expensive but, with its high melting point, it was costly to cast, particularly in the eighteenth century before the complicated process of lost wax casting had been superseded by the cheaper process of sand casting. Vertue records that bronze was 'the rarest and costliest of all materials at all periods',[1] and this can be substantiated by the fact that in 1722 the younger John Van Nost received the princely sum of £500 in part payment for the bronze figure of George I (Plate 3:16),[2] whilst the duplicate lead figure Van Nost supplied a few years later (Plate 3:17) is believed to have cost no more than £150.[3] Consequently, during the eighteenth and nineteenth centuries, other cheaper media such as lead, cast-iron, stone and artificial stone were used far more frequently, many finished in an imitation of bronze.

However, because of its strength (for it is remarkbly robust) and perhaps also because of its cost, bronze was held in high regard as a material and was commonly used for commemorative statues of celebrated figures for display in public places and often paid for by subscription.

Bronze garden statues were only produced on a small scale in England during the eighteenth century, and those that were produced were cast predominantly by the individual sculptors who also modelled them; possibly the Hyde Park lead figure makers may have been involved with some aspects of casting. Even in the early years of the nineteenth century the use of bronze for garden ornament was negligible. The metal was still expensive and, as in the previous century, ornaments in other media were available far more cheaply. Consequently there was a dearth of bronze foundries and when Rundell Bridge & Rundell attempted to find an English foundry to cast their full-size copy of the Warwick Vase (Plate 3:15) they had to resort to a foreign firm. By 1860 several bronze foundries existed in England, while a number of cast-iron foundries were also casting in bronze (see, for example, pages 262-263), but the output from these was slight. The lack of bronze foundries was not, however, a reflection on the metal's popularity, for the demand which grew during the latter half of the nineteenth century was satisfied by a number of sources, the great majority of bronzes coming from Europe, particularly France and Italy, where high quality castings had been and were being produced. This continental source was further augmented by Frédérick Sauvage and Achille Collas' invention in the second quarter of the nineteenth century of a machine which could faithfully reproduce statues in reduced sizes, thereby enabling foundries to provide reduced casts of popular statues and ornaments for even the smallest gardens and conservatories of the rising middle class.

The other main source of supply was of bronze imitations produced both in England and abroad. Cast-iron and cheaper alloys, such as the figure of Mercury in Plate 3:22, were electro-plated in imitation of bronze, whilst zinc and cast-iron were frequently painted to resemble this ever-popular metal.

Despite its infrequent use, bronze must not be underestimated as a medium for garden ornament. Of all the metals it is the most suitable; in comparison with lead it is far stronger and, as a consequence, the considerable weight of a bronze vase will not cause its socle to buckle. It is less brittle than iron and zinc and far more appealing in terms of lustre than both these metals and lead.

When a piece was finished, prospective clients could select from a choice of finishes. Although these were magnificent in their own right, the verdant hues which the metal attains over the years are exquisite, equalled only perhaps by the lichen and verdigris on a Portland stone ornament. Unfortunately, this patination is ultimately detrimental and can cause considerable damage. For their protection, therefore, bronzes should be cleaned and waxed frequently, though owners of bronze garden ornaments are advised to seek expert advice as well.

The comparative wealth of bronze founding in France reflects the French use of the medium over the years. Similarly in Italy, the use of bronze was considerable and although most pieces produced between the fifteenth and eighteenth centuries were intended for interiors, by the nineteenth century great numbers of foundries were producing countless copies both for inside and outside decoration, particularly of the works of famous Italian sculptors, such as Giambologna, as well as copies of the renowned antique works, including those excavated in the second half of the nineteenth century at Pompeii and Herculaneum.

This chapter illustrates the output of French foundries, both in the magnificent bronze vases copied for the gardens of the Chateau of Bagatelle in the late nineteenth century from the originals at Versailles, as well as in the enormous Warwick Vase now at Cambridge. As the use of bronze in this country was limited, only two 'home-made' pieces are included, the bronze statue of George I by the younger Van Nost, and the model of Eos, Queen Victoria's greyhound, by John Francis. Two Italian pieces based on classical figures are discussed, and the chapter concludes with a section on imitation bronze pieces.

The Making of Bronze Ornaments

Bronze ornaments were produced by one of two methods, the predominant method, especially for small works, being the lost wax or *cire perdue* process which is described in its simplest form below. The other method used more frequently for large statues, and which became more commonplace during the nineteenth century, was sand casting. Basically this process is the same as that used to produce cast-iron (pages 316-319). When hollow castings were required, an inner core was needed and this was suspended in the centre of the mould using a similar method to that used in the lost wax process.

Of the two methods, the lost wax process is considered to be superior, but the quality of, for example, the vases in Plates 3:2-13 clearly illustrates the superb details which can be achieved in a sand cast. Distinguishing a model that has been sand cast from one which has been wax cast can at times be difficult, but the presence of screws within the interior of the ornament is often a clear indication that it has been sand cast, for this process frequently involved casting the ornament in sections which were later screwed together.

Lost wax casting
To cast a bronze by the lost wax method, the subject to be reproduced has first to be formed out of wax. The predominant method for reproducing a subject several times rather than a 'one off', which was still used during the nineteenth

century mainly for small sized bronzes, involved covering the original model with gelatine to produce a flexible mould which, for the sake of simplicity, let us say would have been formed in two halves. This gelatine mould was placed within a plaster casing (also in two halves) to keep it rigid and was then left to dry. By dismantling the plaster case and the gelatine mould, the original model was removed. The mould casing and the gelatine mould were then reassembled and fixed firmly together. With smaller figures, either by flicking molten wax inside the gelatine mould or pouring in molten wax and rotating the mould, the inside was covered with a thin even coating of wax. For larger casts a thicker coating was used. The plaster and gelatine were then dismantled to reveal a wax replica of the original subject. Any blemishes on the replica were removed and the necessary finishing carried out. The inside of the wax replica was then filled with a core consisting of grog (brick or clay waste) and plaster which would later be broken up. After the core had set, a variety of wax 'sticks' were attached to the replica to provide runners and risers, through which, respectively, the molten bronze would be poured into the mould and the hot air and steam would come out. The whole wax was then coated with what is known today as an 'investment', an exterior casing of plaster and grog, fine on the inside to follow the contours of the replica, coarse on the outside. Nails were inserted through the investment, through the wax and into the core to keep the core suspended in precise relationship to the investment. After the investment had dried, the whole mould was embedded in sand and heated so that the wax was 'lost', hence the term *cire perdue*. The gap remaining between the investment and the core was filled with molten bronze through the channels left by the melted 'sticks'. After being left to cool the investment was broken away to reveal the cast bronze, and the runners and risers through which the molten bronze had been poured were cut off. The core was removed by breaking it up, either through a hole in the base of the cast or, if necessary, by cutting a hole in the bronze (if allowed to remain it could affect the bronze). Any holes in the bronze left by nails or cutting were filled up by brazing in new sections, and any blemishes, such as those left by the runners and risers or faults in the casting were chased up by hand.

Bronze Copies of Vases at Versailles for the Chateau of Bagatelle

Amongst the magnificent collection of ornaments in the gardens at Versailles are twenty-six bronze vases (thirteen pairs), which surmount marble plinths, and separate the terrace of the Palace from the Parterre du Nord and the Parterre du Midi. These vases, ten of which are illustrated planted with orange trees in d'Etienne Allegrain's famous 1689 painting 'Le Parterre du Nord sous Louis XIV', were designed to be executed in silver by Claude Ballin (1615-1678) the King's goldsmith, but, due to the financial constraints incurred by the war in Flanders, were eventually cast in bronze between 1660 and 1680.[4] (Although the thirteen pairs are traditionally thought to have been designed by Claude Ballin, there is some evidence to suggest this is not the case. Engravings of five of the vases flanking the two Parterres at Versailles survive in the Musée National, Paris. Four of them are recorded as being 'Par Claude Ballin de Paris', but the fifth, the Scroll design (see Plate 3:14), is marked as being 'Par François Anguier de la ville d'Eu'. In the light of this, it may well be that other designs were produced by other artists, indeed the Roundel design (see Plate 3:9) has been ascribed to Michael Anguier.

Louis XIV's gardens at Versailles were inspired by the myth of the Sun God, Apollo, as personified by the King who was dubbed 'Le Roi Soleil'. This symbolic representation of the King recurs in many of Ballin's designs such as that in Plate 3:2 (a nineteenth century copy of Ballin's design, modified by the addition of a square base), which incorporates bas-relief scenes of two of the myths of Apollo: on one side Daphne is being transformed into a tree by her father, the River God, to escape the love-struck Apollo; on the other Apollo, silhouetted against the rays of the sun is slaying the serpent Python. Other motifs sacred to, or connected with, Apollo — the sun, the wolf, the zodiac and the laurel leaf — occur on other vases, whilst as the lion and the sphinx represent the power of the monarch, their incorporation in other designs also symbolises the omnipotent King.

With the exception of other bronze copies at Versailles, Ballin's vases were to remain unique until the third quarter of the nineteenth century, when the 4th Marquis of Hertford (1800-1870), an ardent devotee of Le Nôtre, had bronze copies cast (some of which vary from the originals) for his estate outside Paris, the Chateau de Bagatelle (Plate 3:1). The twelve vases illustrated in Plates 3:2-13 are examples of these vases, whilst the thirteenth (Plate 3:14) is one of the originals at Versailles.

For ease of reference, each basic design is named as follows:

Plate 3:2 Dragon	Plate 3:8 Lion
Plate 3:3 Naiad	Plate 3:9 Roundel
Plate 3:4 Satyr (and	Plate 3:10 Cupid
Colour Plate 38)	Plate 3:11 Wolf
Plate 3:5 Spiral Fluting	Plate 3:12 Janus
and Colour Plate 39	Plate 3:13 Sphinx
Plate 3:7 Satyr Mask	and Colour Plate 41)
	Plate 3:14 Scroll

In an inventory of the contents of Bagatelle, drawn up in 1871, a year after the Marquis' death, a total of forty-six vases was recorded.[5] As these vases are not illustrated in the photographs of Bagatelle circa 1858, they can be dated to within this twelve to thirteen year period. Unfortunately the exact number of copies made of each of Ballin's designs is unknown, and any deductions or assumptions based on illustrations of the gardens in the 1890s[6] are complicated by the fact that the Marquis' son and heir, Sir Richard Wallace (1818-1890), increased the number of garden ornaments in the early 1870s. As there are today more than forty-six documented Bagatelle copies of Ballin's designs, Wallace's additions must have included further models.

None of the Bagatelle copies bears a founder's mark, so it is uncertain at present who cast them. The Marquis was a great patron of the arts, indeed at the 1855 Paris Exposition Universelle he presided over the jury assessing the 'orfèvrerie, bijouterie, industrie des bronzes d'art'[7] and must therefore have been familiar with several of the leading bronze founders. A number of possible foundries have been suggested, but the two most likely were either the prolific bronze manufactory of Ferdinand Barbedienne, from whom the Marquis is known to have purchased a number of items,[8] or the firm of Barbezat, which although renowned for its iron castings had, by the mid-1860s, expanded into bronze casting and, according to the *Gazette des Beaux-Arts,* had exhibited amongst other items 'Des reproductions des vases que Claude Ballin exécuté pour les tablettes des pieces d'eau de Versailles...'[9]

Plate 3:2. Pair of vases, Dragon, bronze, copy of a pair flanking the Parterre du Midi, Versailles, circa 1870, the Courtyard, Hertford House, Manchester Square, London (Wallace Collection). Height approx 35ins.

The bas-relief scenes are symbolic of Le Roi Soleil, depicting as they do two myths of the Sun God Apollo. In a photograph of the Cour d'Honneur at Bagatelle, circa 1890, a pair of vases of this design is clearly visible, but it is not certain that the pair illustrated here is the same one, for a similar pair remains at Bagatelle. Like the pair in Plate 3:3, this pair is one of the three purchased by Colonel Birch from Nether Swell Manor which were sold into a private collection, from which they were obtained by the Wallace Collection. The vases have been slightly modified by the addition of a square base

Permission to take casts from the Versailles vases was only granted as a result of the Marquis' friendship with Napoleon III,[10] and it is highly likely that a document exists recording which firm took the casts, but the relevant Versailles archives have not been put in order at the time of writing, and the document has not as yet come to light. The identification of the foundry is further complicated by the fact that in the mid-1870s Wallace informed the 7th Viscount Powerscourt that 'the models [for the vases] were with "Beurdeley", a dealer in bronzes in the Rue Louis Le Grand, Paris'.[11] This certainly suggests another likely source for the vases, for A Beurdeley (1808-1882) was an important bronze founder, amongst whose clients may be named Napoleon III and the Duc de Nemours; furthermore, at the 1855 Exposition the firm was awarded a bronze medal. Until further information comes to light it is not possible to be definitive in attributing the Bagatelle vases to one particular foundry. However, the fact remains that they are wonderful castings combined with the great variety and richness of Ballin's designs. Lawrence Weaver wrote of them: 'They are goldsmith's work in bronze, and it is doubtful if any sculptor has ever produced a series of garden ornaments more exquisite in modelling and craftsmanship.[12]

By the early 1880s Sir Richard Wallace had removed twelve Bagatelle vases (six pairs) to England: two pairs (Satyr Mask and Cupid — Plates 3:7 and 10) he placed in the courtyard of his London home, Hertford House,[13] and the other four pairs (Naiad, Satyr, Harpy and Satyr Mask — Plates 3:3, 4, 6 and 7, and Colour Plates 38 and 40) at his Suffolk estate of Sudbourne Hall.[14] In 1897 Lady Wallace, who had outlived her husband by seven years, died, and the estate passed to their secretary, Sir John Murray Scott (1847-1912) who, before selling Bagatelle to the City of Paris in 1904, removed many of the garden ornaments to England.

In an attempt to establish how many, and which designs were at Bagatelle, it is necessary to recount the history of their dispersal.

From the illustrations in two *Country Life* articles, one of 1910,[15] and the other of 1912,[16] it is apparent that Scott placed ten pairs (Dragon, Spiral Fluting, Satyr Mask, Lion, Roundel, Cupid, Janus and Scroll — Plates 3:2, 5, 7, 8, 9, 10, 12 and 14 and Colour Plate 39, and two pairs of Naiad — Plate 3:3) in the grounds of his Gloucestershire home, Nether Swell Manor.

Scott also gave a number of Bagatelle copies to his close friend Victoria Sackville-West (1862-1936), who placed several in the grounds of Knole in Kent. Pairs of Satyr Mask, Lion and Janus (Plates 3:7, 8 and 12) adorned the Green Court,[17] whilst a further pair of Satyr Mask and a pair of Wolf (Plate 3:11) flanked the steps approaching the east front[18] (later when Lady Sackville-West left Knole pairs of Satyr Mask, Lion, Wolf and Janus were removed to her daughter's garden at Sissinghurst Castle).[19] However, she was given more than just five pairs, for in 1923 ten vases were sold by Lady Sackville-West — two pairs of Harpy and pairs of Satyr, Spiral Fluting and Satyr Mask.[20] Furthermore the Sackville-Wests owned at least one other pair, for there is today at Sissinghurst Castle a pair of Sphinx vases (Plate 3:13 and Colour Plate 41).

As three pairs of vases (Dragon, Satyr and Cupid) are known to have been left behind at Bagatelle,[21] and the two pairs at Hertford House (Satyr Mask and Cupid) were removed by Scott to Nether Swell Manor, and assuming that the Satyr Mask design sold by Lady Sackville-West in 1923 was one of the pairs at Knole, this makes a total so far of twenty-seven pairs.

However, it is clear that there were others at Nether Swell Manor; five pairs were sold by Miss Katherine Scott (Sir John's sister) in 1925 and passed to an American dealer: three pairs of Cupid, and one pair each of Satyr Mask and Lion,[22] whilst a further seven pairs were purchased in the early 1930s by a certain Colonel Wyndam Birch.[23] Birch sold four pairs to the 7th Viscount Clifden (Satyr Mask, Lion, Roundel and Cupid — Plates 3:7-10) who placed them in the formal gardens of his Cornish estate, Lanhydrock House. Birch sold the remaining three pairs (two pairs of Naiad and a pair of Dragon) into a private collection.

Thus it is apparent that there were at least fifteen pairs at Nether Swell Manor, for none of the pairs of Spiral Fluting, Scroll or Janus illustrated in the *Country Life* articles are accounted for; furthermore, it is clear that there were an extra three pairs of the Cupid design, as well as further pairs of the Satyr Mask and Lion designs.

This brings the grand total of documented copies of Ballin's designs originally at Bagatelle to thirty-two pairs.

Interestingly there is a curious disparity in the numbers of each design copied; for example, five pairs each of Satyr Mask and Cupid designs are known to have been cast, whilst only one pair of the Wolf, Sphinx and Scroll are known to have been copied. As the Marquis was an admirer of Le Nôtre, the designer of the gardens at Versailles, one would have expected complete sets to have been copied, but it would appear that both the Marquis and Sir Richard Wallace favoured certain models above others.

Quite a number of other copies of Ballin's vases are also known to have been in England. The two bronze pairs of Scroll and Janus (stolen from Upton House in 1979) may quite well have come from Nether Swell Manor, for the Scroll pair, illustrated in a *Country Life* article, and described as from 'the Comte d'Artois, Chateau of Bagatelle',[24] together with the Janus pair from Upton, correspond to two of the three pairs which have not been traced from Nether Swell Manor. However, other bronze copies which have appeared on the market, such as pairs

Plate 3:3. One of a pair of vases, Naiad, bronze, copies of a pair flanking the Parterre du Nord, Versailles, circa 1870, the Courtyard, Hertford House, Manchester Square, London (Wallace Collection). Height approx 33ins.

This pair was removed by Sir John Murray Scott to Nether Swell Manor from where it was purchased by Colonel Birch who later sold this pair, a duplicate pair and the Dragon vases (Plate 3:2) into a private collection. They were subsequently purchased by Sir John Stirling-Maxwell (a Trustee of the Wallace Collection) and donated to the Collection in 1950.

The present whereabouts of the Naiad vases at Sudbourne Hall is unknown, but as the house was demolished in 1953, and a pair of this design (together with a pair of the Satyr design) appeared on the market in the 1950s, these vases may well have originated from Sudbourne Hall

Plate 3:4. One of a pair of vases, Satyr, bronze, copy of a pair flanking the Parterre du Midi, Versailles, circa 1870, the Hyacinth Garden, Anglesey Abbey, Cambridgeshire. Height approx 35ins. (See also Colour Plate 38).

Like the vases in Plates 3:5 and 6, this pair was sold by Lady Sackville-West in 1923 and passed into Lord Fairhaven's magnificent collection at Anglesey Abbey. A duplicate pair of this design remains at Bagatelle, and a further pair appeared on the market in the 1950s which may well have been the Satyr pair at Sudbourne Hall

Plate 3:5. One of a pair of vases, Spiral Fluting, bronze, copy of a pair flanking the Parterre du Nord, Versailles, circa 1870, the Dahlia Garden, Anglesey Abbey, Cambridgeshire. Height approx 29ins. (See Colour Plate 39).

Originally part of the Sackville-West Collection, this pair was sold in 1923 and passed into Lord Fairhaven's Collection. The location of the duplicate pair, once at Nether Swell Manor, has not been traced.

The handles are almost certainly derived from the famous Medici Vase, which is interesting, for although several of Ballin's designs include decorative motifs from antiquity, such as the Greek key band on the Janus design (Plate 3:12) and the acanthus leaf on the lower bodies of the Satyr Mask and Lion designs (Plates 3:7 and 8), Ballin did not, with the exception of this pair, draw on the famous works of ancient Greece and Rome.

Although in many respects this is the simplest of Ballin's designs, the complex and dramatic spiral fluting on the body makes it one of the most ornamental

Plate 3:6. One of a pair of vases, Harpy, bronze, copy of a pair flanking the Parterre du Midi, Versailles, circa 1870, the Hyacinth Garden, Anglesey Abbey, Cambridgeshire. Height approx 36ins. (See Colour Plate 40).

Prior to its sale by Lady Sackville-West in 1923, the location of this pair of vases is unknown, but like those in Plates 3:4 and 5 it passed into the Fairhaven Collection at Anglesey Abbey. The duplicate pair, also sold in the 1923 sale, and the pair once at Sudbourne Hall remain untraced.

The intricate detail which can be achieved in a bronze sand cast is clearly illustrated in all thirteen of the Versailles/Bagatelle copies, and it is unfortunate that the foundry has not been identified. On this vase the continuous vines around the rim, the laurel leaves surrounding the escutcheons and the handles in the form of Harpys are all of particular note

THE NATIONAL TRUST: PHOTO PETER GREENHALF

Plate 3:7. Pair of vases, Satyr Mask, bronze, copy of a pair flanking the Parterre du Nord, Versailles, circa 1870, Lanhydrock House, Cornwall. Height approx 33ins.

It is a pity these vases are not on higher pedestals, for it is difficult to see the well-modelled satyr masks at such a low level (though in fact all the Versailles vases are on plinths of a similar height).

As five copies of this design are known to have been at Bagatelle, it would seem that it was one of the 4th Marquis of Hertford and Sir Richard Wallace's favourite designs. The pair at Lanhydrock House came from Nether Swell Manor in the 1930s, while another pair, which was also at Nether Swell Manor, is now in the Cleveland Museum of Art. Of the other three pairs, two were given to Victoria Sackville-West, one of which is now at Sissinghurst Castle, Kent, the other was sold in the 1923 Sackville-West sale and its whereabouts are unknown, while the third pair, at one time at Sudbourne Hall, has also disappeared.

The popularity of this design was to extend well into the early years of this century, for it was being produced in lead by the firm of John P White & Sons Ltd, and was to feature in their 1935 catalogue (Bird Baths, Garden Figures, Vases and Ornaments) in which it was called 'The Covington'

THE NATIONAL TRUST

Plate 3:8. Pair of vases, Lion, bronze, copy of a pair flanking the Parterre du Midi, Versailles, circa 1870, Lanhydrock House, Cornwall. Height approx 33ins.

Whether this pair was removed from Bagatelle by Sir Richard Wallace to Hertford House in the 1880s, or whether they were removed later from Bagatelle by Sir John Murray Scott, is unclear. Two pairs of this design are known to have been at Nether Swell Manor, and these passed through Katherine Scott and Colonel Birch to an American dealer and the 7th Viscount Clifden respectively. The third documented pair now decorates the gateway to Sissinghurst Castle, having been given by Scott to Victoria Sackville-West who passed them on to her daughter Vita

Plate 3:9. One of a pair of vases, Roundel, bronze, copy of a pair flanking the steps to the Parterre du Nord, Versailles, circa 1870, Lanhydrock House, Cornwall. Height approx 49ins.

Of all thirteen Versailles/Bagatelle designs, this austere model is the largest and grandest and carries the most obvious representation of Le Roi Soleil. The lion-head handles stand erect, while between them two reliefs of the sun radiate shafts of light in all directions. The body is decorated with twelve bas-relief portraits, all of which represent not only the King's association with the ancients, but also the wisdom and power of an omnipotent ruler.

Like the other Versailles/Bagatelle vases at Lanhydrock, this pair was sold to Colonel Birch from Nether Swell Manor, and it is interesting to note that, like the Dragon design in Plate 3:2, this pair has been modified by the addition of a square base

139

Plate 3:10. One of a pair of vases, Cupid, bronze, copy of a pair flanking the Parterre du Nord, Versailles, circa 1860, Lanhydrock House, Cornwall. Height approx 34ins.

The most appealing of the thirteen designs, this particular model has been considerably modified by replacing two roundels on the body with swags of fruit and foliage. As a vase with the same modifications can be seen in Plate 3:1, one can assume this pair was amongst those listed in the 1871 inventory, and they are therefore given an earlier date than the other vases. Like the other three pairs at Lanhydrock House (Plates 3:7, 8 and 9) this pair was removed from Nether Swell Manor in the 1930s.

The three pairs purchased from Nether Swell Manor in 1925 are more faithful copies of Ballin's designs, indeed one pair, now in the Cleveland Museum of Art, is an exact copy on which the roundel on one side is decorated with a fasces, and that on the other with laurel leaves. The present whereabouts of the other two pairs is not known, but it is known that they had roundels, though the centres were not enriched.

It is interesting to note that the copies of this vase produced by the iron foundry Dugel in the late nineteenth century were also modified. In one case (illustrated Country Life, *10 April 1986), the decoration of the centre of one of the roundels was replaced with a bas-relief portrait of a helmeted man, a relief which is found in one of the roundels on the vase in Plate 3:9. Patently Dugel had access to models of both Cupid and Roundel vases, and probably others, but the quality of the casting, at least of his Cupid, bears little resemblance either to the vases at Versailles or those formerly at Bagatelle*

Plate 3:11. One of a pair of vases, Wolf, bronze, copy of a pair flanking the Parterre du Nord, Versailles, circa 1870, the Courtyard, Hertford House, Manchester Square, London (Wallace Collection). Height approx 33ins.

By 1912 Victoria Sackville-West had placed this vase and its pair on pedestals flanking the east front of Knole. Later they were removed to Sissinghurst Castle and in 1959, together with the Janus pair (Plate 3:12), they were acquired by the Wallace Collection via the National Art Collections Fund.

Although it would appear this design was not favoured either by the 4th Marquis Hertford or his son Sir Richard Wallace, for they are the only copies known to exist, the fact that a smaller gilt pair (nearly one-third the original size and presumably for interior use) is known to have been at Bagatelle suggests that other full-size pairs were cast but have not yet been discovered

Plate 3:12. One of a pair of vases, Janus, bronze, copy of a pair flanking the Parterre du Midi, Versailles, circa 1870, the Courtyard, Hertford House, Manchester Square, London (Wallace Collection). Height approx 36ins.

This vase and its pair have been modified in that the height of the square base has been increased. Originally part of Sir John Murray Scott's gift to Victoria Sackville-West, for several years they remained at Knole before passing to Sissinghurst Castle. In 1959 they were sold by Sotheby's and passed through the National Art Collections Fund to the Wallace Collection. Another pair adorned the gardens of Nether Swell Manor, and seems likely to have been the pair removed to Upton House, perhaps via Colonel Birch. If there is some symbolism in the design it is not clear, although Janus was the son of Apollo, the Sun God, and is often represented with two heads, here possibly Apollo's sister Artemis and half brother Dionysus

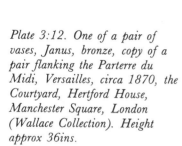

Colour Plate 38. One of a pair of bronze vases, Satyr, copy of a pair flanking the Parterre du Midi, Versailles, now in the Hyacinth Garden, Anglesey Abbey, Cambridgeshire. (See Plate 3:4)
THE NATIONAL TRUST: PHOTO PETER GREENHALF

of Janus[25] and Roundel,[26] may well have come from elsewhere. As has already been mentioned, Sir Richard Wallace had informed Viscount Powerscourt where models of Ballin's vases were, and as Powerscourt is known to have purchased sixteen vases for the two sides of the Perron at Powerscourt,[27] no doubt copies were readily available to other discerning patrons. Furthermore, although one may speculate that such vases, for example the Cupid once at Lynford Hall,[28] were made of bronze and hence from Bagatelle (especially as the owner of Lynford Hall in 1903, H A Campbell, shared the same name as one of Scott's friends, K H Campbell[29]), it may well have been made of cast-iron, for by 1877 the iron foundry of Durenne could offer copies of this model and five others.[30] With the knowledge that another French iron foundry, Dugel,[31] was also producing models, combined with the likelihood that Barbezat et Cie and Barbedienne were

Colour Plate 39. One of a pair of vases, Spiral Fluting, bronze, copy of a pair flanking the Parterre du Nord, Versailles, the Dahlia Garden, Anglesey Abbey, Cambridgeshire. (See Plate 3:5)
THE NATIONAL TRUST: PHOTO PETER GREENHALF

producing bronze copies, it is difficult to establish whether extant undocumented models originated from the gardens at Bagatelle or elsewhere.

The Warwick Vase

With the exception of the Borghese and Medici Vases, the Warwick Vase is, perhaps, the most copied antique vase in Britain. Numerous copies were produced in various sizes during the nineteenth century, both for outside (Plates 3:15 and 4:19 and Colour Plates 42 and 48) as well as for interior decoration. It is therefore fitting that some brief account of the history of the original be given.

In 1770 the Scottish painter Gavin Hamilton (1730-1797) started excavations on the site of Hadrian's Villa, fifteen miles east of Rome. Hamilton had been resident

Plate 3:13. One of a pair of vases, Sphinx, bronze, copy of a pair flanking the Parterre du Midi, Versailles, circa 1870, Sissinghurst Castle, Kent. Height approx 31ins. (See Colour Plate 41).

Like the ten vases sold by Lady Sackville-West in 1923, the history of this pair after its removal from Bagatelle is unclear, and it is therefore tempting to suggest that Sir John Murray Scott's gift to Lady Sackville-West may well have included more than the ten pairs she is at present known to have possessed.

Copies of this design were produced in a terracotta medium by an unknown manufacturer, probably French, and since the 7th Viscount Powerscourt (in Description and History of Powerscourt) refers to copies being 'reproduced in terre cuite', presumably, like cast-iron copies, these were available in the late nineteenth century

NIGEL NICOLSON

Plate 3:14. One of a pair of vases, Scroll, bronze, flanking the Parterre du Nord, Versailles, circa 1670. Height approx 37ins.

Since the Bagatelle pair of vases of this design was stolen from Upton House, and no other copies have come to light, one of the originals at Versailles is illustrated. From an illustration of one of the Bagatelle copies of this design (Country Life, 26 November 1910) it is clear that that pair at least had not been modified

MUSÉE NATIONAL DU CHATEAU DE VERSAILLES

in Italy for many years prior to this, involved not only with his painting but also in the lucrative business of procuring antique statues to decorate the interiors and exteriors of the English aristocracy's country and London houses. These excavations at Hadrian's Villa unearthed a mass of broken statues and marble including several sections of what is now the Warwick Vase. However, these fragmented pieces amounted to less than half the vase, and the enormous expense of recreating it was beyond Hamilton's means.

The renowned collector Sir William Hamilton (1730-1803) was also resident in Italy at the time — as British Envoy Extraordinary to the Court of Naples — and it was to him that the Scottish painter offered the pieces. The exact circumstances surrounding Sir William's acquisition of the remnants of the vase are unknown, but today it is thought that he purchased them rather than just paying for the restoration.[32] By the end of 1775 the restoration of the vase had been completed at considerable cost — the antique pieces had been set into Carrara marble and a new socle carved. Sir William Hamilton offered the vase to the British Museum (which several years earlier had purchased Hamilton's considerable collection of

Plate 3:15. Left, full-size copy of the Warwick Vase, bronze, cast by Charles Crozatier from the antique model, circa 1820, the Senate House, Cambridge. Diameter approx 68½ ins. (See Colour Plate 42).

The eighteenth century engraving by Piranesi of the original (antique) Warwick Vase is also shown to indicate the correct placement of the pedum *and* thyrsus

ENGRAVING SOTHEBY'S BILLINGSHURST: PHOTO PETER GREENHALF

antique vases), but curiously the Museum authorities did not want the vase, seemingly finding it too expensive.[33] Sometime between 1776 and 1778, the vase was sent to England, where it passed into the possession of Sir William's nephew, the 2nd Earl of Warwick (1748-1816). For a few years the vase stood in the courtyard of Warwick Castle before being transferred to a specially built greenhouse. It was to remain there until 1977, when it was sold. Today it forms part of the Burrell Collection, Glasgow, within which it is admirably displayed.

The copy of the Warwick Vase outside the Senate House at Cambridge (Plate 3:15 and Colour Plate 42), is particularly interesting, for although it is a magnificent cast it is, as N M Penzer in his authoritative articles on the vase pointed out[34], incorrect. On the original, the side (illustrated here) with the bearded bust of Bacchus in the centre is decorated to the left with a crooked stick, known as a *pedum,* and to the right with a stick tipped with a pine cone, known as a *thyrsus,* both symbolic of pastoral life and in keeping with the bacchic symbolism on the vase. However, when the Frenchman Charles Crozatier (1795-1855) cast this vase, he evidently confused his moulds and hence two *thyrsi* appear flanking the bearded Bacchus.

The exact date that Crozatier cast this vase remains to be discovered, but it was around 1820. Because no suitable bronze foundry existed in England, Crozatier had been chosen by the renowned London silversmiths, Rundell Bridge & Rundell, to cast two copies from moulds supplied by them. How Rundell Bridge & Rundell obtained these moulds is interesting. In 1813, Lord Lonsdale

Colour Plate 40. One of a pair of bronze vases, Harpy, copy of a pair flanking the Parterre du Midi, Versailles, now in the Hyacinth Garden, Anglesey Abbey, Cambridgeshire. (See Plate 3:6)
THE NATIONAL TRUST: PHOTO PETER GREENHALF

(1757-1844) gained permission from the Earl of Warwick to have a copy of the Warwick Vase cast on the condition that it be cast in silver. Accordingly Lord Lonsdale made arrangements with Rundell Bridge & Rundell, but when the modellers and mould makers started work on a wax model the firm soon realised that it had considerably underpriced the project. Lord Lonsdale was informed, but the proposed increase in price was too much and the vase was not made, the moulds being retained for use in later years.

Charles Crozatier (who is best known today for casting N B Raggi's colossal figure of Louis XIV in 1829) cast two full-scale copies of the Warwick Vase. The one at Cambridge was presented to the University by the 3rd Duke of Northumberland (1785-1847) on the occasion of his first visit as Chancellor in July 1842. The other, which was also cast with the same discrepancy found on the vase at Cambridge, was purchased by George IV in 1822 and now stands on the East Terrace of Windsor Castle.

Colour Plate 41. One of a pair of bronze vases, Sphinx, copy of a pair flanking the Parterre du Midi, Versailles, now at Sissinghurst Castle, Kent. (See Plate 3:13)
NIGEL NICOLSON

Over the years the Cambridge vase, which is known locally as the Northumberland Vase, has formed a beautiful yet damaging patina of black and dark and light greens. Considering the vase has only been situated on its Portland stone pedestal for just over fifty years, there has been extensive verdigris staining.

English Bronze Pieces

During the eighteenth century the use of bronze for statuary in Britain was predominantly restricted to commemorative works, and those that were placed outside tended to be memorials to celebrated figures of the period. The equestrian

Plate 3:16. Life-size equestrian figure of George I, bronze, cast by the younger John Van Nost from a model by Burchard, 1722, the Barber Institute of Fine Arts, University of Birmingham

figure of George I now outside the Barber Institute, Birmingham (Plate 3:16), is a fine example, and although not strictly a garden ornament it is included here because it once stood in the gardens of the Mansion House, Dublin, while the original from which it was copied was produced for the gardens of Cannons in Middlesex.

The bronze figure at Birmingham was commissioned by the Corporation of Dublin which, according to W G Strickland, in 1717 appointed a committee 'to treat with some skilful and able statuary of Great Britain or this Kingdom for such statue [of George I]'[35]. Presumably after some deliberation, for the figure was not finished until four or five years later, the committee chose an English sculptor, the younger John Van Nost. By 1722 the statue had been completed, and on 1 August of that year was unveiled on the Essex Bridge, Dublin, where it remained until 1753 when the bridge was demolished and it was removed to the gardens of the Mansion House. It eventually found its way to England.

Plate 3:17. The lead copy of the bronze equestrian figure of George I cast by the younger John Van Nost and supplied to Stowe in 1723/4. In comparing it with the bronze model (Plate 3:16) note how the horse's tail has slumped and its back legs have bowed

STOWE SCHOOL, BUCKINGHAMSHIRE

Although this bronze was clearly cast by the younger John Van Nost, and the lead copy believed to have been supplied to Stowe in 1723/4 is also thought to have been supplied by him,[36] it is apparent that the original was modelled by a relatively unknown artist, C Burchard (fl1716).

Rupert Gunnis relates that Burchard 'modelled for the Duke of Chandos a large equestrian statue of George I (cast and gilded by Van Nost), which was set up at Canons about 1716'.[37] This predates both the bronze and lead copies. In what medium the Cannons model was made is unknown, for the figure disappeared in the late nineteenth century, but from illustrations of it at Leicester Fields (where it was moved to after the Cannons sale) in the early nineteenth century,[38] it is clear that it was identical to the figures at Stowe and Birmingham.

Comparison of the lead and bronze models clearly illustrates the relative strength of the bronze, for on the lead figure the horse's tail has slumped and its back legs have bowed (Plate 3:17). Damage is also visible on the bronze, but this is almost certainly due to vandalism incurred by being located in a public place.

Plate 3:18. The greyhound Eos, bronze, by John Francis, circa 1848, the Italian Gardens, Osborne House, Isle of Wight. Height approx 31ins
REPRODUCED BY GRACIOUS PERMISSION OF HER MAJESTY THE QUEEN

Evidently the eighteenth century lead figure makers were *au fait* with the casting of bronze ornaments, but, as we have seen, the price and the time required to produce a bronze cast prohibited its frequent use in English gardens. No doubt the lead figure makers' *oeuvre* included a few bronze garden ornaments but, with the exception of a pair of bronze statues in the United States (duplicates of the Shepherd and Shepherdess in Colour Plate 18) which are signed 'J.C.C. 1777', and presumably by John Cheere, no other examples are known.

On 31 July 1844 Eos, one of the Royal family's favourite greyhounds, died. Queen Victoria and Prince Albert were clearly devoted to her, for they had a figure modelled and two copies cast in bronze: one for the dog's grave at Windsor, the other for the Italian Gardens at Osborne House (Plate 3:18).

John Francis (1780-1861), a sculptor popular with the royal family,[39] was chosen to execute the statue, and by late October of the same year he was working on the model at Windsor. An entry in Queen Victoria's diary for that month relates that Francis was working by the kennels, so presumably he was using other royal greyhounds as models for this noble dog. However, it is clear that Francis alone was not completely responsible for the finished work; the Prince Consort, himself a great patron of the arts, was considerably involved with the project. The Queen's diary records that on 1 November '...we walked down to the Kennels, where Francis is getting on with the model of good "Eos",... Albert directs everything, and also works himself at it'.[40]

Colour Plate 42. Full-size bronze copy of the Warwick Vase, cast by Charles Crozatier from the antique model, the Senate House, Cambridge. (See Plate 3:15 and pages 143-147)
PHOTO PETER GREENHALF

The model was probably finished and cast the following year, and it does not seem unreasonable to assume that it was then placed over the dog's grave. At what date the copy at Osborne arrived is as yet unknown; however in 1848 Francis exhibited at the Royal Academy a 'Model of Eos a favourite greyhound of H.R.H. Prince Albert executed for H.R.H. in bronze',[41] and perhaps this was the one now at Osborne.

Both the copies at Windsor and Osborne are raised on unmoulded blocks of granite and, as they form part of the Royal Collection, have been well cared for and show little signs of any weathering.

Unfortunately it is not known which firm was producing zinc copies of Eos in later years, but lead copies are still being produced today by H Crowther Ltd.

Plate 3:19. Statuette of Narcissus, bronze, probably by the Italian firm Chiurazzi, late nineteenth/early twentieth century. Height approx 24½ ins
PRIVATE COLLECTION

Plate 3:20. Reduced copy of the Venus de Medici, bronze, nineteenth century, the Monks' Garden, Anglesey Abbey, Cambridgeshire. Height approx 13ins. (See Colour Plate 43)

THE NATIONAL TRUST

Italian Bronze Pieces

The statuette in Plate 3:19 is a full-size copy of an antique bronze figure discovered in 1862 during excavations at Pompeii. The figure is adorned with a crown of ivy, one of the attributes of Dionysus, and as such perhaps represents that deity; however, soon after its discovery it was deemed to represent Narcissus, and it has retained this name for many years.[42] The pose of the youth, gazing down, would be most appropriate for Narcissus who, having spurned Echo's love, was punished by Hera to fall in love with his own reflection.

The excavations at Pompeii attracted considerable world attention, and by the late nineteenth century this figure had become remarkably popular. It was being produced in great numbers by such notable reproduction firms as Chiurazzi, for its romantic appeal and small size (and consequent cheaper price), meant it could easily be incorporated within even the smallest garden or conservatory. The Chiurazzi 1929 catalogue lists the model (number 91) in three sizes, 62cm (the most popular size and 1cm smaller than the original due to the shrinkage incurred during casting), 39cm and 27cm, and these were available in one of three patinations, 'Pompei', 'Ercolano' and 'Rinascimento'.[43] Although not visibly marked with the firm's name, this figure is probably by that prolific manufactory whose marking appears to have been inconsistent.

The marble statue of the Venus de Medici, now in the Uffizi, Florence, is perhaps the most copied antique statue of all time; certainly it was a particularly popular subject for garden ornament, with a whole range of copies being produced by such manufacturers as the Coades,[44] Blashfield,[45] the Coalbrookdale Company,[46] and Geiss of Berlin,[47] as well as many of the eighteenth century lead figure makers.[48] It is not known where the original statue was unearthed, but in 1638 it was at the Villa Medici in Rome, from whence it takes it name.[49]

No record has come to light to show where Lord Fairhaven acquired the reduced copy (Plate 3:20 and Colour Plate 43) — the original stands 60½ inches high, and

153

as it does not have a founder's mark, by whom and when it was cast are not known. In comparison to the quality of the few eighteenth century full-size casts of the Venus de Medici, such as that by Massimiliano Soldani Benzi (1656-1740) which used to stand in the gardens of Blenheim Palace,[50] it is a poor copy, and this certainly suggests a date in the nineteenth century. As bronze castings of antique statues were rarely produced in Britain, even during the nineteenth century, it seems likely that this figure originated in Europe, probably either Italy or France. Unfortunately this proposition cannot be substantiated by its pedestal of rich red French Languedoc marble, for although well proportioned in height in relation to the figure, it is far too wide, and therefore most unlikely to have been the original one.

It is interesting to note that today the Uffizi Venus de Medici is widely believed to be a copy of a lost Greek bronze.[51] This supposition is based primarily on the inferiority of the treatment of the antique marble putti and dolphin which 'strengthen' the leg of the goddess, for these would have been unnecessary in a bronze casting. Clearly several of the eighteenth and nineteenth century bronze copies cast after the Uffizi marble, such as that at Anglesey Abbey, retain this 'dolphin support', but it is most unlikely that the founders were aware of the irony of including the support within their copies.

Bronze Imitations

Just before reaching the Italian Gardens at Osborne House, the north-eastern avenue divides around a circular fountain border in the centre of which is a mound of granite rocks adorned by a rather charming fountain group of a boy with a swan (Plate 3:21). Unlike many nineteenth century fountains, which often dwarf their borders, it is well proportioned, but unfortunately the unity of the composition is disturbed by the rather awkward combination of the group's stylised base and the contrived naturalism of the rocks below.

This group is a copy of an original plaster model entitled 'The Boy with Swan', which was exhibited at the Berlin Academy by Theodor Kalide (1801-1864) in

Plate 3:22. Reduced copy of Giambologna's Mercury, white metal alloy electro-plated, bearing the Italian founder's mark 'Fonderia Sommez, Napoli', possibly late nineteenth century. Height approx 44ins

H CROWTHER LTD

1834. Two years later he exhibited the same model in bronze, the catalogue entry reading: 'Nr. 1090 Der Knabe mit dem Schwan. Gruppe in Bronze, Lebengrösse, nach eigenem Modell, gearbeitet, um als Fontaine zu dienen. Geformt und in Bronze gegossen von Friedrich Kalide' [The Boy with the Swan. Group in Bronze, Life-size made from his own Design for a Fountain. Fashioned and cast in Bronze by Friedrich Kalide].[52] In 1849 a model was positioned on Peacock Island, but by 1851 it appears to have been removed, for in the *Art-Journal's* illustrated catalogue to the 1851 Great Exhibition, the copy exhibited (which was awarded a medal) is described as being from 'the gardens of Charlottensberg, the summer residence of the King of Prussia'.[53] Unfortunately Kalide's bronze has since disappeared.

The copy at Osborne is one of the zinc casts by Moritz Geiss (1805-1875) of Berlin, whose raised plaque bearing the firm's name (which frequently occurs on models) appears to the left of the group's base. It is included in this chapter, since not only is it a copy of a bronze original, but also because, like many Geiss casts, this model was originally coated with a bronze finish.

The use of zinc for casting statuary was championed by Geiss at his manufactory in Berlin. In its natural state zinc has an unpleasant dull bluish-white colour, but by the 1840s Geiss had successfully perfected a method of bronzing the metal, and the business soon proved to be a success, for zinc ornaments were both cheaper and easier to produce than their bronze counterparts. Geiss expounded the advantages of his products thus:

Zinc is readily melted, liquifies very completely, and, therefore, is better adapted to cover the smallest lines in the mould than metals of a harder and more compact texture. The zinc casting is so pure and so finished on being turned out of the mould that the work requires but very little subsequent chasing. This circumstance, combined wth the cheapness of the metal itself (the cost of a zinc cast being to a cast in bronze only one-sixth or one-eighth), renders zinc an admirable material for statuary.

Geiss went on to relate that his method of bronzing 'gives the cast the perfect aspect of Florentine bronze'.[54]

Among the zinc ornaments displayed at the Great Exhibition were a number of life-size copies of popular statues, including the Boy with Swan, Hebe after Canova and a Kneeling Niobe after the antique. These met with some considerable approval, the *Art-Journal* relating that 'the purity of the casts, the perfection of the chiselling and the durability of the material combine to recommend it...We have no doubt that the exhibition of these statues admirably calculated for gardens in England will be forwarded by a large importation of similar works'.[55] However, one may speculate whether the *Art-Journal* would with hindsight withdraw their reference to the suitability of these statues to English gardens, for the copy of Kalide's group and other Geiss figures both at Osborne and elsewhere, which have been exposed to the elements for many years, have completely lost their original bronze finish, revealing the ungainly colour below.

Queen Victoria and Prince Albert purchased a number of items from the Great Exhibition to decorate their country retreat at Osborne, such as the Coalbrookdale Company's bronze figure of Andromeda, but whether Kalide's fountain group cast by Geiss was also obtained at this time is unclear, for as yet no bill has come to light. However, some idea of its cost can be gauged by the fact that one of the firm's trade catalogues, circa 1850, lists the model at £26.[56]

In 1564, Giambologna (1529-1608), court sculptor to the Medici dukes, executed a bronze statue of Mercury, the mythological messenger of the gods. The deity is represented with many of his attributes. In his left hand he clasps his caduceus (a wand decorated with a pair of entwined snakes, which in mythology induced sleep and was instrumental in the god's slaying of the all-seeing giant Argus), whilst his petasus (the helmet) is decorated with wings to transport him through the skies. The figure is depicted with wings growing from his ankles and not with the winged sandles that mythology records he lent to Perseus.

Giambologna's graceful and athletic work encapsulates a Renaissance idea of the messenger god as an intermediary between human intellect and divine wisdom. The extravagantly styled, yet perfectly balanced figure successfully creates the illusion of aerial agility, and this is accentuated by the contrivance of the 'rush of wind' which lifts the figure both figuratively and in fact; it is of no surprise, therefore, that this figure has been so extensively reproduced over the centuries.

The nature of the pose excluded the statue's reproduction in stone or marble, for, standing on one leg without support, the figure would break, and the addition of any support would have destroyed the composition. Consequently it was copied primarily in bronze and other strong alloys such as the electro-plated model illustrated (Plate 3:22).

The process of electro-plating, which became widespread in the third quarter of the nineteenth century, can briefly be described as follows. A model was cast in a cheap medium capable of conducting electricity, such as iron or, in the case of this figure of Mercury, a cheap 'white metal' alloy. These models were suspended in an acid solution, the positive electrical pole was attached to the figure and the negative to a plate of metal, in this case copper. As the copper decomposes it is deposited on the surface of the model, the greater the time in the solution, the thicker the plating. Very cheap copies could be reproduced by this method, though they are not as well suited as bronze for garden ornament. Many of the alloy casts retain their cores which expand causing fractures and tears, similar but not as dramatic as those that appear on many eighteenth century lead figures; furthermore alloy casts are brittle and difficult to repair.

Copper-plated casts are frequently and easily mistaken for authentic bronzes, although a mark such as 'Fonderia Sommez, Napoli', found on the Mercury in Plate 3:22, does not necessarily imply that the figure is a bronze cast.

The figure is typical of the reduced copies of popular statues available during the latter half of the nineteenth century. It is not dated and it is therefore difficult to attribute it either to the nineteenth or twentieth century with any certainty, for other Italian firms were still producing bronze or electro-plated copies in varying sizes as late as the 1930s.

CHAPTER FOUR

ARTIFICIAL STONE
1760 - 1900

Artificial stone accounts for a considerable quantity of garden ornament. First produced in substantial quantities in the late 1760s, it is still manufactured today and widely used as an alternative to natural stone, primarily because it is cheaper. Numerous different formulae and manufactories have produced artificial stone wares, ranging from those with the weatherproof quality of clay-based pieces, such as Coade Stone, to the often less durable formulae, such as James Pulham's cement-based Portland stone. Indeed artificial stone ornaments can be separated into two groups: those based on a clay formula, which were moulded and then fired in a kiln, such as Coade's or Blashfield's; and those based on a form of cement, which were cast, and hardened without the application of heat, such as Austin & Seeley's limestone, or Pulham's Portland stone cement.

A number of manufactories, producing varying bodies, were in operation during the eighteenth century, the earliest of them being run by Richard Holt who, after five or six years of production, published in 1730 *A Short Treatise on Artificial Stone*[1] explaining the history (he claimed it was based on a lost ancient formula) and advantages of artificial stone over natural stone. He writes: 'Whatever is, or maybe made of Cut Stone, or lead, or of cast-iron for the Embellishment of Houses and Gardens, I am able to make out of my composition of artificial stone — shall run no comparison with either of those substances, nor with the goods made of either of them'.

Unfortunately very little information on Holt's production remains. In 1722 he filed two patents for artificial stone,[2] and we know that by 1730 he employed a number of men at his works near York Building Stairs, Lambeth. His stone must have had some durability, for within his *Treatise* he claims that his goods defied 'All the violence of the Weather as well as the powers of fire', a statement which could, in his own words, be substantiated by the fact that they had been untouched by the severity of the winter of 1728/9. Forty years later, Daniel Pincot, 'Artificial Stone Manufacturer' (fl1767-1797) in his *Essay on ...Artificial Stone*[3] mentions that he possessed some examples of Holt's work, but goes on to say that Holt's models showed 'neither taste in design nor neatness in their execution', a fact which may account for the seeming scarcity of Holt's ornaments today. How long Holt's manufactory continued is not known; according to Pincot the business faded after Holt's death, although, again, it is not known when Holt died. Since no records survive to say otherwise, it does appear that artificial stone was not manufactured again until the mid-1760s when a sale took place by Mr Christie, on 22 and 23 December 1767 of 'The Year's produce of Artificial Stone Manufactory'.[4]

As the manufacturer of the 138 lots is not mentioned, it seems probable that they were the products of Daniel Pincot's manufactory, for in 1767 at the Society of Artists' Exhibition, 'Mr Daniel Pincat [sic], artificial stone manufacturer, in Goulston-Square, White Chapel'[5] exhibited a number of pieces of artificial stone. Taking into account the inconsistent spellings of the eighteenth century, this is almost certainly the same as the manufactory's address given by Christie's as 'Goldston-Square, Whitechapel'.[6] Confirmation of this can be found in Pincot's *Essay* of 1770, where he states that he had exhibited some pieces at the 'New

Auction Rooms in Pall Mall', which almost certainly refers to Mr Christie's auction room which was relatively new in 1767, the first sale having been held in 1766.[7]

Probably, therefore, Pincot was the foremost artificial stone manufacturer of the day, and this can perhaps be substantiated not only by his extensive knowledge of the subject, but also because of the confidence he had in his artificial stone. He writes: 'That kind of artificial stone...is far superior, in strength and durability to white marble or common rock stone'.[8] Further to this his postscript suggests that the manufactory was a success, for a number of masons and workmen were so concerned about the manufactory, and presumably its potential, that they considered it a threat to their livelihood, and in Pincot's words were 'detering modellers from working at the manufactory telling them that they will be despised by the whole trade'. By 1770 Pincot had moved, for his address given in the *Essay* is 'King's Arms Stairs, Narrow Wall, Lambeth', and it is here that the first connection with Coade appears, for the Coade works were established on the same premises in 1769.

Pincot and Coade worked closely together for a few years and though little detail is known of their business relationship, various points of interest are recorded: Pincot received a subscription from Henry Hoare in 1770 for a Borghese Vase, Mrs Coade receiving the balance a few years later;[9] furthermore Mrs Coade advertised in the *Public Advertiser* of 17 September 1771: 'Whereas Eleanor Coade has thought fit to dismiss Mr Daniel Pincot from any further employ in her Manufactory...the Public are desired to take notice that he is not by her to do any Act for her or on any account; and that she has no connection with him in any shape whatever'.[10]

The researches of J A Havill show that Eleanor Coade the younger was born in Exeter where the family remained until the early 1760s when it moved to London.[11] It seems unlikely the Coades had any prior knowledge of the artificial stone business, and probably joined up with Pincot in London, perhaps moving to a more suitable manufactory at Narrow Wall. After a few years' experience, and forseeing the potential of their compound, the Coades split with Pincot. It seems probable, therefore, that the Coade formula was a variation on or possibly even the same formula as Pincot's.

Whatever the case, the Coade manufactory was pre-eminent. What happened to Pincot is not known, though it seems likely, considering his modelling ability and his knowledge of the manufacture of artificial stone, that he would have started another business. If so, perhaps he was one of the producers of artificial stone referred to in Coade's *Descriptive Catalogue* of 1784 which states 'there have been several other Manufactories passing under the same denomination', and goes on to mention that they had been 'extinct for some years past'.[12]

During the nineteenth century the number of manufacturers of artificial stone garden ornaments was extensive, indeed over twenty-five firms are known to have been operating during the period. In the early 1800s the Coade works were predominant, but within a short space of time others, foreseeing the potential of the medium, started producing their own formulae, some of a similar nature to Coade stone (based on a clay formula) and others based on a cement formula. By the 1850s the Coade manufactory had been closed for some years and the gap in the market was soon filled with the clay-based wares of such firms as H M Blanchard, J M Blashfield, and J Pulham, and the cement-based wares of J Pulham and Austin & Seeley. Interestingly, at this date clay formulae were often regarded by contemporary writers as new compounds, which is curious considering that in essence Coade stone, for example, is purely a sophisticated form of the terracotta used by the Greeks and Romans.

By the 1870s the number of manufacturers of artificial stone garden ornaments had multiplied, with items being produced not only in London and the home counties, but throughout the provinces: in Devon by the Watcombe Terracotta Company, in the Midlands by Gibbs and Canning, in Scotland by the Garnkirk Company and in the great pottery centre of Staffordshire by William Baddeley, to name but a few. Of these manufactories, some had been established mainly to manufacture statues, vases and the like (as well as in some cases the associated architectural wares), while others had expanded into this field as a side line to an existing business. Hence one finds such firms as Doulton and the Coalbrookdale Company producing terracotta garden ornaments, whilst a number of cement manufacturers, such as Blashfield's predecessors, Wyatt, Parker & Co, were also producing a range of cement-based garden ornaments.

The large number of manufacturers clearly illustrates the great demand for artificial stone ornaments. There were several reasons for this demand, of which probably the most important was the fact that such pieces could be mass produced much more cheaply than anything carved from marble or natural stone, and could therefore be afforded by the increasingly affluent middle classes. Other factors were also responsible for its popularity, including the quality of the media, especially clay-based forms which were generally well able to resist the ravages of the British climate, and this in itself must have given an added cachet to what was looked on as one of the technical achievements of the century (possibly an exaggerated opinion of its importance). Artificial stone ornaments also had a distinct advantage over their main competitors, cast-iron ornaments, in that they were not prone to the unsightly effects of oxidation.

Relatively little research has been done on artificial stone, and ornaments are consistently mistaken for natural stone, and vice versa. The situation is further complicated by the great mass of artificial stone ornaments, particularly cement-based ones, which do not bear a manufacturer's mark, and by the remarkable lack of manufacturers' catalogues or designs which, when located, are of immense assistance in the identification of wares. Furthermore the history of many of these manufactories is fairly obscure, as are the identities of many of the modellers and designers employed; even the exact constitution of some wares is still unknown.

This chapter concentrates on four manufactories of clay-based artificial stones: Coade stone and the terracottas produced by James Marriot Blashfield, James Pulham, and Doulton & Co. As examples of artificial stone based on cement formulae, examples of the artificial stone produced by James Pulham, as well as several of the limestone ornaments produced by Austin & Seeley, are discussed and illustrated.

Coade Stone

Coade stone is a vitrified ceramic body, with a matt finish and a warm colour which varies from a pale greyish-white to a light yellow or beige. It is a remarkable compound and one to which, not surprisingly, some secrecy was attached: even after fifty years of production there was, according to *The Somerset House Gazette* 'Some shyness about the materials of the composition of this artificial stone, but chiefly in the proportion of the ingredients'.[13]

Coade stone consists mainly of a ball clay (from Dorset or Devon) to which were added grog,[14] flint and sand to reduce shrinkage, and soda-lime-silica glass to

Plate 4:1. Severely damaged Coade stone Water Nymph in the grotto at Croome Court, Worcestershire. The damage, probably caused by falling masonry, has revealed on the interior the finger marks where the clay was pressed into the moulds

help vitrify it.[15] Its manufacture involved not only skilled craftsmen, but also mass-production techniques, both of which allowed for numerous variations on one theme: particular details could be added or subtracted with ease to extend the range of ornaments available (Plates 4:11 and 12). The Coade ornaments were made by forming the clay into sheets of uniform thickness (necessary to reduce the possibilities of distortion) and pressing sections of these into moulds[16] that together would comprise the particular ornament being produced (Plate 4:1). After being left to dry the moulded parts were removed from the moulds and assembled, a process which must have required some considerable skill for the interior often required reinforcing with ribs of clay. Once fully assembled the joint lines were concealed with some form of slip and the whole piece chased up and finished off by hand, which included undercutting and making good those parts which, for example, had been poorly formed or impaired during removal from the mould.

The Coade manufactory had considerable technical control over the clay, so shrinkage and distortion were almost negligible and it was thus possible to produce architectural items of almost precise dimensions and figures as large as the nine foot River God (Plate 4:9).

Plate 4:2. Indentation mark on the base of a Coade keystone
CHRISTOPHER GIBBS ANTIQUES

The most hazardous and complex stage of production was the firing of the ornaments, a highly skilled job undertaken by a fireman. The kiln had to reach a temperature of over 1100°C which was necessary to vitrify the compound, a process which took four days.

Llewellynn Jewitt gives an interesting insight into the firing process at the works, and in particular the ability of one 'fire-man' circa 1790:

There is three kilns, the largest is 9 feet diameter and about 10 feet high, the other two are sizes under; they have only three fire-holes to each, and they are about 14 inches in the clear. They make use of no saggers, but their kilns are all muffled about two inches thick, which was always done by this fire-man. They always was four days and four nights of fireing a kilns, and the moment the goods are fire'd up he always took and stop'd the kilns intirely close from any air whatever without lowering the fires at all. He had been used to fire intirely with Coal. . .He never made use of any thermometer, but depended intirely on his own knowledge. The composition shrinks about half an inch in a foot in the drying, and about the same in the firing. A great deal of the ornaments are 4 inches thick when fired, and he has fired figures 9 feet high. This man has had the intire management of building the kilns, setting and firing them for many years; his wages was one guinea per week, and for every night when he fired he had 2s 6d for the small kiln, 3s for the next size and 3s 6d for the largest.[17]

Coade stone is often, but not always, identified by the presence of one of several indented marks (as Mrs Coade referred to impressed marks): 'COADE', 'COADE & SEALY' or 'CROGGON', frequently accompanied by the marks 'LONDON' or 'LAMBETH', and at times with a date (Plate 4:2). These marks are usually located on the lower part of an ornament, such as the base of a statue or socle of a vase, though this is not always the case — the Lion and Unicorn at the Royal Botanic Gardens, Kew, are not marked at all.

In comparison to natural stones, such as Portland or Bath, Coade stone is distinguished by the fact that it rarely succumbs to moss, has no veining or deposits and above all by the fact that ornaments are virtually unaffected by the weather and remain as crisp today as when they left the manufactory. The compound's quality is suitably summed up by one of the manufactory's advertisements: 'The property which this *artificial* stone has above *natural* stone, of resisting the frost, and consequently of retaining that *sharpness* in which it excels every kind of Stone Sculpture, renders it peculiarly fit for statues in parks and gardens'.[18] Coade stone is, therefore, one of the most suitable media for garden ornaments, its only weak spot occurring on poorly-manufactured items, a small quantity of which have split, or are splitting alone their joint lines (Plates 4:9 and 12 and pages 171 and 172).

The manufactory

As we have seen the Coade Artificial Stone, or Lithodipyra,[19] manufactory was established at King's Arms Stairs, Narrow Wall, Lambeth in 1769. The site is now covered by the Royal Festival Hall.

The manufactory was particularly remarkable in that it was developed and run by two women, Mrs Eleanor Coade (1708-1796) and her daughter (confusingly also called Eleanor, 1733-1821). Mrs Coade's husband had died the year the manufactory was established. In the late 1770s the business (by then probably being run by the younger Eleanor, as her mother was getting on for seventy) published a collection of plates entitled *Etchings of Coade's Artificial Stone Manufactory*[20] which illustrated over 250 items from the extensive range of ornaments available, the majority of which were new designs (as opposed to copies of existing ornaments). This represents a remarkable achievement considering that the business had been established for less than ten years.

By 1784 the accompanying *Descriptive Catalogue. . .* giving prices and dimensions was also available.[21] The bulk of this catalogue consists of architectural items such as keystones, rustic stones (Plate 4:13), coats of arms, capitals, architraves, friezes, pateras, panels and tablets. This side of the manufactory's production was considerable, much larger than that producing garden ornaments, and to a certain extent reflects the growth in the building industry as well as the then developing picturesque taste for relatively ornament free gardens.

There were however over 150 vases, busts and pedestals. According to the catalogue, particular designs could be varied by the addition or subtraction of various sections, and the manufactory boasted that clients' designs 'will be executed with every advantage' and that all the models could be had at a 'considerable saving from the expense of Portland Stone'. It is difficult to generalise about how much cheaper Coade stone was in comparison to other compounds, but some gauge can be found in the cost of the firm's model number 55, a Sphynx. This was a two-third-sized copy of the John Cheere model shown in Plate 1:21, and was priced at £6 6s. Cheere's slightly modified examples, supplied to Somerset House in 1778, cost £31 each. Coade's relatively inexpensive prices — for example a six foot figure of Flora was only £26 5s, a six foot couchant lion only £15 15s, and a fifty-eight inch pineapple and foot (socle) only £2 2s — must have been one of the main reasons for the success of the manufactory in its early years.

By the early 1790s Miss, or rather Mrs Coade (not that the younger Eleanor had married, but this was a title often adopted by women in business) had brought in a relation, John Sealy (1749-1813), to help in the running of the manufactory.[22] When the elder Coade died in 1796, Sealy soon went into partnership with the younger Coade, and although the manufactory was then known as Coade & Sealy, it is often only referred to as Coade. By 1799 the partners had opened an exhibition gallery, not far from the manufactory on the south side of Westminster Bridge Road. The accompanying text in their *Description of Ornamental Stone in the Gallery of Coade and Sealy,*[23] published in the same year, provides a fascinating insight into the business which, after some thirty years of production, was well established, and whose standing had been considerably advanced by the patronage not only of George III but also of the Prince of Wales and Duke of York. Many of the models exhibited in the *Description of Ornamental Stone. . .* were taken from designs executed, in the manufacturers' view, by 'Artists of the highest reputation', and this prudent policy seems to be another reason for the success of the business. The Coade manufactory was thus able to mass produce some of the most fashionable sculptures and ornaments of the day for a discerning and increasingly fashion-conscious clientele. The *Description of Ornamental Stone. . .* reveals that John Bacon (1740-1799), one of the leading neo-classical sculptors at the end of the century, had been extensively employed by the manufactory. Copies of his models formed a considerable part not only of the gallery's exhibits (eight are listed including Urania, and the Water Nymph illustrated in Plate 4:1), but also of the rest of the range. Examples of other leading sculptors' and designers' models were on display, including works by the sculptors John Rossi and John Devaere and the architect James Wyatt. The manufactory did not restrict itself to contemporary artists alone. Several of the gallery's exhibits were modelled on drawings illustrated in popular publications such as *The Antiquities of Athens,*[24] for example the Caryatid from the Erechtheion (six of which flank the Great Avenue at Anglesey Abbey in Cambridgeshire). Copies of other antique subjects were also available, including not only the famous Italian collections (such as the Medici and Borghese Vases, Plates 4:3 and 4), but also copies of antique pieces in English collections, such as a sarcophagus of 'exquisite workmanship' in the Duke of Buckingham's collection. Of course numerous other statues and architectural items were available at the manufactory, based on a variety of other influences, special commissions were still undertaken and, as business prospered and tastes changed, new models were introduced.

In 1813 Sealy died, and the elderly (younger) Mrs Coade (who was then eighty) left the running of the business to a certain William Croggon (fl.1813-1835) whose exact relationship to Mrs Coade is unclear. On her death in 1821, Croggon bought the business, prudently retaining the Coade name, which by then must have carried some considerable design cachet. However, Croggon did diversify the business into the production of scagliola, a form of artificial marble for interior decoration and one which is not at all suited for garden ornament as it deteriorates rapidly. Over the following years the output of Coade stone (although frequently only indented 'CROGGON') was substantial and included major commissions for, amongst other places, Buckingham Palace.[25]

In 1833 Croggon went bankrupt,[26] and died a few years later. His son, Thomas, refounded the business a few years later, but by then the manufacture of Coade stone seems to have been negligible, and the works were soon sold. Croggon first moved into the manufacture or wholesale of Roman stone,[27] and then asphalt,[28] and the Coade works faded into obscurity.

The reasons for the demise of the business are curious, for variations of artificial stone, for example terracotta, were to prove popular throughout the rest of the century. There were perhaps two reasons: imprudent speculation and unhonoured debts incurred by the Duke of York to whom Croggon had supplied a whole range of pieces.[29]

Whatever the case, the manufactory was remarkable. A medium almost totally unheard of prior to 1760 was mass produced to the highest quality for some seventy years. Capable of withstanding the effects of weather, it was cheaper than natural stone, the majority of pieces remaining almost as sharp as when they first left the

Plate 4:3. Vase of Campana form, Coade stone, copy of the antique Medici Vase, not indented, 1826, the Royal Botanic Gardens, Kew. Height of vase approx 50 ins; height of pedestal approx 48ins. (See Colour Plate 44)

Plate 4:4. Vase of campana form, Coade stone, copy of the antique Borghese Vase, not indented, 1826, Wrest Park, Bedfordshire. Height of vase approx 50ins; height of pedestal approx 48ins

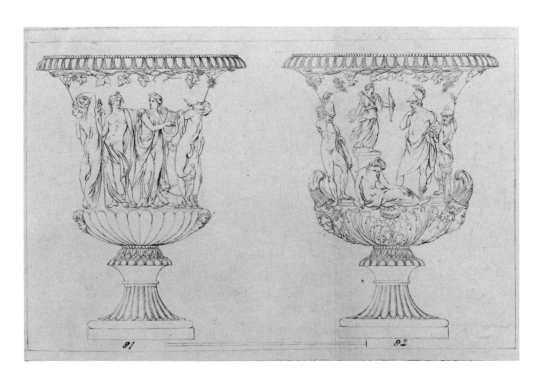

Plate 4:5. The illustrations of the Borghese (left) and Medici Vases in Etchings of Coade's Artificial Stone Manufactory. *Compare these versions with the Kew Medici Vase (Plate 4:3 and Colour Plate 44) on which there are no handles, and the Wrest Park Borghese Vase (Plate 4:4) on which there are handles*

166

Plate 4:6. One of a damaged pair of simple Coade stone pedestals at Chiswick House which support Borghese and Medici Vases. The circular holes at the top of the pedestal between the two rams' heads, clearly show the now missing swag was originally joined to the pedestal
ENGLISH HERITAGE

works. Finally, as a result of the Coade manufactory and its product, a considerable number of artificial stones were developed which were to enjoy popularity till the end of the nineteenth century.

Coade stone garden ornaments

The Medici Vase at Kew which is thought to represent scenes from the Sacrifice of Iphigenia, and the Borghese Vase at Wrest Park, Bedfordshire, which depicts scenes of Bacchanalian revelry, were amongst the manufactory's longest selling models. A huge number of these magnificent, slightly reduced vases (the originals, now in the Uffizi and Louvre respectively, are over five and a half feet high) were more often produced in pairs, though single vases are known.[30]

The modeller who copied the Medici Vase is as yet unknown, though it is almost certain that Daniel Pincot modelled the manufactory's copy of the Borghese Vase. Pincot had exhibited a Borghese Vase in artificial stone at the Society of Artists' 1771 exhibition,[31] and also supplied another to Stourhead for which he was paid £55 in advance, Mrs Coade receiving the balance, inclusive of packing and carriage, of £12 14s 6d in 1772.[32] Mrs Coade and Pincot's business relationship has already been discussed (see page 160), and it seems extremely likely that when the two parted, Mrs Coade retained a mould of Pincot's vase for her own use, a fact which is confirmed by the striking similarities between the Stourhead vase and later Coade copies.

Regettably both the Kew and Wrest vases (Plates 4:3 and 4 and Colour Plate 44) have been extensively restored, the entire rim and socle of the Borghese Vase having been completely replaced in stone; curiously the socle is not a direct copy, while the entire vase has been altered by the attachment of two handles, a peculiar addition, since neither other Coade examples nor the original has them; on the Medici Vase both handles are missing (Plate 4:5). On both vases the heads and several details on the pedestal plaques have been replaced with poorly modelled cement.

Despite these restorations, both vases clearly indicate how impervious Coade stone is to the elements; those sections that have not been damaged still reveal a clarity in the modelling, particularly in the detail of the bas-relief scenes on the main body of the vases. This pair, whose appearance at Kew and Wrest is of some mystery, was commissioned by the architect John Nash (who often used the compound) for George IV. Croggon's 1826 bill for the pair, which was sent from 'Coade's Imperishable Stone, Scagliola, & Marble Works Lambeth',[33] mentions that on Nash's orders they should be 'sent to the Royal Lodge Windsor'. Each vase cost forty guineas (as opposed to £31 10s in 1784[34]), and the total bill including the special modelling of several details for each pedestal came to £293 6s 8d including packing and carriage.

The pedestals are of particular interest, as they are good examples of the adaptability of the manufactory's models. The basic design of the pedestal is illustrated in *Etchings...*,[35] but comparison of this design and George IV's pair reveals considerable variations. On the Wrest and Kew pedestals, the basic form, complete with rams' heads under the cap, has been maintained; however, the floral swag rising in the centre with a ribbon tie illustrated in the design has been replaced with specially modelled swags of laurels and ribbons with the Royal insignia. As in the *Etchings...* illustration, the bas-relief scenes were retained, but on this pair they were specially modelled at a cost of twelve guineas each[36] to portray scenes appropriate to each vase. Of course, numerous other variations on this basic pedestal design were possible, for example the less ornate, and presumably cheaper pedestals (also supporting Borghese and Medici Vases) outside Joseph Paxton's greenhouse at Chiswick (Plate 4:6) where the bas-relief scenes were omitted in favour of plain panels, and the rams' heads united by a single rather than double floral swag.

The pair of Coade stone seats at Parham Park, West Sussex (one of which is illustrated in Plate 4:7 and Colour Plate 45) clearly reflect the neo-classical fashion popular at the end of the eighteenth and beginning of the nineteenth century. The design is modelled from a seat illustrated in C H Tatham's *Etchings of Ancient Ornamental Architecture...*[37] where it is described as 'Grand Antique Chair executed in Parian Marble from the collection in the museum of the Vatican'. However, the Coade seats are far more stylised than Tatham's, the sphinxes more formally arranged, and the uprights, which in Tatham's drawing take the form of a torch, have been replaced with plain architectural supports.

Unfortunately no direct information concerning the origins of the Parham pair seems to have survived, nor have any other examples of these grand seats come to light. However, an almost duplicate pair is illustrated in Thomas Hope's influential book *Household Furniture and Interior Decoration...*,[38] in which they are described as 'Front and side views of stone seats, adorned with sphinxes and Lotus flowers' (Plate 4:8). The sale catalogue of Hope's country house, The Deepdene, lists 'Lot 1188...Fine Pair of Lambeth stone chairs with square seats and winged sphinx arms and slab footrests'.[39] Both Hope and the Coade manufactory (which Hope must have known, as he purchased several items from it) were advocates of applying high quality designs to mass-produced furniture, and it certainly seems likely that Hope could have commissioned the Coade works to execute these seats for him. The indentation of 1800 on the Parham pair certainly coincides with the period Hope was assembling his collection — some four years before he invited members of the Royal Academy to his completed home. It seems likely therefore that the Parham seats are part of Hope's collection; if not, they are strikingly similar.

Plate 4:7. One of a pair of Coade stone seats, indented 'COADE LAMBETH 1800', flanking the Temple, Parham Park, West Sussex. Height approx 45ins. (See Colour Plate 45)

Plate 4:8. Illustration of 'front and side views of stone seats, adorned with sphinxes and Lotus flowers', from Thomas Hope's Household Furniture and Interior Decoration...

169

Plate 4:9. Larger-than-life figure of a River God, Coade stone, indented 'COADE LAMBETH', circa 1800, the Forecourt, Ham House, Richmond. Width approx 94ins

Whatever the case, the Parham pair are admirably modelled and, with the exception of the fact that the uprights lack their lotus flower finials, they are in perfect condition.

The Coade models differ from Hope's seats in three ways: the delicate details below the seat of Hope's chair are missing; the positioning of the sphinxes tails is slightly different; and a moulding is missing from the base of the Parham pair.

One further point is worth noting; the seats are only marked 'COADE LAMBETH 1800'. This is strange, for one would expect the Sealy mark to be present (by 1800 Sealy had become a partner); in view of this, the exact dating or placing of undated Coade ornaments into particular periods of the manufactory's history is clearly not always possible.

The superb figure of a River God at Ham House, Richmond (Plate 4:9), of which probably only one other Coade example exists (heavily vandalised, in the Terrace Gardens, Richmond[40]), was the largest figure available in the early years of the manufactory. Graciously reclining on an urn (through which, according to the 1784 *Descriptive Catalogue. . .,* water could pass), this robust figure, with his delicately modelled beard and hair embellished with aquatic flora, must be one of Coade's finest pieces. The technical ability and control needed to fire a figure as large as this in one piece was remarkable, and even more so when one considers

Plate 4:10. Illustration from Etchings of Coade's Artificial Stone Manufactory *showing John Bacon's design of a River God*

that a thermometer was probably not used and the largest kiln was only nine feet in diameter.[41]

The figure is in perfect condition with the exception of a broken finger, a few fractures on the base (not to be confused with the roughly hewn natural stone plinth) clearly defining where the pieces of clay were joined during assembly, and conspicuous repair joints where the left leg and arm have broken off along their original assembly joints.

Illustrated in the *Etchings. . .* (Plate 4:10) it was, according to the 1784 *Descriptive Catalogue. . .,* available for £105, the most expensive and impressive ornament available. The figure is taken from a model executed by the sculptor John Bacon, RA (1740-1799), who was to use the same figure at least once, in later years, in his bronze group of George III in the courtyard of Somerset House.[42]

Although not indented with a date, it seems probable that the figure was purchased at the same time as the other Coade ornaments at Ham (twelve pineapples) some of which are indented 'COADE & SEALY LAMBETH 1800'.[43]

The basic design for the finial or vase (the lids are frequently removable for floral display) in Plates 4:11 and 12, was one of the manufactory's more popular models. Numerous variations on it were available, and comparison of the two shown here illustrates the versatility of the compound in that particular enrichments or details,

Plate 4:11. One of a pair of Coade stone vases or finials, not indented. Height approx 26ins

T CROWTHER & SONS LTD

Plate 4:12. One of a pair of Coade stone vases or finials, indented 'COADE & SEALY LAMBETH 1800'. Height approx 26ins

PRIVATE COLLECTION

usually on the frieze, could be added or taken off during construction. The 1784 *Descriptive Catalogue...* lists four variations of this one design, not only in enrichments but also in the sizes available:

88 A Vase with Lions' Heads, much enriched	2' 2"	1' 11"	£2 12s 6d
89 Ditto with Drapery Festoons	2' 2"	1' 11"	£2 8s 0d
90 Ditto same pattern larger	2' 7½"	2' 2"	£2 15s 0d
777 A Vase as No 90; with Rams' Heads	"	"	£3 10s 0d

A number of examples of these survive: 88 (Lions' Heads) (Plate 4:12) is in a private collection; four examples of 89 (Drapery Festoons) and two examples of 90 (Ditto same pattern larger) decorate the gateway at Easton Neston, Northamptonshire (now the entrance to the Towcester Races Car Park), while examples of the other common design, 777 (Rams' Heads), appear with dealers from time to time. It is easy to believe that given this ability to vary designs by the addition of certain details, other variations were also manufactured, such as the Horses' Heads illustrated in Plate 4:11.

The basic model seems to have been one of the cheaper Coade finials available, and it is a fine example of the versatility of the mass-production techniques employed by the firm. The example in Plate 4:12 must have been poorly manufactured for it is in a poor state and clearly shows how the various components (now splitting along their construction joints) were joined.

The keystone and rustic stones (Plate 4:13) which are part of an arch at Croome Court, Worcestershire, clearly show the architectural side of the Coade business, which was substantial. Unlike the larger Coade ornaments, each part of the

Plate 4:13. Coade keystone and rustic stones, the keystone indented 'COADE LONDON 1797', the Dry Arch, Croome Court, Worcestershire. Height of keystone approx 19ins

keystone was formed in one mould, the clay being pushed into the mould in one lump; on removal the inside of the clay was carefully cut out to produce walls of an equal thickness, hence reducing the chances of distortion during firing.[44]

A huge range of these facings for arches was available, the 1784 *Descriptive Catalogue*. . . listing twenty-six keystones, many of which were variations in size on one theme: the rustic stones, for example, were available in four different lengths — 10¼ins, 13½ins, 14ins and 17ins, and in one of two forms — 'For an Arch' or 'Jaumb [jamb] to ditto'.

With the exception of the damage to the face of the keystone (almost certainly deliberate as its pair on the other side of the arch has been damaged in a similar way) it clearly shows not only the smooth finish of the stone in comparison to the natural stone above it, but also its durability. If the keystone and rustic stones had been made from a natural stone the deep and clearly cut details would no doubt have been considerably worn down by exposure to the elements over the last 180 years.

Also at Croome Court are two Coade stone terms (Plate 4:14). During the Regency (1811-1820) many such terms were produced by the Coade manufactory which would have been able to produce them comparatively cheaply, for a single mould could be used for the shaft, while the nature of the unfired medium would have made it easy to adapt extant busts to the form of a term, thereby allowing a huge range of models.

Apart from the fine quality and relative cheapness of Coade stone another and an important reason for the success of the manufactory in its early years was the close attention paid to prevalent fashion. This feature of the firm's wares can be seen in the four Egyptian Lionesses illustrated in Colour Plate 46.

The style of these magnificent recumbent models is closely associated with the Regency period, although the lionesses are, in fact, copies of a famous pair of

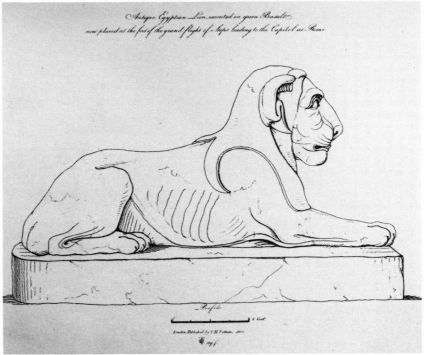

Plate 4:14. *Two of the original set of four Coade stone terms on the approach to the Rotunda, Croome Court, Worcestershire*

Plate 4:15. *Illustration from C H Tatham's* Etchings of Ancient Ornamental Architecture, *1799-1800, showing one of the classical antique granite lions on which the Coade examples in Colour Plate 46 are based*

antique granite models which still flank the steps leading to the Capitol in Rome. However, instances of the models' considerable popularity in the first quarter of the nineteenth century can be seen in, for example, C H Tatham's highly influential publication, *Etchings of Ancient Ornamental Architecture...*,[45] which includes an illustration showing one of the antique originals (Plate 4:15). Furthermore, several reduced-size copies of these lions were important elements of the interior decoration used by the leading exponent of the Regency style, Thomas Hope, for his house in Duchess Street.

However, some sixteen years before the turn of the century the Coade manufactory was producing copies, for the 1784 *Descriptive Catalogue...* includes: '53 An Egyptian Lioness. (Plinth) 4ft 0in, by 1ft 4in. 5 5s 0d',[46] and this must refer to the same model as those shown in Colour Plate 46, not only because of the similar dimensions, but also because the manufactory's late eighteenth century publication showing their etched designs, *Etchings of Coade's Artificial Stone Manufactory* (copy in the Sir John Soane's Museum), includes a drawing of the Egyptian Lioness, the plinth of which is marked 53.

It should, however, be noted that the majority of extant Coade models of these Lionesses which have been seen, including these, which are indented 'COADE & SEALY LAMBETH 1810', tend to date more towards the Regency period rather than earlier. It is also interesting to note that David Watkins' research on Thomas Hope shows he visited the manufactory in 1818 and a year later purchased a model of a 'Lion'. This seems likely to have been one of these Egyptian Lionesses, for an identical model is known to have adorned the gardens of his country house, The Deepdene.

This set of four Lionesses again clearly illustrates the great versatility the manufactory was capable of, for as can be seen in Colour Plate 46, models could be had with or without the simple plinth. One other point of interest is the joint line between the body and the extended front paw on the Lioness on the right. This paw now detaches completely from the body, and must have been modelled separately from the main body and only joined together with slip later in the process of manufacture.

Blashfield's Terracotta

Like Coade stone, Blashfield's terracotta is a vitrified ceramic body with a matt finish. It has a smooth granulated surface and varies in colour from a light yellow or beige to a dull orange (Colour Plates 47 and 48). Some of the ornaments are identifiable by the presence of an often small indented mark: 'J.M. BLASHFIELD', 'BLASHFIELD STAMFORD', 'BLASHFIELD MILLWALL' or 'J.M. BLASHFIELD, STAMFORD' (Plate 4:16), at times accompanied by the model number.

After 1872 the indentation is: 'THE STAMFORD TERRA COTTA COMPANY (BLASHFIELD'S) LIMITED', (Plate 4:17). These indentations are often difficult to distinguish, for the lettering is only one quarter of an inch high and often over or under pressed into the terracotta. Other models are not marked at all, such as the finial in Plate 4:18, whilst a few, such as the pair of fountains at Castle Ashby, are indented with a much clearer and larger mark. Few Blashfield ornaments are dated.

In line with many of the other clay-based artificial stones, Blashfield's terracotta is quite durable and has none of the veining or deposits that occur in a natural stone. In comparison to Coade stone, it is not quite as durable a compound, for although several Blashfield ornaments, such as the tazza vase in Plate 4:21, still retain much of their crisp details, others, such as the vase in Plate 4:20 are beginning to deteriorate.

Plate 4:16. Detail of the interior of a tazza bowl at Kew Gardens. The indentation 'J.M., BLASHFIELD. STAMFORD' dates it to between 1858/9 and 1872

Plate 4:17. Detail from the base of a vase, now used as the centrepiece of a fountain, illustrating the small indentation found on wares produced by Blashfield between 1872 and 1875

Blashfield's method of manufacture was very similar to that of the Coade works, in that a special clay formula was pressed into plaster moulds and allowed to harden sufficiently for the pieces to be removed and assembled. After a further period of drying the terracotta was fired in a muffled kiln until vitrified. Blashfield certainly admired the durability of the Coade wares for in *An Account of the History and Manufacture of Ancient and Modern Terra Cotta...*[47] he relates that Coade pieces 'are in as perfect condition as when first made, while it is common to observe the stone-work adjoining or supporting them in a state of mouldering decay'. Blashfield goes on to describe in some detail his method of manufacture:

The plaster moulds should be tolerably dry (that is, the water used in mixing the plaster, with which they are made, should have partially evaporated) before they are used. For terra cotta work, sheets of clay are beaten on a bench to the consistency of painter's putty, and pressed by hand into these moulds. According to the magnitude of the work and the weight it may have to sustain, the thickness of the clay is determined and arranged, and here consists a part of the art it would be impossible to describe, and which requires years of experience in such matters to produce great works, and fire them with certainty of success.

After the clay has been allowed to dry a little in the plaster mould, the latter is removed, and a clay *moulded* article is exhibited — more properly speaking, a clay casting or impression is exhibited, but moulding is the potter's term for such work. Upon this clay article the joints and seams of the mould are seen as upon a plaster cast, and the same amount of care and skill is required for their removal. In all works of art this is done by a skilled workman or artist, who at the same time carefully goes over the work, and undercuts such parts as are necessary, and repairs any defects which appear on the surface of the impression. The work is then left to dry gradually, and lest it should become twisted it must be carefully watched, and in the case of statues props and supports will be required. The drying of large and valuable works, their subsequent removal to the kiln and the process of burning will cause much anxiety to the manufacturer. One mistake or slight accident may totally destroy an original work of several hundred pounds' value.

After the moulded article has become sufficiently dry for baking, it is conveyed to a kiln, and requires careful handling, as it is very fragile and easily chipped; and when the kiln is filled with articles, a slow fire is at first made, and gradually quickened; the articles are baked and become terra cotta. The heat should be of sufficient intensity to blend and partially vitrify the materials of which the mass is composed without melting or distorting the ware. As soon as this temperature is obtained, the firing is stopped, and all apertures closed, to prevent the admission of cold air. When the kiln has cooled, the articles are withdrawn, and unless requiring to be painted and glazed, are finished.

Great destruction sometimes takes place in the burning, and considerable care is required in the management of stacking the kiln, and in protecting the goods from violent contact with the flame. The kilns are reverberatory, and require to be of great thickness, and well bound together with iron to keep them from bursting asunder when red hot within.[48]

From further publications, often compiled from information supplied by Blashfield, more is known about his method of manufacture than that of similar manufactories' methods. His wares, which consisted of 'clays of Dorset and Devon, with silica, and other fusible bodies',[49] were relatively non-porous. This was achieved by carefully washing the formula and passing it through a sieve, comprising forty meshes per square inch for the fine ware, and twenty-eight meshes per square inch for the ordinary ware,[50] and the subsequent firing of the clay which vitrified the surface. The clay (which at first appears to have been obtained on the Earl of Leicester's estate at Holkham Hall in Norfolk) was left in the plaster moulds for 'about an hour's time',[51] and once the various parts were assembled to form the complete ornament, any 'twisting' was generally caused by it being 'imperfectly dressed'.[52]

By 1866 Blashfield had patented his own kiln, a diagram of which is illustrated in 'Terra Cotta Work at the New Dulwich College. . .'[53] Like that of the Coade works, this was a muffled kiln and the wares were placed within a brickwork lining so protecting them from 'violent contact with the flame'.[54] Charles Barry, the architect (1795-1860), relates that this method of firing produced wares that were 'more uniformly burnt, and never discoloured by the sulphur from the coals',[55] but the process required 'a little more coal'.[56]

The manufactory

Little is recorded of the early years of James Marriot Blashfield (1811-1882). He is known to have been a partner in Wyatt, Parker & Co a firm producing building and other associated materials. During the nineteenth century Wyatt, Parker & Co was run by various members of the Wyatt family, and although in the early years they were primarily involved with the manufacture of Roman Cement (which Parker had invented), by 1840 the business had expanded into the manufacture of plaster, mastic, scagliola and tessellated pavements as well as the importation of marble.[57] The company had substantial premises in London at Blackfriars and Millwall, as well as at Northfleet in Kent, but in 1846 it was sold for unknown reasons (perhaps due to the increase in the number of other firms producing cement), and Blashfield purchased the Millwall works.

The precise nature of Blashfield's involvement in Wyatt, Parker & Co is unclear. He assembled a variety of ornamental works for the company's catalogue of *Figures, Vases, Fountains &c. . .*,[58] and may have worked as a designer, but he was also involved with several independent commercial ventures. During the late 1830s, perhaps in connection with Wyatt, Parker & Co, he had been making tesserae and tiles, but in his own words was forced to 'surrender all interest in it to the manufacturer Herbert Minton'.[59] Blashfield was also involved in the purchase of several leases in Kensington Palace Gardens between 1843 and 1847 with the intention of building, but this venture, too, was to prove unsuccessful, and in 1847 he was declared bankrupt.[60]

His bankruptcy must only have been a minor set back, for he managed to retain his works at Millwall which, in 1848 according to an advertisement in *The Builder,* was still producing 'ROMAN CEMENT', which 'made according to the specifications of Parker's Patent may be had genuine of J M Blashfield. . .Also Plaster, Mastic, Terras, Bricks, Tiles etc'.[61] In the same year Blashfield was to start producing a compound he had been interested in for some years, terracotta. As early as 1839 he had, according to Charles Barry, 'employed Bubb' (James George Bubb, one of the Coade manufactory's modellers who had set up a short-lived terracotta manufactory[62]) 'to make experiments at Canford, for Sir John Guest, on Lord de Manley's clays, for making terra cotta for use in building model cottages, and a small quantity of moulded bricks, tiles and ornaments were made at that place',[63] but Bubb's health was deteriorating and Blashfield temporarily gave up this attempt to establish a terracotta manufactory.

During the following years Blashfield maintained his interest in terracotta, continuing experiments with different formulae,[64] even supplying moulds of the Borghese and Medici Vases to Herbert Minton in the mid-1840s.[65]

In 1854 he took out a patent for 'Improvements in the Manufacture of China, Pottery, Bricks, and other Articles manufactured for the most part of Clay',[66] and in the following year published *An Account of the History and Manufacture of Ancient and Modern Terra Cotta,* to which was subjoined *A Catalogue of Five Hundred Articles, made of Patent Terra Cotta, by J M Blashfield.* This descriptive *Catalogue. . .* included a few architectural items such as chimney pots, capitals and brackets, but consisted mainly of ornamental items such as vases, fountains, busts and statues. Like those of the Coade manufactory, these ornamental items were taken from a variety of sources including both antique and contemporary sculpture, as well as models copied from those produced by Wyatt, Parker & Co, whilst others were designed by Blashfield himself. Furthermore some of the models in the *Catalogue* feature designs by Owen Jones[67] and C R Cockerill[68] as well as works derived from or by the sculptors (or modellers) John Bell,[69] James Pulham,[70] Fiamingo,[71] Weigall,[72] Roubiliac,[73] Chantrey,[74] Nollekens,[75] Cellini,[76] Pitts,[77] Nixon,[78] Rauch,[79] and Woodington.[80] To accompany the *Catalogue. . .* Blashfield also published the first of many booklets of engravings which illustrated these models, and declared them all to be 'warranted to stand both heat and frost'.[81]

These ornamental items were available relatively inexpensively. A 'Statue of Venus, 38 inches high. . .', for example, was available for £5 5s; John Bell's life-size statue of Erin could be had for £31 10s, whilst vases were available from £1 1s for a design by Owen Jones to £12 12s for a 'Large Roman Vase, with allegorical figures from an antique'.[82] Unfortunately, it has not been possible to discover comparative prices between Blashfield's ornamental wares and pieces executed in stone or marble, but Charles Barry indicates the relative inexpensiveness of Blashfield terracotta by comparing the principle floor windows made by Blashfield for Dulwich College, which cost £41 each, whilst the equivalent in Bath stone would have cost £57, and in Portland £86.[83]

Blashfield produced several garden ornaments for the Crystal Palace including a colossal nine foot figure of Australia, modelled by the sculptor John Bell (1812-1895), and four Tritons, also by Bell (an example of this model is seen in Plate 4:23). He also exhibited within the Palace a selection of his wares, including a fountain in the Renaissance Court (surmounted by a copy of Verrochio's Boy with a Fish), and these were favourably looked upon according to an article in the *Art-Journal:*

> It is, however, undoubtedly due to Mr Blashfield to say of him that he has carried his art beyond his competitors, and has achieved much that gives it the high character it may be made universally to assume. Several of his productions are copies, but many of them are original — designed, modelled, and 'baked' in his own establishment; and we rejoice to know that his efforts are appreciated, and that his trade in these works is very considerable. An examination of his stall will show that 'wants' in this way may be here supplied. All his productions are good; some of them being exceedingly beautiful as examples of design as well as workmanship.[84]

In 1858 Blashfield sold his works at Millwall and moved to Stamford in Lincolnshire. The reasons for this move are unclear, but it was probably due to the fact that a splendid clay existed at Stamford, and also because the town had to a certain extent been left behind by the Industrial Revolution and could provide a cheaper source of labour. An advertisement in *The Builder* provides an interesting insight into the sheer size of the Millwall works which, according to Blashfield, included 'The largest manufactory of Plaster of Paris in England'.[85] The advertisement reads:

TO CEMENT and PLASTER MANUFACTURERS, POTTERS, &c — TO BE SOLD or LET, with immediate possession, the whole of the valuable PLANT and MACHINERY known as 'BLASHFIELD'S CEMENT and TERRA COTTA WORKS', situate at Millwall, Isle of Dogs (nearly opposite the East Country Docks). The works have a river frontage of 180 feet, and a depth of 480 feet, with a back frontage to the West Ferry road. The quay has a depth of water in front of 9 feet at ordinary tides, upon which is a crane, worked by steam, capable of lifting and landing half a ton in one minute from shipping or craft. The cement and plaster works consist of two Roman cement and two Portland cement kilns, seven plaster ovens, three coke ovens with large drying floor over for cement slip, four large backs or reservoirs, with connected wash-mill, for washing and mixing clay and chalk for Portland cement, mill house with four floors and two pair of horizontal stones for grinding cement or coprolites, large vertical crushing mill, with sifting machinery for grinding and sifting plaster, a 20-horse high-pressure steam-engine, with boiler, supply pumps, and well, and also tank for a supply of fresh water for engine from the Thames. The whole complete, and in good working order. There are five large dry store vaults, capable of storing 500 tons of ground material. The chimney-shaft is about 100 feet above ground and is well executed in brickwork. The terra cotta works consist of three large pottery kilns for burning terra cotta (or, if required, stone-ware); two pug mills and sifting machinery, clay baths and bins, slip kiln, ten large workshops fitted with shelves and benches, large warehouse room, drying floor and experimental kiln, &c. There is a cooperage and carpenter's shop, lime shed, and stable, a dwelling house, with five rooms, kitchen and water-closet, counting-house, with three rooms and four dwelling-rooms for clerk or foreman above; smith's shop and forge, coal vaults, &c. The whole of the premises are in good condition, and securely enclosed, and are capable of being adapted to any large general business. In connection with the above an inland wharf and warehouse in the north-west part of London can be had at a moderate rent...[86]

On 14 March 1859 Blashfield's new works in Wharf Road, Stamford, were officially opened by a local dignitary, the Marquis of Exeter.[87] Production increased, new models were introduced to both the architectural and ornamental sides of the business and, as at Millwall, special models could be executed to clients' requirements. Like the Coade manufactory, Blashfield employed a large workforce of modellers (several Italian[88]) and firers, many of whom were skilled workmen. C F Hayward (who used Blashfield's terracotta for the Duke of Cornwall Hotel in Plymouth) says of the workmen: 'I was much pleased with the artistic skill displayed by the workmen — in fact I ought to say sculptors, for I believe there were several first-rate artists of the classic school engaged upon statues, vases &c, but the way in which my suggestions were met, and the ready adaptation of skill to the kind of work I wanted, enabled me effectually to co-operate with the workmen.'[89]

Like many of the nineteenth century manufacturers of art works, Blashfield exhibited at the international exhibitions, receiving two medals in the 1862 exhibition: one 'For Terra Cotta', the other 'For perfection in Manufacture and Beauty of Form'. Blashfield's stand (somewhat reminiscent of Sir John Soane's Museum) was recorded in a stereoscopic photograph by William England in which many of his garden ornaments were seen. These included a copy of the frieze from the Borghese Vase, a colossal bust of Homer, statues of Ceres and a maiden holding a ewer from models by Henry Hale, a life-size dog by Mrs Henry Heathcote, as well as several vases, including his copy of the Duke of Buckingham's vase and the Tempest vase, designed by Blashfield and modelled by Samuel Nixon (1803-1854). This photograph also showed Weigall's bust of Queen Victoria as well as the wide variety of other wares Blashfield was producing, including items for the interior and exterior of houses, such as figurines and cornices. Three years later he received a further medal for 'Fine Terra Cottas for Architectural Purposes', whilst at the 1867 Paris Exhibition he was awarded a Silver Medal, and he proudly advertised these achievements on the covers of his booklets of engraved designs. By 1870 his range of wares extended to over 1,400 pieces, vases of tazza form could be manufactured up to six feet in diameter, and ornaments had been supplied to, amongst others, the Royal Mausoleum at Windsor, Buckingham Palace, and even as far afield as Bombay, New Zealand and Australia.[90]

In 1872 Blashfield ran out of money and once again was declared bankrupt. The business was bailed out by several local businessmen including the Marquis of Exeter,[91] and was resurrected as The Stamford Terra Cotta Company (Blashfield's) Limited, still under Blashfield's control. This brief reprieve did not last long. The country was in recession, and cheaper terracotta, which did not require the considerable amount of preparation used by Blashfield, was being produced. In 1875, the firm finally went into voluntary liquidation. Two sales were held at the works,[92] and the following year Blashfield returned to London, where he died in 1882.

There were several reasons why Blashfield was able to enjoy so many successful years in business, the most important of which was the quality of his terracotta, with 'its indestructibility and freedom from decay by the action of the weather'.[93] Other facts were also to play an important part: his many and varied connections with, for example, architects and members of the gentry, provided several lucrative commissions; and by prudently employing some of the leading sculptors of the day, or being allowed to take casts from works executed by them, Blashfield could offer the most fashionable wares to Victorian society.

Blashfield's terracotta garden ornaments

The finial (or, as Blashfield described it, a terminal) in Plate 4:18 and Colour Plate 47 is particularly interesting for it does not correspond exactly to any extant design published by Blashfield, but is a combination of several models. The main body, decorated with festoons and ribbon ties, and perhaps also the lower half (modified by the addition of ribbing) is taken from Blashfield's Terminal No 1321,[94] whilst the other components are variations on the socle of vase No 632,[95] and the cap from vase No 193.[96] The cap is surmounted by a finial of natural form which, like the lower half of the body, does not seem to correspond to any of Blashfield's designs, but this may be due to the fact that the upper half has been replaced with cement, so making identification difficult.

The festoons on the main body of the vase clearly indicate both the technical achievements possible as well as the durability of the terracotta. These would have

Plate 4:18. One of a set of four finials, Blashfield's terracotta, not indented but dating from between 1858/9 to 1872, Royal Botanic Gardens, Kew. Height approx 46ins. (See Colour Plate 47)

been separately moulded and applied to the vase prior to firing. Normally, building up in this way causes uneven thickness in the terracotta and so makes it more difficult to fire, but despite this such decorations were successfully produced and the terminal has stood the test of time, both retaining its crispness and remaining almost completely undamaged.

The colour fluctuations of Blashfield's terracotta are quite apparent when comparing this terminal (Colour Plate 47), which is much beiger in colour, with the vase and pedestal in Colour Plate 48.

None of the four Kew terminals is indented, but they are flanked by several vases which are indented 'J.M. BLASHFIELD. STAMFORD' on both the socles and the bowls (Plate 4:16). This suggests that if both vases and finials were supplied at the same time, which seems likely for they are all located in line on raised stone curbs, then they probably date from between 1858/9, the date Blashfield moved to Stamford, and 1872 when the business became limited.

The vase in Plate 4:19 and Colour Plate 48 is a reduced copy of the famous antique marble Warwick Vase (extensively reproduced during the nineteenth century), described as follows by Michaelis:

> The vase is in the shape of a large krater, the foot having been added by Piranesi. The lower half of the main body is very much rounded, and decorated all round the foot with acanthus leaves and above with a panther's skin. Above this part the vessel is compressed so as to give the effect of a shelf covered with a skin, and on this shelf lie on either side four Bacchic masks; in the centre, on a separate, low plinth, are Dionysus himself, crowned with

Plate 4:19. One of a pair of Warwick Vases raised on a pedestal, Blashfield's terracotta indented on the socle of the vase 'THE STAMFORD TERRA COTTA COMPANY (BLASHFIELD'S) LIMITED', dating between 1872 to 1875, the Private Gardens, Burghley House, Lincolnshire. Height of vase approx 24½ins; height of pedestal approx 32ins. (See Colour Plate 48)

Plate 4:20. Illustration of the engraving of the Warwick Vase in Blashfield's A Selection of Vases, Statues, Busts &c..., *1857*

ivy, the second with pine-sprays. On the opposite side, also on a low plinth, is Dionysus in the centre, bearded, without a wreath, and the bald-headed Silenus, crowned with ivy; beside them on the left is a pedum, on the right a thyrsus; at either end is a bearded Satyr-head, that on the left hand bald-headed and crowned with ivy, that on the right hand crowned with pine-leaves. Underneath the main body of the vase are attached strong handles, which are much twisted and finally run into delicate vine-sprays, and are so continued round the uppermost edge of the vessel. The vase, of very fine marble, is 1.70[m] high and has a diameter of 2.11[m]; its capacity is 81½ gallons.[97]

The Warwick Vase was discovered by Gavin Hamilton at Hadrian's Villa in 1771, and by 1778 had been brought to England (see pages 143-145).

The appearance of a pair of Blashfield's Warwick Vases at Burghley House is not unexpected for its owner, the Marquis of Exeter, had been associated with the works since its move to Stamford between 1858 and 1859. Indeed the Marquis had even presented a bust of Queen Victoria, made by Blashfield, to Prince Albert[98] and, as has already been mentioned, the Marquis was also involved in the refinancing of the business in the early 1870s. It is not known how much the Warwick Vase cost, but according to the indentation on the socle it must have been supplied after the business became limited in 1872. The model was available for many years prior to this and described in the *Catalogue*. . . 'Pattern. . .332. The Warwick Vase, 3 feet 7 inches in diameter. The heads upon this copy of the Warwick Vase were modelled by the late celebrated Mr PITTS, from the original antique marble now at Warwick Castle. . .£12 12s'. Blashfield also lists a small version of this vase 'Pattern. . .221. The Warwick Vase. . .Diameter 2 feet. . .£4 4s'. A single engraving for both vase patterns was used in his later illustrated booklets, such as that in the 1857 illustrated catalogue, *A Selection of Vases, Statues, Busts &c*. . . (Plate 4:20).

Blashfield's reference to William Pitts (1790-1840) is of interest, for Pitts had died some eight years prior to Blashfield starting his manufacture of terracotta, and Blashfield must, therefore, have obtained his copy from another source. So far there is no information as to when or for whom Pitts modelled the heads, but it is suggested that Blashfield, whilst assembling Wyatt, Parker & Co's catalogue of statues and ornaments,[99] had previously employed Pitts on behalf of that company to model the heads. If this was the case, then it seems likely that Pitts would have modelled them in the last years of his life.

The pedestal of the Warwick Vase in Plate 4:19 is decorated in relief with a floral wreath; also by Blashfield, this was one of his most common pedestal designs and was available in several sizes.

Blashfield's greatest ornamental commission was undertaken between 1861 and 1867 for the Marquis of Northampton's estate at Castle Ashby, Northamptonshire. Working in connection with the architect Digby Wyatt (1820-1877) and W B Thomas, the landscape gardener, Blashfield supplied a whole mass of architectural and ornamental items at a cost of £5,000.[100] Of the ornamental items, some were stock models that had been produced for many years, whilst others, such as the figures in the niches of the house, were specially modelled. Blashfield's balustrading (which extends to several hundred feet) is broken in a few places revealing marks where the clay was pressed into the moulds similar to that in the Coade figure in Plate 4:1. The balustrading is surmounted by numerous models of his vases, which also proliferate throughout the garden. Two examples are shown here. The design in Plate 4:21 was one of Blashfield's commonest models and many can be seen not only in the grounds of Castle Ashby, but also on several other estates. It is of tazza form (a shallow bowl and circular foot), and described in the *Catalogue*. . . as being taken 'from an antique at Bologna, surrounded by laurel leaves at top, and supported by acanthus and water leaves', priced in 1855 at £3 3s.[101] Fifteen years later the same design was still available, but it had been duplicated in two larger sizes, 'No 517, Height 46ins' and 'No 719, Height 54ins'.[102]

This Castle Ashby vase illustrates the most common form of deterioration of Blashfield's work; the vitrified surface, in this case the rim, has started to disintegrate revealing the less durable terracotta below, which is a palish-white speckled with pink fragments.

The second example (Plate 4:22) was produced by Blashfield from moulds taken from an antique marble vase discovered by Gavin Hamilton in 1773, and purchased a year later for £250 by the renowned collector Charles Townley (1737-1804). On Townley's death he left it, and the rest of his substantial

Plate 4:21. *Tazza vase, Blashfield's terracotta, not indented but dating between 1861 to 1867. Height approx 17ins. One of numerous tazza vases made by Blashfield for the Marquis of Northampton's estate, Castle Ashby*

THE MARQUIS OF NORTHAMPTON

Plate 4:22. *One of a pair of Townley vases, Blashfield's terracotta, not indented but dating from between 1861 and 1867, flanking the steps to the Formal Garden, Castle Ashby, Northamptonshire. Height approx 37ins*

THE MARQUIS OF NORTHAMPTON

collection, to the British Museum where it it now displayed in the Townley Room.[103]

Blashfield's copy varies from the original in that the socle, which does not have the bronze decoration found on the original, has been raised on a three inch plinth; furthermore the bas-relief scene which depicts Bacchanalian revelry, described by Blashfield in the *Catalogue...* as a 'Faun clothed in a panther's skin, holding a thyrsus; a Satyr bearing an amphora, and four male and four female Bacchantes', has been rotated in relation to the handles by approximately seventy degrees, probably due to the haphazard assembly of the clay impressions from the mould. In 1855 the model (No 151) was priced at twelve guineas, though it is not known how much this pair cost the Marquis of Northampton.

Plate 4:23. *Life-size figure of a Triton, Blashfield's terracotta, no visible indentation, 1857, the Radcliffe Infirmary, Oxford. Height originally 72ins*
THE RADCLIFFE INFIRMARY, OXFORD

Plate 4:24. *Illustration from Blashfield's* A Selection of Vases, Statues, Busts &c..., *1857, showing the base, now hidden, of the Triton in Plate 4:23*

The subject of the figure in Plate 4:23 is derived from a marble figure of Triton (the mythological son of the sea goddess Amphitrite) executed by the seventeenth century Italian sculptor Giovanni Lorenzo Bernini (1598-1680) for a fountain in the Piazza Barberini, Rome. Blashfield's Triton, which varies noticeably from that of Bernini, was modelled by the sculptor John Bell for the Crystal Palace Company, and, according to Blashfield's *Catalogue...*, weighed 'one ton before burning'. Blashfield's 1857 book of engravings, *A Selection of Vases, Statues, Busts &c*, describes No 171: 'Colossal statue of Triton...executed...in one piece...',[104] but this is misleading. Bell's original figure was no doubt hewn out of solid clay, but it is unlikely that it was ever fired, for it would have distorted as some parts 'burned' faster than others. Instead plaster moulds would have been taken and once the plaster had dried, the still malleable clay could then be picked from the newly formed moulds. Sheets of Blashfield's clay of an even thickness would then be pressed into these moulds and, after being left to dry and contract, removed. The now moulded pieces could then be assembled to form the complete figure and any finishing such as chasing or undercutting carried out. Although the original figure was executed from one block, Blashfield's copies were produced from many pieces, only the finishing and firing being done 'in one piece'.

This method, used for many of his ornaments, enabled Blashfield not only to produce four examples of this Triton for the Crystal Palace (a fact he was proud of advertising in most of his publications), but also to offer the model for sale in later years, such as the example shown here which he supplied to the Radcliffe Infirmary in 1857. *The Builder* reported: 'The fountain at the Infirmary is now completed...surmounted by a figure of a Triton, 6 feet high, modelled by Mr Bell, and executed in one piece of terra cotta by Mr Blashfield'.[105] It is not known exactly how much this cost,[106] but it seems likely to have been in the region of £50, for this is the price given in Blashfield's *Catalogue...* published two years earlier. The Triton is in remarkable condition, particularly for a fountain figure which is exposed not only to the weather but also to water; it has not cracked and the clarity of the details appears as fine as when it let the kiln, marred only by a thin layer of lichen.

Much of the Triton's tail, and all of its naturalistic base (clearly visible in Plate 4:24) has been lost by covering the plinth in the centre of the fountain with cement, which presumably hides any indentation.

Pulham's Artificial Stones

In the early 1840s James Pulham (1820-1898) established a manufactory at Hoddesdon in Hertfordshire for the production of Portland cement and the manufacture of garden ornaments in this medium. By 1843 the business had moved to Broxbourne, a few miles south of Hoddesdon, and it was here that the firm expanded into the production of terracotta ornaments.

James Pulham's connection with this line of work stems from his father (circa 1788-1838), also called James, who worked for a builder in Woodbridge, Suffolk, William Lockwood. Like his son, the elder James Pulham, seems to have been a competent modeller as well as a good businessman, and he was put in charge of Lockwood's new cement works in London which was established around 1820 at 22 Elder Street, Spitalfields. The business, which was involved with the production of a wide range of garden and architectural ornaments, blossomed and by 1827 the firm had moved to new premises on the Great Northern Road in Tottenham, north London. By this date the works were being run by Lockwood, whilst James and his brother Obadiah were doing much of the modelling. When Lockwood retired in 1834, Obadiah left and James took over much of the London business. On his death in 1838, his son followed in his footsteps.[107]

The manufactory

James Pulham's manufactory at Broxbourne took the form of a mock Elizabethan factory with several kilns, but much of this has been demolished and today only one kiln and the horse-driven grinding machine for pulverising the grog and components of the cement remain (Plate 4:25).[108]

The manufactory is particularly interesting, for not only was it producing two forms of clay-based artificial stone, but also a cement-based artificial stone. The

latter, Pulham's Portland cement, had, as Pulham wrote in 1845:

> A near resemblance to Portland stone in colour, hardness, and durability; its natural colour is that of Portland stone, and therefore it requires no artificial colouring. It has stood the test of twenty-four years' use, and remains perfect; it has even deceived the trade, the imitation is so complete; it is excellent both for exterior and interior purposes of stucco and mouldings, and for fountains, vases and even floors, &c; is capable of being trowelled to a very smooth face like marble, and hardens by the influence of the atmosphere. Simple washing is sufficient to clean it when dirty, and it does not vegetate so much as stone.[109]

Interestingly, very few of Pulham's garden ornaments in this medium have come to light, and this is perhaps due to its 'near resemblance to Portland stone'. However, it should be noted that weathered cement is easily identifiable once one knows what to look for, the two most obvious characteristics being pronounced airholes on the surface and reinforcing materials (often slate) where damage has occurred.

Of the clay-based artificial stone, which was no doubt produced using a similar method to that used by Coade or Blashfield, that which is most commonly found is of a buff colour, a little darker than Coade stone, whilst the other is of a rich pale red. The great difference between Pulham's cement and clay-based artificial stone is clearly seen in the discussion on one of Pulham's fountains (pages 196-197 and Plates 4:32 and 34).

Plate 4:26. View of part of the artificial stone rocks created by Pulham at Madresfield Court, near Malvern, in the late 1870s

The range of wares produced by the firm was considerable and included not only garden ornaments and architectural works, but also the formation of great cement rockeries, cliffs, ravines and bridges.[110] Although not strictly within the scope of this book, an examle of these great cement works is illustrated in Plate 4:26. The stone rocks at Madresfield Court form one of Pulham's most impressive creations with its cyclopean size boulders.

At the 1851 Great Exhibition, Pulham exhibited a variety of wares, including subjects in terracotta and cement. The *Art-Journal* was particularly enthusiastic about one Gothic terracotta vase, describing it as 'excellent in design and admirable workmanship...It stands on a granulated pedestal of similar character, which, like the vase, shows great sharpness and delicacy of execution.'[111] The design for this vase, which according to the *Art-Journal* was modelled by 'Mr J Pulham', is shown in Plate 4:27.

In 1859 Pulham's manufactory was the subject of an article in the *Art-Journal* and this provides some insight into the firm:

In the terra-cotta works of Mr James Pulham, at Broxbourne, there is very gratifying evidence that the science of his manufacture has received due attention. Hence he has been enabled to produce his 'granulated stone-like

188

terra-cotta', and his 'natural stone-colour cement'. Both are materials of great value and importance — both have already proved their practical capabilities, and, without doubt, when they become better known, both will be brought into widely extended use. The former of these materials, however, is the more valuable of the two, since, from the physical constitution of the mass, objects produced in it have less contraction, coupled with more general uniformity in texture, than can be obtained in any other clay.

In the matter of the applicability of terra-cotta to various purposes, which shall all of them be consistent with the qualities of that material, Mr Pulham finds before him a wide field, and one that has been but little explored. We were glad to observe that here, as in the case of scientific inquiries, Mr Pulham is acting upon sound principles. His kilns are employed for the production both of the commoner classes of articles for builders, and of those which may claim a more intimate association with Art. Thus it is, probably, that he obtains such employment, and realises those profits which enable him to issue from his establishment productions that, in a commercial sense, cannot 'pay', although it is through the instrumentality of these 'better things' that a reputation is often made, and so encouragement is given by which perseverance is ultimately rewarded. In both classes of objects Mr Pulham may widely extend the range of his operations with the utmost advantage; and, more particularly, he may anticipate the most gratifying results from the production of a class of works in which the distinctive qualities of both classes may be combined...The pages we have devoted to this subject contain engravings of about twenty of Mr Pulham's productions; and we have selected those examples which, for the most part, more particularly illustrate the terra-cottas of the higher order as works of Art. The selection was made from a very large number of works, of all classes and orders — some original and others copies — with but few (perhaps none) that can be considered objectionable to the instructed eye and the artistic mind. Amongst the vases there are two or three that will at once be recognised as having been familiar favourites for centuries; while others which will be no less readily distinguished, have been designed expressly for the manufacturer. These vases have been exclusively used, we believe, as decorations of gardens and conservatories, for which office they are eminently qualified, from the good tone of their colour and the sharpness of their manipulation. It would indeed have been a fortunate circumstance had a large number of these vases in terra-cotta occupied the places now filled in the gardens of the Crystal Palace with cold duplicates of some of the coldest and feeblest productions ever *manufactured* from marble.[112]

As mentioned in this article the great majority of Pulham's garden ornaments were taken from contemporary designs, rather than based on earlier works. To what extent these were modelled by the elder or younger James Pulham is unclear, for the only trade catalogues the author has seen date from the early years of this century, and these make scarce reference to the artists responsible. In the catalogue of the Great Exhibition Pulham was described as both a 'Designer and

Plate 4:27. The vase and pedestal by James Pulham exhibited at the 1851 Great Exhibition. According to the Art-Journal *the subject was modelled by 'Mr J Pulham'. So far no extant examples have come to light, but it is worth noting that four years later Blashfield's descriptive* Catalogue of Five Hundred Articles made of Patent Terra Cotta... *listed 'No 180. Gothic Vase, by PULHAM, exhibited at the Great Exhibition, 1851...£12 12s 0d'*

Colour Plate 44. Copy of the Medici Vase, Coade stone, not indented, the Royal Botanic Gardens, Kew (See Plate 4:3 and pages 167 and 168)

Colour Plate 45. One of a pair of Coade stone seats, indented 'COADE LAMBETH 1800', flanking the Temple, Parham Park, West Sussex. (See Plate 4:7 and pages 168 and 170)

Manufacturer', and this combined with the *Art-Journal* reference to him being the modeller of the Gothic vase (Plate 4:27), would suggest that he was responsible for at least some of the firm's designs.

Of the 142 ornaments illustrated in one of the firm's catalogues (which dates to around 1925), quite a number were models being produced by the 1870s, including the Preston Vase exhibited at the 1867 Paris Exhibition. Of copies of 'previous' works may be mentioned the antique Diana de Gabies, Antoine-Laurent Danton's Neapolitan Girl, Giambologna's ever popular statue of Mercury (Plate 4.28), and a rather extraordinary subject, the elder John Van Nost's figure of a kneeling Indian supporting a sundial (see page 48).

At the 1862 Exhibition, Pulham exhibited a number of vases and several fountains, including that illustrated in Plate 4:32, and a curious terracotta fountain consisting of four columns, each surmounted by a shell, surrounding a larger column, surmounted by a copy of Verrochio's famous bronze Putto with a Dolphin in Florence. Pulham, unlike one of his competitors, J M Blashfield, was not awarded a medal, but he was commended for his 'architectural decorations in terra-cotta and for a sound and durable material'.[113]

Three years later Pulham was joined by his son, and the firm became known as Pulham & Son. In 1871 they were employing forty men and nine boys, seemingly not that substantial a workforce, and this was perhaps due to James' policy: 'Mr Pulham aimed more at the quality than the quantity made: and it is said that he still carries out the rule he laid down, not to extend his business, but to keep it so that it is not too large to be under his own personal supervision'.[114]

191

Plate 4:28. Mercury, Pulham's terracotta, after the original by Giambologna, dating from the late nineteenth century, Madresfield Court, near Malvern. Height approx 84ins

By the 1880s the firm was primarily concerned with the garden ornament and landscape side of the business rather than the production of more architectural wares. The business grew from strength to strength, due not only to the nature and quality of the wares, but also to the services it could provide; complete grottoes could be created for clients, whilst the firm could also supply all the necessary components for formal gardens and terraces, such as balustrading statuary, fountains and urns.

An office was opened in London, first in Marylebone Road, then Finsbury Square and later Newman Street. In 1895 the firm's standing was greatly enhanced by the granting of a Royal warrant for its work for the Prince of Wales (later Edward VII) at Sandringham. In 1898, James Pulham died, and the business was continued by his son and grandson, James Robert Pulham (1873-1957).

The firm, which later extended into nurseries, continued in production until 1945 and was still producing cement wares during the twentieth century. However, the catalogue of circa 1925[115] mentions that cement was not used in their composition, and thus the firm must still have been producing terracotta ornaments at this date. This is interesting, for by then great numbers of cheaper and less durable terracottas were being imported, particularly from Italy.

The test of time has proved Pulham's terracotta to be as durable a compound as, for example, Blashfield's, a fact which is well illustrated by the tazza vases in Plates 4:30 and 31. These are both over 120 years old and clearly justify one contemporary account that Pulham's wares were 'so 'baked' as to be uninfluenced prejudically by weather'.[116] However, like other clay-based artificial stones, Pulham's terracotta is not invulnerable, and on some ornaments the semi-vitrified surface has weathered away, while on others, such as the fountain in Plate 4:32, damage has occurred as the result of sharp blows.

Pulham's cement-based artificial stone, although an adequate weather-resistant compound, is by no means as durable as his terracotta. This is clearly illustrated by the detail of the fountain bowl (Plate 3:34), which, although cracked and pitted (both of these being features which frequently occur on cement-based artificial stones), is in otherwise reasonable condition.

Plate 4:29. The Mercury fountain at Madresfield Court as it appeared in the early years of the twentieth century, showing the undamaged terracotta statue in the centre of Pulham's cement surrounding border

Manufacture of cement-based artificial stone ornaments

Unlike clay artificial stone, there are no contemporary descriptions of how cement-based artificial stone was produced. All one can say for certain is that ornaments were produced without being fired. However, something similar to one of the following methods may have been used.

Cement-based artificial stone ornaments are still manufactured today using a process which, for a life-size statue, for example, requires many separate rigid moulds (made nowadays from fibreglass), which are joined together to form the whole mould. After the relatively dry cement formula has been inserted into this mould and allowed to 'go off' (dry), the mould is dismantled piece by piece to reveal the completed ornament. However, this process does not easily allow the intricate undercuts found on many nineteenth century cement-based artificial stone ornaments, and although it could be that they were produced using a similar process, it seems unlikely.

Probably one of the two following processes was used. The first was similar to that used by the Coade and Blashfield manufactories for the production of their clay-based artificial stone, whereby the many components of one ornament were formed in plaster moulds and, after being allowed to dry and contract, were then joined together prior to being fired in the kiln. If this was the process used for cement-based stone, the problems involved with, for example, assembling a life-size statue must have been considerable, for unlike clay-based artificial stone ornaments, cement ones tend to be solid, and great difficulties would have arisen in trying to assemble a large semi-dry cement ornament, for even with an interior armature and reinforcing bars or slates (which frequently feature in these ornaments), the weight would have been considerable and extremely likely to distort the shape of the figure. Perhaps this method was used for smaller pieces, such as Austin & Seeley's entwined dolphin fountain in Plate 4:36, which is constructed from a number of separate pieces which have been cemented together.

The second method may have been similar to that used by bronze foundries, whereby the mould comprises a flexible compound (in the nineteenth century probably gelatine) held rigid by plaster. Once the formula had been allowed to dry the sectional plaster mould could be removed, followed by the flexible mould, which faithfully followed the contours of the original model. This flexible mould

could be twisted and contorted in order to free it from the cast statue. This process would certainly have allowed Austin & Seeley to produce the magnificent Triton in Plate 4:41 in one piece, complete with intricate details.

Pulham's artificial stone garden ornaments

The firm supplied a variety of their wares to Earl Beauchamp's estate at Madresfield Court, near Malvern. The impressive rock garden (Plate 4:26) was created in the late 1870s and is signed 'This Work by M.J. Pulham Broxbourne AD 1878.79...Fini July 18'.

The firm was also employed in later years at Madresfield. One of the twentieth century catalogues cites as testimony to their success a number of extracts from satisfied clients' letters, including one dated 1890 from 'The Rt. Hon. Earl Beauchamp', which reads 'I am well satisfied with what you have done'.[117] Unfortunately no reference to what work was done has been discovered in the archives, but perhaps the Earl was referring to the over-life-size terracotta statue of Mercury after Giambologna, which still survives in the gardens (Plate 4:28).

This statue and its border had been erected by 1918, when it was featured in Gertrude Jekyll's *Garden Ornament*[118] (Plate 4:29), but was almost certainly supplied earlier than this, for the book is comprised predominantly from photographs published in earlier *Country Life* articles.

The Pulhamite cement-based stone border, which surrounded the statue, remains *in situ*, although crumbling in places, but the Mercury has since been removed to another part of the garden.

As is clearly apparent, the Mercury has suffered extensively at some point, all the limbs have been broken and repaired, Mercury's caduceus (wand) has been lost and, interestingly, an iron bar is visible in the left leg. This must be a later addition to strengthen the figure, for if it had been fired with the iron bar, the intense heat would have caused the figure to blow up. It could be that this iron

bar is part of a comparatively modern restoration, but it is more likely that it was inserted after the figure had been fired and cemented in place to reinforce the statue which, standing on one leg, would have been particularly vulnerable to damage.

Vases of tazza form were immensely popular during the Victorian era, and this is reflected in the *oeuvre* of Pulham's manufactory. Indeed, in the firm's circa 1925 catalogue, of the forty-seven vases illustrated over half were of this form, and two of the more commonly found terracotta tazzas are illustrated in Plates 4:30 and 31. The former is described in the circa 1925 catalogue as the 'Westonbirt Vase', priced at £13 10s. It was also available in a slightly smaller form (twenty-one and a half inches higher rather than thirty inches) as the 'Moreton Vase', priced at a mere £6.

The second vase, with its typically Victorian heavy relief on the frieze, clearly bears the firm's oval indented stamp mark, 'PULHAMS TERRA-COTTA BROXBOURNE' on the base. Thus the vase must date to some time prior to 1865, for the firm's mark was replaced at this date with 'PULHAM & SON BROXBOURNE'. Like the terracotta vase in Plate 4:30, this model was still being produced in 1925, when it was listed as the 'Newport Tazza' costing £8 5s. The same model was also available in a more ornate form, whereby for an extra £1 it could be produced with rams' heads extending from the lower body of the vase. The moulding on the base beneath the socle is interesting. On the right and left a moulding is clearly visible which does not appear on the front and back. It thus seems probable that the tazza was originally intended to surmount a pedestal which formed part of a balustrade, with the coping (also produced by the firm) fitting up flush on each unmoulded side.

As has already been mentioned, the way these clay-based artificial stones were manufactured enabled infinite variations to be made; thus the varying mouldings and optional rams' heads would have been an easy matter for the manufactory to produce.

Plate 4:30. One of a pair of vases of tazza form, the 'Westonbirt Vase', Pulham's terracotta, circa 1860. Height approx 30ins
SOTHEBY'S, SUSSEX

Plate 4:31. One of a pair of vases of tazza form, the 'Newport Tazza', Pulham's terracotta, bearing the firm's oval indentation mark 'PULHAM'S TERRA-COTTA BROXBOURNE', circa 1860. Height approx 27½ins
SOTHEBY'S, SUSSEX

Plate 4:32. Fountain in Pulham's terracotta and Pulhamite stone, after a fountain by Tribolo in the Villa Petraia, near Florence, 1862, Dunorlan Park, Tunbridge Wells. Height approx 15 feet
TUNBRIDGE WELLS BOROUGH COUNCIL

One of the firm's monumental garden ornaments was exhibited by Pulham at the 1862 exhibition. Standing over fifteen feet in height, it was derived from a marble fountain by Niccolo Tribolo (1485-1550) now in the Villa Petraia, outside Florence, which is surmounted by a bronze statue by Giambologna of Florence Rising from the Waves. However, Pulham's form of this fountain (Plate 4.32) has many variations. Giambologna's statue was replaced by a terracotta figure of Hebe after Canova, which Jewitt described as 'a perfection in burning...very sucesful'.[119] Other variations include the upper bowl, which on Tribolo's fountain is in the form of an inverted platter; the putti decorating the side of the main bowl on Pulham's fountain are kneeling as opposed to standing, whilst the upper base of this fountain is decorated with four duplicate Naiads, as opposed to the different

196

Plate 4:33. Pulham's fountain at Dunorlan Park in 1872 showing the statue of Hebe after Canova and the four kneeling Triton figures, now disappeared

TUNBRIDGE WELLS REFERENCE LIBRARY

Plate 4:34. Detail of the Dunorlan fountain illustrating the difference between Pulham's clay-based medium (the garlands of flowers, for example) and the cement-based medium (the bowl) which is of a much coarser nature

TUNBRIDGE WELLS BOROUGH COUNCIL

water deities found on Tribolo's. Furthermore Pulham accentuated and altered the bas-reliefs between the Naiads, as well as those on the column supporting the upper bowl, and he exchanged the hexagonal panelled base, for one of a very curious style, almost of an engineering nature, with tremendously deep grooves.

By at least 1867, probably soon after the exhibition, the fountain had been supplied to Henry Reed's estate of Dunorlan, just outside Tunbridge Wells, where it remains today (Plate 4:33). Unfortunately it has suffered extensive damage. The border, which is made of Pulhamite stone (cement), used to be adorned with four identical kneeling Triton figures which spouted water into the pool, and were no doubt made of terracotta, but these have since disappeared. So far no extant examples of the figures have been traced, which is a pity as a model of a kneeling Triton figure (raised on a tazza bowl), together with a number of other items, was awarded a medal at the 1871 Paris Exhibition. As is also clearly visible in Plate 4:32, the statue of Hebe has disappeared — with the exception of her ankles. Furthermore, quite a number of pieces have broken off due, no doubt, to vandals; indeed the first time the fountain was examined by the author he found several throwing stones at it.

The detail of the fountain's main bowl (Plate 4:34) clearly illustrates the difference between Pulham's clay- and cement-based media. The Pulhamite stone bowl is of a much coarser nature than the delicate and smooth buff-coloured terracotta, with its fine details, such as the garlands of flowers, which have been almost unaffected by exposure to the elements.

The terracotta decoration on this bowl is applied and must have been fired separately. Apart from this the bowl and base are totally undecorated. Whether Pulham considered it unnecessary to make the main bowl in the same medium is unclear, but both the bowl and the base are of massive proportions, and were perhaps too large for him to fire in one piece.

Colour Plate 47. One of a set of four finials, Blashfield's terracotta, not indented, Royal Botanic Gardens, Kew. (See Plate 4:18 and pages 180-181)

Austin & Seeley's Artificial Limestone

Austin & Seeley's artificial limestone, unlike the clay-based artificial stones such as Blashfield's, is a cement substance with a granulated, pitted surface, a little similar to coarse sand. The compound consisted of 'Portland cement, (first patented by Aspdin & Beverley of Wakefield), combined with broken stone, pounded tile, and coarse sand',[120] and was no doubt formed in moulds, for it was manufactured without the 'application of heat'.[121] Their ornaments, which vary in colour from a dull grey-white to a light brown-yellow, are rarely marked and those that are were only crudely indented by hand.

In comparison to natural stones such as Portland (which the manufactory claimed its compound most closely resembled) and Bath stone, Austin & Seeley's ornaments are distinguishable by the fact that they have no veining or deposits and, unlike many other cement artificial stone compounds, are quite durable

Colour Plate 48. One of a pair of Warwick Vases raised on a pedestal, Blashfield's terracotta, indented on the socle of the vase 'THE STAMFORD TERRA COTTA COMPANY (BLASHFIELD'S) LIMITED', the Private Gardens, Burghley House, Lincolnshire. (See Plate 4:19 and pages 182-183)

However, they are not always identifiable, for they can easily be mistaken for natural stone. Indeed, at times, only the presence of joint lines and the excessive cracking that so frequently occurs in cement-based artificial stones (and on occasion heavy weathering uncovering the larger particles below the surface), reveal their true nature. Despite this detrimental cracking, which accelerates deterioration, it is a fairly weatherproof compound, and an 1851 advertisement claimed that 'being *waterproof* [it] is safer to use for fountains than any stone, excepting granite'.[122] Although this claim has been partially proven by the test of time, it is somewhat exaggerated, as the fountain in Plate 4:36 reveals. It still retains remarkable detail, for example in the dolphins' heads and scales, but the broken bowl and damage to the thinner parts clearly illustrate the structural weakness of the compound. In comparison to the durability of Coade stone or Blashfield's terracotta, Austin & Seeley's limestone is not as fine a compound

The manufactory

Exactly when Felix Austin, a sculptor,[123] started manufacturing his artificial stone ornaments is unclear. According to Charles Barry[124] it was around the late 1820s, and this can be substantiated by an advertisement placed in *The Builder* in 1857: 'During 30 years this material has been in use in the highest quality residences'.[125] However, the business, which was based at 1-4 Keepell Row, New Road, Regent's Park (later 371-375 Euston Road), is first recorded in the Post Office directories in 1825.[126] Whether the ornaments were actually produced at this address is doubtful. According to one of the firm's later advertisements, the manufactory of the cement was located near 'the Thames Tunnel, Rotherite',[127] and thus it seems reasonable to assume that only the finished ornaments were displayed at Keepell Row.

Unlike other major manufacturers of artificial stone who published catalogues of engraved designs, such as Coade or Blashfield, Austin & Seeley appear to have marketed their wares on a more economical basis. One advertisement states that 'a list of designs... [could] be forwarded',[128] and these appear to have been supplemented by either sending drawings or, much more frequently, tracings of drawings, to perspective clients. A small selection of these drawings and tracings, from the firm's correspondence with Lady Pembroke at Wilton House in the 1840s, is reproduced in Appendix II. The seeming failure to publish sets of designs is unfortunate and must account to a great extent for the considerable lack of information on the manufactory.

On the demise of the artificial stone manufactory owned by Van Spangen Powell & Co[129] in the late 1820s, Austin is known to have purchased 'a large number of [their] models and moulds'.[130] What subjects these moulds and models represented is unknown, but they presumably provided the bulk of Austin's models in the early years.

A short article on Austin's artificial stone in the 1834 edition of *The Architectural Magazine* provides some information on the business. The compound's hardness and durability were admired, and items could be supplied 'at a price (as may easily be conceived) extremely moderate when compared with that of real stone'.[131] This article is predominantly concerned with the manufactory's fountains, and several designs are illustrated, many of which could be seen at 'Mr Austin's very interesting Museum'[132] (presumably the showroom at Keepell Row). However, several of these fountains incorporate similar features, suggesting that at this date Austin's range was limited. The text goes on to relate that Austin had supplied many such items to numerous customers, but only two are cited: a fountain comprising a tazza bowl surmounted by a foliate stem and a crystal upper bowl, for the Pantheon Bazaar; and a fountain comprising three herons or cranes, supporting a tazza bowl, for Lady Amherst at Montreal House, Kent.

Sometime between 1836 and 1843, Austin went into partnership with another sculptor, John Seeley (born 1789), and the firm became known as Austin & Seeley. Coinciding with this, the *oeuvre* of the manufactory increased to the extent that a two page advertisement in *The Builder* lists 'Pier ornaments, such as Pine-Apples, &c...Tazzas, and Vases, to the extent of nearly One Hundred Models... Fountains from £6 and upwards; Monumental Urns; Figures — Statues from the Antique, as well as some chaste subjects of modern design, Animals, Birds, &c',[133] and it illustrates a number of these, including several animals and fountains as well as a number of modern and classical inspired urns. It is likely that the number of 'Pier ornaments' is misleading, for it suggests that nearly one hundred completely different models were available. Considering that many of the manufactory's

82.   FOUNTAIN. MESSRS. SEELEY & CO.

Plate 4:35. Seeley & Co's fountain exhibited at the 1851 Great Exhibition as illustrated in The Official Descriptive and Illustrated Catalogue of the Works of Industry of all Nations

fountains frequently incorporated the same elementary parts, it is probable that nearly one hundred models *were* available, but that many of these were basically of the same design, with slight variations, for example, in the treatment of the socles, caps, handles, etc.

At the 1851 Great Exhibition the firm exhibited a monumental fountain 'suitable for the market-place of a provincial town'.[134] Designed by J B Papworth (1775-1847) it was clearly a remarkable exhibit, standing over twenty feet high,

Colour Plate 49. Thalia (the Muse of Comedy), one of a set of ten figures of Apollo and the Nine Muses, Doulton's terracotta. (See Plate 4:43 and page 211)
SOTHEBY'S

Colour Plate 50. Apollo, one of a set of ten figures with the Nine Muses, Doulton's terracotta. (See Plate 4:44 and page 211)
SOTHEBY'S

Colour Plate 51. Melpomene (the Tragic Muse), one of a set of ten figures of Apollo and the Nine Muses, Doulton's terracotta. (See Plate 4:45 and page 211)
SOTHEBY'S

with water dropping through four levels before pouring out on to free-standing Naiads (Plate 4:35). The other exhibit, a Mercury after Giambologna, was located outside the building. Curiously, only Seeley's name is recorded in the official catalogue, and Austin's name is again omitted from the firm's advertisements of that year. Consequently it seems reasonable to suppose that by this date Austin had either died or been bought out by Seeley. Whatever the case, the manufactory was to resume trading under the name of Austin & Seeley in later years.

Like many of the artificial stone manufactories, the firm was also producing a range of architectural fittings such as chimney pots, although the majority of the business was involved with the manufacture of garden ornaments. The many models encompassed a wide range of stylistic influences. Apart from those acquired from Van Spangen Powell & Co, both Austin and Seeley no doubt modelled their own pieces for reproduction in their artificial limestone, for both were sculptors in their own right. These models would obviously have included modern designs, but other designers were also used to reproduce fashionable designs, amongst whom

Colour Plate 52. Ornate fountain and border, Doulton's terracotta. (See Plate 4:46 and pages 213 and 215)
SOTHEBY'S, SUSSEX

may be mentioned Papworth, Barry and Smirke. Popular antique works were still in demand during the period, and the firm was consequently supplying models of such subjects as the Warwick and Borghese Vases and the Calydonian Boar. Of the many varied designs produced some, such as the fountain or jardinière in Plate 4:36 and the Eagle in Plate 4:40, are of reasonable artistic merit, but others, such as the atrocious figure of Ceres (advertised by the firm in 1843), leave much to be desired.

The firm is believed to have continued production at least until 1872.[135] Although its output does not seem to have been substantial, this may be due purely to the lack of documentation on the firm, and the author believes that many models survive today, incorrectly identified as freestone ornaments.

Plate 4:36. Jardinière or fountain, Austin & Seeley's artificial limestone, not indented, mid-nineteenth century, the Swiss Garden, near Biggleswade, Bedfordshire. Height approx 72ins
BEDFORDSHIRE COUNTY COUNCIL

Plate 4:37. Detail of dolphin scales illustrating the durability of Austin's formula
BEDFORDSHIRE COUNTY COUNCIL

Austin & Seeley's artificial limestone garden ornaments

In the Swiss Garden, near Biggleswade, Bedfordshire, stands a damaged artificial stone jardinière or fountain (Plate 4:36). Raised on a natural stone plinth, it is in a dilapidated state, the mouths of the three entwined dolphins and their tails have been seriously damaged, and the tazza bowl which used to surmount them now lies shattered beside it on the grass.

The fountain is not marked, and to date no information has come to light indicating when it was supplied; it can, however, be identified as one of Austin & Seeley's products by the fact that it corresponds to one of Austin's models. It was available by at least 1834,[136] and from one of the firm's later advertisements it appears that it was designed by one Barry, presumably the architect Charles Barry. The advertisement reads: 'The fountain as designed by Mr Barry for the Queen's Park, Brighton, viz, a pair of Grecian Tazzas resting on the tails of three entwined dolphins. . . £90 0s'.[137]

Whether the Swiss Garden model (which, if it did have the second tazza mentioned in the advertisement, has since lost it) was originally used as a fountain is unclear. Austin certainly intended it to be, for the design is illustrated in several contemporary publications[138] with water spouting from each dolphin's mouth and nostrils, as well as pouring over the upper bowl. However, the Swiss Garden example does not have a surround or basin, and as such may well have been intended only for use as a jardinière, although the possibility that the basin was filled in in later years cannot be ruled out.

The surface of the dolphins (Plate 4:37) clearly illustrates the durability of Austin's formula, each scale remains remarkably crisp, as is also the case with the features on the heads. Even the squat naturalistic plinth which supports the entwined dolphins has been almost unaffected by exposure to the weather, and a section of egg-and-dart moulding on the bowl (not visible in the photograph) is also in fine condition.

The ornament was constructed comparatively simply: each of the three dolphins was produced individually (allowing the manufactory to offer single dolphins as free-standing fountains) and formed in two pieces, the head and the tail. The three tail sections were cemented together, and the heads then attached: these joint lines are clearly visible running horizontally just above the head of each dolphin. The bowl appears to have been formed in one, as was the plinth.

One of the firm's more common architectural fountains can be seen in the Italian Gardens of Tottenham House, Wiltshire. This is a simple design comprising a tazza bowl raised on a socle and pedestal, surrounded by a border twenty feet in diameter and made in sections which, like the rim of the bowl, is decorated with an egg-and-dart moulding (Plate 4:38).

Tazza bowls were one of the mainstays of the firm's production, and were produced in a whole range of forms and sizes, ranging in diameter from two feet five inches to fifteen feet, for use either as vases or, as is the case in the Tottenham model, as the bowl for a fountain. Indeed of the seventeen fountains listed in one of the firm's advertisements, at least ten incorporated one or more tazzas.

The date this fountain was supplied is unclear, but it was certainly in place by 1851, for the firm advertised a fountain 'as erected for the Marquis of Ailesbury, at Tottenham Park'[139] in that year. Thus it has been exposed to the elements for at least 130 years and, although damaged in places, retains much of its original detail; the bowl for example (Plate 4:39), despite having cracked in several places (on the side not visible in the illustration) remains in remarkable condition, the moulding on the rim retaining a clarity comparable with an iron casting or even Coade stone. However, the overall deterioration does not justify one of Austin's more extravagant claims, that his compound was 'more durable, and considerably superior to Portland stone'.[140]

Flanking a lawn at the Swiss Garden at Biggleswade is a pair of majestic eagles (Plate 4:40). These are indented with half-inch letters on the base 'F. AUSTIN LONDON 1836'. They are the only examples of the manufactory's models the author knows of which are marked, suggesting that either this pair, or at least the original pair, may well have been modelled by Austin himself. Unfortunately, there is no known information which corroborates this, but the fact that the

Plate 4:38. Fountain, Austin & Seeley's artificial limestone, not indented, circa 1845, Tottenham House, Wiltshire. Diameter approx 20 feet

THE EARL OF CARDIGAN

Plate 4:39. Detail of the fountain in Plate 4:38. Although cracked in several places the bowl is still in remarkable condition, the egg-and-dart moulding on the rim retaining much of the original crispness

THE EARL OF CARDIGAN

206

Plate 4:40. One of a pair of eagles, Austin & Seeley's artificial limestone, indented 'F. AUSTIN LONDON 1836', the Swiss Garden, near Biggleswade, Bedfordshire. Height approx 36ins
BEDFORDSHIRE COUNTY COUNCIL

manufactory appears rarely to have marked its ornaments does suggest that there was something special about this model.

Both figures have been extensively repaired (including a protective layer of paint), but much of the original detail remains in remarkable condition, in particular the head and the flowing feathers on the chest and wings.

The fact that the eagles wings are spread out would tend to make them more vulnerable to damage, but this weakness is the statues' strength, as they are far grander than they would be in a more conservative pose which would, of course, have been easier to manufacture.

The impressive over-life-size figure of Triton raised on three dolphins and blowing his conch (Plate 4:41) could easily be (and was when it was sold in 1984), mistaken for natural stone, for its artificial nature was particularly well camouflaged by a combination of moss and mineral deposits remaining from the days when it spouted water.

The figure is particularly interesting, for according to one of the firm's advertisements in *The Builder* (which was accompanied by a line drawing of the Triton), it was 'copied from a fountain in the Barberini Palace; the height is 7ft. 9in...£21 02'.[141] This is puzzling, for the statue of Triton by Bernini which surmounts the fountain in the Piazza Barberini, Rome, bears no resemblance to the manufactory's Triton, and one must look elsewhere in an attempt to discover why it was described as such.

Plate 4:41. Larger-than-life figure of Triton, Austin & Seeley's artificial limestone, not indented, circa late 1800s, originally at Marchmont, Berwickshire. Height approx 91ins
CHRISTOPHER HODSOLL: PHOTOGRAPH PETER HODSOLL

Plate 4:42. The Coade stone figure of a Triton at Petworth House, West Sussex, on which Austin & Seeley may have based the Triton in Plate 4:41. The right arm and conch have been restored in cement LORD EGREMONT

In the private gardens of Petworth House stands a Coade stone figure (Plate 4:42) which, although smaller than Austin & Seeley's figure, depicts the same subject. Unfortunately the bill for this figure has not been traced, but it seems most probable that this Triton is the same as that listed in the firm's 1799 publication, *Description of Ornamental Stone in the Gallery of Coade & Sealy* as '55. The Triton — A 6ft. statue for a fountain sitting on three dolphins from the Piazza Barberini, at Rome'.[142] Perhaps Austin & Seeley's figure was modelled from the Coade model, which would perhaps account for the firm's description of it being a copy from the Barberini Palace. However, it may well have been modelled from an engraving of a bronze figure attributed to Battista Lorenzi (1529-1594) in the Museo Archeologico, Palermo, for both the Coade and the Austin & Seeley models are reversed copies of this subject. As the Coade figure is some twenty-one inches smaller than the Marchmont figure, this would add weight to the proposition that Austin & Seeley's model was taken from an engraving rather than an extant Coade figure. However, the firm's description accompanying the figure in the advertisement in *The Builder* goes on to say that 'The same figure and several others may be had of a smaller size', which further complicates the situation, for Austin & Seeley's figure in the 'smaller size' may have been the same height as the Coade figure, six feet.

Whatever the source of Austin & Seeley's figure, it is impressive and clearly shows the remarkable size of ornaments the manufactory was capable of producing at a decidedly inexpensive price, even if it bears little comparison to the Coade figure.

Doulton's Unglazed Terracotta

The original Doulton pottery was established in Vauxhall in 1815 under the name of Jones, Watts & Doulton, but by 1826 Mrs Jones had left, and the remaining partners, John Doulton (1793-1873) and John Watts had moved to larger premises on Lambeth High Street. At this point the pottery was predominantly involved with the manufacture of salt-glazed stoneware items for household and laboratory use. However, by the late 1820s the company had started producing a small range of terracotta building materials. With the apprenticeship of Doulton's son (Henry, 1820-1897) in 1835 this side of the business was to increase and by 1840 a new terracotta kiln had been built. It seems probable that by this date the firm had started producing a range of garden ornaments, for one contemporary illustration of the pottery shows a number of statues and vases on display in the courtyard.[143]

At the 1851 Great Exhibition the majority of Doulton & Watts' exhibits were samples of industrial and domestic ware, but a few small garden vases and a figure of Father Time, fired in one piece, were also exhibited.[144] In 1854 Watts retired and the business continued to be run by John Doulton in partnership with his sons, Henry in the manufacturing department, Frederick and James working in the office. The business soon became known as Doulton & Co.

With the increasing demand for architectural and sculptural terracotta during the third quarter of the nineteenth century, the firm's range of terracotta ornaments increased considerably and its catalogues were packed with large numbers of designs for garden ornaments. These were generally available more cheaply than anything carved from stone or marble and, at times, were even cheaper than the wares of manufactories of terracotta garden ornaments. The fine quality wares were described by Llewellynn Jewitt in 1883:

> In terra-cotta, Messrs. Doulton's works rank high, both for the beauty of their products, the variety of designs they have introduced, and the durability and excellence of their material. In vases for gardens, &c. — ...pedestals, fountains, garden-seats, flower-boxes and pendants, brackets, &c... — they produce a large number of exquisite patterns. In statuary and architectural decorations the productions consist of figures, busts, and medallions; keystones, arches, trusses and string-courses; capitals, bases, and finials; rain-water heads, of marvellously bold and effective design; parapets and balustrades; panels of coloured stoneware and terra-cotta, modelled in very high relief, for out-door decoration; and everything requisite for the architect or builder. Some of the highest achievements in art, as applied to original conceptions modelled in the most masterly manner in terracotta.[145]

The firm's stock terracotta ornaments encompassed a wide variety of subjects, ranging from such items as edgings for flower gardens, to vases, from under six and a half inches to over four and a half feet in height. Its statues and fountains included small models such as entwined pelicans supporting bowls, and small figures of girls under three feet high, to statues and ornate fountains over six feet high. These were produced in a buff coloured terracotta, but many could also be had in a deep red (according to later catalogues these red terracotta ornaments were fifteen percent more expensive than those in buff). A few items were also available in a glazed finish, whilst in later years finishes such as bronze, ivory and silicon were applied to a number of ornaments.

By the 1890s a great many more terracotta models were available, among them several vases identical to those produced by Blashfield, suggesting that the firm had purchased several moulds from the Stamford firm which went into voluntary liquidation in 1875. Whilst all the stock items illustrated in the catalogues could be made to order, Doulton also executed special commissions, such as the three figures illustrated in Plates 4:43, 44 and 45 (Colour Plates 49, 50 and 51) as well as exhibition works, for instance the replica of the America group on the Prince Albert Memorial exhibited at the 1876 exhibition, and the Biblical Fountain shown two years later in Paris.

In 1901 the firm was awarded a Royal warrant, together with authorisation to describe their products as 'Royal'. This was a considerable honour for one of the largest pottery manufacturers in the world, whose output not only included a range of garden ornaments, but also such items as sanitary fittings, fireplaces, stoves and baths, as well as glazed tableware and figurines of the highest quality.

The firm's early twentieth century catalogues still featured a considerable range of garden ornaments, but the majority of these were new, smaller models, created for the new and fashionable small uncontrived gardens, although some fairly large figures were also available. The majority were small quaint statues — almost figurines in fact, depicting such subjects as Puck, elves, hares, rabbits, foxes, ducks, pelicans, while the ornate predominantly Italianate-style vases of the previous century were largely replaced by small bird baths and simple flower pots.

The firm seems to have continued producing garden ornaments into the 1930s, but after the Second World War appears to have stopped. In 1956 the Lambeth works closed and the business transferred to one of the firm's other manufactories outside Stoke-on-Trent, where it remains today.

Modellers at the Doulton works

The number of modellers employed by Doulton from the 1840s through to the 1930s was considerable, and the quality of their work greatly contributed to the success of the business. One of the earliest sculptors employed was Samuel Nixon (1803-1854), a friend of Henry Doulton, but the most important influence on the firm's production stemmed from the friendship between Henry Doulton and John Sparkes, headmaster at the local Lambeth School of Art, a man who was to become heavily involved with the pottery. One of the earliest Sparkes protégés employed by the firm was Percival Ball who executed a series of heads depicting great potters for the façade of the works. George Tinworth (1843-1913), another of Sparkes' protégés, who was taken on as a resident sculptor in 1867, was also involved with this commission. One of the most famous terracotta sculptors of the period, Tinworth is best known today for his bas-relief panels. He produced a number of garden ornaments for Doulton, including several aquatic creatures, fountain figures and fountains, the most famous being that designed for the 1878 Exhibition in Paris. Another important modeller at the works, and an accomplished sculptor, designer and decorator, was John Broad (1837-1919) who modelled several voluptuous statues for the firm, including such subjects as the Four Seasons,

Pomona, Ariadne and Flora. (Amongst Broad's better known works may be mentioned the sculpture on the façade of Harrods in London). Other sculptors and modellers employed by the firm include Beere, Ellis, Frith, Pomeroy and Hornsby. In the early years of the twentieth century new sculptors, such as H Simeon and Mark Villars Marshall, were brought in. They were responsible for the manufactory's new quaint models, such as the sets of girls entitled Reflections on Childhood, and the Dutch boy and girl Bird Feeders, as well as for many of the small animal figures.

Most of the firm's terracotta ornaments bear indented marks, which occur in varying forms, usually on the lower part of the item in question. Items dating prior to 1854, are usually marked 'DOULTON & WATTS', at times accompanied by wording such as 'LAMBETH POTTERY LONDON' or 'HIGH STREET LAMBETH'. Articles produced after 1854 usually bear the indented mark 'DOULTON LAMBETH' (although it is interesting to note that the 'DOULTON & WATTS' mark may have continued to be used several years after this date). These occur in a variety of forms, often with accompanying words, and predominantly set in oval or oblong frames.

Doulton ornaments were produced using a similar process to that used by Coade and Blashfield, whereby sheets of uniformly thick clay were pressed into plaster moulds. After being allowed to dry and shrink, the various parts were joined together prior to firing. Both the buff and red coloured ornaments are fairly weather resistant and robust, but it should be noted the firm's catalogues advised clients: 'As a matter of precaution during winter months, fountains, basins, vases &c., should be emptied of water or earth, as the expansion resulting from frost is liable to cause injury'.

Doulton's terracotta garden ornaments

The figures of Apollo and two of the Muses, Thalia and Melpomene (Plates 4:43-45 and Colour Plates 49, 50 and 51), were never originally intended to be used as garden ornaments. They were produced as architectural decorations for the façade on the Apollo public house in Tottenham Court Road, London, which was built in 1898. The unusually deep buff colour of these three figures (much darker than most Doulton items) can be explained by the fact that they were used as architectural decorations, and in the polluted atmosphere of London have become stained, as well as accumulating black discoloration in some parts.

These figures and the other seven Muses were modelled by one of the firm's leading artists, John Broad, who, as we have seen, produced a considerable number of figures for the firm including one off models such as these, as well as a number of stock garden statues. His ability as a modeller of garden statuary has received acclaim in the past, but the quality of these three is certainly questionable. Of the three, the most appealing is Melpomene (Plate 4:45), which was inspired by an antique statue,[146] for there is an awkwardness in the stance, proportions and drapery of Thalia (Plate 4:43), and Apollo (Plate 4:44) is bulky and lacks much of the elegance befitting a deity of his grandeur. Furthermore, there is an unfinished feel to the figures; the treatment of Apollo's hair, for example, is by no means as fine as it could have been, bearing in mind the detail in the Muses' ivy garlands. In spite of their shortcomings, these figures clearly illustrate the capabilities of the firm, for it would have been no easy matter to mould, dry and fire such large pieces.

Interestingly, and perhaps appropriate for figures which adorned the façade of a public house, both the Muses were modelled complete with several bacchic

Plate 4:43. Thalia (the Muse of Comedy), one of a set of ten figures of Apollo and the Nine Muses, Doulton's terracotta, by John Broad, 1898. Height approx 72ins. (See Colour Plate 49)
SOTHEBY'S

Plate 4:44. Apollo, one of a set of ten figures with the Nine Muses, Doulton's terracotta, by John Broad, 1898. Height approx 74ins. (See Colour Plate 50)
SOTHEBY'S

Plate 4:45. Melpomene (the Tragic Muse), one of a set of ten figures of Apollo and the Nine Muses, Doulton's terracotta, by John Broad, 1898. Height approx 72ins. (See Colour Plate 51)
SOTHEBY'S

Plate 4:46. Ornate fountain and border, Doulton's terracotta, probably modelled by George Tinworth, circa early 1890s. Approx overall diameter 17 feet. (See Colour Plate 52)
SOTHEBY'S, SUSSEX

212

TERRA COTTA FOUNTAINS, POND RIM AND
CONSERVATORY EDGINGS.

Fig. 149.

Fig. 147.

Fig 148.

Conservatory Edging, 3/6 per foot run.
Fig. 39.

Pond Rim for Fountain, 7 ft. 6 in. diam.,
15 in. high, 4/- per foot run.

Fig. 145

7½ in. high, 2/6
Fig. 45.

Pelican Fountain, complete, £3 10s.
Lower Reservoir, 3 ft. diam., 35/- ; Upper Reservoir, 17 in. diam., 7/6.
Pelican Standard, 25/; Jet, 4/-

8 in. high 2/6.

Fig. 150.

Mignonette Box, 14/-

Fig. 73.

Crane Fountain, complete, 63/-
Upper Reservoir, 2 ft. diam., 10/6
Lower Reservoir, 2 ft. 8 in. diam., 25/-
Crane Standard, 2 ft. 1 in. high, 30/-

Mignonette Box, 3 ft. long, 12/-
Ditto, without Pendants, 10/-

34...7

Plate 4:47. A page from Doulton & Co's catalogue Terra Cotta Garden Vases, Pedestals, Flower Pots, and Every Other Description of Horticultural Terra Cotta, *1893. The illustration includes the pelican column, bowl and spout which would have surmounted the bowl in Plate 4:46 (centre), as well as the surround section of the pond rim (top right)*

emblems: both have ivy garlands around their heads, and the mask each clasps, showing Comedy (Thalia) and Tragedy (Melpomene), have bacchic connotations.

The manufacture of relatively small-sized fountains was an important part of Doulton's garden ornament business. During the nineteenth century, these tended to be of a formal symmetric nature, such as that illustrated in Plate 4:46 and Colour Plate 52. Unfortunately it is not known who modelled this centrepiece, but stylistically it seems probable it was one of Tinworth's works. The model was in production by at least the early 1890s, but the six pedestals between the decorative border (or rim as it was called) suggest that the fountain dates more towards the turn of the century, for this type of pedestal does not feature in earlier catalogues.

The fountain clearly illustrates the buff colour of Doulton's terracotta ornaments as well as the durability of the compound, for it is in remarkably good condition.

213

Terra Cotta Eagle Terminals.

Fig. 563.

Fig. 564.

3 ft. 5 in. high.

3 ft. 1 in. high.

Plate 4:48. Illustration from Doulton & Co's catalogue Architectural Terra Cotta for Construction and Decoration *showing two of the firm's designs for stock eagle figures*

Plate 4:49. One of a pair of eagles, Doulton's terracotta, indented 'DOULTON LAMBETH LONDON', late nineteenth/early twentieth century. Height approx 37ins. The figure is taken from the smaller of the two models in Plate 4:48, with the head turned to the bird's right. The firm's characteristic oval stamp mark is just discernible on the left of the base

T CROWTHER & SONS LTD.

TERRA COTTA FOUNTAINS, GARDEN-SEATS AND VASES.

Fig. 189.

Fig. 157.

Fig. 154.

22 in. diameter, 20 in. high, 25/-

2-ft. 3-in. high, 45/-

20/-

Fig. 156.

Fig. 62.

Glazed Garden Seat,
19½ in. high,
Plain, 10/-, Perforated, 15/-
May also be had Unglazed.

Fig. 61.

Glazed Garden Seat,
19½ in. high,
Plain, 10/-; Perforated, 15/-
May also be had Unglazed.

Fig. 53.

Fig. 54.

8 in. high 5/-

Complete £9
Reservoir, 3 ft. 9 in. diameter ... £3
Dolphin Standard, 3 ft. 2 in. high ... £6

11 in. high, 7/6

Plate 4:50. A page from Doulton & Co's catalogue Terra Cotta Garden Vases, Pedestals, Flower Pots, and Every Other Description of Horticultural Terra Cotta. *The small vase in the bottom left-hand corner (Fig 53) was one of the models shown by the firm at the Great Exhibition of 1851*

However, it is worth noting that part of the fountain is either missing, or was never supplied. According to catalogue illustrations, the fountain centrepiece was surmounted by a column decorated with three pelicans, which supported a further bowl and spout. The design for this, which was also available complete with bowl (or basin) as a free-standing fountain, together with the sections of pond rim, is shown in Plate 4:47.

Although Doulton's twentieth century catalogues continued to illustrate a number of fountains similar to these, by the late 1920s they had been replaced by new coy fountain statuettes holding urns or fish from which water issued, several of these models being reproduced today by H Crowther.

Among the firm's varied range of stock architectural items were terminal decorations for use on top of piers and walls, and these included such pieces as

TERRA COTTA VASES.

Fig. 179.

Fig. 64.

Fig. 153.

1-ft. 5-in. high, 30/-

17 in. high, 7/6

16 in. high, 27/6

Fig. 4.

Fig. 144.

Fig. 10.

20 in. high, 10/6

3ft. 6 in. diam. over handles, 2ft. 2½in. high, £5 5s.

19 in. high, 10/-

Fig. 60.

Fig. 78.

Fig. 77.

Large size, 28 in. high, 20/-
Small size, 23 in. high, 15/-

Large, 34 in. high, 30/-   Small, 25 in. high, 17/6
With Handles, 33/6   With Handles, 20/-

30 in. high, 22/6

34—

Plate 4:51. A page from Doulton & Co's catalogue Terra Cotta Garden Vases, Pedestals, Flower Pots, and Every Other Description of Horticultural Terra Cotta. *The vase in the top row, centre (Fig 64), was one of those the firm exhibited at the Great Exhibition of 1851. Also illustrated are the designs for the campana-shaped vase in Plate 4:52 (Fig 60), and the Warwick Vase in Plate 4:53 (Fig 4)*

spheres, pineapples and urns. By the early 1890s this range had been enlarged to include figures of eagles, and designs for these are illustrated in Plate 4:48. An example of the smaller of these two models, with its head turned in the opposite direction, is shown in Plate 4:49. It has weathered poorly; much of the vitrified surface has been eaten away taking with it huge quantities of the original detail in the wing and chest feathers, whilst even worse damage in the form of breakages has occurred on the beak and wing tips. As can be seen, Doulton's terracotta is

Plate 4:52. *Campana-shaped vase and pedestal, Doulton's terracotta, circa 1880. Approx height including pedestal 60ins*
SOTHEBY'S, SUSSEX

Plate 4:53. *One of a pair of vases, Doulton's terracotta, oblong indented stamp 'DOULTON LAMBETH', copy of the antique Warwick Vase, circa 1880. Height approx 26½ ins*
PRIVATE COLLECTION

not totally impervious to the weather, and in this case certainly seems to have been a less durable formula than Doulton's competitors, such as Pulham and Blashfield, were using.

Vases were one of the firm's earliest garden products. At the 1851 Great Exhibition several small vases were exhibited, including designs shown in Plates 4:50 and 4:51. By the 1890s a great number of other vases were available, two examples of which are shown here (Plates 4:52 and 53), together with the design illustrations in the early 1890s catalogue (Plate 4:51, Fig 60 and Fig 4 respectively). The vase in Plate 4:52, the larger version of the two available, is loosely derived from the famous antique Medici and Borghese Vases, but of a much plainer nature. This type of campana-shaped vase was enormously popular during much of the nineteenth century and early years of the twentieth century, as was the pedestal with its relief of laurel garlands. Numerous models of this type were produced both by Doulton and a number of other manufactories. The vase illustrated in Plate 4:53 is a copy of the famous antique Warwick Vase. As it is almost certain that the Doulton pottery bought up a number of the Stamford Terra Cotta Company (Blashfield's) Ltd moulds in 1875,[147] one would perhaps expect Doulton's copy of the Warwick Vase to be exactly the same as that produced by Blashfield (see page 182). As this is not the case, Doulton must have had his own copy modelled, presumably by one of his modellers, presumably prior to 1875. It is interesting to note that in 1893 the Doulton works were pricing their copies of the Warwick Vase at £5 5s, less than half the price Blashfield was charging thirty-five years earlier for a similar-sized model.

Plate 5:1. Detail of one of a pair of Statuary Carrara marble vases, circa 1800, formerly in Thomas Hope's house in Duchess Street. These have been in an exterior location for about seventy-five years and have consequently deteriorated considerably. (See Colour Plate 53)

SOTHEBY'S, SUSSEX

CHAPTER FIVE

MARBLE
As seen in British gardens
from the early nineteenth century

Since antiquity, sculptors have favoured marble because of its beautiful surface textures, though continental use of marble for garden ornament has always been far more widespread than in Britain. In gardens such as Versailles and Vaux-le-Vicomte in France, and in the grounds of Italian villas, such as the Borghese, Albani and d'Este, great numbers of marble statues, vases and fountains were used to adorn the walks and vistas. It was not until the early to middle part of the nineteenth century that the use of marble in Britain became widespread, though it was never to achieve the same popularity the medium had in Europe. Probably this is just as well, for most of the marble garden ornaments found in British gardens (including the type which occurs with the greatest frequency in this country — white marble) are carved from imported marble and, contrary to widespread belief, this is not well suited to our climate. Indeed, many of the marble garden ornaments introduced into uncovered or unprotected parts of British gardens, even as late as the end of the last century, are today extensively corroded. Some examples which have been outside even longer (such as the figure of Sir Hans Sloane, carved in 1737 and formerly in the Physic Garden, Chelsea) are in a horrific state of decay.

Although marble pieces only started being extensively used as garden ornaments in Britain from the middle of the nineteenth century, quite a number made before this are found today in our gardens. While some were imported from continental sources, many others were originally executed by sculptors for the sculpture galleries of patrons' houses and other interior locations, and were only placed outside when they fell from favour.

A good example of this can be seen in a pair of marble vases or finials on pedestals, formerly in the grounds of Parham Park, West Sussex (Plate 5:1 and Colour Plate 53). These date to around 1800 and seem likely to have originated from the interior of Thomas Hope's London mansion in Duchess Street, for they are shown flanking the entrance to the Statue Gallery in Hope's influential publication, *Household Furniture and Interior Decoration,* 1807 (Plate 5:2). In the early nineteenth century Thomas Hope transferred some of the interior furnishings from Duchess Street to his country house near Dorking, The Deepdene, the contents of which were sold in 1917 and the items dispersed. As a pair of Coade stone seats with a striking similarity to a pair once at Duchess Street now flank the Temple at Parham Park (Plate 4:7), it seems most probable that this pair of vases also once graced the interior of the famous mansion in Duchess Street.

Closer examination of one of the vases (Plate 5:1), which cannot have been located in an outdoor setting for more than seventy-five years, clearly shows that the lid and upper parts of the body have badly corroded. The rest of the piece is in relatively good condition, but left in an outdoor setting, it is merely a matter of a few years before the rest of the marble deteriorates similarly.

The relatively small use of marble for garden ornament in this country can be explained by a number of factors. Firstly the main source of good quality marble (including the white particularly favoured for statuary and vases) was in the vicinity of the Apuan Alps, north of Pisa. The problems involved in removing good

Plate 5:2. An illustration from Thomas Hope's Household Furniture and Interior Decoration, *1807, showing the design for the vase in Plate 5:1 and Colour Plate 53. The vase is a copy of an antique original, said by Hope to have originated from the Albani or Barbarini Collection. The pedestal is copied from an original in the Albani Collection, and may well have been inspired by an engraving by Piranesi*

quality blocks from the quarries high up in the hills, coupled with the immense cost of transporting such a heavy material to Britain made it an extremely expensive commodity. Secondly these imported marbles were rarely suited to our climate, and unless properly cared for (regular cleaning, waxing and, at times, repolishing) most had a poor ability to withstand the elements. This characteristic feature of foreign marble in British gardens had been observed as early as the seventeenth century. When Evelyn described the famous antique Arundel marbles in the grounds of Arundel House he stated that they had been 'exceedingly impaired by the corrosive air of London'.[1] It is not recorded how they were 'impaired', but Evelyn was probably referring to the breakdown of the surface of the marble, an effect commonly known today as 'sugaring' after the similarities the granules have to grains of sugar, for when rubbed these grains literally crumble off the corroded surface.

For this reason, during the eighteenth century many marble works were found in sheltered and protected environments. For example, in the gardens of Stourhead, Wiltshire, John Michael Rysbrack's figure of Hercules was placed in the Pantheon, whilst at Stowe, Buckinghamshire, the figure of Venus Arising from her Bath was located in an upper basin in the grotto.

During this period the preferred media for garden ornaments were lead and stone, though a few marble pieces were also to be found. Some of these were original Greek or Roman antiquities imported into this country, among them the life-size figures (thought to be Cicero, Pompey and Caesar) which were incorporated into the Exedra at Chiswick, and part of the Arundel Collection which liberally decorated the grounds and garden buildings of Easton Neston in Northamptonshire. Others were specifically commissioned for garden locations, such as the two magnificent pairs of Carrara marble vases carved at immense cost at the end of the seventeenth century by Caius Gabriel Cibber and Edward Pearce (circa 1635-1695) for the gardens of Hampton Court (now at Windsor Castle). Another small but important source of marble garden ornaments during the period came from marble quarried in Britain. However, these pieces (which tended to be far hardier than their foreign counterparts) were usually only found within the environs of the quarries or their market areas, and even then they were rarely more than architectural pieces. The reasons for this were, again, the problems involved in transporting marble, together with the fact that British marbles, often being of a dark or sombre colour (for instance Purbeck and Ashford Black — see Appendix I), tended to be inappropriate for figurative work.

As we have seen, from the early years of the nineteenth century, the popularity of marble garden ornaments grew considerably. Many of the lead statues so extensively found in eighteenth century gardens were replaced with marble statues, as was the case at Chatsworth and Wrest Park, Bedfordshire. However, it was still a much more expensive form of garden ornament than both cast-iron and artificial stone and, as such, large works tended to be commissioned by particularly wealthy patrons such as Sir Samuel Peto at Somerleyton Hall, Suffolk, or Baron Rothschild at Waddesdon Manor, Buckinghamshire.

Precisely what is and what is not marble has in the past been a matter for debate, but today it is generally agreed that marble is a hard crystalline metamorphic rock resulting from the recrystallisation of a limestone and that its surface is capable of taking a high polish. However to define or illustrate typical examples is complicated, because being a natural deposit it is possible for one type of marble to occur in a great variety of forms. For example, in a particular quarry one sort of marble with a light vein may be found in one place, whilst in another place, say several hundred yards away, it may be found more heavily veined and with a slightly different tone. This effect is caused by slightly different geological conditions when the limestone was recrystallised, the change in tone being due to various chemical impurities — thus, for example, red tones are caused by the presence of iron oxides, purples by manganese oxides. The problems of correct identification are even more complex when one considers that some quarries have been worked for hundreds of years and the best quality deposits have been extensively removed. Furthermore, many marbles look completely different in their natural state than they do in a polished state.

Types of Marble

Carrara

The marble which is most commonly found decorating British gardens is the white Carrara marble found in the Apuan Alps. Like other marbles it occurs in a multitude of forms. No less than six types — white Carrara, Altissimo, Streaked (green streaks), Statuary (of Carrara), Calacatta (yellowish streaks), and Arabesqued (pink stripes) — are mentioned as being white marbles coming from the area of the Apuan Alps,[2] and there are numerous other terms for various forms of Carrara marble, including Sicilian, Second Statuary, Bastard Statuary and Statuary Vein to name but a few.[3] However, generally speaking the creamy-white Statuary or Statuario marble tended to be used for more important works, such as figurative sculpture, statues and vases, whilst lesser, often harder wearing and cheaper marbles (for instance those with more veining, discolorations, flaws) tended to be used for items such as pedestals.

Whilst white marble is the predominant colour, there are may different types of coloured marble and the most commonly found are listed here.

Rosso Verona

Quarried from the vicinity of Verona in northern Italy, this marble has been in use since the first century AD and is still obtained today. It is a mottled red-orange colour when polished or wet; when unpolished tints of orange are just discernible behind its grey-white colour (see Plates 5:18 and 19, Colour Plate 67 and Appendix I).

Istrian

In reality a stone, quarried in the old Venetian province of Istria, this was extensively used for the buildings of Venice, and has been employed since the first century AD. Examples of Istrian stone or marble (as it is sometimes called) are shown in Plate 5:20 and Appendix I.

Verde Antico

Sometimes known as Antique Green, this marble has been in extensive use since the middle to last quarter of the nineteenth century. Obtained from quarries near Larissa in Thessaly, it was available in three shades of green — light, medium or dark. Similar green coloured marbles were also quarried at an earlier date in Italy at Prato, Tuscany (Verde de Prato), and in the Turin area (Alps, a more streaked form).

Languedoc

This French marble is a wonderful rich red interspersed with whites and greys. In use since the sixteenth century, it was extensively used at Versailles (the

Colonnade columns and Water Avenue basins). Quarried from the vicinity of Carcassone in southern France, its varied colours are illustrated in the pedestal in Colour Plate 43.

Breccia Violette
Sometimes known as Breccia de Seravezza, after the town in the Apuan Alps from which it is quarried, this is a Brecciated marble (a polychrome marble made up of angular fragments of marble of various colours and recemented many thousands of years ago into solid rock or embedded in different molten marble during the process of cooling). The main colours found are violet, brown, red, green and white. It has been quarried since the sixteenth century, and an example of drapery is illustrated in Plate 5:12 (see also Appendix I). Deposits of a lighter tone, known as Breccia Africano, are obtained from the vicinity of Pietrasanta.

Belgian Fossil
This is easily confused with the strikingly similar Kilkenny marble found in Ireland and is jet black in colour when polished. Unlike the pure Ashford Black (which was much worked during the nineteenth century), it is full of fossilised shells and deposits. After exposure to the elements the three marbles mentioned here lose their black tone, changing to a light grey-white. (See Appendix I.)

Dove Grey
An Italian marble quarried from Carrara, Seravezza and Massa in the Apuan Alps.

Rouge Royal
This Belgian marble, sometimes known as Rouge Griotte, Rouge Byzantine or Rouge Imperial, is a pale red colour, sometimes interspersed with veins.

Purbeck
A light grey marble with numerous fossils and hints of green and brown which has been quarried since before the thirteenth century from the isle of Purbeck near Poole, Dorset.

Carving Marble Sculpture

The process of carving in marble changed little during the eighteenth and nineteenth centuries, the two major advances being the improvements during the latter century in pointing machines which enabled sculptors to pass much of the work of cutting unwanted sections of marble on to masons or apprentices, and a move (also generally effected by the nineteenth century) from fired clay models to plaster ones.

Although sculptors frequently modelled items in clay (an essential part of any sculptor's training), it was common practice before starting a work in marble for the sculptor to find a patron willing to spend the often considerable amount of money on commissioning a work. Assuming that the patron did not already favour one of the sculptor's existing models, and that he did not want a facsimile of some other artist's creation, the first step of the commission usually involved the supplying of a drawing or drawings. Once these had been approved and some form of contract agreed, work could start on modelling the subject in clay. This process, common since before the Renaissance, had the advantage that any corrections or alterations could easily be made in such a malleable material. The clay model was built up on a wood or iron skeleton or armature (on large works of some considerable size). These armatures were essential structural features, and the consequences if they were not used were at times disastrous, as is recorded in the biography of John Gibson (1790-1866), a Victorian sculptor:

> Up to this period [1817] I never had received any instructions from a master, nor had I studied in any academy. At my own request Canova allowed me to copy his fine Pugilist, the marble statue is in the Vatican. I began to model my copy from the cast at the studio. After I had worked at the clay a few days down it all fell. It seems that my Master had observed to his foreman, Signor. Desti, that my figure must fall, 'for', said he, 'you see that he does not know anything about the skeleton-work; but let him proceed, and when his figure comes down show him how the mechanical part is done.' So when my model fell, a Blacksmith was called, and the iron work made, and numerous crosses of wood and wire. Such a thing I had never yet seen. One of his pupils then put up the clay upon the iron skeleton and roughed out the model before me, so that the figure was as firm as a rock. I was enchanted and worked a long time upon my copy.[4]

While work was in progress and on completion it was essential to keep the model damp, for if left to dry out it would crack and soon crumble apart. During the eighteenth century it was common practice to fire the completed clay models, but this was a risky business, for the natural clay was of an unequal thickness and so was prone to contract unevenly, sometimes twisting or even breaking when being fired. Since clay models were so accident prone they were gradually abandoned in favour of plaster reproductions. Reproduction of a plaster copy (known as the original plaster model) of the sculptor's original unfired clay model was often done by specialists, and involved the destruction of the clay original. The clay model was first coated with a thin layer of oil, then with a coat of coloured plaster. Many further coats of uncoloured plaster were then built up on top of this. Having been left to dry the mould could be split apart and the clay model, complete with armature, picked out of the mould. The sections of the mould were then reassembled and held firmly together whilst enough white plaster was poured into the interior, the mould being rotated to coat the inside walls to some depth. This was preferable to filling the inside of the mould completely with plaster, as it reduced the chance of air bubbles being caught against the side of the mould. Once the plaster inside the mould, together with any further plaster deemed necessary to reinforce the interior of the cast, had been allowed to harden, the outer mould could be chiselled off. The first coloured plaster layer provided the chiseller with a means by which to identify where the original plaster model started. This process of reproducing sculptors' models in plaster enabled works of a much greater size to be produced than had been possible with clay models.

Having produced a model (whether plaster, clay or some other medium), the next stage of the operation was to select a suitable block of marble, and the most

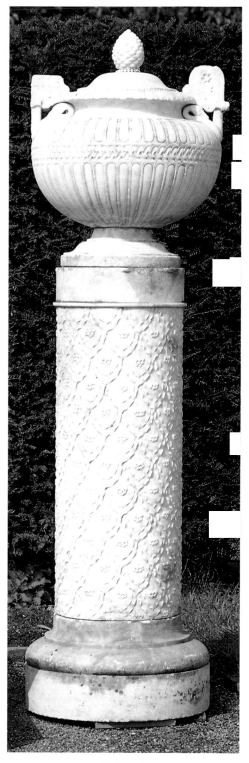

Colour Plate 53. One of a pair of Statuary Carrara marble vases, formerly in Thomas Hope's house in Duchess Street, London. Approx height with pedestal 53ins. (See Plate 5:1 and page 219)
SOTHEBY'S, SUSSEX

223

important aspect here was to ensure the block contained no flaws or fractures (both natural or sustained during quarrying, cutting or in transit). White Italian marble, particularly the type known as Statuario or Statuary, was the preferred type because of its pure, clean nature and its inherently beautiful creamy colour and surface. It was one of the more expensive marbles quarried in Italy due to the fact that it was extracted underground. Like all marbles, Statuary is an extremely dense material, and the problems involved with transporting it, either in block form or as a finished statue from Italy to England, contributed to the considerable cost.

The method of reproducing the sculptor's original model in marble evolved over the ages. In 1568 Bartoli published his translation of Alberti's highly complex process *De Statua*.[5] This required numerous co-ordinates and a complicated system of set squares. On top of the model rested a calibrated disc; from the centre of this radiated sticks of various lengths along which ran plumb lines which dropped to the various points of the model. By the nineteenth century a variety of different, less complex systems had evolved. In Italy a simple system known as *macchinetta* or *crocetta*[6] was used which enabled the sculptor (or more correctly his apprentice or workmen), to determine by the use of a slide-rule the position of any point within a given area defined by three principal points. In Britain a device known as a pointing machine was used. These machines consisted of a needle, or pointer, calibrated to a fixed axis, which could transfer measured three dimensional points from the model into the block of marble, entry into the marble being achieved by the use of drills.[7]

These new processes had great advantages for the nineteenth century sculptor. Before this, although sculptors could leave apprentices to cut the overall outline of a piece roughly, during the nineteenth century, sculptors' apprentices could be left to produce almost complete works on their own, with the master adding just a few finishing touches. The mechanical system was described by Count Hawks Le Grice in his *Walks Through the Studii of the Sculptors at Rome* of 1841:

> This cast [plaster] now becomes the model, according to which the workman cuts from the solid marble its imitation. The process of this imitation is entirely mechanical, and is effected by measurement until the work is chiselled nearly to the form of the original one in plaster. The workman is then dismissed from his mechanical labour; and the master hand of the sculptor is now employed to impart fidelity, life and spirit to the mechanical imitation. The accessories introduced merely to embellish are executed by the scarpellino or carver, for they require nothing but servile imitation and the work of the chisel.[8]

However, it should be noted that the quality of some signed (and many unsigned) nineteenth century marble works is so poor and so lacking in vitality, depth and movement that it is doubtful whether the sculptors who signed them actually ever worked on them.

The final stage in completing a marble piece was polishing. This involved the removal of chisel marks and small scratches with abrasive stones of decreasing coarseness, such as, respectively, sandstone, pumice and emery.

Nineteenth Century Marble Garden Sculpture at Chatsworth

One of the leading British collectors of marble statuary during the first half of the nineteenth century was William Spencer Cavendish, 6th Duke of Devonshire

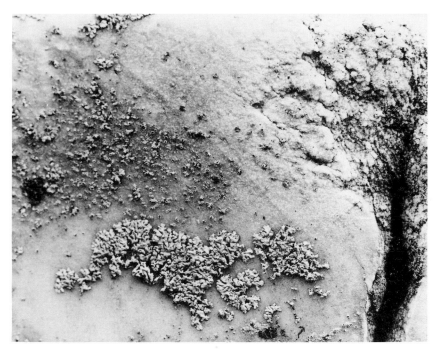

Plate 5:3. Detail of the base of a Carrara marble statue by Bienaimé, circa 1835, Chatsworth, Derbyshire. The accumulation of lichen and 'sugaring' of the marble are both signs of the material eroding. Deterioration is far more widespread in the vein of much softer marble which has literally been 'eaten' away by frost damage

(1790-1858), whose patronage of several renowned as well as a number of lesser European and English sculptors resident in Rome was considerable. Like many other British patrons, many of his purchases (including nearly all the important ones) were intended for placement within a specially constructed interior sculpture gallery, but the Duke also purchased quite a number of life-size marble statues and vases specifically for the pleasure gardens at Chatsworth.

In his account of Chatsworth, written in 1844, the Duke mentions that 'Eight statues and two vases have been worked for me by Francesco Bienaimé at Carrara, of hard marble of that place, that appears to defy the climate of the Peak, and to resist all incipient vegetation on its surface'[9] (Colour Plate 54). This reference is noteworthy, for it reflects an awareness in nineteenth century Britain that white Carrara marble was not suited to the climate and prone to deteriorate. These 'hard marble' works were placed outside on pedestals of local Bakewell sandstone in the gardens south of the house where they remain today set back into a row of lime trees. As would be expected, parts of the surface of these figures have begun to deteriorate, and most have accumulated a layer of lichen which can be seen in the detail of the base of one of the figures (Plate 5:3). Lichen is clearly visible at the bottom of the illustration, whilst above it the marble has begun to erode and sugar. However, the overall condition of Bienaimé's works is by no means as poor as some nineteenth century garden pieces, and this can perhaps be explained both by the fact that they were carved from hard marble, as well as in the attention they seem to have received in the form of cleaning.

The pieces executed by Bienaimé at Chatsworth include a copy of the Borghese Vase, and a similar sized campana shaped urn. The statues include copies of a number of famous antique works, such as the Diana de Versailles, the Farnese Hercules (both seen in Colour Plate 54) and the Amazon (illustrated in Plate 5:4 and Colour Plate 54) which is a copy of the original Wounded Amazon, thought to be a work by the Greek sculptor Polycleitus (fl 232 BC). An interesting feature

Colour Plate 54. Six of Bienaimé's Carrara marble statues in the Private Gardens at Chatsworth, Derbyshire. From left to right, top to bottom: copy of the antique Apollo Belvedere in the Vatican Museum; copy of the antique Minerva Giustiniani in the Vatican Museum; copy of the antique Wounded Amazon in the Museo Pio Clementino, Rome (see also Plate 5:4); copy of Thorvaldsen's original neo-classical Adonis (see also Plate 5:5); copy of the antique Diana de Versailles in the Louvre; copy of the antique Farnese Hercules in the Museo Nazionale, Naples

of Bienaimé's copy, which is often seen on other marble figures, are the horizontal marble supports which connect the Amazon's bow to her body. Although they detract from the composition, they would have been retained by the sculptor to reduce the probability of breakage whilst carving as well as in transit. It seems likely that if this statue had been intended for an interior location, these supports would have been removed on arrival, but as an exposed and vulnerable garden figure their retention has obvious advantages.

Other statues at Chatsworth executed by Bienaimé are copies of famous works by more contemporary artists, such as Bertel Thorvaldsen (1770-1844) and Antonio Canova (1757-1822). They reflect not only the prevalent taste between 1820 and 1840, but also the 6th Duke's, for he was a great collector of neo-classical sculpture, even purchasing several important works from Thorvaldsen and Canova to decorate the interior of his Sculpture Gallery. Bienaimé's copy of Thorvaldsen's Adonis is shown in Plate 5:5 and Colour Plate 54. Interestingly his portrayal of the youth so beloved in mythology by Venus, is slightly different to Thorvaldsen's. Here Adonis' head is turned to his left as opposed to the right as is the case with the original plaster model of 1808.

Although Bienaimé's works, together with a number of the other marble pieces in the gardens at Chatsworth, were purchased by the 6th Duke for use as garden

Plate 5:4. Larger-than-life statue of a Wounded Amazon, Carrara marble with slight blue-grey veining, by Bienaimé after the antique, circa 1835, the South Gardens, Chatsworth, Derbyshire. Height approx 72ins. (See Colour Plate 54 and pages 225-226)

Plate 5:5. Larger-than-life statue of Adonis, Carrara marble with slight blue-grey veining, by Bienaimé after a model by Thorvaldsen, circa 1835, the South Gardens, Chatsworth, Derbyshire. Height approx 72ins. (See Colour Plate 54 and page 226)

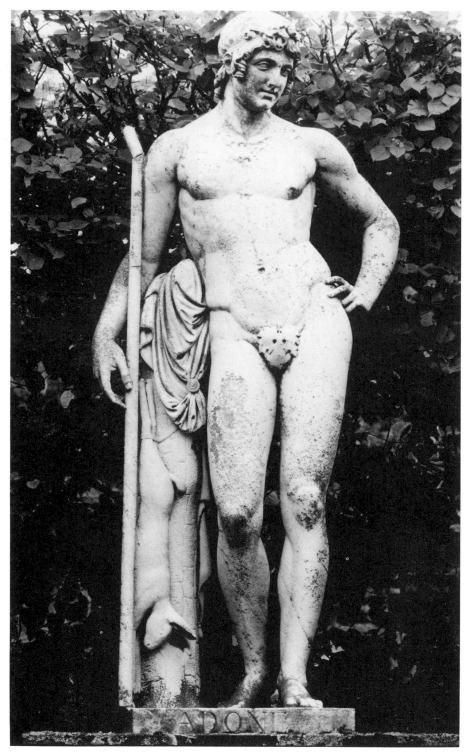

ornaments, a few of the pieces he originally placed inside the house are now outside. One example of this can be seen in the pair of Carrara marble lions outside the Orangery (Plates 5:6 and 7 and Colour Plates 55 and 56). These are full-scale reproductions of the originals at the base of the monument to Clement XIII in St Peter's, Rome, executed between 1783 and 1792 by Canova. They were ordered by the Duke in 1823,[10] and were executed from plaster casts taken from the originals by Rinaldo Rinaldi (1793-1873 — the Sleeping Lion) and Francesco Benaglia (the Waking Lion). Eventually erected in the Sculpture Gallery in 1833,

Plate 5:6. Waking Lion, Statuary Carrara marble, by Benaglia after the original by Canova, circa 1830, outside the Orangery, Chatsworth. Length approx 105ins. (See Colour Plate 55)

Plate 5:7. Sleeping Lion, Statuary Carrara marble, by Rinaldi, after the original by Canova, circa 1830, outside the Orangery, Chatsworth. Length approx 87ins. (See Colour Plate 56)

they were placed in similar positions to the pair at St Peter's (facing each other on pedestals backing against the wall), where they were to remain until they were moved outside the Orangery during the 9th Duke's time (sometime between 1908 and 1938).

The lions are, therefore, in a far better condition than other Carrara marble works that have been outside since the 6th Duke's time. However, both are beginning to accumulate a thin covering of lichen (particularly in crevices in places like the mane), and this will doubtless prove destructive in years to come.

Although the 9th Duke may well have had a specific purpose for moving these two stupendous and immensely heavy beasts outside, their removal to the garden in the early years of the twentieth century is worthy of comment, particularly since great numbers of interior marble pieces were moved to garden settings during this period. A partial explanation is the change in sculptural taste away from the classical past.

Allowing for fluctuations in style, it was common during much of the eighteenth century for many sculptors to be influenced by antique Roman pieces in Italy. Thus numerous figures were modelled after antique originals, or portrayed in the garb of, for example, Roman senators or soldiers. However, by the end of the century, widespread acknowledgement that Roman sculpture had been extensively based on previous antique Greek works, produced a disctinct new style — the neo-classical. This continued in popularity until the early years of the Victorian era, but was soon replaced by a new fashion, still associated with symbols from antiquity, but at the same time much divorced from it. This new style was described thus:

> To an English farmer, a plough boy in a smock-frock, guiding his team along the furrow, conveys the idea of agriculture. To the educated fancy all over the world the same idea is conveyed, in a more universal sense, by the benign maternal Ceres, holding her wheat-sheaf... Half a century ago the fashion was all in favour of paganism in sculpture; now the popular feeling runs so against it that it gives rise to the most obvious absurdities. Sculptors who have seized and worked out classical ideas are afraid to give them classical names; a figure of Orpheus is a 'Violin Player'; a Cupid and Psyche becomes 'A Boy with a Butterfly'; Apollo, as the Shepherd, is 'A Boy at a Stile'; and instead of the Oread and Dryad Fleet, or Naiad of the Stream we have 'Nymphs Preparing to Bathe'.[11]

Colour Plate 55. Waking Lion, Statuary Carrara marble, by Benaglia after the Canova original in St Peter's, Rome. Both this and the Sleeping Lion in Colour Plate 56 were removed to their present garden setting outside the Orangery, Chatsworth, in the early years of the twentieth century. (See Plate 5:6 and pages 228-229)

Of course, some classical works continued to be produced, but these tended to owe little to antiquity. By the end of the nineteenth century a new fashion for sculpture had come to the fore, the 'new sculpture'. Even more divorced from the antique and neo-classical, and more refined than earlier Victorian taste, this style developed into the abstract. Thus, marble sculptures collected in Italy or carved for patrons' houses during the eighteenth and much of the nineteenth century were, to the descendants of the original owners, generally considered unfashionable, if not downright ugly. During both Edward VII and George V's reigns, the banishment of many marble pieces to a garden setting was often a direct consequence of this change in taste.

Colour Plate 56. Sleeping Lion, Statuary Carrara marble, by Rinaldi after the Canova original in St Peter's, Rome, outside the Orangery, Chatsworth. (See Plate 5:7 and pages 228-229)

Other Marble Pieces and the Problem of Weathering

A good example of the 'mass production' of marble statuary during the nineteenth century can be seen in the pair of groups by the Italian sculptor Giovanni Maria Benzoni (1809-1873) — Fidelity and Gratitude (Plates 5:8 and 9). To date, no less than a total of thirteen examples of each of these two pieces are known, most of them signed 'G M BENZONI ROMA', with dates varying from between 1846 and 1853. The proliferation of copies in Britain (whose popularity can perhaps be explained by the fact that pairs were amongst the exhibits on display at the Crystal Palace in 1851)[12] suggests that most of the models were produced by Benzoni's assistants (using the *macchinetta* or *crocetta* process), Benzoni only adding the finishing touches.

Plate 5:8. Fidelity, Statuary Carrara marble, signed 'G M BENZONI 1852 ROME', formerly at Stoneleigh Abbey, Warwickshire. Height approx 32ins
CHRISTIE'S, LONDON

Plate 5:9. Gratitude, Statuary Carrara marble, signed 'G M BENZONI 1852 ROME', formerly at Stoneleigh Abbey, Warwickshire. Height approx 31ins
CHRISTIE'S, LONDON

Comparison of these two interior marble groups (formerly at Stoneleigh Abbey), with a duplicate pair (Plates 5:10 and 11) which has been outside for a number of years, clearly shows the poor weathering ability of Statuary marble. The smooth, polished, waxed and (with the exception of a few natural flaws in the marble) relatively unblemished surface of the interior models is in sharp contrast to the pitted and discoloured weathered pair. Particularly noticeable are the missing fingers, the damaged floral wreath in the lap of Fidelity (Plate 5:10) and the broken hind paw on the 'grateful' dog (the circular hole in the centre of the break being a dowel hole from an earlier restoration) (Plate 5:11). All of these defects were undoubtedly caused by leaving such delicate and intricate work outside. What is less apparent is that although the pieces in Plates 5:10 and 11 still retain relatively precise and clear outlines, the surface of the marble is beginning to rot, or sugar, and disintegrate. For example, many of the details on the dog in the weathered Fidelity group (Plate 5:10) — the upper muzzle, the eyes and the lower part of the ear (the more exposed parts) — have, in comparison to the duplicate interior figure, lost much of their original definition. It is difficult to generalise, for the speed of weathering varies depending on location, but it is likely that if either of these weathered pieces were returned to a garden setting without undergoing any restoration or protection, then within a relatively short space of time, say twenty years, none of the detail on the exposed sections would remain — if indeed the pieces were still recognisable.

The failure of Italian marble to withstand the British climate is further illustrated by three other examples, all of which seem to have been in British gardens for no more than about fifty years.

Plate 5:10. Fidelity, weathered Statuary Carrara marble, signed 'G M BENZONI FA 1853 ROMA'. Height approx 32ins
SOTHEBY'S, SUSSEX

Plate 5:11. Gratitude, weathered Statuary Carrara marble, signed 'G M BENZONI FA 1853 ROMA'. Height approx 31ins
SOTHEBY'S, SUSSEX

The first example (Plate 5:12) shows a Statuary Carrara and Breccia Violette marble bust of the Roman Emperor Aurelius Antoninus (called Caracalla) (AD 188-217 — Emperor from 211), who is best known today for his tyranny and the murder of his brother, Geta. This bust, removed from the gardens of Wilsford Manor, Wiltshire,[13] was, in 1988, cleaned and in parts repolished and waxed and this has accentuated the effects of weathering. The top of the bust has started to sugar and much of the original carving, particularly the hair, is decidedly blurred, whilst the softer veins in the Breccia Violette marble drapery have been eaten into. The bust's face, protected from the elements by the angle at which it was positioned, has remained relatively untouched. It is this part which has been repolished, and it provides a stark comparison with those weathered parts, particularly the hair. The

Plate 5:12. Bust of the Roman Emperor Aurelius Antoninus, head Statuary Carrara marble, drapery Breccia Violette marble, after the antique original, circa eighteenth century, formerly in the gardens of Wilsford Manor, Wiltshire. Height approx 30ins
CHRISTOPHER HODSOLL: PHOTO PETER HODSOLL

*Colour Plate 57.
Narcissus, Statuary
Carrara marble on
Portland stone pedestal,
signed 'W THEED FECIT
ROMA 1848', Anglesey
Abbey, Cambridgeshire.
Height approx 49½ ins.
(See pages 235-236)*
THE NATIONAL TRUST: PHOTO
PETER GREENHALF

234

Colour Plate 58. Set of four vases and pedestals, vases Statuary Carrara marble, pedestals Portland stone, by Delvaux and Scheemakers, Anglesey Abbey, Cambridgeshire. (See Plates 5:13-17 and pages 236-238)

THE NATIONAL TRUST: PHOTO PETER GREENHALF

subject is derived from antique Roman examples. The Statuary Carrara marble head is similar to the most famous representation of Caracalla, now in the Museo Nazionale, Naples, but the Breccia Violette drapery is treated completely differently, and bears more of a resemblance to other antique examples, such as the bust now in the Museum of Fine Arts, Kansas City.[14]

This particular example probably dates from the eighteenth century when busts of Caracalla were particularly popular.[15] It is not signed, but one may speculate that it was carved by a sculptor with access to antique prototypes and Italian marbles, possibly operating from the vicinity of the Apuan Alps, where both the Statuary and Breccia Violette marbles used in it were quarried.

Another example of weathered marble garden ornaments is the neo-classical statue of Narcissus, peering enchantedly into a pond, beyond the Hyacinth Garden at Anglesey Abbey in Cambridgeshire (Colour Plate 57). This was carved by the Victorian sculptor William Theed the younger (1804-1891), and except for the fact that it does not have a fig leaf is an almost exact replica of the original (1847) work commissioned by the Prince Consort for Osborne House.[16]

From where Lord Fairhaven (1896-1966) acquired this Statuary Carrara marble figure is unclear, for many of his papers were destroyed on his death, but it could possibly be the same statue exhibited by the sculptor at the Exhibition of Art Treasures in Manchester in 1857.[17] It is known to have been erected outside at Anglesey Abbey on its Portland stone pedestal in 1947, and since then,

Plate 5:13. Set of four vases and pedestals, vases Statuary Carrara marble, pedestals Portland stone, by Delvaux and Scheemakers, circa 1725, Anglesey Abbey, Cambridgeshire. Height each vase approx 40ins; each pedestal approx 30ins

unlike its infinitely more robust pedestal, it has deteriorated considerably. Much of the exposed parts, the tree stump, legs, shoulders and head, have begun to sugar. Only those particularly well protected areas, for example under the left arm and the neck, retain the smooth finish the piece would have had (as an interior figure) prior to 1947. The statue has also started to accumulate lichen and moss which will be the cause of further destruction in the future. As is clearly apparent from this and many of the preceding examples in this chapter, most types of Italian marble are completely inappropriate additions to British gardens.

We have seen that such marbles are unable to withstand the ravages of our climate. But they are also inappropriate aesthetically, particularly in the case of white marble, for there are few worse combinations than the glossy white of marble and the brilliant, almost fluorescent green of the moss it is so often prone to attract in the British climate.

The four vases in Plates 5:13-17 and Colour Plate 58, also in the gardens of Anglesey Abbey, are more fortunate than Theed's Narcissus, for much of the vases, including the socles, handles, and intricately carved reliefs on the friezes, has been protected from the elements by the projecting rims of the lids.

This is fortunate, for they form an important set of early eighteenth century vases carved by two sculptors who were partners for most of the 1720s — Laurent Delvaux (1696-1778), who carved the vases in Plates 5:14 and 15, and Peter Scheemakers, who carved those in Plates 5:16 and 17. The set was carved for the interior of Wanstead House, Essex, and must have been executed prior to 1728, for in that year the partners set out together to study sculpture in Rome. Delvaux only stayed there for a few months before returning to his native lowlands, whilst

Plate 5:14. One of the four vases in Plate 5:13, based on the Borghese Vase, by Delvaux

Plate 5:15. One of the four vases in Plate 5:13, based on the Medici Vase, by Delvaux

Plate 5:16. One of the four vases in Plate 5:13, by Scheemakers

Plate 5:17. One of the four vases in Plate 5:13, by Scheemakers

Scheemakers was to spend several studious years in Rome before returning to London to set up a thriving business of his own.

All four vases are inspired by antique originals, and in particular the famous Medici and Borghese Vases, indeed the frieze on Delvaux's two vases are almost direct copies. That in Plate 5:15 varies from the Medici Vase primarily in the more compact and, at times, more flamboyant reproduction of the frieze, whilst that in Plate 5:14 is similar to the Borghese Vase, though varying notably in the addition of handles and the use of a different lower body. Both vases have been further modified in the substitution of the thin egg-and-dart mouldings found on the lips of the originals by large bold carving on the lids which are themselves additions.

Scheemakers' companion pair of vases (Plates 5:16 and 17) are similarly treated with a free composition of heroic scenes depicting classical figures worshipping deities.

When the contents of Wanstead House were sold in 1822, these vases, together with their superb quality Portland stone pedestals (the dies of which are carved from one whole block), were moved to the great hall of Leigh Court in Somerset. Sometime during this century they passed via a dealer's hand into Lord Fairhaven's outstanding collection of garden ornaments.

Today, during the worst months of the year, these vases are protected by 'sentry boxes' (see page 22), though these essential protective measures have only recently been introduced, and the consequences of leaving the marble vases out prior to this, as well as during the 'unguarded' summer months, is visible on each of the vase lids.

Venetian Marble Well-heads

Until the turn of the twentieth century, when aqueducts and piped water were introduced, the geographical location of Venice in a salt water lagoon obliged the population to rely on cisterns for the supply of water. In almost every square, piazza and public as well as private courtyard, cisterns were to be found (at least until the early 1900s), their tops decorated with raised marble well-heads. Some idea of the great numbers of these well-heads can be gauged from an early seventeenth century account that 'over one hundred and fifty wels [sic] for the common use of the people'[18] existed, whilst a census over two centuries later, in 1858, recorded more than six thousand in private hands alone.[19] These well-heads featured prominently in Venetian life, to the extent that laws were passed concerning their usage. The majority were executed from the marble available locally, particularly the robust white Istrian marble, whilst a few were executed from the red or orange-coloured marble found in the vicinity of Verona and known as Rosso Verona.

The vast majority of well-heads, such as can be seen in Canaletto's famous view of a Venetian stone mason's yard in the National Gallery, London, appear to have been executed by local craftsmen. These unique Venetian well-heads reflect the changing shape of the city's art and architecture, ranging as they do from richly carved examples from the Veneto-Byzantine period to the often simple forms which were produced during the nineteenth century. It is these varying styles, combined with the quality of carving and any wear visible, that provide the best means of dating otherwise undocumented examples.

With the introduction of modern systems of water supply at the end of the nineteenth and beginning of the twentieth century, many of these well-heads were no longer required, their wrought-iron over-throws were removed and the apertures boarded up. The plethora of now defunct well-heads coincided with the demand from Europe and elsewhere for works of Venetian art, and many were removed from the courtyards and piazzas of Venice and passed into the hands of collectors. In Britain the use of these well-heads as garden ornaments became popular at the end of the nineteenth century, and numerous examples (together with many fakes), found their way into British gardens. Few were used for their original purpose, but were placed in ornamental settings and filled with displays of flowers and foliage.

One of the most notable collections of Venetian well-heads in Britain is to be found in the Italian Gardens of Hever Castle, Kent. This was assembled during the latter years of the nineteenth and early years of the twentieth century by the immensely wealthy American, William Waldorf Astor, and three examples of this collection are illustrated.

The well-head in Plate 5:18 is carved from Rosso Verona marble. This relatively robust marble from the locality of Verona, west of Venice on the river Adige (which provided easy access to Venice), is perhaps best described as being of a mottled or 'blotchy' nature. After exposure to the elements it develops numerous horizontal and vertical crevices as the softer veins are eaten away. Its colouring is quite dramatic, for when unpolished and dry the colour of the varying blotches ranges from a white-grey to a light just discernible pink or red, but when damp or polished it blossoms into a superb range of reds, oranges and pinks (see Colour Plate 67 and Appendix I).

The treatment of this well-head would seem to date it to the late fourteenth or fifteenth century, for other documented examples of this date are similarly carved with vertical bands terminating in scrolls and dividing the head into sections. The use of acanthus leaves below each of the four heraldic shields probably dates it to around the fourteenth century rather than earlier. This well-head bears little comparison to early twentieth century examples, such as those being sold by J P White (see Chapter 7, pages 302-305), for the undercutting of the leaf bands, rosettes and armorials is vastly superior. Unfortunately it is poorly situated, having no form of step to set it off, and this not only detracts from its grandeur, but also puts it in direct contact with the ground making the piece especially vulnerable to deterioration, for the crevices at the bottom are particularly prone to frost action.

The most ornate well-head in the Italian Gardens at Hever Castle is also carved from Rosso Verona marble (Plate 5:19). Its treatment is similar to the bronze well-head by Jacob Sansovino (1486-1570), in the courtyard of the Doge's Palace in Venice (a reproduction of which is shown in Plate 7:16), and this fact, combined with the treatment of such features as the armorial cartouches, would certainly suggest a date around the fifteenth or sixteenth century. It is likely that this example originally adorned a private courtyard in Venice, for the armorials of the old order on many of the well-heads in public places were extensively removed in 1789 when the Republic of Venice was declared.[20]

The third well-head at Hever Castle (Plate 5:20) also features vertical leaf bands terminating in scrolls and dividing the drum of the well into sections, and so probably dates to roughly the same period as that illustrated in Plate 5:18. However, the leaf bands on this example (in the form of acanthus leaves) are far bolder and more luxuriant, so making it probably slightly later. Noticeable on the top of the well-head are the remains of wrought-iron fixtures leaded into holes chipped out of the marble. These are frequently found on genuine well-heads, being the remains of over-throws, protective grilles, and fixings to which ropes were attached. At times these sort of fittings are found on twentieth century examples, while their absence on poorly carved examples is often evidence of a twentieth century date.

Plate 5:18. Well-head, Rosso Verona marble, Venetian, late fourteenth/early fifteenth century, the Italian Gardens, Hever Castle, Kent. Height approx 35ins
HEVER CASTLE LTD

This well-head is carved from Istrian marble (or stone), a remarkably strong, relatively unporous stone. When newly cut or chipped it is bright white and shiny, which is why it is often referred to as a marble. It was obtained from quarries in the Venetian province of Istria (located opposite Venice, on the peninsula below Trieste, in what is now Yugoslavia) and was extensively used in the building of Venice. Its characteristic colour of a bright, almost bleached white, as well as its varying weathered grey-black tones, can be clearly seen on the facing scroll. The other main characteristic, hair line crevices running horizontally, can also be seen. Some idea of the durability of this immensely tough marble can be gauged from an event the author witnessed several years ago, when a larger-than-life statue weighing several tons fell over five feet on to a York stone pavement. With the exception of a few chips, the figure was untouched, whilst most of the York stone slabs it had come into contact with had been smashed. This makes Istrian marble one of the few suited to our climate, though it is not indestructible for, as with other soft veined marbles, the action of frost in the crevices of veins can cause catastrophic damage.

Plate 5:19. Well-head, Rosso Verona marble, Venetian, fifteenth or sixteenth century, the Italian Gardens, Hever Castle, Kent. Height approx 34½ins

HEVER CASTLE LTD

Plate 5:20. Well-head, Istrian marble/stone, Venetian, fifteenth century, the Italian Gardens, Hever Castle, Kent. Height approx 48ins including step (not seen)

HEVER CASTLE LTD

CHAPTER SIX

CAST- &
WROUGHT-IRON
1840 - 1900

The use of cast-iron for garden ornament became widespread in the early years of the nineteenth century, and in a short space of time a thriving business had blossomed with a proliferation of foundries also producing everything from inkstands to railway stations.

The medium had been used ornamentally for many years prior to this, but mainly for architectural work, such as the railings around St Paul's Cathedral,[1] or the fanlights and lamp-holders designed by Robert and James Adam. It was, however, generally frowned upon in favour of the more 'delicate' wrought-iron: 'There is a neatness and finished look... that will never be seen in cast'.[2]

However, with the increase in building at the turn of the century, the need for cheap ironwork rose dramatically. Cast-iron could be mass-produced at a fraction of the cost of wrought-iron work; furthermore cast-iron could be used to reproduce items impossible to manufacture in wrought-iron, such as vases, and so great numbers of foundries sprang up, or extended their range of castings, to meet this increased demand. Very soon 'frowned upon' cast-iron had superseded wrought-iron.

A natural progression from architectural castings was interior work, and by 1830 several booklets of 'tasteful' designs had been published such as Lewis N Cottingham's *The Smith and Founder's Director,*[3] which contained, 'A Series of Designs and Patterns for Ornamental Iron and Brass Work'. The preface states: 'The great improvement that has taken place in our Brass and Iron Foundries within these last twenty years, has elevated this branch of English manufacture far above that of any country, and raised the articles which were formerly considered as merely gross and ponderous, into the scale of ornamental embellishment, in which utility and security are united with the lightness and elegance of classical design'.[4] Although illustrating many designs for architectural castings, Cottingham's publication also includes such subjects as pedestals and vases, a number of which could be used both for interior and exterior use.

As cast-iron was cheap to produce, and therefore readily available to both the rising middle- and landed-classes, its use in gardens for ornamentation (for example vases) as well as for architectural features (for example conservatories) became extremely popular.

But there are two drawbacks; the first of these, and cast-iron's greatest disadvantage, is that it rusts. The Victorians were only too well aware of this problem, indeed Digby Wyatt looked forward to the day when 'scientific chemists shall have discovered a material which, superseding paint, shall effectually protect iron from oxidation',[5] but the only real remedy, paint, had the disadvantage that, as the anonymous author of the *Art-Journal* recounts, 'however carefully laid on [it] must fill up the details of ornamental casting'.[6] The second drawback is that cast-iron, unlike its wrought counterpart, is brittle, and if struck with a heavy blow will fracture, the subsequent repair proving both difficult and expensive.

In spite of this, cast-iron has distinct advantages over other materials: castings of some considerable strength can be produced, for instance ornate seats with elaborately pierced backs, which would be almost impossible to reproduce in other media such as stone or lead; the weight of a cast-iron vase will not damage its socle, as is so often the case with lead models; and fountains, as long as they are drained during the winter months, will not fracture by the action of ice, as is frequently the case in fountains made from stone or marble. If properly cared for with paint, cast-iron provides a cheaper alternative to bronze.

The number of foundries (such as the Carron Company, Charles D Young & Company, the Eagle Foundry and the Saracen Foundry) producing ornaments for parks and gardens was considerable, but this chapter is focused on the two most prolific manufacturers of cast-iron garden ornament: the Britannia Iron Works and the Coalbrookdale Company, whilst an example of a chair made by the Lion Foundry is included to illustrate the quality of casting of which even the smallest foundries were capable.

Also included is a short section on the iron-castings of two leading French establishments, Barbezat & Cie (who in later years traded under the names of, first, Houille & Cie, then Société Anonyme . . . du Val d'Osne), and A Durenne. Although not strictly within the environs of a book covering British garden ornament, both foundries produced a variety of wares which found extensive use in several British gardens, indeed Barbezat & Cie is known to have had an agent in England, as probably did A Durenne.

This chapter concludes with a brief discussion of wrought-iron work. Although stronger and less liable to fracture than cast-iron, wrought-iron does tend to deteriorate faster in places. Nevertheless, charming wrought-iron pieces, mostly chairs, were produced during the nineteenth century.

Plate 6:1. Detail of the design registration diamond, or lozenge, on the armchair illustrated in Plate 6:25
MILES D'AGAR AND NICK GIFFORD-MEAD ANTIQUES

Registration Marks

Many of the British manufacturers of cast-iron ornaments advertised their names by incorporating within the cast their own trade mark, though its presence did not legally prevent other foundries deleting it and copying the design. To safeguard designs, a system of registration was introduced in 1842 whereby designs could be registered at the Patent Office. Thus it is possible to identify the British manufacturer of an ornament that has no trade mark but does bear a registration mark. These registration marks take the form of a lozenge or diamond surmounted by a circle within which is coded the date of registration (Plate 6:1). In this example, the circle has the Roman numeral I, to denote its class (I indicating iron). Until 1867, the letter below this circle gave the year of manufacture, that in the left-hand corner of the diamond indicated the month, whilst the number in the right hand corner referred to the day of the month. The mark at the bottom indicated the bundle number, which was used to differentiate designs registered on the same day. From 1868 to 1883 the class reference remained the same, whilst the mark below indicated the day, the right-hand corner the year, the left-hand corner the bundle number and the bottom the month.

The lists overleaf show the year letters for the two periods; the month letters remained the same for both periods.

1842-1867		1868-1883		Months (both periods)	
A	1845	A	1871	A	December
B	1858	C	1870	B	October
C	1844	D	1878	C or O	January
D	1852	E	1881	D	September
E	1855	F	1873	E	May
F	1847	H	1869	G	February
G	1863	I	1872	H	April
H	1843	J	1880	I	July
I	1846	K	1883	K	November (and December 1860)
J	1854	L	1882	M	June
K	1857	P	1877	R	August (and 1-19 September 1857)
L	1856	S	1875	W	March
M	1859	U	1874		
N	1864	V	1876		
O	1862	W	1-6 March 1878		
P	1851	X	1868		
Q	1866	Y	1879		
R	1861				
S	1849				
T	1867				
U	1848				
V	1850				
W	1865				
X	1842				
Y	1853				
Z	1860				

Thus the registration diamond in Plate 6:1 reveals that the design was registered on 24 May (E) 1859 (M), and from this it is possible to discover the name of the manufactory, and possibly the designer, from the register in the Public Record Office.

From 1884 to 1907, a numerical system of registration was used.

Making Cast-Iron Ornaments

During the nineteenth century, iron was obtained by placing the iron-containing ore between layers of coke in a furnace. (Prior to the eighteenth century, charcoal had been used as a fuel but, because the weight of the ore crushed the charcoal, this restricted production to small furnaces.) Once the furnace was lit, air was blasted in to attain the immense heat necessary to melt the iron. The pig-iron which is the result of this process contains some impurities, primarily carbon, and it is this iron that is used for casting.

To obtain a cast, an original pattern was required. Depending on the subject, these were carved in wood or modelled in clay by a pattern maker, a highly skilled artist, for not only did he have to carve the pattern, but he also had to take into consideration the fact that molten metal contracts during cooling. Once carved or modelled, the pattern was sealed to prevent distortion when exposed to a damp mould. Considering the intricacy and size of some iron castings, such as the seat in Plate 6:16, the pattern maker's abilities cannot fail to be admired.

Each ornament was cast in a frame which comprised a lower half (drag) and upper half (cope). The drag was partially filled with coarse sand and then topped up with facing sand (a much finer sand) and compressed. The pattern was embedded into this. The cope was located on top of the drag, and the process of sand filling was repeated. Facing sand was required in order to obtain a finer mould, whilst coarse sand facilitated the escape of any air or gas generated during casting. After being left to consolidate, the cope and drag were separated, the pattern removed, and the formed mould dusted with powdered charcoal to allow a finer textured cast to be taken. The pattern was then reintroduced to the mould, pouring and breathing holes were located, and the whole mould recompressed. After separating the cope and drag again, the pattern was finally removed and the mould reassembled. The molten iron was poured in and, after cooling, the cast removed.

Easy as it may sound, the whole process was highly technical and not without mishaps. 'Washing' could occur if the sand was not sufficiently tenacious, causing details in the mould to be literally washed away when the molten iron was poured in. Furthermore castings were easily spoiled, for if the air or gas was unable to escape from the mould, the resulting bubbles would produce either a pitted surface or even cause the mould to explode. Whilst these were but a few of the problems of casting, the careless construction of a mould could also ruin the cast, and unlike softer metals such as lead or bronze, where defects in the cast could easily be remedied, 'the chaser's tools will not touch iron; the cast once made remains — no blemish in the casting can be removed — no disturbance in the proportions can be altered. An iron-casting is, therefore, a more wonderous work of mechanical art than a cast of brass or bronze; there are more difficulties to be overcome in the preparation, there is more nicety in the process, and there are no earthly means of changing the result'.[7]

Although many of the moulds were of some considerable size, such as that used to produce the main bowl for the Chateau Impney fountain (plate 6:10 and Colour Plate 60), which must have been over six feet in diameter, the great majority of garden ornaments were cast in several sections, and then joined together. In the case of chairs for example, the back, seat and each arm and leg were cast separately and then bolted together.

The Britannia Iron Works

The Britannia Iron Works, which stood on the bank of the river Derwent in Derby, are known today predominantly for their engineering and architectural castings. In 1850 the foundry was employing between 220 and 250 men at the works which covered 'at least three acres of ground'.[8] Iron was obtained both locally (Derbyshire and Staffordshire), and from as far afield as Yorkshire, south Wales and Scotland, and cast in moulds made from a red Mansfield sand combined with charcoal and coal dust. Amongst the many castings being produced, girders, columns, axles, pipes, wheels and locomotive cylinders may be mentioned. By 1898, the foundry was employing about one thousand men and had produced a whole range of enormous castings; its bridges, for example, had been erected not only in England, but also in Russia, Austria, Spain, Portugal, Denmark, Italy, Sardinia, Canada, Australia, South America and Africa.[9]

The foundry was also producing a range of ornamental castings. This side of the business was started by the firm of Weatherhead & Glover, which had established a foundry in 1818 and is known to have supplied several ornamental castings to Alton Towers.[10] In 1843, Weatherhead & Glover's interest was taken over by Thomas Wright, who expanded the castings to meet the increased demand for railways and associated products. Wright's concern was short-lived, for in 1848 the works were taken over by a Scotsman, Andrew Handyside (1806-1887), who was to expand both the engineering, architectural and ornamental sides of the foundry.

By 1850, according to the *Art-Journal,* Handyside was producing several 'ornamental vases...many of which are remarkable for their classic purity of form and ornament', and at least one fountain which, like several of the vases, was illustrated. The *Art-Journal* went on to describe the fountain as 'of very graceful design, capable of much enlargement and enrichment of detail'.[11]

The following year at the Great Exhibition, Handyside exhibited a selection of ornamental wares, including two reduced copies of the Medici Vase, two bacchanalian vases, two antique vases with scrolls and a superb 'bronzed' vase (the design is illustrated in Plate 6:5) which, according to the *Art-Journal* catalogue, was 'deserving of much attention' and an 'excellent design'.[12] It was perhaps due to this vase, decorated with an interlaced design and busts of Peel, Nelson, Watt, Wellington, Stephenson, Scott, Shakespeare and Milton,[13] that the foundry was awarded a medal for 'Iron Castings'.[14]

At the International Exhibition in London eleven years later, the foundry, still 'more renowned for its machinery — huge powerful "utilities" — than for its Art-issues',[15] gained a further medal for 'Iron Castings' as well as one for 'Machinery'.[16]

In 1868, presumably to celebrate fifty years of casting at the Britannia Iron Works, 'Andrew Handyside & Co.' of the 'Britannia Iron Works, Derby and 32, Walbrook, London' published a short booklet entitled *Works in Iron.*[17] Atlhough this is mainly concerned with the firm's engineering and architectural castings, the booklet contains some information on the ornamental side of the foundry. Of cast-iron vases and fountains we read: 'The Britannia Iron Works have long been well known for the production of these articles, so useful and effective in garden decoration. The use of cast iron permits a delicacy of outline which is impossible in cheap stone or terra-cotta, and the fine moulding sand obtained at Derby allows a smoothness of surface otherwise unattainable'.[18]

In 1873, the business became a limited company and the following year published a catalogue of its ornamental wares. Entitled *Handyside's Ironwork,* and proclaiming the firm's achievements not only at the two exhibitions, but also the other medals it had won,[19] the introduction expounds the advantages of cast-iron over other media:

> Ornamental fountains and vases may be carved in Marble or Stone, moulded in Terra-Cotta and Stucco, or cast in Iron or Bronze. The finest works are those carved in Marble by skilled artists, but the very great cost which is involved renders their use rare. Stone, though not so expensive a material as marble cannot be sculptured well without considerable cost, but Fountains, and other similar objects, are sometimes made at a comparatively low price by men who are rather masons than sculptors, and who produce inartistic designs in a coarse and rude style. Cheap stone will crack and decay when exposed to wet weather. The art of moulding in Terra-Cotta has been revived and much improved during the last few years, and the most beautiful objects are produced from this material. Fountains are, however, seldom made of Terra-Cotta, and vases of this material are easily chipped and broken. Fountains and Vases made of this material will crack and crumble away, when exposed to wet or frost... The use of cast-iron or bronze permits a sharpness and delicacy of outline which is impossible in Stone or Stucco, and the fine moulding-sand and iron obtained at Derby allows a smoothness of

surface not otherwise easily attainable. Cast-Iron Fountains and Vases, if occasionally painted, are imperishable, and will not crack when exposed to wet or frosty weather.[20]

The catalogue illustrates a huge range of ornamental wares, including, amongst other items, gates, railings, lamp pillars, balusters, columns, conservatories, fountains and vases. The company's achievements can perhaps be gauged by the fact that it could offer a total of thirty-three free-standing and seven wall fountains, as well as forty-nine different vases. However, many of these are variations or adaptations of one model.

In 1887 Handyside died. The works, whose site is now covered by a housing estate,[21] continued in production until 1911 when it closed.

The foundry's vases and fountains are often difficult to identify, for many of them, even monumental works such as the fountain in Plate 6:10, do not display the firm's name. Those that are marked either have a plaque riveted to them (usually on the base), bearing words such as 'A HANDYSIDE & CO DERBY & LONDON', or a similar inscription incorporated within the cast (Plate 6:2).

Like the Coalbrookdale Company, Britannia Iron Works ornaments are known to have been available with a 'bronzed' finish but were, without doubt, also painted. The precise colours are not listed in the 1874 catalogue, but they probably included 'Dark green, indigo green or dark brown' and 'Bronze green',[22] the colours suggested by Ewing Matheson (an employee of the firm).

The following pages examine in some detail a few of the works executed by the company, which is not as yet renowned (though should be) for its garden vases in the way the Coalbrookdale Company is renowned for its garden chairs.

Handyside vases

The Britannia foundry, unlike that at Coalbrookdale which was mainly producing modern designs, was predominantly involved with producing copies or variations of antique vases. Indeed Handyside relates that 'Amongst the best forms of vases are those which are oldest, and which reproduce with fidelity the most famous classical designs'.[23]

The Handyside vases illustrated are only a selection of the many models available. The great majority of these are often poorly cast and bear little resemblance to any original they were copied from. Price-wise, they appear to have been more expensive than, for example, Blashfield's terracotta, for in 1857 Blashfield could offer a copy of the Warwick Vase, two feet in diameter for £4 4s (see page 183), whilst eleven years later Handyside's similar-sized copy could be had for £6.[24]

Number 23 in the company's 1874 catalogue, the vase in Plate 6:3, was exhibited by Handyside at the 1862 exhibition. It had been 'designed especially' and the foundry's efforts were suitably rewarded when it 'obtained a prize medal'.[25]

The relief on the frieze is copied from a pair of marble plaques entitled Night and Morning by the Danish sculptor Bertel Thorvaldsen. These reliefs were popular during the period, indeed the *Art-Journal,* illustrating a marble pair purchased by the Duke of Devonshire went so far as to describe them as:

> Among the most exquisitely poetical conceptions of a mind whose constitution was eminently of a poetical order, as evinced in nearly the whole

of its productions. The former [Night] is symbolised by a winged figure bearing two infants, floating rather than flying through the air; they are asleep, and an air of repose is felicitously given to the composition by the quiet attitudes assumed by the figures, even to the lower limbs of the principal one, crossed as at rest: the companion of their shadowy flight is the 'bird that loves darkness'. 'Morning' on the other hand, is full of light... Thorwaldsen [sic] must ever be regarded as one of the great lights of an enlightened age.[26]

It is not surprising, therefore, that the two figures were reproduced by an 'art' manufacturing company such as Handyside's, both on a vase and in their original form as a pair of bas-reliefs.[27]

Unfortunately the Swiss Garden vase (Plate 6:3) which ironically turns Morning towards the darkness of a hedge leaving Night in the full light of day, has been altered by the addition of an unsightly and evidently modern plate between the main body and foliage below. Like many of the firm's ornaments it lacks any identifying mark. Despite this, it must have been one of which Handyside was rightly proud, for he illustrates both aspects of the vase in the catalogue (Plate 6:4).

Plate 6:5 includes model 'No 3A' in the company's 1874 catalogue. This vase, raised on pedestal 'No 5A', is an adaptation by the foundry of a 'famous classical design'.[28] It is a smaller-size copy of the famous Borghese Vase, but unfaithful in that the lower half, decorated with acanthus leaves and two handles, is taken from another vase, perhaps its pair, 'No 3', the Medici Vase.

Plate 6:4. Page 60 from Handyside's 1874 catalogue (C). It illustrates several of the firm's designs, including both sides of the Night and Morning Vase in Plate 6:3, and the smaller copies (top left and right) of the Medici and Borghese Vases

DERBY LOCAL STUDIES LIBRARY

It is not clear when Handyside produced his Borghese Vase (Plate 6:6), certainly by 1868 a model had been cast for it is illustrated in *Works in Iron*.[29] Its companion, the Medici Vase, was being produced by at least 1850,[30] but may well have been available earlier than this, as L N Cottingham included the design in his publication dated 1824 to 'introduce such a collection of Designs and Patterns as may well be a guide to them [smiths and ornamental metal-workers] in forming correct and tasteful compositions'.[31] There is no documentary evidence to support this theory, but Cottingham's work was influential and it may have inspired the foundry to produce not only the Medici copy, but several other models.

Examination of the Borghese Vase reveals that the socle and its square base were cast separately from the main body, as was the decorative beading surmounting the egg-and-dart moulding on the rim. As a piece of cast-iron work it is notable for its depth, the frieze, for example, is over one and a half inches in relief in a few places; however, much of the modelling is poor, the faun playing misshapen pipes, for example, leaves much to be desired (Plate 6:7).

Both the company's copies of the Medici and Borghese Vases were also available in a smaller size of one foot five inches, respectively models 'No 3 Small' and 'No 3A Small', the designs for which are illustrated in Plate 6:4 (top left and top right). However, these smaller-sized models are frequently even more poorly cast than the larger examples.

The vase in Plate 6:8 is perhaps one of the commonest produced by the company. It was available in two sizes, two feet high, as illustrated, and two feet six inches high. According to the 1874 catalogue, they were respectively models 'No 1 Small' and 'No 1 Large'.[32] The foundry was also producing a range of other vases of a similar campana form. For example model 'No 2' is the same as model 'No 1 Large', but cast with a circular rather than square base and bolder

Plate 6:5. Page 66 from Handyside's 1874 catalogue (C). This also illustrates several of the company's designs, including the Borghese Vase (bottom right) seen in Plate 6:6, and the vase for which the company was awarded a medal at the Great Exhibition in 1851 (bottom centre). A model of this can be seen at the Erewash Museum, Ilkeston

DERBY LOCAL STUDIES LIBRARY

Plate 6:6. Smaller-size copy of the Borghese Vase on a contemporary pedestal, cast-iron, Britannia Iron Works (Handyside), no founder's mark, circa 1870. Height of vase approx 32ins; height of pedestal approx 26ins

PRIVATE COLLECTION

decoration on the frieze, whilst model 'No 10' is the same as model 'No 1 Large', but with the handles exchanged for interlocking dolphins and the relief on the frieze replaced by dolphins and putti. Numerous other variations were also being produced, such as vases 'No 6' and 'No 6A' which retain the form and much of the design, including the socle and lower half found on models 1, 2 and 10, but the main body is decorated with broad vertical reeding, while the lobed moulding on the rim is replaced with egg-and-dart moulding, similar to that found on the Borghese Vase in Plate 6:6. Furthermore, model 'No 6' was decorated with handles in the form of foliage, and was two feet six inches high, whilst model 'No 6A' had no handles and stood three feet six inches high.

At what date the foundry started producing casts of model 'No 1 Small' is unclear. A pair of 'vases with Scrolls'[33] was exhibited at the Great Exhibition, but it has not been possible to ascertain whether these were examples of model 'No 1 Small', 'No 1 Large', or another model.

This particular casting of model 'No 1 Small' can be dated to after 1873, for it carries an oval plaque (not visible in the photograph) marked with the company's limited name.

Plate 6:7. Detail of the vase in Plate 6:6 showing the poor modelling of the figures and the misshapen pipes

Plate 6:8. One of a set of four 'No 1 Small' vases, cast-iron, with cast mark on base of 'A Handyside & Co Ltd, London and Derby', after 1873. Height approx 24ins

Handyside fountains

The fountains in Plates 6:9 and 10 and Colour Plates 59 and 60 clearly illustrate the company's use of the same patterns to produce different models. From their architectural pedestals upwards the fountains are almost exactly the same; that at Temple Newsam (Plate 6:9 and Colour Plate 59) is a less ornate and, therefore, presumably cheaper fountain than that at Chateau Impney (Plates 6:10 and 11 and Colour Plate 60). The main bowl and its support, decorated with acanthus leaves, is the same on both models, with the exception that water flows over the rim at Temple Newsam, whilst at Chateau Impney it issues from decorated outlets in the rim. Continuing up the fountain the dolphin support and upper bowl are again similar, but the example at Chateau Impney is more elaborate with foliage behind the dolphins. The surmounting figures are also interesting, for although both were no doubt interchangeable, that at Temple Newsam (which has been extensively copied in lead this century) seems too small, whilst that at Chateau Impney far too large.

A variety of sections from these two fountains were also duplicated in several other of the company's castings. Fountain number 12, for example, is almost exactly the same from the lower bowl up as that at Temple Newsam, whilst the dolphins were not only incorporated in the fountains in Plates 6:9 and 10 and in fountain number 12, but also in fountain 15 and flower stands 28 and 29. This practice of using the same pattern in several models was employed by many cast-iron foundries as a great saving of time and money, for pattern making was an expensive operation.

The Chateau Impney fountain probably dates from the mid-1870s, for by 1875 the building was complete, and it seems reasonable to assume that the fountain was supplied at this time.[34] In the company's 1874 catalogue it was model 36 (Plate 6:12), the most ornate design available, and it remains today in remarkably good condition. The present colour scheme is unlikely to have been original (Colour Plate 61).

The Temple Newsam fountain (model number 19 in the company's 1874 catalogue) must have been supplied some time before the company became limited in 1873, since the foundry's name, incorporated in the cast, reads only as 'A HANDYSIDE & Co'. Although one can speculate that the fountain had been cast earlier, and then supplied at a later date, it seems improbable since two vases at Temple Newsam also supplied by the foundry bear a similar legend.[35]

The basic design was being produced at the foundry by at least 1862, for a model, modified by the use of a more ornate upper bowl, is illustrated in *The Art-Journal Illustrated Catalogue of the International Exhibition 1862*.[36] This illustration reveals that the fountain was originally designed to issue water on a grander scale than it does at present; the two cherubs surmounting the fountain were plumbed to spout water both horizontally and vertically, whilst twin jets of water arose from the lips of each dolphin. Furthermore the water which today merely trickles from each lion's mouth is depicted as gushing forth.

The Coalbrookdale Company [37]

Perhaps the most renowned foundry for cast-iron garden ornaments, particularly garden chairs, is the Coalbrookdale Company. The works were established in 1709 by a Quaker, Abraham Darby (1678-1717), at Coalbrookdale on the river Severn in Shropshire, and were run during much of the remaining century by successive Darbys. During this period the business, involved primarily with engineering

Colour Plate 59. Fountain, cast-iron, 'A HANDYSIDE & Co' raised in relief on the pedestal, the South Garden, Temple Newsam, Leeds

LEEDS METROPOLITAN DISTRICT COUNCIL: PHOTO PETER GREENHALF

Plate 6:9. Fountain, cast-iron, 'A HANDYSIDE & Co' raised in relief on the pedestal, circa 1865, the South Garden, Temple Newsam, Leeds. Height approx 14 feet 4½ins. (See Colour Plate 59)
LEEDS METROPOLITAN DISTRICT COUNCIL

Plate 6:10. Fountain, cast-iron, Britannia Iron Works (Handyside), no foundry mark, circa 1875, the Formal Garden, Chateau Impney, Droitwich. Height approx 15 feet 9ins. (See Colour Plate 60)
CHATEAU IMPNEY HOTEL, DROITWICH

castings and household wares, established a firm reputation for fine quality castings, and this reputation was further advanced by the foundry producing the first iron rails, in 1769, and bridge, in 1799.

By the turn of the century, the business had expanded from Abraham's original furnace at Coalbrookdale to numerous works, not only at Coalbrookdale but also Horsehay (a short distance up the Severn). In 1827 the management of the Horsehay works was taken over by Abraham IV (1804-1878) and Alfred Darby (1807-1852), sons of Edmund Darby, a nephew of Abraham III, whilst those at Coalbrookdale were run (since 1810) by Francis Darby (1783-1850). Unlike the earlier Darbys, Francis was not a strict Quaker, and indulged a love of the arts. According to John Randall, he 'filled his rooms with costly paintings which he felt a pride in shewing to his friends',[38] and it is perhaps above all due to him that the works moved into the relatively new field of art castings. This prudent expansion was a well-timed economic move; the recession of the early years of the century had passed, and a new demand for ornamental wares was developing, caused not only by the increase in building, but also by the emergence of the middle-class. Cast-iron wares were well suited to meet this new demand, for they could be reproduced to a high quality and at a reasonable price. Indeed Digby Wyatt in 1851 relates that 'every possible variety of those smaller articles which enter into the daily consumption of the great mass of the middle classes, are made at Coalbrookdale. Stoves, fenders, chairs, vases, etc'.[39]

By 1846, the company, according to an article in the *Art-Union,* was employing between three and four thousand men, and had 'produced castings of iron which challenge competition with the most perfect bronzes'.[40] Numerous garden

Plate 6:11. Detail of the fountain in Plate 6:10. (See Colour Plate 61)

Plate 6:12. Page 14 from Handyside's 1874 catalogue (C), illustrating the design for the Chateau Impney fountain in Plate 6:10 and Colour Plate 60

ornaments were available such as vases (which were not so keenly admired) and fountains, but none were 'more popular than the garden and hall chairs, which generally combine great lightness with great strength and stability'.[41] The article goes on to say that 'no works in the kingdom have done more to combine art with the productions of our native mines',[42] and it concludes:

> The Coalbrookdale works are the first of the empire in the artistic excellence of their productions, and the conductors are exerting themselves to maintain this superiority by sparing no expense in procuring the best models at home and abroad. They have succeeded in casting figures of most complicated detail, and we doubt not that they will continue to make new applications of iron to objects both of ornament and utility, so as at once to extend the domain of art, and increase domestic convenience.[43]

New models were introduced and, with the increase in technical skill of the casters, pattern and mould makers, the faith in the firm's future expressed by the *Art-Union* was fulfilled and the foundry expanded into larger art works.

In 1851 the company exhibited a selection of castings at the Great Exhibition, receiving a prestigious council medal awarded for, according to the report of the jury, 'their variety and very general excellence, whether as objects of utility or ornaments...'.[44] These exhibits included not only several smaller articles, such as fire-grates and garden chairs, but also some monumental works including the ornate gates, designed by one of the company's designers, Charles Crookes, which stand today by the Albert Gate in Hyde Park, and the life-size models of John Bell's (1812-1895) Cupid and Swan and Eagle Slayer which met with some

Colour Plate 60. Cast-iron fountain, Britannia Iron Works (Handyside), no foundry mark, the Formal Garden, Chateau Impney, Droitwich. (See Plates 6:10 and 11 and page 252)

CHATEAU IMPNEY HOTEL, DROITWICH

considerable approval. Digby Wyatt referring to Bell's works relates that 'the beauty of such productions...do credit alike to Mr Bell...and to the company'.[45]

By 1852, Abraham Darby had retired, and both Francis and Alfred were dead. The management of the works, which by 1855 was producing two thousand tons of finished iron a week,[46] was left to Charles Crookes. Under his control new castings were produced, such as John Bell's Deer Hound table which was exhibited at the 1855 Paris Exhibition, and as business prospered the works continued to expand. In 1859 the company, which took considerable care of its workforce, opened a new building to form an educational centre for its employees and to house a school of art and a literary and scientific institute. At the International Exhibition of 1862 the company, which by then, according to J B Waring, was 'so well known in the world of industrial art that any eulogium on their productions is quite unnecessary',[47] gained a further medal for 'excellence of workmanship and artistic design in the articles exhibited by them'.[48] Among the many castings exhibited were an ornate set of gates designed by Bell & Crookes, some fifty-four feet long;[49] two fountains, one designed by 'that eminent sculptor M. Carrier-Belleuse',[50] the other in bronze by Mr Kershaw; and 'some cleverly-designed

Colour Plate 61. Detail of the Chateau Impney fountain. This colour scheme is unlikely to have been the original finish

garden-seats, ornamented with natural foliage, olive, fern, passion flower, &c.'.[51] Waring concluded that the firm's 'present high state of excellence is mainly due to the energy, judgment, and good taste of Mr. Crookes, who for many years has acted as manager to the company'.[52]

The company also exhibited a new, short-lived range of terracotta. Several of these vases and flower pots are illustrated in the *Art-Journal* catalogue of 1862,[53] whilst examples can be seen at, amongst other locations, the Ironbridge Gorge Museum and Regent's Park.[54] This expansion into the production of a different medium was, no doubt, due to the increasing popularity of the compound, and was facilitated at Coalbrookdale by the fact that since the early years of the century a brick works had been operating, supplying bricks to house the increasing workforce.

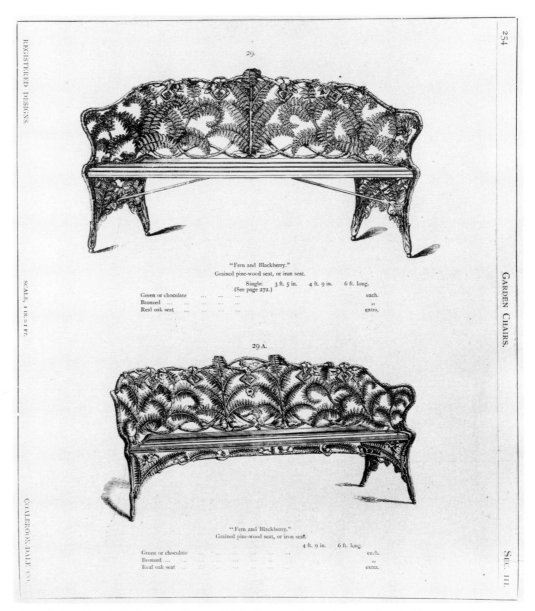

29.

"Fern and Blackberry."
Grained pine-wood seat, or iron seat.

Single. 3 ft. 5 in. 4 ft. 9 in. 6 ft. long.
(See page 272.)

Green or chocolate	...	...	...	each.
Bronzed	...	...	...	,,
Real oak seat	...	...	...	extra.

29 A.

"Fern and Blackberry."
Grained pine-wood seat, or iron seat.

4 ft. 9 in. 6 ft. long.

Green or chocolate	...	...	...	...	each.
Bronzed	...	...	...	...	,,
Real oak seat	...	...	...	...	extra.

Plate 6:13. Page 254 from the Coalbrookdale Company's catalogue of 1875, illustrating the designs of the Fern and Blackberry garden chair
IRONBRIDGE GORGE MUSEUM TRUST

In 1866 the management of the works was taken over by William G Norris, whose family had been associated with the company for many years, and under his control the expansion of both the ornamental and engineering sides of the business continued. In 1875 the company published an enormous illustrated catalogue, comprising twelve sections, of which Section III, *Garden and Park Embellishments,* covers over one hundred pages, and provides a considerable insight into Coalbrookdale's range of garden ornaments. A great number of designs are illustrated, including a total of forty-one garden chairs and park benches, forty-two vases (or finials), fifty fountains and seventeen pedestals. However, several of these different designs incorporate the same model, such as the figure of Cupid, which occurs in fountain numbers 8 and 26, and flower stands 112 and 125. Other designs are extensions of one particular design, such as that of the Fern and Blackberry garden chair, which was illustrated in three forms but was available in a total of six different sizes (Plate 6:13). Despite this, it was a remarkable

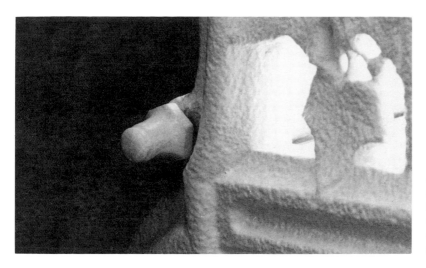

achievement, and one that can perhaps be gauged by the sheer number of products available; for example, of the twenty-seven basic designs for garden chairs and park benches illustrated, the company could list a total of over 130 different models.

The ornaments were available in a number of finishes, perhaps the most common of which was paint, the most popular colours being green, chocolate (these two mostly offered for garden chairs), or white (mainly for fountains and vases). Other paint finishes included oak[55] and marble[56]. Several alternative finishes to paint were used: bronzed[57] and electro-bronzed,[58] whilst less common were Berlin blacked and japanned and gilt.

In 1881, the business became a limited company, and a few years later leased and then sold the works at Horsehay, which are still in production today. Five years later Alfred Darby II (1850-1925) became chairman of the company, although Norris continued to manage the works until 1897 when Duncan Sinclair took over. In 1922 the firm merged with several other foundries to form Light Castings Ltd, and seven years later became an autonomous subsidiary of Allied Ironfounders Ltd. The foundry continued in production until 1969 when the works were taken over by Glynwed Foundries Ltd. Some of the remaining works, the furnace and the Great Warehouse are now run by the Ironbridge Gorge Museum Trust, in which a number of the company's castings are displayed, including, amongst other items, a number of garden chairs, and copies of Bell's Swan and Boy fountain, Andromeda and Deer Hound table.

The success of the company was due primarily to the quality of its castings, which won many exhibition awards. Like so many other manufacturers of art works, the company, by employing a number of eminent sculptors and modellers, could offer not only high standards of craftsmanship, but also models which reflected the popular fashions of the period. These facts, together with the publicity consciousness of the company, promoted its name as the leading nineteenth century foundry and, considering the volume of its output, particularly of garden chairs, it is no surprise that so many examples survive today.

Coalbrookdale garden chairs

The company's garden chairs are usually identifiable by the presence of its name, such as 'C.B. Dale Co' or 'COALBROOKDALE', found mainly on the front or rear of the chair back. These marks are predominantly indented in the casting, but a few have the inscription raised in relief on a plaque, also incorporated in the casting (rather than attached to it). Some of the models, particularly the more ornate chairs, are characteristic in that they were assembled using moulded bronze nuts (Plate 6:14). Other examples of the firm's castings are identifiable through

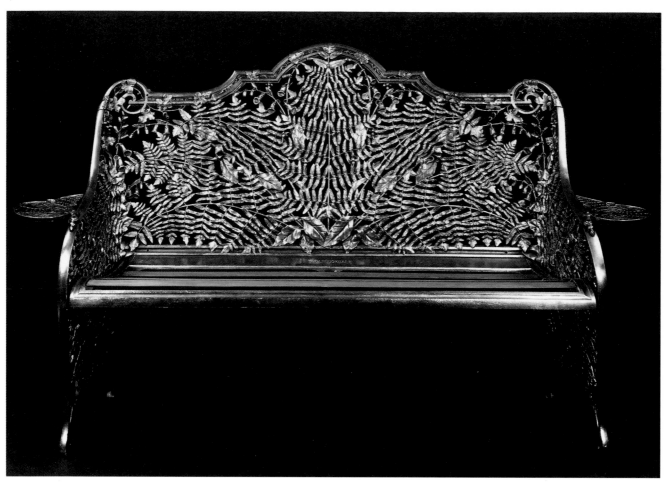

Colour Plate 62. Two-seater bronze version of the Coalbrookdale Company's Osmunda Regalis chair complete with bracket shelves — an optional extra, late nineteenth century. Width approx 58ins. (See also Plate 6:16 and pages 262-263)

WILLIAM BEDFORD PLC

the registered designs illustrated in the company's catalogues, but this method of identification should be treated with caution, for several of the designs appear to have been reproduced by other foundries. An example of this is the chair in Plate 6:15 which does not carry the company's name, yet corresponds both in design and dimensions to that illustrated in the 1875 catalogue, entitled 'Fern and Blackberry' (Plate 6:13). Unfortunately no information concerning the origins of this particular example has come to light,[59] and although it may be possible that the seat passed through the Coalbrookdale works unmarked, it seems most unlikely, for the original pattern would no doubt have been carved with the company's name, which would inevitably occur, as with all genuine Coalbrookdale Fern and Blackberry chairs, in the casting. It was probably produced by another foundry, for although all Coalbrookdale designs were registered under the 1842 Design Act, this only provided protection for three years, and it was therefore possible for other foundries to make copies quite legally after that time.

A number of companies operating in the nineteenth century are known to have featured copies of this design in their catalogues, including Val d'Osne, Watson Gow & Co of the Etna Foundry, and Thomas Hyde.

Generally speaking, the naturalistic and Gothic chairs tend to date from the early years of production, though some of the more orderly naturalistic models, such as Christopher Dresser's Horse Chestnut and Water Plant (Plate 6.19) chairs, date from the 1870s.[60]

Colour Plate 63. An almost identical Valet de Limiers (Bloodhound Groom) to that in Plate 6:29. The cast-iron group, from the Val d'Osne foundry, is fully signed 'A JACQUEMART', and from the quality of the casting is circa 1870. This model shows signs of the original paint and, unlike the model at Anglesey Abbey (Plate 6:29), the standing hound bears a hunting brand
MILES D'AGAR AND NICK GIFFORD-MEAD ANTIQUES

Plate 6:15. Although corresponding to the Coalbrookdale Fern and Blackberry chair, this example is unlikely to have been cast at Coalbrookdale, since it is unusual to find unmarked chairs from this company
CHATEAU IMPNEY HOTEL, DROITWICH

The chair in Colour Plate 62 and also illustrated in the Coalbrookdale Company's 1875 catalogue (Plate 6:16) is of particular interest, for no bronze chairs are referred to in any of the company's literature or extant catalogues; furthermore this particular model, even executed in iron, is rare. Entitled Osmunda Regalis,[61] and with the design number 57A it was available in one of two sizes: '6ft. 4in. long'[62] as illustrated in Plate 6:16; or 'About 4ft. 10in. long',[63] a slightly modified version of the larger size, as illustrated in bronze in Colour Plate 62. Iron models were available in one of a number of finishes: 'Bronzed' or 'Painted green or chocolate', and came with either a 'Grained pine-wood seat, or iron seat', or at an extra cost a 'Real oak seat'.[64]

The use of bronze for a garden chair, although unusual, is not totally unexpected, for the foundry, as well as being renowned for its iron castings, had also been casting in bronze for many years. Indeed bronze castings had been exhibited at, amongst others, the 1851[65] and 1855[66] exhibitions and, as has already been mentioned, the use of bronze nuts to secure the various components

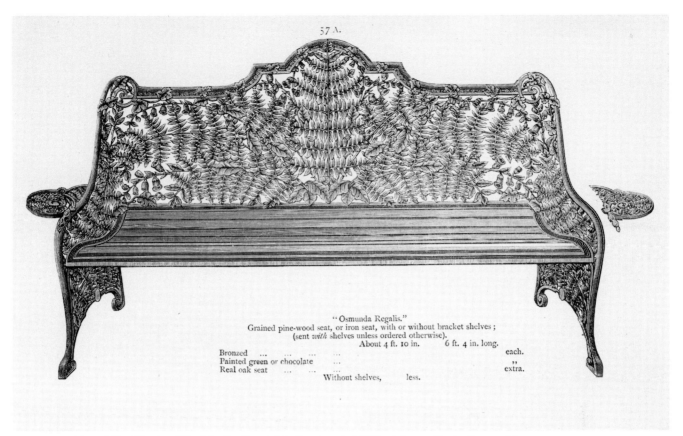

57 A.

"Osmunda Regalis."
Grained pine-wood seat, or iron seat, with or without bracket shelves;
(sent *with* shelves unless ordered otherwise).
About 4 ft. 10 in.   6 ft. 4 in. long.

Bronzed	...	...	...	each.
Painted green or chocolate	...			„
Real oak seat	...	...		extra.

Without shelves,   less.

Plate 6:16. Page 262 of Section III of the Coalbrookdale Company's 1875 catalogue, illustrating model number 57A, the Osmunda Regalis chair. A bronze version is shown in Colour Plate 62

IRONBRIDGE GORGE MUSEUM TRUST

of the more ornate seats had been a practice at the firm for some time. Considering this, and the fact that the company had also been casting other metals, such as brass,[67] it does not seem quite so odd that the seat in Colour Plate 62 was cast by the company, perhaps as a one off.

The seat's provenance is unknown, but it can be dated to the last quarter of the nineteenth century by the design registration mark of 1875, and the fact that the design is illustrated both in the 1875 and spring 1893[68] catalogues. However, in this case the design registration date may be misleading, for the smaller of the two Osmunda Regalis seats is listed as 'About 4ft. 10in. long',[69] a curious statement considering that all the other designs have precise dimensions.

It can therefore be assumed that when the 1875 catalogue went to press, the smaller version had probably not been produced (hence the vagueness of the measurement), and that the registration of the design applied to the overall design of both the larger and smaller chair.

Like many of the company's designs for garden chairs the Osmunda Regalis is composed with natural foliage forms, idealised and manipulated to create symmetry and pattern. It is a wonderful chair, one of the most ornate, and certainly the most intricate, designs illustrated in the catalogue. The detail and crispness of the casting is superb, and one is left wondering at the skill not only of the pattern and mould makers, but also of the casters: to form such a delicate mould with so much pierced work is remarkable enough in itself, but the ability to cast it without incurring washing or other defects is an even more notable achievement, and clearly reflects the technical heights to which the company had risen.

Of the three different Medallion design chairs illustrated in the company's 1875 catalogue, models number 34 (Plate 6:17) and 35 (Plate 6:18) are good examples of the chaotic designs at times implemented at the foundry. The birds in the back and arms of model 35 (Plate 6:18) link in with the medallion of a seated girl cooing at a bird resting on her raised hand in the centre of the seat back. However, the hoof feet (which are incorporated in other chairs such as Midsummer Night's Dream, from which they were, perhaps, borrowed) and the rope work and finials on the top of the chair back, seem to be at odds with what one would deem the overall theme — birds. This curious concoction is taken to even further lengths in model number 34 (Plate 6:17), a more elaborate version of model 35. The theme of birds also occurs here but is lost in the vulgar (yet ingenious) castings of draping rope work, grotesque beasts and a protruding shield all coexisting in romantic free association. Although one may consider these two typically Victorian seats aesthetically displeasing, they are still fine pieces of cast-iron work.

The adaptation of model 35 to a more ornate version (or perhaps it was the case of adapting model 34 to model 35), clearly shows the versatility of the patterns. Particular parts, such as the decoration in the arm rests, legs and much of the chair

back, could be used for both models. As such it does not seem unreasonable to assume that various parts, such as the shield, could be altered to suit a particular client's requirements, for example, in the addition of a coat-of-arms.

Both models 34 and 35, and the third Medallion chair (model 33 incorporating the same central bas-relief scene) were, according to the 1875 catalogue, supplied with a grained pine or iron seat (oak was extra), and a bronzed finish, each measuring five feet six inches in length. As ornate chairs, all three were assembled using moulded bronze nuts, which are just visible on the inside of the chair in Plate 6:18. This chair, which has recently been repainted white (a colour more frequently used by the company for fountains and vases) also illustrates the main weakness of cast-iron: it fractures easily, and has done so on both the lip and rear left-hand leg of the chair, hence the rather awkward wooden support at the back.

The company's 1875 catalogue illustrates on page 271 five of its designs for single seats, all of which were also produced in larger sizes.

Although not mentioned in the accompanying literature both model 'S18 Rustic' and 'S22 Gothic' (respectively top right and left of Plate 6:19), were available not only 'Bronzed' or 'Painted' (presumably green or chocolate), but

Plate 6:17. Detail from Section III of the Coalbrookdale Company's 1875 catalogue, showing model number 34, the most ornate of the three Medallion designs

IRONBRIDGE GORGE MUSEUM TRUST

Plate 6:18. Three-seater Medallion chair, cast-iron, the Coalbrookdale Company, circa 1865. Width approx 66ins. This is model number 35 which, with models 33 and 34, included the same central bas-relief medallion

SEAGO ANTIQUES

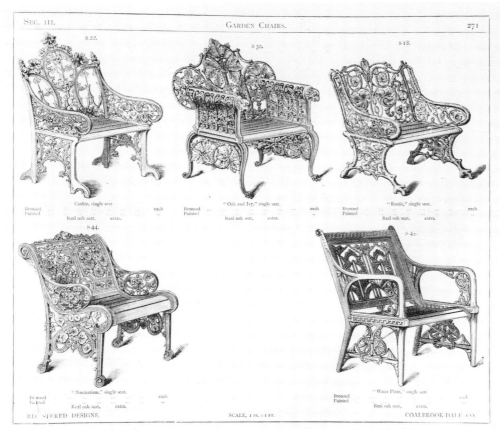

S 22.   S 30.   S 18.

S 44.   S 45.

Plate 6:19. Page 271 of Section III of the Coalbrookdale Company's 1875 catalogue, illustrating single, or armchair, models of the Gothic, Oak and Ivy, Rustic, Nasturtium and Water Plant designs (the latter designed by Christopher Dresser)
IRONBRIDGE GORGE MUSEUM TRUST

Plate 6:20. A three-seater version of the Coalbrookdale Company's Oak and Ivy design, marked 'C.B. Dale', late nineteenth century. Width approx 72ins
SEAGO ANTIQUES

Colour Plate 66. Two seater games chair on wheels and with foot rest, wrought-iron. (See Plate 6:41 and pages 287-288)

PRIVATE COLLECTION

also, no doubt, in a 'Painted Oak' finish, for this is a finish listed for the larger companion chairs, model '18 Rustic' and model '22 Gothic'.[70] These larger models tend to be more commonly found than the single seats, and each could be had, according to the 1875 catalogue, in sizes of three, four, five or six feet long.

The Nasturtium design 'S44' (Plate 6:19 bottom left) ranks with the Fern and Blackberry design (Plate 6:13) as the firm's most commonly found, and hence popular, chair. It was available in numerous sizes; models incorporating extended variations of the design on the single chair's back could be had at lengths of '3ft. 3in., 4ft. 7in., 6ft. 1in.', whilst models with a plain wooden back (no doubt cheaper) could be had at lengths between three and nine feet. Like the Fern and Blackberry, this chair's design incorporates a literal form of contrived naturalism, in contrast to the Water Plant and Medallion designs.

The Water Plant design 'S45' (Plate 6:19 bottom right) was available in three larger sizes than the single chair model: '3ft. 8in., 5ft. 4in., 6ft. long'. Unlike the earlier designs produced by the company, its designer, Dr Christopher Dresser, tended towards a stricter formalisation of nature, and this is clearly reflected in the stylisation of this chair, whose design probably dates from the 1870s.

The design 'S30. Oak and Ivy' (Plate 6:19 top centre) was available in four larger sizes than the single chair: '3ft., 4ft., 5ft., 6ft. long'. Like the majority of garden chairs these were available either bronzed or painted green or chocolate. Of those that survive today few retain the decorative lip which hangs below the seat, as is the case in the six foot long version in Plate 6:20. Marked on its back 'C.B. Dale', this chair illustrates the way the design of the back is extended from a single chair model to larger sizes. As a garden seat it is not that practical, for the hollow interior of the arms are inaccessible when painting, and one consequently finds considerable rusting within and residue stains below. A model of this chair was still being produced in the late 1920s, for it is illustrated in Coalbrookdale's *Allied Ironfounders' Export Catalogue.*[1]

Coalbrookdale fountains

Predominantly finished bronzed or white, these can be separated into five categories.

The first category includes those of between two and three feet in height, of a simple architectural design and single bowl, produced presumably for the lower end of the market.

The second includes those of between three and six feet in height, incorporating two bowls; the lower frequently supported by aquatic creatures such as swans or dolphins, the upper either by an architectural support or figure. These figures vary from charming plump cherubs to totally incongruous characters, such as the Falconer who, seemingly unaware, balances the bowl on his head.

The third category which, like the second, was produced for the middle market for use in conservatories or gardens, may be deemed to include those more ornate designs of between five and six feet in height, incorporating a single bowl and several points where water issues forth horizontally, rather than the smaller models which were designed to spout vertically.

The fourth category comprises monumental fountains of huge proportions, designed to be impressive for use in large estates and municipal architecture. These incorporate a variety of decorations clustered around the central support, and huge bowls which, unlike the previous categories, allowed controlled cascades from decorated apertures in the rim, similar to the Handyside fountain in Plate 6:10.

The fifth category includes fountains of a more naturalistic character, designed for such settings as lakes rather than confined borders. It includes free-standing ornaments such as mermaids, naiads, cherubs, bulrushes and rocks to form variable rustic compositions. A particularly fine example is illustrated as design 46 in the company's 1875 catalogue (Plate 6:21). The centrepiece of Cupid riding on a swan is raised on naturalistic iron rockwork decorated with three groups of bulrushes. These bulrushes do not visibly issue water, but were probably able to, for the catalogue illustrates a larger model: '48. Group of Bulrushes, to form fountain...can also be had in various other small sizes'. Outlying this are five naiads blowing conch shells. The whole group measured 'about 8ft. 6in. high in extreme', and was available finished either 'bronzed or painted white, the rockwork and bulrushes, &c. in natural colours'.

The company's policy of using one pattern in several different designs also extended to fountains. The centrepiece in Plate 6:21, modelled specifically for the company by John Bell, was exhibited at the 1851 Great Exhibition on a tazza bowl, and in 1875 the design as exhibited was still available as model 5. It was also available as model 10, on a naturalistic base, or as illustrated here incorporated within a rustic scene. Similarly the naiad figures were also used as decoration for several of the monumental fountains, or were available individually.

Plate 6:21. Page 296 of Section III of the Coalbrookdale Company's 1875 catalogue, illustrating a proposed design for a fountain for 'a lake or ornamental water'. A model of the centrepiece, Cupid Riding on a Swan by John Bell, was incorporated within another fountain and exhibited at the Great Exhibition of 1851

IRONBRIDGE GORGE MUSEUM TRUST

Coalbrookdale vases

Unlike the company's iron chairs, huge numbers of which survive today, its vases are very few and far between, and who can say why? Great numbers of vases produced by other foundries (often incorrectly referred to as Coalbrookdale models) survive today, and one can only assume that either the designs were unpopular, which seems unlikely, or that the prices were too high for any but richer clients. From the forty-two designs in the 1875 catalogue, five of the more ornate models are discussed.

Model '24. Night and Morning' (Plate 6:22 top left). A model of this vase, designed by 'M. Carrier, the renowned designer of Paris',[72] was exhibited at the 1862 exhibition. According to the *Art-Journal* both this and the accompanying pieces illustrated, were 'so sharp and delicate in finish as to bear comparison with productions in bronze. The vases for gardens and conservatories are of beautiful design'.[73] Finishes listed in the 1875 catalogue included, 'High finished and bronzed' or, according to the introduction, 'electro bronzed or partially so'.[74]

The model '36 Stag's Head Vase' (Plate 6:22 centre top) was perhaps one of the earliest vases cast by the company, for a pair are incorporated in the gates exhibited at the Great Exhibition, now in Hyde Park, which *The Official Descriptive and Illustrated Catalogue of the Great Exhibition of the Works of Industry of all Nations* described as an 'Ornamental park entrance of cast iron, bronzed...terminating in stag's head vases... English design: C. Crookes'. It therefore seems probable that the vases were also designed by the company's leading designer, Charles

24.
"Night and Morning."
30 in. high, 28½ in. diameter across top ; fitted masks, panels, and
handles applied, medallions, and wreaths.
Highly finished and bronzed ...

36.

"Stag's Head" Vase.
44 in. high, 24 in. wide across top extreme ; fitted heads and applied
ornamentation.

25.
"Cupids."
36 in. high, 32 in. diameter across top ; fitted panels, handles, and
applied ornamentation.
Highly finished and bronzed ...

Highly finished and bronzed ...

18. (Obverse.)
The "Milton" Vase.
Representing, in *alto relievo*, "The Expulsion of Adam and Eve" on
the obverse, and "The Expulsion of Satan" on the reverse ; the
handles with finely-modelled masks applied ; the pedestal
formed of coiled serpents.
Highly finished and bronzed ...

18. (Reverse.)
The "Milton" Vase.
48 in. high, 31 in. across top, 19½ in. square at base.

37.

"Cupids."
48 in. high, measuring pedestal, 32 in. diameter across top ; fitted panels, handles, and applied
ornamentation.
Highly finished and bronzed ...

Pedestal No. 8.
Enamelled in imitation marble

Bronzel

REGISTERED DESIGNS.   SCALE, 1 IN. = 1 FT.   COALBROOK-DALE CO.

Plate 6:22. Page 326 of Section III of the Coalbrookdale Company's 1875 catalogue, illustrating some of the more ornate vases available
IRONBRIDGE GORGE MUSEUM TRUST

Crookes. The accompanying information on this vase reads '44in. high, 24in. wide across top extreme; fitted heads and applied ornamentation'.[75] It has not been possible to examine the insides of any models of these vases, but the fact that the decoration is applied suggests that the stags' heads, for example, were, in fact bolted to the main body, and therefore cast separately. The pattern of the stag's head is incorporated within another, particularly peculiar, vase, model 7 'Deer's Head' (presumably so called to prevent confusion between the two designs) in which a basket rests on the stag's head, the handles formed by the antlers.

Of the two vases which have duplicate bodies, models '25 Cupids' and '37 Cupids' (respectively top right and bottom centre in Plate 6:22), model 37 (which is raised on pedestal number 8) is perhaps the most pleasing, for its socle is more in keeping proportionately with the main body. It is not known who designed this model, but it is interesting for it illustrates the use of different patterns, in this case for the socle, on similar models. Model 37's socle corresponds to a pair of vases exhibited at the Paris Exhibition,[76] which in turn correspond to the cast-iron models 12A and 14, whilst the same socle is incorporated in the ram's head vase, model 13. This policy of using the same socle for different vases was often implemented by the foundry.

The Milton Vase, '18' (Plate 6:22 bottom left obverse, and right reverse), which depicts scenes of Adam and Eve (obverse) and Satan (reverse) being expelled from the Garden of Eden, was available either 'Highly finished and bronzed' or 'electro bronzed or partially so'. A model was exhibited at the 1862 exhibition and is illustrated in front of Bell & Crookes's gates in J B Waring's *Masterpieces of Industrial Art and Sculpture in the International Exhibition, 1862*. Unfortunately Waring does not refer to the designer of this vase, but it was no doubt a work of which the company was proud, hence its illustration from two sides in the catalogue.

Coalbrookdale animals

Models of English cast-iron animals are unusual, for unlike their French counterparts, such as Durenne and Barbezat, English foundries rarely produced these subjects; indeed the Coalbrookdale Company's 1875 catalogue only illustrates three life-size models, the two dogs in Plates 6:23 and 24, and a lion.[77]

The Setter (Plate 6:23), number 160 in the 1875 catalogue, is cast from a model by the French sculptor Christophe Fratin (1800-1864), whose indented signature appears on the base. It is well modelled, and was no doubt cast, as were the bird and damaged foliage on the base, in several sections, the join marks being almost undetectable on the finished work. The identity of the modeller of the Pointer and Hare, number 159 (Plate 6:24), is less certain, for similar objects were produced by Fratin and other prominent sculptors such as Pierre-Jules Mêne (1810-1871). As Mêne is also known to have produced models for the company,[78] it might well be by either one of these renowned animal modellers. The pointer despite looking, like many French dogs, as though it is starving, is as admirably modelled as the setter. It too seems to have been damaged, for the positioning of the head, which in the catalogue is illustrated pointing forward, has been altered. Although this may have been a variation possible when the components of the dog were assembled, this is probably not the case, there being a joint line visible on the neck suggesting that the head has been disturbed and incorrectly relocated.

This pair, now on the steps of Belton House, originally stood in the hall of Ashridge Park, Hertfordshire,[79] and were removed to Belton, presumably when Ashridge was sold in the 1920s. At what date they were originally at Ashridge is unknown, nor is it known when these dogs were first being produced, for they are two of the very few Coalbrookdale castings that do not bear a registration mark. Curiously, and of particular note, is the fact that the company's name is not present on either model.

The Lion Foundry

The armchair in Plate 6:25 illustrates the technical abilities of one of the smaller and less renowned foundries operating during the nineteenth century, the Lion Foundry in Northampton. It had been established by John Brettel as the Beehive Foundry in the early 1830s, but in 1849 Brettel took William Roberts into partnership and renamed the company the Lion Foundry. The works were more involved with the production of household and agricultural castings than garden seats, all of which were exhibited at the 1851 Exhibition.[80] By 1852 Roberts had taken over the foundry, and it was he who registered on 24 May 1859 the design for the chair illustrated here.

Plate 6:23. Life-size figure of a setter, cast-iron, the Coalbrookdale Company, circa 1865, Belton House, Lincolnshire. Height approx 32ins
THE NATIONAL TRUST

Plate 6:24. Life-size figure of a pointer with a hare, cast-iron, the Coalbrookdale Company, circa 1865, Belton House, Lincolnshire. Height approx 35ins
THE NATIONAL TRUST

Plate 6:25. Autumn pattern armchair, cast-iron, the Lion Foundry, Northampton, circa 1860. Height approx 39ins

MILES D'AGAR AND NICK GIFFORD-MEAD ANTIQUES

It is a superb piece of casting, the back is highly decorated in relief and bows forward, whilst the bas-relief scene is even more remarkable, faithfully capturing the chase marks from the pattern. Since the word Autumn appears at the top of the back of the chair, it is almost certain that it was originally one of a set of four representing the seasons, but unfortunately the whereabouts of any of its companions are as yet unknown.

Bearing in mind the elaborate casting, it seems likely that the Spring, Summer and Winter chairs were taken from the same pattern, the indented cartouche and bas-relief scenes on the chair back being exchanged during mould making for the appropriate patterns. Roberts must either have been concerned about the seat being copied, or just proud of it, for not only does the indented inscription 'LION FOUNDRY NORTHAMPTON REGISTERED BY W. ROBERTS' occur in the back of the casting, but a plethora of registration design marks appear on the legs, arms and seat.

Roberts died in 1868 and the foundry was taken over by Henry Mobbs. It continued production into the twentieth century.[81]

French Cast-Iron

Barbezat & Cie

The firm of Barbezat & Cie was formed in 1855. It succeeded an earlier atelier, that of André (J P Victor), which could perhaps be regarded as the French equivalent of the Coalbrookdale Company, for it too, at the 1851 Great Exhibition, was awarded a prestigious council medal.

André, not having a foundry of his own, first started contracting work out to the foundries in the Champagne area, east of Paris. In 1835 he established his own iron works in the Val d'Osne, at first casting more architectural items such as pipes and balconies, but he soon progressed to more ornate art castings, which seem to have been of a higher quality and cheaper than his competitors. Describing the firm in 1851, Digby Wyatt relates:

> He [André] was enabled, by the excercise of activity and intelligence, to introduce the best system of moulding, which besides ensuring perfect execution, led to a great economy of production...By allying himself to the most skilful designers and the best modellers of the French metropolis, he has evinced, in the prosperity of his career, how valuable good taste may become as a commercial commodity. Fully appreciating the advantages of education, he has attached to his establishment in the Val d'Osne a gratuitous school, in which he provides the best instruction for his apprentices; and a savings'-bank and benefit society also form part of his establishment. Upwards of two hundred workmen are constantly employed in his *atelier,* and in busy times his manufactory may be regarded as giving employment to at least double that number.[82]

André's achievements gained him a silver medal at the 1839 exhibition, gold medals in 1844 and 1849 and a medal d'honneur at the 1855 Paris Exhibition. These awards were proudly displayed on the outside of the firm's showroom in the Rue Neuve, Ménilmontant, Paris. When Barbezat & Cie took over, the name of their predecessor obviously held much cachet, and in the following years André's achievements and name were to be used extensively by the firm.

By 1858 Barbezat had brought out a substantial catalogue, entitled *Barbezat & Cie Ancienne Maison André, Hauts Fourneaux &c. Fonderies du Val d'Osne.* This illustrates a whole range of ornaments which could be obtained both in France as well as in England from Carlhian and Corbiere, of 68 Cannon Street, St Paul's, London, presumably Barbezat's agents. It includes such castings as balustrades, columns and chimney-pieces, but also fountains, vases, chairs and statues, many of which were originally André's castings, such as the fountain designed by Liénard which had been exhibited at the Great Exhibition of 1851 (Plate 6:26).

In the light of this it seems probable that the pair of bloodhounds illustrated in that catalogue (Plate 6:27 top), were originally part of André's *oeuvre.* A pair of these, bearing the firm's raised oval foundry mark, 'BARBEZAT & Cie VAL D'OSNE' are shown in Plate 6:28. Just visible beside each animal's haunch are the raised

Plate 6:27. A page from the 1858 Barbezat & Cie catalogue, illustrating the designs (top) on which the models for the bloodhounds in Plate 6:28 are based
SCIENCE MUSEUM LIBRARY

marks 'A.J.', the initials of the French animalier Alfred Jacquemart (1824-1896). There are many other examples of this model in England, for instance at Woburn Abbey and Bicton. (Another pair of these hounds used to stand outside the church in St George's Street, London, but unfortunately they have been mistaken for works by Adrian Jones and removed to a new veterinary college dedicated to this English animalier.)

Alfred Jacquemart seems to have been a popular artist with both André and Barbezat, for the heads of the two hounds illustrated here were available as wall mounts, and reduced-size models were incorporated within a fender, whilst the ferocious boar and wolf models (typical of French animal statues) illustrated at the bottom of Plate 6:27 were also designed by this artist. At the 1867 exhibition, Barbezat, exhibited a model of 'Valet de Limiers de Mr Bracquermart',[83] (Bracquermart being a spelling mistake for Jacquemart). An example of this

Plate 6:28. Life-size figures of a bloodhound dog and bitch, cast-iron, initialled 'A.J.' for Alfred Jacquemart and marked 'BARBEZAT & Cie VAL D'OSNE', circa 1865.

The impressed initial 'B' on the dog was an adaptation available to individual clients. Presumably whoever purchased these figures owned a pack of dogs branded with their initial to identify the hounds easily after the hunt or if they got lost. Another adaptation available was a base of geometric form (as found on the pair at Bicton which does not have the respective belt and game on the bases as here)

THE SLADMORE GALLERY

Plate 6:29. The Bloodhound Groom, cast-iron, marked 'VL D'OSNE', late nineteenth, possibly early twentieth century, Anglesey Abbey, Cambridgeshire. Height approx 70ins. (See Colour Plate 63)

THE NATIONAL TRUST

fantastic model stands in the gardens of Anglesey Abbey (Plate 6:29), bearing testament to the extraordinary talents of the French iron foundries. However, this particular model seems unlikely to have been cast by Barbezat & Cie, for it only carries the foundry mark 'VL D'OSNE' (just discernible on the corner of the plinth). The explanation is that in 1867 Barbezat & Cie changed its name to Houille & Cie, and then again, some three years later in 1870, to the Société Anonyme... du Val d'Osne. As the foundry changed its name, so too did the casting marks found on the surface of the casts, and thus the appearance of only the Vl d'Osne mark would

Plate 6:31. Two of the many designs for chairs illustrated in Barbezat & Cie's 1858 catalogue. Both were still being manufactured in later years by the Société Anonyme...du Val d'Osne
SCIENCE MUSEUM LIBRARY

Plate 6:32. Three-seater Gothic Tracery chair, cast-iron, Val d'Osne, no founder's mark, late nineteenth century. Width approx 56ins
CHRISTIE'S, SOUTH KENSINGTON

suggest that the model dates to some point after 1870, Val (or Vl) d'Osne being an abbreviation commonly used by the foundry after this date. (Another model of the Valet de Limiers (Bloodhound Groom) can be seen in Colour Plate 63.)

Three further plates are included from Barbezat's 1858 catalogue, one representative of the vases they were producing (Plate 6:30) in which the Villa Albani Vase (bottom centre) is of particular note as it is frequently mistaken for the Warwick Vase. Plate 6:31 illustrates two of the firm's garden chairs, many of which were still being produced by Val d'Osne in later years. Of these the most commonly found in England is the Gothic Tracery design, an example of which is illustrated in Plate 6:32. The third example from the catalogue, Plate 6:33, illustrates several of Barbezat's designs for medium-sized fountains.

Plate 6:33. Plate 277 of Barbezat & Cie's 1858 catalogue, illustrating several of the firm's smaller-sized fountains. A variation of the top right-hand example formed the upper stem and bowl of the fountain exhibited at the 1851 Great Exhibition (see Plate 6:26)

Durenne

The other major French manufacturer of art castings during the nineteenth century was the firm started by Antoine Durenne. In 1847 he bought a small foundry at Sommevoire, not far from the Val d'Osne works in the Haute-Marne. The business grew from strength to strength, in 1855 blast furnaces were installed and by the early 1860s the foundry could offer a considerable array of statuary, vases and fountains. Like other British and French foundries the firm exhibited at the many international exhibitions held during the period, and one of the chief exhibits at those held in the 1860s was a set of four over-life-size groups depicting

Plate 6:34. Plate 185 of Durenne's catalogue of circa 1880

animals. These groups, which were stock figures and could be ordered from the firm's illustrated catalogues (Plate 6:34), are copies of bronze originals commissioned for the piers flanking the ramp leading to La Cour des Écuries de l'Empereur at the Louvre.[84] These magnificent groups, which now adorn La Cour Lefuel, were modelled by the French sculptor Pierre-Louis Rouillard (1820-1881) and cast by the bronze foundry of Eck & Durand.[85]

At what precise date and how Durenne obtained permission to reproduce Rouillard's work is unknown, but as Rouillard exhibited a plaster model of the 'Chienne dogue de forte race avec ses petits' (Mastiff Bitch and Pups, Colour Plate 64) at the Salon in 1859, and as it is clear from a stereoscopic view of the firm's stand at the 1862 International Exhibition (Plate 6:35) that at least three of these groups (probably all four) were on display, then it must have been within this three year period. Whatever the case, Durenne's casts of Rouillard's models attracted considerable attention in the press, the *Art-Journal* stating that 'his groups, statues, vases, bas-reliefs, and more especially animals, are marvellous achievements in design, modelling and casting, being generally as sharp and brilliant in manipulation as they could have been in bronze'.[86] Of the four magnificent groups the figure of the Wolf Stealing a Mastiff Pup (left in Plate 6:35, and Colour Plate 65) is an unusual iron cast in that it not only bears the sculptor's signature, but also, and even more unusual, a date — 1860 (Plate 6:36). This suggests that the Durenne pair (of the Mastiff Bitch and Pups and Wolf Stealing a Mastiff Pup)

Plate 6:36. Rouillard's signature found on the base of his cast of Wolf Stealing a Mastiff Pup while undergoing restoration

whose provenance is uncertain, other than it is known to have decorated the grounds of Wynnstay Hall, Wrexham, probably date to 1860, and this can perhaps be substantiated by the superb quality of the casts, which still clearly define, for example, the hairs on both the bitch's and the wolf's back. Animalier subjects such as these, showing nature in its bestial form, were immensely popular subjects with French sculptors and patrons during the nineteenth century, and although groups as large as these are comparatively rare, an enormous quantity of small table-top bronzes were manufactured for interior use.[87]

Wrought-Iron

The use of wrought-iron for garden ornament, with the exception of such architectural features as gates and gazebos, was limited. Its predominant use was for garden chairs in the early nineteenth century but, with the technical advances of iron casters, these often charming wrought-iron chairs were soon superseded by cast models which could be made with far more ornate designs at a cheaper price. However, a number of plainer models continued to be produced by such firms as Barnard, Bishop & Barnard Ltd (Plate 6:43).

Wrought-iron is obtained by resmelting pig iron and removing most of the impurities. The result is that the iron is far more malleable than cast-iron and when heated can be beaten or hammered into the desired shape. In comparison to cast-iron, wrought-iron when struck with a heavy blow does not fracture but merely bends. Although there are obvious advantages in this, especially for something as exposed as a garden seat, wrought-iron chairs can be more susceptible to rust and deteriorate faster than a cast model. For example, if not properly cared for, the strips of wrought-iron are liable to break loose from their rivets. Chairs with paw feet are particularly susceptible to rust, for each paw is formed by beating part of the bottom of the leg into a wider, and therefore thinner, shape. As these chairs are frequently placed in damp areas, such as lawns, one frequently finds that they have rusted beyond repair, as is the case with the chair in Plate 6:42.

Wrought-iron chairs

Wrought-iron chairs were produced comparatively simply, the components being lengths or strips of wrought-iron of varying width and thickness, frequently decorated with reeds, with plain bars and strips being used for the less visible parts such as stretchers. Sections of these pieces were individually wrought into the desired shapes that would, when riveted together, constitute a complete chair. Taking the chair in Plate 6:37 as an example, a tell-tale hole where the top horizontal bar has broken free from the central vertical bar indicates where a rivet was located. On the seat, however, the seven horizontal slats were designed to flex. Each slat is held firmly to the central bar in the middle of the seat by a rivet but the free ends are merely slotted into wedge-shaped cuts (visible in the detail in Plate 6:38), thereby permitting them to flex when anyone sat on the seat. These wedge-shaped cuts are usually a sign of an earlier chair, for on later models, such as that by Barnard, Bishop & Barnard (Plate 6:43), the slats are riveted at both ends, while bars flanking the central structural bar are only present to prevent overflexing. On the rest of the chair in Plate 6:37 the wider sections, such as those forming the legs and back uprights, are decorated with five reeds, whilst the thinner strips which constitute the decoration and the central horizontal bar on the back are decorated with three reeds. The front legs terminate in wrought paws, whilst those at the rear terminate in scrolls. On this example, the seat slats are also reeded, but one frequently finds more practical slats, curved in section to prevent water collecting and thus avoiding rusting iron, peeling paint and a soaked bottom!

This chair resembles that in Plate 6:39, which has a similar finial and scrolls, but it is not as pleasant a design, for the back, although symmetric, seems to be lacking continuity. As it is curved, it almost certainly originally comprised part of a set, perhaps surrounding a flowerbed, and if this was the case, which seems likely, then it would, together with its companions, have been far more pleasing, for the scrolls in each corner, instead of terminating at the back of the arms, would have continued on to the flanking chairs.

Plate 6:37. Three-seater garden seat, wrought-iron, early nineteenth century. Width approx 65ins. Since it is curved in form, the seat was probably part of a set surrounding a tree or flowerbed

PRIVATE COLLECTION

Plate 6:38 Detail of the seat in Plate 6:37 illustrating the location of slats into wedge-shaped cuts, and the use of an iron bar for the stretcher below. The central slat is secured following late twentieth century restoration

Plate 6:39. One of a pair of four-seater chairs, wrought-iron, early nineteenth century. Width approx 70ins

PRIVATE COLLECTION

Plate 6:40. Four-seater chair on wheels, wrought-iron, early nineteenth century. Width approx 80ins

PRIVATE COLLECTION

Plate 6:41. Two-seater games chair on wheels and with foot rest, wrought-iron, early nineteenth century. Width approx 41ins. (See Colour Plate 66)
PRIVATE COLLECTION

Another of the weaknesses of wrought-iron chairs is apparent in this model, for several of the seat slats have been damaged and are now bent. Among considerable restorations may be noted the rather poorly finished joint where the two centre scroll sections meet at the seat.

The elaborately segmented back of the chair in Plate 6:39 is particularly ornate and was constructed from lengths of three- and six-reeded strips, forming a lyre in the centre.

The back is curious, however, in that many of the strips are riveted together on the front with short pieces of iron. Whilst this was obviously necessary (for unlike the seat in Plate 6:37, the scrolls do not overlap a structural strip), one may wonder why these were not placed on the rear where they would have been less obtrusive. Despite this, it is still a fine seat, the slats are well fitted into the sides, and the paw feet (not visible in the photograph) admirably worked.

The chair in Plate 6:40 is unusual, for not only is it particularly wide (hence the necessity to rivet the slats on to two central seat supports), but it is also one of the few models which incorporates wheels but no foot rest (see Plate 6:41).

The geometric design on the chair's back was an immensely popular one, and is found on a variety of chairs, such as those in Plates 6:41 and 42. It is interesting to note that the three vertical uprights do not rise to the same level as the top of the back leg uprights, nor to a level flush with the highest point of the back, but stop abruptly without embellishments half-way between. Despite this, it is not an unattractive chair, and one on which the use of rivets to secure the seat back is quite apparent.

The chair in Plate 6:41 and Colour Plate 66 incorporates the same popular geometric design in its back as those in Plates 6:40 and 42, but it has the structural characteristics of a games chair since it is on wheels which, when the foot rest pivots up, enables it to be moved easily to another viewing position. Comparison of the chairs in Plates 6:41 and 42 clearly reveals that the latter has suffered extensive damage, the most prominent being the loss of the curved strips at the top of the

Plate 6:42. Two-seater chair, wrought-iron, early nineteenth century. Width approx 44ins
SOTHEBY'S, SUSSEX

chair's back. Less obvious, and illustrating one of the main weaknesses of wrought-iron chairs, is the deterioration of the legs which should terminate in paw feet at the front and scrolls at the back. These have rusted away and been crudely restored by bending the bottom of each leg out, so lowering the height and ruining what would otherwise be a rather charming and well-proportioned chair.

Structurally the games chair (Plate 6:41) is far stronger, for it has rising stretchers of bar form, but is less decorative, for it is mostly plain iron, reeded sections being used only for the back, whilst the chair in Plate 6:42 is almost completely constructed of reeded sections.

The three-seater chair in Plate 6:43 is particularly interesting, for in comparison with the construction of the wrought-iron models of the early nineteeenth century it is much cruder. It was almost certainly produced by the firm Barnard, Bishop & Barnard Ltd which produced a whole range of wrought-iron chairs from the mid-nineteenth century. The great majority of the firm's models are much plainer than that illustrated, and tend to have crudely wrought legs and wooden slats. This particular chair corresponds to the firm's model 'No 506' which is described in the 1930 catalogue as one of the 'most comfortable and graceful seats yet introduced',[88] though it is more elaborate in that it has vertical interwoven slats forming the back.

Although no doubt a practical, comfortable and reasonably cheap seat, in its design it bears little comparison to earlier seats. Of particular note is the use of rivets to attach the slats to the chair's legs.

Plate 6:43. Three-seater chair, wrought-iron, Barnard, Bishop & Barnard Ltd, circa 1930. Width approx 48ins
SOTHEBY'S, SUSSEX

CHAPTER SEVEN
TWENTIETH CENTURY GARDEN ORNAMENTS

A number of pieces which are today sold as period garden ornaments were, in fact, produced in the early twentieth century. Originally manufactured and sold as reproductions of genuine period pieces, they are now frequently still mistaken as period works. To add to the confusion, during the last fifty years or so, original twentieth century pieces (as opposed to reproductions) have been dated earlier than is actually the case. Examples of works that have been mistakenly identified as period pieces are featured in this chapter.

Up to this point we have been discussing persons or firms who made a living manufacturing their own wares, many of which produced other goods as well as garden ornaments, for the success of a business often relied on diversification; for example, cast-iron foundries also produced engines, railway tracking, chamber pots and other items.

The late nineteenth/early twentieth century saw the development of a new phenomenon in the world of garden ornaments, namely the growth of firms which not only manufactured them, but also relied heavily on acting as retailers of ornaments produced all over Europe. (This period also saw the growth of a number of firms dealing in antique garden ornaments.)

This new breed of retailers was to have an impact which can still be seen in gardens today, and one of the most important was the company established by J P White at the end of the nineteenth century in Bedford.

The diverse range of ornaments handled by this firm bears detailed discussion and illustration, and the following pages on the company's activities are divided into two sections: imported ornaments (including the popular Italian well-heads) and ornaments produced in Britain.

This is followed by sections on the types of material most commonly used for garden ornament during the twentieth century by other firms: lead (notably by the Bromsgrove Guild and H Crowther Ltd), Vicenza stone, Italian marble and cast-iron.

J P White

John Parish White (1855-1917) served his apprenticeship with a builder in Biggleswade, Bedfordshire, and afterwards set up his own business at Dunmow in Essex. However, by the mid-1880s he had taken over the Bedford building firm of John Hull, and in 1896 he established the Pyghtle Works on the Bromham Road, Bedford. It was here that the business was to be permanently based.[1]

By at least 1900 it is apparent that White had developed interests beyond the building industry, for he had expanded into the manufacture of carved wooden chimney-pieces, gates and garden seats.[2] The manufacture of these garden seats proved profitable for, according to his obituary, his first model, the Peacock, sold with 'instant and rapid success'.[3] This seems to have prompted White to expand into other areas of garden ornament, for within six years the range of pieces he was able to offer both from the Pyghtle Works and a new showroom in London (134 New Bond Street) was considerable. The variety of these ornaments is clearly illustrated in White's Christmas 1906 catalogue.[4] Not only were numerous designs for wooden garden seats shown, there was also a variety of other wooden ornaments including oak sundial pedestals and a variety of planters known as palm boxes. These ornaments are of more interest than the seats and included fountains, statues, animal figures, vases, well-heads, bird baths, seats, etc, all available in a range of media including marble, bronze, lead, terracotta and a variety of English and Italian stones. The catalogue also illustrates larger features such as wrought-iron umbrella rose trainers and even complete garden houses. As White resigned from most of his public appointments in 1906,[5] it would seem that the business had taken off with remarkable speed.

By late 1938, the firm had stopped producing both lead and carved English stone ornaments.[6] However, it would seem that the range of items in stock at this date must have been considerable for the contents of the works garden were slowly dispersed over later years, the last being sold off at the sale when the works closed in 1960-61.[7] It is interesting to note that towards the end of this period the firm may well have been buying genuine antique garden ornaments, such as the lioness in Plate 7:14, seemingly the same model now at Anglesey Abbey (see Plate 2:39).

Identifying White's ornaments is often difficult, for the firm never seems to have marked its pieces. Although catalogues can be consulted, this is of limited value, for these were only representative of the firm's continually changing stock. The ornaments can be broadly divided into two groups: those imported, such as terracotta, marble, Vicenza stone and most bronze pieces; and those produced at the Pyghtle Works, such as those carved from English stones, and those cast in lead.

Imported ornaments

From the illustrations in the firm's 1906 catalogue it is apparent that in the early years of the twentieth century the majority of White's statues, vases, fountains, etc, were imported from Italy. It seems improbable that White would have had the necessary funds available to establish his own factories in Italy, and it therefore seems reasonable to assume that he bought his ornaments direct from established firms. Unfortunately we do not know which firms were involved, but before proceeding it is worth mentioning the considerable size of the sculpting and casting industry in Italy in the early 1900s.

There are numerous photographs from about this time showing craftsmen at work at the quarries in Carrara, transforming blocks of marble into copies of famous statues. In the background their many plaster models are often to be seen, dotted with protruding measuring points. Throughout the country similar work was carried on at other marble quarries and their environs, whilst in the area of Vicenza the soft local limestone was being carved into countless forms of garden and other ornaments.

The bronze casting industry was also considerable, involving numerous firms. A good example of one of these is the Naples firm of Chiurazzi Societa Anonima, whose early twentieth century catalogue illustrates over three hundred examples of statues, vases, animals and busts, etc, from collections all over the world. These included antique subjects, as well as more modern pieces, such as copies of

Plate 7:1. Two terracotta vases from White's 1906 catalogue; that on the left was the most ornate in the catalogue and stood 40ins high

Cellini's Perseus, and Canova's Three Graces. Many of these were available not only in the same size as the original, but also in reduced forms. This was also the case with copies of Giambologna's Mercury, which was available in five further sizes, ranging in height from 22 to 100cm. Several pages from this catalogue are reproduced in Appendix II.

The manufacture of terracotta pieces at the turn of this century was also considerable, one of the main centres of production being Tuscany.

It is worth noting several points regarding these sculptural works. Firstly, although White may have had agreements with Italian manufacturers to supply him with certain stock items, these would have been carved by individual sculptors, to whom some artistic licence should be allowed. This would account for, for example, the varied treatment of the limbs and drapery found on some stock statues. Secondly, towards the middle of the twentieth century, the general standard of craftsmanship dropped, and this would certainly account for several of the poorer quality pieces illustrated here.

One further more general point is worth noting when considering White's imported items. As the firm never marked pieces and as, as has already been mentioned, it seems improbable that the Italian suppliers were actually owned by White, then these suppliers would have been in a position to sell what one would deem 'stock White garden ornaments' to other clients both in Italy and abroad. Hence extant undocumented garden ornaments carved from marble, Vicenza stone, terracotta or bronze, which correspond to designs featured in White's catalogues, may not actually have passed through the hands of this prolific retailer. The resultant problems of correctly identifying White's imported ornaments are manifold, but for simplicity's sake, I have assumed, rightly or wrongly, that all those illustrated in the following pages, did pass through the hands of the firm.

THE PISTOJA DESIGN.

A garden seat with beautifully modelled ends in Tuscan terra-cotta (see p. 113).

Seat and board at back in oak or teak.

Total length	...	5 ft.	
Oak	...	£18 10	0
Teak	...	£19 0	0

Plate 7:2. Terracotta Pistoja seat from White's 1906 catalogue
BEDFORDSHIRE RECORD OFFICE

Terracotta

A substantial part of White's 1906 catalogue is devoted to the firm's terracotta ornaments, which he referred to as 'Tuscan pottery'. The pieces were imported from an area in northern Italy, described in his introduction to the section thus: 'In no other place is it possible to find the particular clay used in the production, the preparation of which is a very lengthy and important process, and must be carried out with great care, in order to secure that distinctive appearance and exquisite softness of colour, which can be obtained from no other material'.[8]

The terracotta had a buff finish, but most of the models were also available either slightly more cheaply in a red, or slightly more expensively in an 'Antique Bronze' finish. Of the pieces featured in the catalogue, the majority are vases, and these included copies of 'Antique' examples, as well as models of a more contemporary nature and a number of relatively plain tubs. Two of the vases are reproduced in Plate 7:1. That on the left, the most ornate of all those shown and the tallest, was available for £10, whilst that on the right, one of the twenty or so storage jars or tubs illustrated, was priced at £6 16s. Other terracotta items included such pieces as a reproduction of Donatello's ornate stand and bowl in the Duomo, Sienna, several ornate well-heads, some statues and a few bird baths. The catalogue also shows two unusual terracotta seats, one of which is reproduced in Plate 7:2. An extant buff-coloured example is shown in Plate 7:3. Although by no means corresponding exactly to the catalogue illustration, the similarities suggest that it came from the same supplier. Perhaps confirmation of this can be found in the similarly buff-coloured terracotta ornament in the foreground of Plate 7:3 which corresponds exactly to a pedestal (for a Byzantine vase) shown in White's catalogue; listed as No 1275, it was available for £6. The quality of these pieces is reasonable, the modelling good, and they have clearly withstood the worst extremes of our climate. However, as a general rule, Italian terracottas are not well suited to our climate, a situation White was clearly aware of, for in the introduction to the catalogue he advised his clients:

293

Plate 7:3. One of White's 'Tuscan pottery' garden seats; in the foreground, one of the firm's stock pedestals

The following points should be carefully noted in making use of this ware:
(1). That when the Vases or Jardinières are to be used for growing flowers or plants of any kind, the earth should never be placed directly into the vases or jardinières. A strong zinc or galvanized iron lining can be made to fit exactly the interior of the vessel, at a very small cost, or an ordinary garden pot can be placed inside to receive the earth. When the earth is placed directly inside the vase the contraction and expansion caused by cold and heat are liable to crack it.
(2). That none of the pieces should be placed in direct contact with the ground, as the material, being naturally porous, readily absorbs the moisture from the damp earth, which is often injurious. It is therefore advisable that all such pieces as are required to stand on or near the ground should be placed on a base of stone or some non-absorbent material.
(3). Owing to the delicacy of the colour and the modelling it is advisable to cover the pieces up, or to store them undercover, during a severe winter.
All goods are priced in 'buff' finish, as illustrated, but nearly all of them can be finished in red or an antique bronze, the red costing 10% less and the bronze 10% more, but for ordinary use the 'buff' finish will be found the most serviceable and pleasing in appearance.[9]

These suggested precautions provide a notable comparison to the claims of earlier English manufacturers such as Coade and Blashfield, who went to great lengths to expound the resistant nature of their wares to this climate.

THE LEGHORN SEAT.

Semi-circular seat, 7 ft. 6 in. diameter.

Richly carved.

Price £87 10 0

Not including the stone or marble paving.

No. 8471.

Plate 7:4. The Leghorn seat as illustrated in White's 1906 catalogue. This was one of the firm's more ornate examples of Carrara marble garden seats
BEDFORDSHIRE RECORD OFFICE

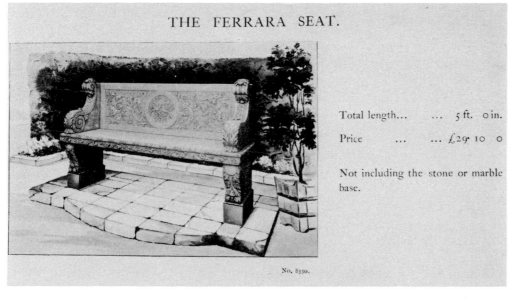

THE FERRARA SEAT.

Total length... ... 5 ft. 0 in.

Price £29 10 0

Not including the stone or marble base.

No. 8330.

Plate 7:5. The Ferrara seat; like all the firm's marble Carrara seats this could be ordered with the whiteness of the new marble toned down
BEDFORDSHIRE RECORD OFFICE

Marble

A large proportion of the garden ornaments illustrated in White's 1906 catalogue were carved from the white marble of Carrara. A selection of seats, all of which were made to order, were illustrated. These could be obtained with the whiteness of the new marble toned down, and such items were recommended as architectural statements, even though less comfortable than wooden seats. All the models were named after locations in Italy and ranged from simple benches comprising supports in the form of brackets supporting slabs of marble with carved or moulded rims, to more substantial decorative seats, such as the Ravenna. Six foot six inches long, the highly carved brackets of this seat supported a carved and moulded bench, the back was decorated in relief below a scrolling top, while the arm rests were in the form of winged beasts. Two examples of these more ornate seats from White's 1906 catalogue are shown in Plates 7:4 and 5.

The majority of Carrara marble statues offered by White were reproductions of, to quote the 1906 catalogue, 'Some of the best known examples of sculpture in the

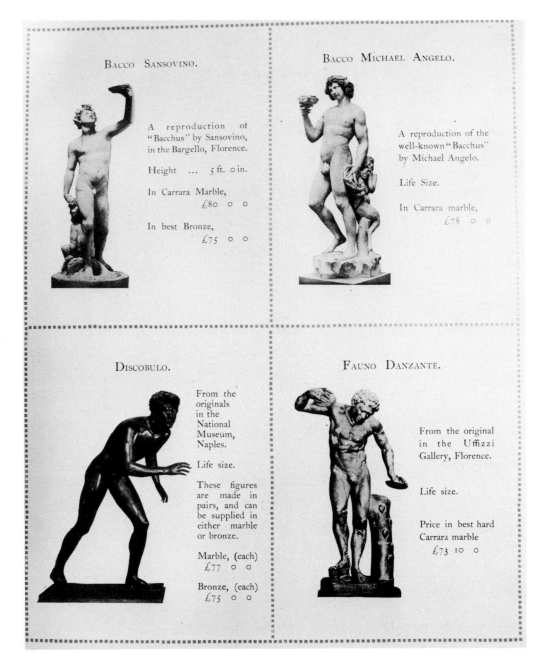

BACCO SANSOVINO.

A reproduction of "Bacchus" by Sansovino, in the Bargello, Florence.

Height ... 5 ft. 0 in.

In Carrara Marble, £80 0 0

In best Bronze, £75 0 0

BACCO MICHAEL ANGELO.

A reproduction of the well-known "Bacchus" by Michael Angelo.

Life Size.

In Carrara marble, £78 0 0

DISCOBULO.

From the originals in the National Museum, Naples.

Life size.

These figures are made in pairs, and can be supplied in either marble or bronze.

Marble, (each) £77 0 0

Bronze, (each) £75 0 0

FAUNO DANZANTE.

From the original in the Uffizzi Gallery, Florence.

Life size.

Price in best hard Carrara marble £73 10 0

Plate 7:6. Page 141 of White's 1906 catalogue showing reproductions of four famous sculptures which the firm could supply

BEDFORDSHIRE RECORD OFFICE

world'. Few of these statues, which were 'Carved by some of the best sculptors on the Continent', are illustrated, but White was able to provide quotes for reproductions of 'any of the well-known examples of sculpture in the museums of Florence, Naples, Rome, etc'. As can be seen from the 1906 catalogue, the firm's reproductions included copies of antique statues as well as Renaissance works by such sculptors as Michelangelo and Sansovino (Plate 7:6). Among other statuary offered by White may be mentioned eagles and several pairs of sphinxes and lions, including reduced copies of Canova's famous models. The 1906 catalogue also illustrates a number of less than life-size statues, but these were of a more contemporary style, such as the Four Seasons illustrated in Plate 7:19, which were also available in lead and Vicenza limestone. In later years it seems that the firm

Plate 7:7. Simple campana-shaped vase, Carrara marble, J P White. Height approx 36ins. According to the 1906 catalogue this vase could also be had in two smaller sizes — 2 feet and 2 feet 6ins
SOTHEBY'S, SUSSEX

also started selling smaller statues, again of a contemporary nature, such as figures of satyrs, similar to the set of four lead Musicians illustrated in the 1935 catalogue (see Appendix II).

The firm's Carrara vases were loosely based on a variety of styles, including the antique as well as French and Italian. As illustrated in the 1906 catalogue, the firm's *oeuvre* included a number of plain vases of the tazza form which had been so popular in the nineteenth century, as well as a number of campana or tulip form vases, all of which could be had in a great number of sizes, such as the three foot high campana model in Plate 7:7. There were also more ornate models available, such as the four illustrated in Plate 7:8. An extant example of one of these is shown in Plate 7:9. Like many examples of White's ornaments, this vase varies considerably from the catalogue illustration, in particular in the different handles and the omission of carving beneath the rim. These variations can, however, be put down to artistic licence on behalf of the Italian sculptor, as well as to the economies found in carving towards the middle of the twentieth century, the probable date this model was executed. It is by no means an accomplished work; the egg-and-dart carving on the rim is shallow, as is the decoration on the socle. Furthermore the relief on the body of the vase is extremely crude in comparison to anything produced in the previous two centuries, so prompting us to question the ability, at least in this case, of some of the Italian sculptors producing such items for White. One further point is worth noting: the vase was executed from a considerable number of pieces of marble — the rim, body, lower part of the vase, handles and socle are all separate. This is a feature often found on such large examples of twentieth century vases, for earlier marble vases tended to be cut from only two pieces, a block for the socle and another for the body and any handles.

Other marble garden ornaments illustrated in the 1906 catalogue included a few Carrara and Istrian marble sundial pedestals, several Carrara marble fountains, as well as a number of other models of a more contemporary nature. White did however make a point of offering to submit special designs for clients, as well as providing quotes to copy any existing 'old examples'.

No. 8448.
In best hard Carrara marble.
4 ft. 2 in. high ... £42 0 0
5 ft. 0 in. „ ... £57 10 0

No. 8446.
In best hard Carrara marble.
3 in. 0 in. high... ... £32 0 0
4 in. 0 in. „ ... £47 10 0
5 in. 0 in. „ ... £65 0 0

No. 8351.
In best hard Carrara marble.
1 ft. 6 in. high ... £7 15 0
2 ft. 0 in. „ ... £10 10 0
2 ft. 6 in. „ ... £12 15 0

No. 8343.
In best hard Carrara marble.
3 ft. 0 in. high ... £21 0 0

Plate 7:8. Four ornate Carrara vases illustrated in White's 1906 catalogue
BEDFORDSHIRE RECORD OFFICE

Vicenza stone

White's range of garden ornaments included a number of Vicenza limestone pieces (see also pages 325-330). In 1906 a few baskets of fruit cut from this stone were available from the firm, but the range of models was mainly made up of reproductions of famous statues in museums in Italy. However, no examples of these are shown, and no prices are given. Stock models, not listed in the 1906 catalogue, did become available in Vicenza stone in later years and the set of figures of the Four Seasons (Plates 7:10 and 11) is an example. Again these statues do not correspond exactly to the design of the equivalent marble and lead ones shown in the 1906 catalogue. In the catalogue (Plate 7:19) Summer (far left) is shown supporting a basket of wheat, and Autumn (centre right) grasping a bunch of grapes. In the stone set illustrated here, the figure that should, according to the catalogue, be Autumn (Plate 7:11 left) has been reversed and the bunch of grapes replaced with the attribute of Summer, wheat, whilst the figure that should be

Plate 7:9. Campana-shaped vase, Carrara marble, J P White, mid-twentieth century. As is the case with many of White's pieces, this vase varies considerably from the firm's catalogue illustration (Plate 7:8, top left), while the quality of carving bears little comparison with marble pieces produced in the eighteenth and nineteenth centuries

T CROWTHER & SONS LTD

Plate 7:10. Spring and Summer, two of the Four Seasons figures, Vicenza stone, J P White. The figure of Summer (right) is shown here supporting a large bunch of grapes, in fact the attribute of Autumn. The statues do not correspond to the design of the equivalent marble and lead figures of the Four Seasons in the firm's 1906 catalogue (see Plate 7:19)

T CROWTHER & SONS LTD

Plate 7:11. Autumn and Winter, two of the Four Seasons figures, Vicenza stone, J P White. Here the figure of Autumn (left) is reversed and carries a wheat sheaf, the attribute of Summer. Winter (right) is the most skilfully carved of the four figures, all of which have suffered the effects of the British climate

T CROWTHER & SONS LTD

DESIGN No. 71   Height, 1′ 7″

DESIGN No. 73   Height, 1′ 7″

DESIGN No. 72   53   Height, 1′ 7″

DESIGN No. 486   52   Height, 1′ 3″

Plate 7:12. Two of the many Vincenza stone flower and fruit baskets illustrated in White's 1935 catalogue. The catalogue recommended them 'for placing along terrace walls, piers and flank walls to flights of steps'

Plate 7:13. Two further Vicenza stone flower and fruit baskets from the 1935 catalogue. One of the advantages of this soft limestone is that bold carving is easily achieved

Summer (Plate 7:10 right) now supports a large bunch of grapes, the attribute of Autumn. Of the four Winter is undoubtedly the most skilfully carved. The other figures are decidedly inferior. All four statues, which are typically unmarked, have clearly suffered from the effects of our weather: considering the figures are less than one hundred years old, the legs of Winter and much of the lower half of Spring are showing signs of serious deterioration.

By 1935 the firm's range of Vicenza stone ornaments had increased considerably with, in particular, great numbers of flower and fruit baskets available (Plates 7:12 and 13). These were recommended in the 1935 catalogue for their suitability 'For placing along terrace walls, piers and flank walls to flights of steps'.[10] The catalogue goes on to state that 'They are finely and boldly carved and are a most effective form of decoration in the garden at all times of the year',[11] and concludes that they 'weather very nicely'. Bold carving was certainly easy to

Plate 7:14. A photograph from White's 1935 catalogue illustrating the firm's 'unique collection of Garden Ornaments on View at Bedford, consisting of several thousand pieces, comprising Well-heads, Fountains, Vases, Sundials, etc., etc.'

achieve in this soft stone, which, it is true 'weathers very nicely', but can easily 'overweather'! A few other Vicenza stone ornaments are illustrated in the catalogue, but it seems likely that many other items illustrated, including more architectural pieces, such as the garden temple visible in the general view of the Pyghtle Works (Plate 7:14), were also carved from this soft limestone.

Bronze

The small quantity of bronze ornaments illustrated in White's 1906 catalogue suggests that the material was, for many clients, still restrictively expensive. Some idea of the medium's considerable cost can be gauged from the price of the firm's full-size copies of Verrochio's famous putto clasping a fish surmounting the fountain in the courtyard of the Palazzo Vecchio, Florence. The model could be obtained in buff coloured terracotta for £6 6s (for an extra £1 4s it could also be finished in an imitation of bronze), in lead for £10, but for real bronze the model cost the considerable sum of £25.

However, in a similar manner to his marble reproductions, White was able to offer quotations for reproducing examples in bronze of any of the famous sculptures in the museums of Florence, Naples, Rome, etc, and two of these bronze statues are illustrated on page 141 of the 1906 catalogue (Plate 7:6). The variety of other bronze statuary was negligible, with the exception of a typical early twentieth century bronze fountain figure of a boy riding a dolphin, clasping seaweed in one hand and a fish in the other. No bronze vases, seats, or well-heads are illustrated in the catalogue. By the 1930s the quantity of bronze figures available had reduced still further, and those that were available tended to be figurines, rather than statuary, ranging in height from seven inches to one foot four inches.

Well-heads

One of the most popular and better selling forms of garden ornament offered by the firm were Italian well-heads. At least ten can be seen in the photograph of the stock at Bedford in 1935 (Plate 7:14), and a similar quantity are illustrated in the 1906 catalogue. From the introduction to the section on well-heads in the 1906 catalogue, it is apparent that the bulk of the firm's stock consisted of copies of well-

Plate 7:16. Well-head, white Verona marble, J P White, reproduction of Sansovino's bronze well-head in the courtyard of the Doge's Palace, Venice. This finely-carved model was offered in the firm's 1906 catalogue

T CROWTHER & SONS LTD

Plate 7:17. Well-head, Istrian marble, J P White. The standard of carving here is more representative of the craftsmanship found on the firm's wares

BEDFORDSHIRE COUNTY COUNCIL

Plate 7:15. This photograph from White's 1906 catalogue of a well-head illustrates the fine carving which could be found on the Italian imports earlier in the century

known Venetian models, and this also seems to have been the case in later years. The materials used for these reproductions were generally the same as those used for the originals — the marbles of Verona (red, pale yellow and white) and Istria; a few were also available in terracotta. These were often supplied complete with ornate wrought-iron overthrows, or, as White referred to them, iron hoods. A further line offered by White in 1906 was well-heads formed from both old and new capitals (from columns), the centre of which had been hollowed out, but these are rarely found.

An example of one of White's reproduction well-heads, carved from Rosso Verona marble is shown in Colour Plate 67. It is not an accomplished work, the masks and scrolling acanthus leaves on the corners, and the armorials in between, can just be made out, whilst the rope work decoration running around the rim is barely visible. The quality of this well-head, one of the worst pieces of carving the author has come across, suggests that it dates not from the early 1900s, but nearer the middle of the twentieth century, and this can perhaps be substantiated by comparing it to the vastly superior model, illustrated in the 1906 catalogue (Plate 7:15).

Of the examples of well-known Venetian well-heads shown in the 1906 catalogue may be mentioned reproductions of the fine originals in the Campo San Giovanni e San Paolo, and in the Palazzo Vanasse and Palazzo Bernardo. But the two most ornate models were the copies of Sansovino's bronze models in the courtyard of the Doge's Palace. According to the catalogue, two feet six inch diameter reproductions in terracotta could be had for £15, whilst both could also be had in Istrian marble. A magnificent example, four feet in diameter and carved from white Verona marble is shown in Plate 7:16. It is one of the best examples of the firm's wares, and clearly shows the high quality of some of its garden ornaments. It is much more finely carved than the well-head illustrated in Colour Plate 67, and this probably means it was made during the first twenty years of the twentieth century.

However, the two well-heads in Plates 7:15 and 16 are extreme examples, for the overall standard of carving workmanship found in most of the well-heads imported by White is of a more intermediate quality, as exemplified by the Istrian marble example in Plate 7:17. Here, although the scrolling acanthus leaves are bold, and the carving clearly visible, it is not an outstanding work. The winged Lion of St Mark in the centre, for example, is decidedly uninspiring (though much superior to the masks found on the well-head in Colour Plate 67). There is one point which firmly dates this well-head to the twentieth century — the crisp edges. Istrian marble is a tremendously resilient medium, and as such the almost clinical clarity found, for example, on the rim of this piece, is perhaps to be expected. However, on genuine fifteenth, sixteenth and seventeenth century marble well-heads (such as those illustrated in Plates 5:18-20), no such edges are to be found, for they have been exposed to the elements for hundreds of years. As can be seen this is not the case with this example, which is clearly twentieth century, despite the fact that gouge marks have been made all around the rim to simulate, somewhat unconvincingly, the wear caused by the action of ropes and chains hauling up water over the centuries.

Ornaments produced in Britain
Stone
The stone garden ornaments carved by the sculptors and masons working at White's Pyghtle Works were of English stone, and were thus quite distinct from the firm's imported marble and stone ornaments. English stone was mainly used for items of a more architectural nature, such as pedestals and a few vases, rather than statuary. Portland limestone was most commonly used, and an example can be seen in the sundial pedestal in Plate 7:18 In the 1906 catalogue the model was described as the 'Chepstow Dial', and was available complete with an ordinary brass dial for £22 10s, whilst for an extra £2 14s it could be obtained with a 'Special Dial'. Of the ten or so Portland sundial pedestals illustrated in the catalogue it is one of the most ornate, and the carving is certainly reasonable. It is a pity it is not raised on a step for this would certainly add to its grandeur.

Two other English stones were also used by the firm. Ketton stone was recommended 'on account of its durability and good weathering qualities',[12] and Hornton (quarried near Banbury) was recommended for its unobtrusive brown to bluish-grey colour which lent itself well to the English garden. By the 1930s the

Plate 7:18. A sundial pedestal, called the Chepstow, made at White's Pyghtle Works in Portland stone, the stone most commonly used by the firm for garden ornaments produced in Britain
ANTIQUE COLLECTORS' CLUB

craftsmanship found in the sundial in Plate 7:18 had been replaced by a more mechanical process.

Lead
With the exception of wooden garden seats, by far the largest number of items manufactured by J P White were of lead. The quality of these pieces is generally inferior to anything produced during the eighteenth century — the previous period lead garden ornaments were manufactured in England in any substantial numbers. White's pieces seem to have been produced by a crude process of sand casting, and although some time was spent chasing up the details of some of the pieces, the quality of craftsmanship that went into the majority of them was often poor.

In the 1906 catalogue the stock lead items illustrated included a sundial pedestal, a few small bird baths and several vases, but the majority of pieces were figurative subjects of a contemporary nature. The material was recommended, for 'although in the first instance rather more costly than stone or terracotta [it] will be found by far the most satisfactory material for garden vases or ornaments, as it is practically unbreakable, and almost everlasting, and in a few months even new lead work will assume the lovely grey-green colour of work hundreds of years old'.[13]

By the 1930s the firm's range of lead items had increased considerably, many new figurative models had been introduced and a great many more vases were available.

THE FOUR SEASONS.

A finely sculptured Set of Figures representing the four seasons.   Each 2 ft. 6 in. high.

In best hard Carrara Marble (each) £18 18 0
In Lead (each) £15 15 0

Plate 7:19. White's set of four figures, representing the Four Seasons, illustrated here in the 1906 catalogue, was available in Carrara marble and Vicenza stone (see Plates 7:10 and 11) as well as in lead (Colour Plate 68)

BEDFORDSHIRE RECORD OFFICE

Like most of the lead figures produced during the twentieth century, White's figurative lead figures were almost all cast complete with a lead base, as opposed to the stone base so frequently used by eighteenth century lead figure makers. These characteristics can be clearly seen in the illustration of the Four Seasons in the 1906 catalogue (Plate 7:19, Colour Plate 68). An extant set (Plate 7:20) shows the poor quality of workmanship, while the detail of Winter's head (Plate 7:21), particularly the unworked hair, is typical of the sort of treatment found on many of the firm's lead figures.

Another feature of the figurative subjects illustrated in the firm's catalogues is that they tended to be small works, indeed none measured over three feet in height. However, while all the stock models were under life-size, given the versatility of the firm and its repeated claims to be able to reproduce almost any form of garden ornament in any medium, it may have produced a few life-size models.

By the 1930s the firm's range of lead garden figures had increased considerably. Amongst their many new additions was a range of fountain figures. The 1935 catalogue illustrates four of these (Plate 7:22), examples of which occur on the market with remarkable frequency, and hence must have been particularly saleable pieces. An example of the Teme group is shown in Plate 7:23. The treatment of the hair and its chasing up is vastly superior to that of Winter (Plate 7:21), but the figure lacks quality, the arms are awkward, and the waves breaking on the base are only just distinguishable.

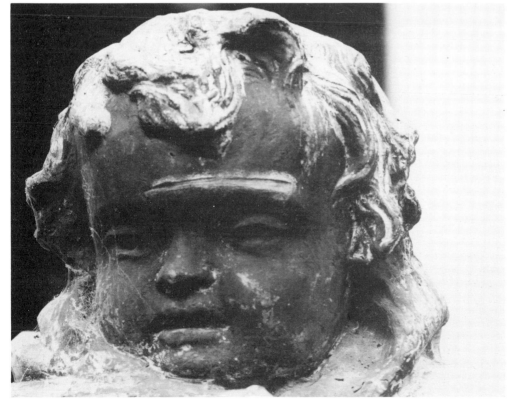

Lead Figures

THE "TEME" GROUP

Height of Figure   -   -   2′ 0″

THE "KENNET" GROUP

Height of Figure   -   -   2′ 0″

Two finely modelled figures which can also be used as fountain or bird bath figures, the water in each case being projected from the mouth of the Duck or Dolphin.   The "Kennet" group is illustrated in conjunction with a Lily Pool on the opposite page.

THE "BOY AND TORTOISE" (upright)

Height of Figure   -   -   2′ 3″

THE "BOY AND PYTHON"

Height of Figure -   -   -   2′ 6″

Both figures are fitted for water, the "Boy and Python" being shown in conjunction with a pool on the opposite page.

11

Plate 7:22. Page 11 from White's 1935 catalogue showing four of the fountain figures manufactured by the firm

Plate 7:23. The Teme group fountain figure, lead, J P White. Height approx 24ins. The quality of this figure is much finer than is usually found in the firm's lead work. Compare the figure's hair with that of Winter in Plate 7:21
AUTHOR'S COLLECTION

The firm's stock lead vases tended to be relatively small in size, few being over two and a half feet in height. Only three are illustrated in the 1906 catalogue, but this is probably an unrealistic representation of the range, for in the introduction White mentions that a variety of patterns were always kept in stock at New Bond Street. He also offered to reproduce any old examples. The firm's 1935 catalogue illustrates many more examples, and these included copies of antique seventeenth century French and eighteenth century English models, as well as a few of a contemporary nature. Identifying the firm's copies of earlier works is generally easy for, like most of White's figures, they tend to be of a poor quality. This is well illustrated by an example of the Highgate model (Plate 7:24) which, according to the catalogue was copied from six vases found in an old garden in Highgate. On the separately cast and applied relief on the frieze reclining cherubs are recognisable almost only by outline, whilst the moulding on the socle is so barely proud that it could not possibly be mistaken for a genuine antique model. Several further pages showing some of the other patterns that could be produced in lead are illustrated in the 1935 catalogue and reproduced in Appendix II, as are several other pages from the 1906 catalogue.

Plate 7:24. One of J P White's lead vases, known as Highgate, in the gardens of Lanhydrock House, Cornwall. The quality of casting leaves much to be desired

THE NATIONAL TRUST

Other Manufacturers and Commonly Used Materials

Lead

J Lewis André, writing in 1888 was 'compelled to come to the conclusion that most of the applications of ornament to leadwork belong to bygone times'.[14] This was certainly the case during much of the nineteenth century, when the manufacture of lead garden ornaments was negligible. The exact reasons for its revival in the very last years of the century are still unclear, but with the increasing demand for garden ornaments at this time there were obvious advantages in using such a relatively robust metal such as lead, which could be melted at a low temperature and also easily worked.

By the early 1900s a number of firms were producing lead garden ornaments. In London the three most notable lead foundries were H Crowther, Petretti, and Vangelisti. The Italian Petretti started a high-class foundry in Battersea, and was responsible for casting, among other works, W Fagan's lead Tritons for the dome of the American Steamship Offices in Pall Mall.[15] His stock garden ornaments included such popular models as Verrochio's Boy Clasping a Fish, and the infant Hercules strangling a snake. Examples of his work, the majority of which were one-off casts, are notable because of the fine chasing and considerable thickness of the cast.[16] Vangelisti, another Italian, worked with his son and daughter in premises at the Putney end of King's Road (the site is now occupied by Garden Crafts Ltd). He produced a limited range of models, mostly for garden settings, of which the most common is the small figure of Cupid clasping a bowl, basket or sundial above his head. An example of this type of model, which was also produced by other foundries, including J P White and H Crowther, is shown in Plate 7:25.

Plate 7:25. The commonest example of twentieth century lead statuary is this figure of a Cupid clasping a bowl above its head. The model, which was manufactured by many lead foundries, is often found supporting other features, such as the bowl of a fountain, a basket and, at times, a sundial
H CROWTHER LTD

Plate 7:26. Garden vase, lead, cast by the Morris Singer Foundry from a model by John Belcher, RA. The quality of casting and detail is vastly superior to many twentieth century lead vases, such as the Highgate model produced by J P White (Plate 7:24)

PRIVATE COLLECTION

Plate 7:27. The Morris Singer Foundry's archives could not confirm whether this vase was also cast by the firm, but the similarities in casting and detail with the smaller, squatter vase in Plate 7:26 certainly suggest that this piece also came from the famous foundry

PRIVATE COLLECTION

The ornaments produced by the other major London lead foundry, H Crowther, are mentioned in more detail below, as are the casts of the Worcestershire-based Bromsgrove Guild.

Lead was also used by other foundries, such as the famous Morris Singer Foundry of Basingstoke and Frome. Among its more notable works in this material was the magnificent Welsh dragon at the Cardiff Law Courts which was cast in ten pieces and soldered together — the total figure weighing some four tons.[17] The foundry was also producing some garden vases, such as the squat example modelled by John Belcher, RA, illustrated in Plate 7:26. The similarities between this example and the larger vase shown with it (Plate 7:27), suggest that this too came from the Morris Singer Foundry.

The Bromsgrove Guild

Of the English manufacturers of lead garden ornaments during the first half of this century, one of the most notable was the Bromsgrove Guild of Applied Arts. Established in 1894 by Walter Gilbert, who took over a foundry in Bromsgrove, Worcestershire, it was at first involved with decorative ironwork, but the business soon expanded into a great many other fields, including the manufacture of stained glass windows, as well as decorations for the interior of houses, ships and churches. By 1900 Gilbert had gone into partnership with a Mr McCandlish and had taken over further premises in the town which housed bronze and lead foundries, as well as wood and stone carving studios. In the same year the Guild won a prize medal at the Paris Exhibition for its art nouveau-style bedroom. By 1908 the firm had established an outlet in London (at Fenchurch House in Fenchurch Street), and as a result of their most famous commission, the iron and bronze gates outside Buckingham Palace, they were issued with a Royal Warrant appointing them metal workers to Edward VII (an honour repeated two years later under George V).[18]

The firm's catalogue of garden ornaments of this date (a copy of which survives in the Hereford and Worcester Record Office) illustrates a few of its items. Although these include several wooden garden seats, the majority of items illustrated are lead figures and vases, whilst a few of these lead subjects were also available in a cement-based artificial stone medium.

The lead figures were mostly under four feet in height, but a few larger examples were available, including one particularly magnificent work, a terminal figure of Pan playing a syrinx, some six feet in height. The Guild also offered to execute larger works for clients, and one of these, a heroic-sized mermaid clasping a fish, which had been modelled to the designs of R S Lorrimer and cast for a garden in the west of Scotland, is illustrated in the catalogue.[19]

Unlike the majority of other contemporary English manufacturers of garden ornaments, most of the Guild's figurative subjects were modelled in the popular styles of the day. This is well illustrated in the two art nouveau Snake Charmers illustrated in the 1908 catalogue (Plate 7:28). That on the right, playing a syrinx, shows a common characteristic of the Guild's lead statuary, the shaped lead base. An extant example of the left-hand snake charmer, typical in that it displays no identifying marks, is shown in Plate 7:29. In comparison to models cast at other works at this date, such as J P White, this is a vastly superior piece of casting, a fact which is reflected by its considerable price of thirty guineas, as opposed to a similarly-sized copy of Thorvaldsen's Cupid, which could be had from White, complete with a two foot six inch Portland stone pedestal, for a mere £18 17s 6d. Two further statues, also illustrated in the 1908 catalogue, are shown in Plate 7:30,

SNAKE CHARMER. (a)

No. 3.   Height, 3ft. 6in.

(including base)

SNAKE CHARMER. (b)

No. 4.   Height, 3ft. 6in.

(including base)

PRICE of either, Cast in Lead - 30 GUINEAS

*Plate 7:28. Snake
Charmers illustrated on
page 2 of the Bromsgrove
Guild's 1908 catalogue*
HEREFORD AND WORCESTER
RECORD OFFICE

BOY AND FISH.

No. 8.   Height, 3ft. 6in.

PRICE:

Cast in Lead - 35 GUINEAS.

Cast in Cement 15 „

SUNDIAL.

No. 9.   Height, 3ft. 10in.

PRICE:

Cast in Lead - 40 GUINEAS.

Cast in Cement 17 „

Prices in Stone and Bronze on Application.

*Plate 7:29. Snake Charmer,
lead, the Bromsgrove Guild.
This figure, which corresponds to
the left-hand figure in Plate
7:28, is, like most of the firm's
lead statues, unmarked*
SOTHEBY'S

*Plate 7:30. Figures featured on
page 5 of the Bromsgrove
Guild's 1908 catalogue*
HEREFORD AND WORCESTER RECORD
OFFICE

Plate 7:31. Garden vase, lead, the Bromsgrove Guild. This delightful example is unusual in that the separately cast and applied mice beneath the rim are all intact

T CROWTHER & SONS

Plate 7:32. A French-influenced garden vase illustrated in the Bromsgrove Guild's 1908 catalogue

HEREFORD AND WORCESTER RECORD OFFICE

GARDEN VASE.

No. 31. Height, 3 feet.

PRICE - Cast in Lead - 25 GUINEAS.

both of which again show the art nouveau style of the Guild's work. Which artist was responsible for the modelling of the four figures, illustrated here from the catalogue, or indeed any of the other figures produced by the Guild, will probably never be known for, like other Guilds, the identity of the artists remained anonymous.

Only a few lead vases are illustrated in the Guild's 1908 catalogue. All the models are, as would be expected, of a contemporary nature, such as the octagonal vase illustrated in Plate 7:31. This is characteristically unmarked, while the varying reliefs of animals and foliage within rope work borders are admirably modelled. Lawrence Weaver, a great advocate of the firm's lead work, writing in 1909, described the model as 'a perfect ornament for a modern garden'.[20]

Another influence on the firm's garden vases can be seen in the illustration of a garden vase, 'No 31' in the 1908 catalogue (Plate 7:32). This is French in style, and was perhaps modelled by one of the Continental craftsmen known to have been attracted to the Guild. According to the catalogue, this vase could be obtained in lead for twenty-five guineas, but the basic model was also available in several further forms. As number 32, it could be obtained in a cement medium for twelve guineas, modified by the removal of the ornate scrolling handles, and the addition of decoration rising from the sides of the lower half of the body. The charming relief on the frieze, depicting on one side two putti carrying home game, was also incorporated into a number of smaller vases. Finally, the overall outline of the vase was used for another model (available both in lead and cement), but this had a different, higher relief frieze of plump cherubs frolicking with satyrs, and the mouldings found on the socle, lower half of the body and rim of vases 31 and 32 were absent.

In 1921 the Guild became a limited company, but by this date some of the members had left to start their own companies. Amongst these was Gilbert, who had set up business in Birmingham with a certain L Weingartner, selling lead, stone and reconstituted stone sculpture for the garden. However the Guild continued to produce a variety of garden ornaments for many years, finally closing in 1966. Amongst the firm's better known works were the beaten copper Liver Birds on the Royal Liver Buildings in Liverpool and the lamp standards in Parliament Square.[21]

H Crowther Ltd[22]

The Chiswick lead foundry of H Crowther was established in 1908 by Oxford Cole, an accomplished lead sculptor and founder, and Henry Crowther. As a result of Cole's knowledge and experience and Crowther's access to a variety of eighteenth and nineteenth century patterns (through his father's antique garden ornament business) the foundry blossomed until the outbreak of the First World War. In 1918 the partnership broke up. Cole established his own short-lived foundry, whilst Crowther, together with his three sons, Jim, Leslie and Ronald, retained the original premises. With the onset of the depression in the early 1930s (which saw the demise of many small lead factories) the firm survived thanks mainly to its now considerable collection of patterns, which had been greatly extended by the acquisition of many German terracotta animalier works, as well as a number of magnificent pieces of lead work.

During the Second World War little was produced, but afterwards Leslie was responsible for the great improvements in the firm's patterns and casts. In 1960 the firm became a limited company. A year later Leslie died, followed six years later by Henry and the business continued to be run by the remaining two sons, though owing much of its continuity to Jim who, after sixty years' experience of production and restoration, retired in 1988. His two sons, Paul and David, continue to produce a vast range of lead garden ornaments at the same foundry in Chiswick.

Unlike many other lead foundries, most of the firm's business has been involved with supplying ornaments to established dealers and retailers. Among these may be mentioned two of the leading London antique garden ornament dealers, as well as such firms as Pearsons Page of Birmingham. The firm has also supplied a number of American firms including Hoben Fack & Keller of Pennsylvania, the Manheim Gallery in New Orleans, Jack Patla & Co in Charlestown, and Kenneth Lynch of Connecticut, who purchased a number of pieces from the firm and used them for his own patterns. Today the foundry is reaching a wide clientele, including both private individuals and architects.

In the early years the foundry was manufacturing its ornaments by a process of sand casting, but the considerable time involved soon made it prohibitively expensive, and a process of open flask casting was introduced. Using sand and clay, this process did not require an inner core, and it is still frequently used by the firm today. The process is described below, while Plates 7:33-45 illustrate the method of manufacture on the torso of a lead cast of Theodore Kalide's group of a Boy with Swan (Plate 7:46; see also Plate 3:21).

The pattern, an original nineteenth century zinc cast by M Geiss of Berlin (see page 157), is cut into a number of pieces. The pattern (in this case the torso section) is then placed face down in a wooden casting frame filled with loose, damp casting sand and half buried in the sand. The sand surrounding the pattern is pressed firmly down, and more put in around until it is compact and the surface flat and flush with the top of the casting frame (Plate 7:33).

Very carefully, and this is a skilled art, pieces of modelling clay (a block of which is visible on the side of the casting box in Plate 7:34) are pressed layer by layer into any undercuts or important details on the back of the pattern. Known as inserts, these can be seen in the crevice betwen the boy's head and left arm, as well as on the back of his neck and in between the legs (Plate 7:34). Once all the necessary inserts have been located, checked that they faithfully follow the contours of the pattern, and that each can easily be removed both from one another and the pattern, all the insert sides are dusted with dry casting sand to ease separation at a later point. The inserts are then gently heated *in situ* to harden them, and the whole surface of the casting frame dusted with dry sand to create a barrier for ease of separation later.

The top half of the casting frame is then placed over the lower half. Damp casting sand is sifted (Plated 7:35) on to the exposed surface of the pattern and its clay inserts, followed by coarse damp sand which is evenly compressed into the remaining gaps, so that eventually the whole frame is full of compressed sand level with the top of the frame (Plate 7:36). To help retain the sand in position a piece of wood is firmly secured to the top of the frame. The whole mould is then turned upside down, and the bottom frame (now the top frame) removed. The sand within this frame is broken away, to the level of the bottom of the frame (defined by the thin barrier layer of dry sand), so revealing the front of the pattern (Plate 7:37). A similar process of making clay inserts is undertaken (Plate 7:38). The top half of the casting frame is replaced and sieved damp sand (Plate 7:39) followed by coarse sand is firmly pressed into the frame till it is full and flush with the top. Another piece of wood is then placed on to this to help retain the compressed sand.

The next step is to separate the two frames of the mould, an important and difficult process, for if the surrounding sand has not been sufficiently compressed, the mould will fall apart. Other problems include uneven lifting, or sections of sand within the top and bottom frames adhering either to the pattern or each other, all of which will distort the mould and ruin the cast. When the top frame has been removed, the pattern, complete with clay inserts, remains in the bottom frame, and the top frame with its mould is placed beside it (Plate 7:40). The clay inserts located on the front of the pattern are carefully eased off one by one, and replaced in their correct position on the mould in the top frame (Plate 7:41). The pattern is then gently removed and the clay inserts on the back of the pattern are positioned in the mould in the bottom frame. To retain the inserts in position in relation to the rest of the mould, nails are pushed through the inserts and into the damp sand at varying angles (a tray of these can be seen in the foreground of Plate 7:42, resting between the top and bottom halves of the casting frame). The heads of these retaining nails are embedded into the clay inserts and the resultant holes, as well as any blemishes or tiny joint lines are later worked on by a skilled craftsman. On both moulds, at the end of the impression left by the pattern's thighs, a large hole is wittled out of damp sand to provide a runner into each thigh through which the molten lead will be poured. The now completed mould is again checked for any blemishes, and any residue grains of sand removed by blowing them out with bellows.

Finally, those sections of the mould with little in the way of undercutting, such as the back and chest, are pierced at varying angles with a sharp point, to aid the adhesion of the lead to the mould and so prevent the cooled lead from falling in on itself. In several places the mould is pierced completely through to provide an outlet for the hot air and steam caused by the action of the molten lead on the damp sand and clay.

The top casting frame is very carefully lifted back over the bottom casting frame and the whole lashed firmly together. A specific quantity of molten lead, in this

Plate 7:33. The zinc pattern half embedded in damp sand within a wooden casting frame

Plate 7:34. Applying clay inserts into the details and undercuts on the back of the pattern

Plate 7:35. The top half of the casting frame located on to the bottom half. Damp casting sand is being sieved on to the pattern

Plate 7:36. The casting frame full of compressed sand, prior to securing a piece of wood over the top to keep the sand in position

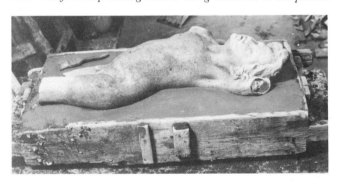

Plate 7:37. The casting frame has been turned over and the top (formerly the bottom) half of the frame and surrounding sand removed to reveal the front of the pattern

Plate 7:38. Applying clay inserts into the details and undercuts on the front of the pattern. All the inserts are dusted with dry sand before being pressed into position

Plate 7:39. The top half of the casting frame is replaced and damp casting sand is sifted on to the front of the pattern and its inserts

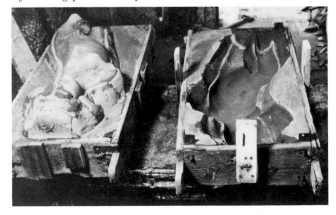

Plate 7:40. The two frames of the mould separated. In the right-hand frame the impressions left by the clay inserts are clearly visible

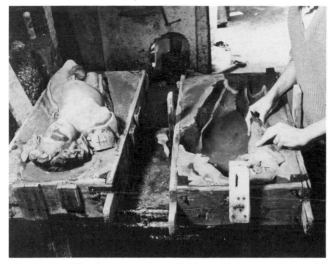

Plate 7:41. The clay inserts from the front of the pattern are eased off and replaced in the respective locations in the top half of the casting frame

Plate 7:42. To retain the inserts in position in relation to the rest of the mould, nails are pushed through the inserts and into the damp sand of the mould. A large hole is whittled out of the sand on both moulds to provide a runner through which the molten lead will be poured

Plate 7:43. Pouring molten lead through the runner into the mould. Special casting boots are worn because of the obvious dangers from spilt molten metal

Plate 7:44. The cast torso within the mould. Some of the nails which hold the inserts to the damp sand and spurs caused by piercing the mould can be seen

case 850lbs, is ladled into a cast-iron copper, which is rested on the casting frame to facilitate the pouring of the lead into the runner. The lead is then left to cool to a point where it is just beginning to harden on the edges of the copper, when it is carefully poured down the runner into the mould (Plate 7:43). When the copper is empty it is removed and the casting frame turned through 180 degrees to allow the considerable quantity of molten lead in the mould to flow back through the runner, leaving a hollow shell of lead between three quarters of an inch and one inch thick within the now spent mould.

After being left to cool for some time the casting frames are separated to reveal the cast torso (Plate 7:44). As can be seen in Plate 7:45 (overleaf), the cast does have blemishes and will require considerable finishing by hand to remove the spurs. These are first removed with a file and then burnished with silver steel rods to create a smooth finish, whilst the details are chased up by hand. To complete the copy of Kalide's original, the limbs of the boy and the sections of the swan (some fifteen pieces altogether) are cast in a similar way and then soldered together. Finally, the completed model is treated with a specially formulated antique finish of acids and pigments which help speed the ageing process. An example of a complete group is shown in Plate 7:46.

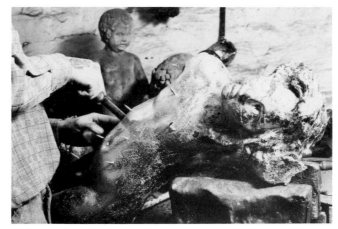

Plate 7:45. Working on the cast to remove the blemishes

Plate 7:46. A completed lead reproduction of Kalide's Boy with Swan, cast from sixteen pieces, Castle Hill, Devon

LADY MARGARET FORTESCUE

Weathered examples of the firm's casts are often incorrectly identified by both dealers and auction houses as genuine antiques, partly because, until recently, the firm never marked its items, and partly because most of the patterns used are original models dating from the eighteenth and nineteenth centuries. The firm's wide range of patterns include cast-iron examples, including French works such as the Val d'Osne's cast of Mathurin Moreau's Enfant au Canard, as well as vases produced by Barbezat & Cie. English cast-iron patterns include several architectural fountains by the Coalbrookdale Company, as well as a number of fountain figures. Zinc patterns include a number of M Geiss subjects, such as Kalide's Boy with Swan, and a pair of Eagles, whilst bronze models include a number of twentieth century works including the famous Doe discovered during excavations at Herculaneum. The artificial stone patterns include several Coade stone vases and plaques, and an impressive cement-based relief of a crowned River God. However, by far the largest quantity of patterns are made of lead. These include patterns from genuine eighteenth century models, such as John Cheere's Shepherd and Shepherdess, and a number of vases. The firm also uses a number of contemporary patterns including models produced by other twentieth century lead manufacturers, such as J P White and the Bromsgrove Guild, as well as a number of pieces modelled by various members of the Crowther family.

Determining the difference between a genuine antique item and a Crowther model can be difficult. It is not easy to generalise, but there are, as with much twentieth century leadwork, points to look out for. One is to beware of nineteenth century lead garden ornaments, for the material was rarely used during this period. Another is the firm's extensive and predominant use of lead rather than stone bases. Furthermore, since the firm does not use an inner core during casting, there should be no indication of one on a Crowther model. One of the areas which causes great difficulty in identifying the firm's products is in the copies of genuine eighteenth century leadwork. The problem can be seen in the less than half life-size figures of the Shepherd and Shepherdess illustrated in Plate 7:47 which were copied from a pair of eighteenth century models. On close examination it is clear that, despite some disfiguration caused by poor restoration, they are well cast statues, but there are differences between them and the features one would expect to find on an eighteenth century pair. Firstly they are located on lead bases, and although these could be later additions it is unlikely. The second most important point is that the quality of casting is not quite fine enough. On an eighteenth century pair one would expect finer detail in, for example, the clothes. On this pair the buttons and belt on the Shepherd and the bodice and fruit in the apron of the Shepherdess are not finished to a high enough standard. Confirmation of their Crowther origins can be found in an illustration in one of the firm's early catalogues (Plate 7:48) in which they are described as 'Watteau figures'.

At Polesden Lacey, Surrey, the over life-size statue of Diana de Versailles dominates the croquet lawn (Plate 7:49). It differs from the original antique marble in the Louvre primarily in the addition of a large bow (cast from a wooden bow whittled by one of Henry Crowther's sons). The figure was cast from a plaster pattern comprising many pieces but, due to the considerable time involved in casting such a piece, copies are no longer being produced.

A good example of how even experts can be fooled by the firm's work can be seen in the set of figures of the Four Seasons in Plate 7:50. In 1985 these were catalogued by a leading auction house as eighteenth century, but the very same models are still being produced today. The original patterns were terracotta, but these were broken many years ago and lead patterns are now used. From time to

*Plate 7:47. Shepherd and
Shepherdess, lead,
H Crowther Ltd,
reproductions of eighteenth
century originals,
mid-1950s. Height approx
35½ ins*

SOTHEBY'S, SUSSEX

*Plate 7:48. Detail from an H Crowther catalogue of
the mid-1920s showing the designs for the Shepherd
and Shepherdess in Plate 7:47. The pedestals were in
stone or artificial stone and were not included in the
price*

H CROWTHER LTD

Plate 7:49. Life-size figure of Diana de Versailles, lead, H Crowther Ltd, modified reproduction of the original antique marble in the Louvre, early twentieth century, Polesden Lacey, Surrey. The most notable variations between this statue and the one in the Louvre are the addition of a bow (made by one of Henry Crowther's sons), the use of a lead rather than a stone base, and the inferior quality of the casting

time the patterns have been chased up and the details altered, as can be seen by comparing them with the more recently cast set illustrated in Plate 7:51.

Perhaps the best gauge of the firm's success over the last eighty years is the number of estates to which examples of its work have been supplied. These, to name a few, include Burton Agnes Hall, West Wycombe Park, Bicton, Misarden Park and Blenheim Palace.

Plate 7:50. Set of four figures representing the Four Seasons, lead, H Crowther Ltd, circa 1970. Height approx 19ins. This set was sold at auction in 1985, catalogued as eighteenth century

Plate 7:51. Set of four figures representing the Four Seasons, lead, H Crowther Ltd, 1987. Height approx 19ins. Note the recent chasing up in the detail of this set of figures when compared with the earlier cast set in Plate 7:50

H CROWTHER LTD

Plate 7:52. Half-size figure of Water, Vicenza limestone, circa 1950, Polesden Lacey, Surrey
THE NATIONAL TRUST

Vicenza stone

Among the garden ornaments that have been imported into Britain since the beginning of this century, probably the greatest quantity are stone pieces from northern Italy. Examples are often of sufficient quality and in such condition that they confuse both layman and expert alike into imagining them to be of a much earlier date, and horrific but unprintable stories are told of vetting committees at prestigious antique and fine art fairs failing to spot them.

The main centre of production (which still exists today) is around Vicenza, where a number of manufacturers still turn out a considerable range of ornaments from the local limestone. When newly carved, Vicenza limestone is white in colour (see Appendix I), but after a few years' exposure to the British environment the surface takes on a yellow hue. It is a notably soft stone, and this is one of the main

Plate 7:53. The roadside display of a Vicenza limestone works, with row upon row of modern statues, many of them copies of antique pieces
MILES D'AGAR AND NICK GIFFORD-MEAD ANTIQUES

reasons why so many pieces are still carved from it for, with the aid of pneumatic chisels, it can still be produced remarkably cheaply. Unfortunately the stone is not well suited to the British climate, as can be seen in the photograph of a figure of Water in the grounds of Polesden Lacey (Plate 7:52). Most of its face has been destroyed by the action of frost, and whilst the covering of moss and lichen is pleasing, this will soon have a detrimental effect. The main reason for the unsuitability of Vicenza stone in the British climate stems from its porosity. Its ability to absorb water is best illustrated by an event witnessed by the author when a gallon bucket of water was tipped into a Vicenza stone bird bath. Four hours later, the bird bath, which was inside a warehouse, had completely sucked up the water like a sponge. Of course, Vicenza stone is well suited to its natural environment, where it rains little and any rain that is absorbed by the stone is easily evaporated by the heat generated from the sun. However, in Britain the stone absorbs as much water as it can, making it particularly prone to the action of frost during the winter months. Consequently the use of Vicenza stone for fountains in Britain is quite inappropriate. Most examples that have been in use for as little as three or four years have either broken or the bowls have cracked, or they are completely encased in a bed of moss which hides much of the carving. However, the stone is quite appropriate for use in such protected locations as conservatories.

One of the larger producers of these ornaments, and one that has been in business since at least the 1930s, is Laboratorio Morseletto SRL. Clearly visible from the nearby autostrada, the large premises in west Vicenza are surrounded by rows of ornaments. Amongst these are figures of lions, dogs, birds, statues, etc, as well as items of a more architectural nature such as columns, temples, vases, baskets of fruit, well-heads, seats and tables. Inside the workshops, numerous masons using pneumatic chisels can be seen at work carving countless different pieces. The firm (whose lengthy name has led to the stone acquiring the nickname in the antique trade of 'Mozzarella') has been supplying British clients for a

Plate 7:54. Single fountain, Vicenza limestone, circa 1980. Height approx 53ins
SOTHEBY'S, SUSSEX

number of years. Other stone carving firms in and around Vicenza produce items of a similar nature (Plate 7:53), and as neither Laboratorio Morseletto nor any of these other firms ever appear to have marked their wares, identifying the firm responsible for a particular item is difficult. Consequently, although the items illustrated in this section are all carved from Vicenza stone, their precise origins are not known.

An example of an almost new fountain (as opposed to a brand new one, which would either be completely white or white spotted with yellow, green and black dots of water paint to simulate lichen) is shown in Plate 7:54. Like many Vicenza stone fountains the bowl is in the shape of a scallop shell and supported by a pedestal of Baroque form. This type of fountain is still manufactured today in a great variety of sizes (this example being one of the smallest), some having as many as three bowls and standing as much as eight feet high.

Plate 7:55. Set of four Musicians, Vicenza limestone, circa 1980. Height approx 46ins
SOTHEBY'S, SUSSEX

The most common size of Vicenza stone standing statue is around three feet in height. Countless subjects have been produced, such as dwarfs, sets of the Four Seasons, elements and arts, as well as numerous individual allegorical figures. A typical example of one of these sets is seen in the four Musicians in Plate 7:55. The plump, almost 'Flemish', treatment of the limbs, poorly worked details and proportions, as well as the crude nature of the instruments, are all typical features of Vicenza stone manufactories.

Whilst Vicenza stone figures of around three feet in height seated on naturalistic bases are infrequently found, more formal statues abound. A good example is a pair of figures at Parham Park, West Sussex (Plate 7:56). Again, these figures have plump 'Flemish' limbs, and although of a superior quality to the Musicians in Plate 7:55, the quality of sculpture is still poor. The bases of the two statues at Parham Park show a feature frequently to be found on Vicenza stone ornaments — the numerous raised thin parallel lines, running horizontally in this case, are the marks left by multi-pronged chisels. Plate 7:56 also illustrates one of the most common types of pedestal. Both capital and base are each carved from one piece (with the outline of the mouldings carved by a machine), whilst each die with its incised panel is also carved from one piece. As is typical of Vicenza stone in the British environment, both figures and pedestals are beginning to accumulate a heavy layer of lichen.

The larger figures produced by the Vicenza stone carving firms also encompass a wide range of sizes, and include pieces much larger than life-size. Copies of famous originals in Italy, such as antique models, works by artists like

Michelangelo and Bernini, as well as French pieces and copies of originals at Versailles, are all popular. Of the large-scale models, the most popular are sets of the Four Seasons (Plate 7:57). Assuming that the two figures in this illustration have not been inside for some years, they must be relatively new (possibly five to ten years old), and bear many of the characteristic features found on smaller models, for example the multi-pronged chisel marks on the bases. Both figures also illustrate the poor quality of carving of more modern works: both are awkwardly posed, badly proportioned and lack any feeling of movement or life.

Plate 7:57. Two of a set of figures representing the Four Seasons, Vicenza limestone, circa 1980. Height approx 72ins; height of pedestals 42ins

Italian marble

Italy, with its great deposits of white marble in the Apuan Alps and a long sculptural tradition, has been the predominant source of marble garden ornaments during the twentieth century. In the early years the production of marble vases, statues, etc, was still much as it had been in the previous century. Numerous sculptors and masons in *studii* in Florence, Rome and Naples, to name the larger centres, as well as, of course, the villages around Carrara, continued to produce pieces, many of which were copies of works by earlier artists. Production techniques had also changed little, and although some mechanical tools had been introduced, chisels, mallets and drills still tended to be used by the marble workers. The fine quality Statuary marble was also still available, although at some considerable premium.

The quality of marble pieces at this date differed considerably. Some poor quality carvings were produced, for example some of the items imported by the firm of J P White, but whilst these were probably made by masons, quite a number of ornaments were still carved to a standard comparable with that found during the last fifty years of the nineteenth century.

An example of one of the better quality works produced at the beginning of the twentieth century can be seen in the slightly weathered figure of Bacchus treading grapes (Colour Plate 69). This copy of an early nineteenth century work by the Italian sculptor Lorenzo Bartolini (1777-1850) was carved by Pietro Barzanti, one of a number of sculptors operating in Florence whose copies of famous works were displayed at his gallery in the town.[23] The piece is carved from a fine quality block of Statuary marble and is excellently worked, the detail of the hair and grapes being particularly notable. It is in stark comparison to the crude carving on the frieze of a J P White marble vase (Plate 7:9) which was carved from a inferior marble. Although the surface of the Bacchus figure is slightly pitted, it has not as yet begun to sugar, and is still in relatively good condition, suggesting that, in the past, it has either been well cared for or been in an outside environment for a short time.

By the middle of the twentieth century, new more efficient means of working marble had been devised. Blocks could be obtained more cheaply and could be easily carved into ornaments using the new pneumatic chisels and electric saws and drills. Coinciding with these advances was the decline in the standard of craftsmanship. Already apparent at the beginning of the century, this decline steadily increased, so that many ornaments produced during and after the 1950s are easily distinguishable from pre-war productions. Again, the main characteristics of these pieces are poor proportions and an unfinished appearance, but a clearer gauge can usually be found in the marble used. During the eighteenth and nineteenth centuries and into the early years of the twentieth century, the beautiful, translucent, creamy white Statuario or Statuary marble was still readily available, but these supplies were not inexhaustible, and one finds ornaments dating from around the middle of the twentieth century, and sometimes slightly earlier, cut from lesser quality marbles. Some of these have pronounced coloured veins running through them, others are grey, but the marble most commonly used was white crystal. White crystal marble (which at times has veining running through it) is easily recognisable when compared to Statuary marble, for it has large, easily discernible crystals which glisten in the light, as opposed to the compact dull white quality of Statuary marble (see Appendix I). It is this sort of marble which carvers in Italy still use today.

As before, the main centres of marble production are Florence, Naples and Rome, but the largest group of workers is to be found on the coast running between Pisa and La Spezia, and in particular in the small town of Pietrasanta. Here, white crystal marble copies of the world's most famous statues and ornaments can be purchased for use either as interior marbles or as garden ornaments. These are often extremely expensive and frequently of such a poor quality that collectors would be better advised to find old pieces. Illustrations of the sort of pieces available are shown in Plates 7:58 and 59.

Cast-iron

At the beginning of the twentieth century, production of cast-iron garden ornaments in Britain was still considerable. The method of manufacture of many foundries continued unchanged from the previous century, still using the same patterns and techniques. This often causes confusion today, for many models that were, in fact, originally made in the first twenty or so years of the twentieth century are commonly indistinguishable from pieces produced in the latter half of the nineteenth. This point is particularly well illustrated by comparing the Coalbrookdale Company's 1907 catalogue with its 1875 edition, in which many pieces are exactly the same.

Plate 7:58. Detail of the interior of a marble workers' shop in the environs of Pietrasanta, Italy. The figures include, from left to right, reproductions of the antique Venus de Medici, a Venus discovered at Pompeii, Michelangelo's David, and an artist's impression of the Botticelli Venus
ANTIQUE COLLECTORS' CLUB

Plate 7:59. Marble workers' display area near Pietrasanta showing, among other pieces, several Venuses, including a copy of Canova's Venus (far left), a reduced-size copy of the Borghese Vase (centre left), and a copy of Sansovino's Bacchus (centre), as well as a mass of architectural marble pieces

ANTIQUE COLLECTORS' CLUB

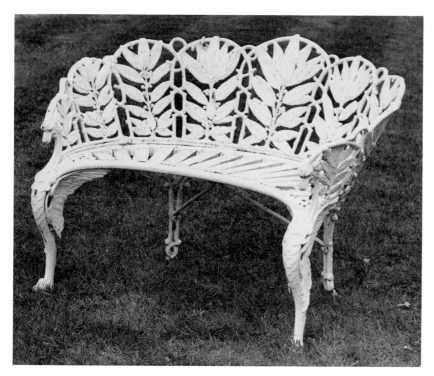

Plate 7:60. Laurel two-seater chair, cast-iron, the Coalbrookdale Company, originally featured in the company's 1875 catalogue and still in production in 1907. Width approx 46ins
SOTHEBY'S, SUSSEX

Plate 7:61. Fountain, cast-iron, the Coalbrookdale Company, another example of a piece originally featured in the 1875 catalogue and still in production in 1907. Height approx 52ins
SOTHEBY'S, SUSSEX

An extant example of one of these designs is shown in Plate 7:60. Known as the Laurel design, the chair was still available in 1907, complete with a grained pine seat, in either a bronzed, brown or chocolate paint finish. It seems likely, although this is not mentioned, that the chair could also be had with the optional iron seat mentioned in the 1875 catalogue. Another example of a nineteenth century model still being produced in the early twentieth century is the small architectural fountain in Plate 7:61. This was still available in 1907 for £5 6s painted, or £5 10s with a bronzed finish. (It should, however, be noted that the upper and middle supports as well as the top bowl are later additions to the original nineteenth/early twentieth century base.)

Some new designs had, however, been introduced by the Coalbrookdale Company in the early years of the twentieth century, and extant examples of two of these are illustrated in Plates 7:62 and 63. It seems probable, however, that these two designs were first brought into publication in the twilight of the nineteenth century, for both, like Christopher Dresser's Water Plant design (Plate 6:19), are notably formal and organised.

An interesting addition to the Coalbrookdale Company's range of garden furniture in the early 1900s were simple yet functional and cheap wrought-iron and wooden park chairs. This type of seat had been in production since around the middle of the nineteenth century (produced by such firms as Barnard, Bishop & Barnard Ltd) and was particularly popular; designs from the Coalbrookdale 1907 catalogue are shown in Appendix II.

By 1929 it would seem that much of the firm's diverse range of ornaments had been dramatically reduced, for by then the Coalbrookdale Company had become part of Allied Iron Foundries, and the 1929 catalogue shows only a few garden chairs.

Plate 7:62. Single-seater chair or armchair, cast-iron, the Coalbrookdale Company, a design introduced at the end of the nineteenth century and still in production in 1907. The model was available in a number of sizes (see Plate 7:63). The broken front of the seat is a particularly common occurrence on many of the firm's chairs
SOTHEBY'S, SUSSEX

Plate 7:63. Four-seater chair, cast-iron, the Coalbrookdale Company. Width approx 76ins
CHRISTIE'S, SOUTH KENSINGTON

The continuation of the production of cast-iron garden ornaments into the early years of the twentieth century was a feature of many British foundries, but after the First World War demand for ornate relatively expensive pieces dropped in favour of cheaper wrought-iron seats and imported ornaments.

French Cast-iron

At the turn of this century, the production of cast-iron garden ornaments in France was on as large a scale, if not larger, as in Britain. By the early 1900s the Société Anonyme... Val d'Osne (see pages 279-280) could offer an immense range of cast-iron (and bronze) ornaments. These, which could be selected from lavishly illustrated catalogues, included not only many of the models which had been available during both André and Barbezat & Cie's control of the foundry, but also many of those which had been produced by another large French cast-iron foundry, J J Ducel at Pocé (in 1878 on the death of Monsieur Ducel, the Val d'Osne foundry had purchased the firm's patterns).

334

An example of one of the Société's pieces, together with an illustration from an early twentieth century catalogue, can be seen in Plates 7:64 and 65. This group, which formerly decorated the grounds of Lynford Hall and is now in America,[24] is a slightly modified copy of the original lead group made by J Hardy (1653-1737) for the gardens of Versailles and known as L'Ile des Enfants. The exact date it was supplied to Lynford Hall is unclear; it does not feature in the numerous illustrations in the 1903 *Country Life* article on Lynford,[25] and so was presumably a later addition. However, castings of this model seem to have been available from the foundry several years earlier, for amongst the items exhibited by the Société at the 1893 Chicago Exhibition were copies of a number of originals at Versailles.[26] It is an outstanding piece of cast-iron work, over five feet wide and four feet high, and clearly shows the quality of casting of which the foundry was capable.

Plate 7:66. Detail from a Durenne catalogue circa 1880 illustrating a design for a fountain. Copies of this fountain are still produced by GHM today
GHM

Although many copies of seventeenth century ornaments at Versailles feature in the Société's catalogues at the turn of the century, these were by no means the only new additions to its *oeuvre*. Up to the beginning of the First World War, new models in the popular styles of the day were constantly being introduced by artists such as Perron and Dame.

It is clear that the Société's range of models, circa 1910, was enormous, and when this large foundry merged with another similarly large French iron foundry, Antoine Durenne, the combined collection of patterns far outnumbered that of any other foundry in the world. The exact date the Société Anonyme des Établissements Métallurgiques A Durenne et du Val d'Osne was formed is unclear, certainly prior to 1930. As we have seen in Chapter Six, the firm of Durenne had been started in 1847 at Sommevoire in the Haute-Marne. By the 1870s it was producing a massive range of statues, vases, fountains, etc (several pages from the firm's 1889 catalogue are illustrated in Appendix II), as well as numerous other castings such as fireplaces, lamp posts, balustrades, balconies, etc. With the outbreak of the Second World War, the production of art castings stopped, and although production was resurrected afterwards, it was never on

Colour Plate 67. An example of a Rosso Verona marble well-head imported by J P White. The quality of the carving is so poor that it suggests the piece was manufactured around the middle of the twentieth century. The well-heads imported by the company early in the century (Plates 7:15 and 16) are much more finely carved

SOTHEBY'S, SUSSEX

Colour Plate 68. Spring, one of the Four Seasons, lead, J P White, circa 1910. Height approx 30ins. (See Plates 7:19 and 20 and page 306)

PHOTO BRIGITTE THOMAS

Colour Plate 69. Statuary Carrara marble Bacchus, carved by Pietro Barzanti after an original by Lorenzo Bartolini, probably early twentieth century. Height approx 53ins. Although slightly pitted, the surface has not yet begun to sugar and is still in relatively good condition. (See page 331)

Plate 7:67. Interior of one of the magasins at the old Durenne foundry at Sommevoire, showing plaster patterns of a pair of Lions and of the famous antique Diana de Versailles
GHM

Plate 7:68. Interior of one of the magasins at the old Durenne foundry at Sommevoire showing some of the cast-iron copies of the original seventeenth century bronze vases at Versailles
GHM

anything like the scale of the pre-war years, the main emphasis being placed on castings of a more practical or engineering nature. In 1969, the Société Anonyme des Établissements Métallurgiques A Durenne et du Val d'Osne was bought out by the Société Générale de Fonderié and, due to its main activities at that time, took the name of Société Nouvelle Générale d'Hydraulique et de Mecanique (GHM). Today, however, GHM continues to produce both art and industrial castings at Antoine Durenne's original foundry at Sommevoire, and still uses many of the original buildings.[27]

The present quality of the firm's ornamental castings, as would be expected in today's mechanised less labour-intensive world, is not as fine as it was in either the nineteenth century or the early years of the twentieth century (a phenomenon found in the majority of cast-iron pieces manufactured today). Although some sand moulding is still done by hand, most is now formed by machine. Unfortunately, this process of mould making is prone to leave thin seams in the mould (where the various parts of the mould join) which appear in the cast, and these have to be removed with electrical power tools. It is these two features, poor detail and marks left on seams by such implements as grinders, that provide the best means of identifying modern casts.

However, the overall quality of casting in comparison to similar products is good. Although mainly involved with the production of copies of the foundry's original nineteenth century lamp posts, GHM still casts a variety of vases and fountains, including copies of the famous Wallace fountains in Paris. Another fountain, which has been in production since at least 1876,[28] is shown in Plate 7:66. Despite bankruptcy in the late 1970s GHM (which is now operational again) managed to retain some of the original nineteenth century patterns. Many of these patterns such as the pair of Lions and copy of the famous antique Diana de Versailles illustrated in Plate 7:67 are made out of plaster. Others, such as those illustrated in Plate 7:68 are made of cast-iron and come apart in sections. Of particular note in Plate 7:68 are the cast-iron copies of the original seventeenth century bronze vases at Versailles which were copied in bronze for Bagatelle (see pages 133-142).

APPENDIX I
Common Stones and Marbles

Stone

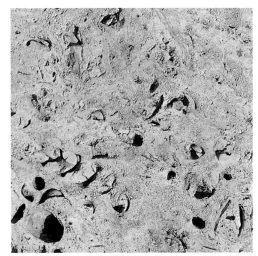

1 *Portland stone (Roach — unsuitable for carving)*

2 *Portland stone (Whit — with the form known as Base, this is the type of Portland stone used most extensively for sculptural work in the eighteenth and nineteenth centuries)*

3 *Bath stone*

4 *Vicenza limestone (unweathered, no more than two years old)*

5 *Hornton stone*

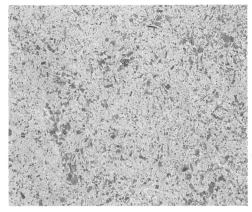

6 *Hopton Wood stone (polished)*

7 Ketton stone (showing the petrified cod's roe nature of the stone)

8 Roche Abbey stone

Artificial Stone

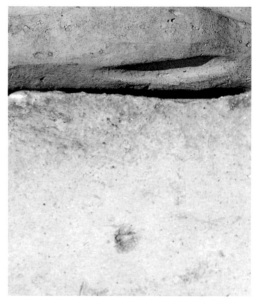

9 Coade stone

10 Coade stone, below, and Blashfield's terracotta, top (showing the varying nature of the two materials, both samples weathered)

11 Cement-based artificial stone (showing characteristic air holes)

12 Statuary Carrara marble (lightly veined, heavily weathered)

13 Carrara marble (heavily veined)

14 Crystal marble (modern, unweathered)

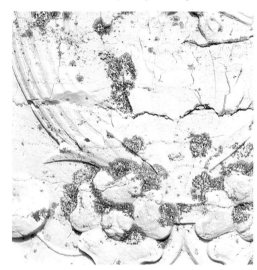

15 Istrian marble or stone (weathered)

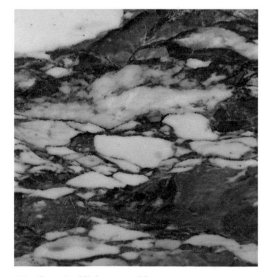

16 Breccia Violette marble

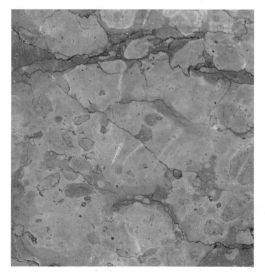

17 Rosso Verona marble

CONTINUED

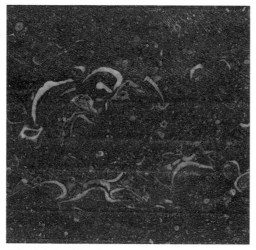 

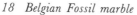

18 *Belgian Fossil marble*   19 *Ashford Black marble (polished)*

APPENDIX II
Manufacturers'
Catalogue Illustrations and Drawings

Illustrations from Etchings of Coade's Artificial Stone Manufactory, *taken from the copy in the Sir John Soane's Museum, London. Although undated, some of the pages in the Soane copy are marked with various dates in 1778, although the British Museum copy has dates of 1777, 1778 and 1779*

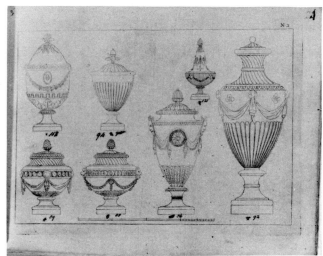

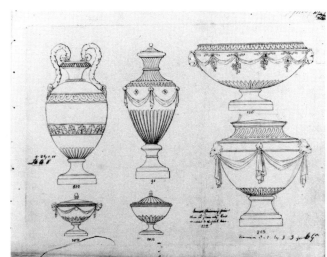

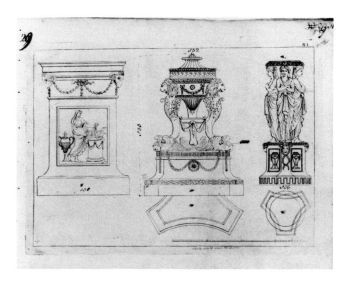

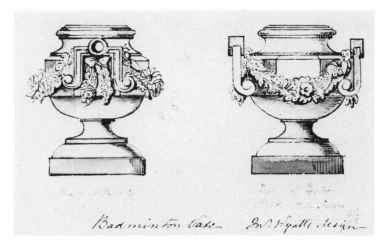

Badminton Vase

3.6 diam

D

2 ft

2.2/

Square Handled Urn. Pompeian

Drawings and tracings included in Austin & Seeley's correspondence with Lady Pembroke in the 1840s
Wilton Estate

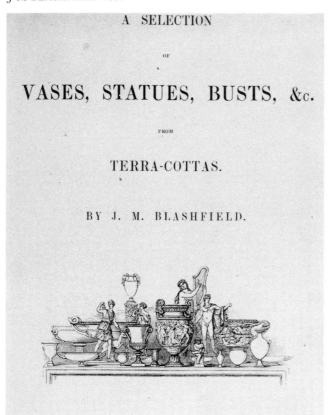

A SELECTION

OF

VASES, STATUES, BUSTS, &c.

FROM

TERRA-COTTAS.

BY J. M. BLASHFIELD.

No. 151.—VASE FROM THE ANTIQUE, IN THE BRITISH MUSEUM.
Height, 34 inches.

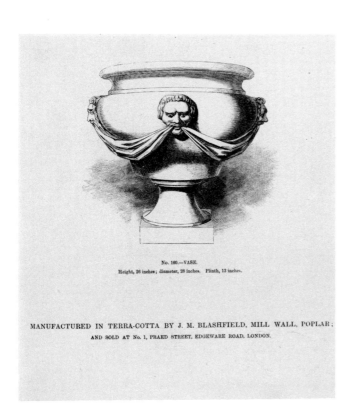

No. 160.—VASE.
Height, 26 inches; diameter, 28 inches. Plinth, 13 inches.

MANUFACTURED IN TERRA-COTTA BY J. M. BLASHFIELD, MILL WALL, POPLAR;
AND SOLD AT No. 1, PRAED STREET, EDGEWARE ROAD, LONDON.

No. 153.
APOLLO.
Height 33 inches.

Manufactured in TERRA-COTTA by J. M. BLASHFIELD, Mill Wall, Poplar,
AND SOLD AT No. 1, PRAED STREET, EDGEWARE ROAD, LONDON.

Nos. 195 AND 356.—TAZZA AND PEDESTAL.
Height, 2 feet 11 inches.

MANUFACTURED IN TERRA-COTTA BY J. M. BLASHFIELD, MILL WALL, POPLAR;
AND SOLD AT No. 1, PRAED STREET, EDGEWARE ROAD, LONDON.

Nos. 350 AND 213.—VASE AND PEDESTAL FROM THE ANTIQUE.
Height of Vase, 37 inches; diameter, 31 inches.   Height of Pedestal, 21 inches.

MANUFACTURED IN TERRA-COTTA BY J. M. BLASHFIELD, MILL WALL, POPLAR;
AND SOLD AT No. 1, PRAED STREET, EDGEWARE ROAD, LONDON.

Nº 444.
"GIRL AT THE SPRING," by W. F. WOODINGTON.
4 feet 7 inches.

Nº 445.
NAIAD by W. F. WOODINGTON.

Illustrations taken from A Selection of Vases, Statues, Busts &c From Terra Cottas by J M
Blashfield, *1857*
Rarereserve Ltd

349

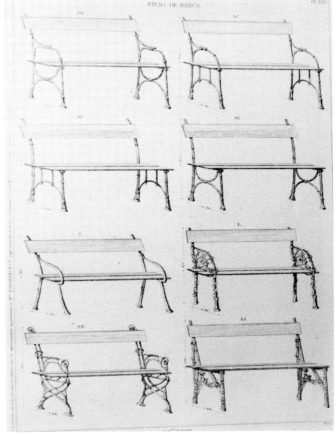

Items from Barbezat & Cie's illustrated catalogue of 1858

Illustrations from Morris Geiss' catalogue Zinkguss — Ornamente, Statuen und Sculpturen, *1863*
Rarereserve Ltd

For price see Appendix.

Illustrations from Handyside's Ironwork (Catalogues B & C): Ornamental Ironwork
Manufactured by Andw Handyside & Co Ltd, *1874*
Derbyshire Local Studies Library

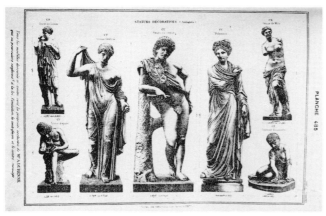

Illustrations from Durenne's illustrated catalogue, Fonte der Fer. A. Durenne, Maitre de Forges:
Edition de 1889 (Serie R.)
GHM

THE CHEPSTOW DIAL. THE YEOVIL DIAL.

Height of Pedestal ... 4 ft. 0 in.
Square at base 1 ft. 7½ in. top 1 ft. 3 in.
In Portland stone, richly carved.
Price including square brass engraved ordinary
dial and gnomon £22 10 0
Do. do. with special dial and
gnomon £25 0 0

Height of Pedestal ... 4 ft. 2 in.
Square at base 2 ft. 3½ in. top 1 ft. 5 in.
In Portland stone richly carved.
Price including ordinary square brass engraved
dial and gnomon £22 0 0
Do. do. with special dial and
gnomon £24 10 0

THE COLWICK DIAL. THE KESWICK DIAL.

Height of Pedestal
3 ft. 2 in.
Made in Tuscan
Terracotta
(see page 126).
Price with ordinary
dial ... £6 0 0
Price with special
dial ... £7 10 0

Height of Pedestal
3 ft. 8 in.
1ft. 3 in. square at top,
1 ft. 6 in. square at base.
Made in Portland
stone.
Price with ordinary
dial ... £12 0 0
Price with special
dial ... £14 5 0

THE SMETHWICK DIAL. THE ELSWICK DIAL.

Height of Pedestal
3 ft. 6 in.
Price in Portland
stone with ordinary
dial ... £13 0 0
Do. do. with special
dial £15 0 0

Height of
Pedestal 3ft. 4 in.
Price in Portland
stone with ordinary dial ...
£18 10 0
Do. do. with
special dial ...
£21 0 0

A reproduction from Gian Bologna's (John of Bologna's) famous "Mercury" in the
Bargello, Florence.

Height ... ... 6 ft. 0 in.
Price in best bronze as original £57 10 0

Quotations for Pedestals on application.

A MARBLE FOUNTAIN.

Total Height ... ... 7 ft. 4 in.
Price in best hard Carrara Marble (not including marble rim) £49 10 0

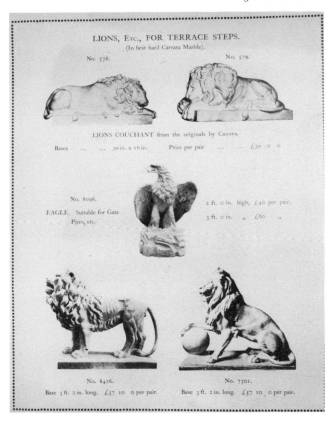

Stone and marble items from J P White's A Complete Catalogue of Garden Furniture and Garden Ornament, *1906*
Bedfordshire Public Record Office

ORNAMENTAL FOUNTAINS.

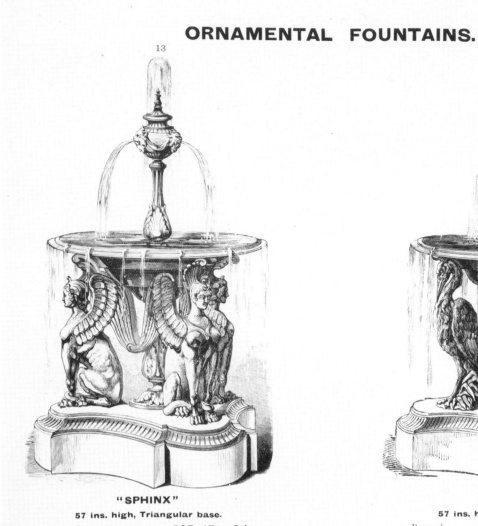

"SPHINX"

57 ins. high, Triangular base.

Bronzed ... ... **£35 15s. 0d.**

"HERON"

57 ins. high, Triangular base.

Bronzed ... ... **£29 15s. 0d.**

ORNAMENTAL   **FOUNTAINS.**

VASES and PEDESTALS.

VASES and PEDESTALS.

VASE No. 45.
17½ ins. diameter, 27 ins. high.
Painted, **65/-**   Bronzed, **67/-**
PEDESTAL No. 27.
17 ins. diameter, 30 ins. high.
Painted, **78/-**   Bronzed, **79/9**

VASE No. 46.
28 ins. diameter, 21 ins. high.
Painted, **64/3.**   Bronzed, **66/-**
PEDESTAL, No. 28.
19 ins. square, 30 ins. high.
Painted, **59/-**   Bronzed, **61/6.**

VASE, No. 43.
18½ ins. diameter, 17 ins. high. Base, 9 ins. diameter.
Painted, **38/6**   Bronzed, **40/6**
PEDESTAL No. 19.
38½ ins. high. Base, 17½ ins. wide, top 12 ins.
Painted, **75/6**   Bronzed, **77/-**

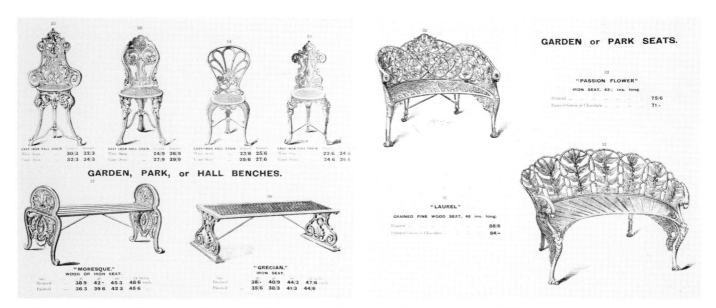

GARDEN or PARK SEATS.

"PASSION FLOWER"
IRON SEAT, 43½ ins. long.
Bronzed — 75/6
Painted Green or Chocolate — 71/-

"LAUREL"
GRAINED PINE WOOD SEAT, 48 ins. long.
Bronzed — 88/6
Painted Green or Chocolate — 84/-

GARDEN, PARK, or HALL BENCHES.

"MORESQUE."
WOOD OR IRON SEAT.

"GRECIAN."
IRON SEAT.

Items from The Coalbrookdale Illustrated Catalogue of Garden and Park Furniture, *1907*
Ironbridge Gorge Museum Trust

GARDEN or PARK SEATS.

58.

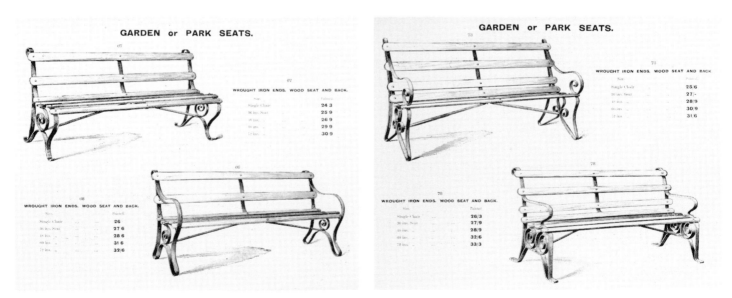

"BOYS AND GRIFFINS"

GRAINED PINE WOOD SEAT, 76 ins. long.

Bronzed ... **100/-** each.

Items from The Coalbrookdale Illustrated Catalogue of Garden and Park Furniture, *1907*
Ironbridge Gorge Museum Trust

No. 361
WORTH PARK SUNDIAL
Height of pillar with star base 3ft. 10ins.
Diameter of lower base 4ft.
Price complete £18 10 0
Pillar with star base
£11 15 0
Base only 6 15 0
Takes a 12in. dial plate.

No. 361

No. 364
KINGSDOWN SUNDIAL
Height of pillar 4ft.
Diameter of base 3ft. 9ins.
Depth of base 6ins.
Price complete £14 5 0
Pillar only 8 15 0
Base only 5 10 0
Takes a 10in. dial plate or smaller.
Inscription—Raised Letters 1 6 each.
Incised Letters 9d. each.
If desired provision can be made in
the base for planting.

No. 405
BLENHEIM SEAT
Length 6ft. 9ins.
Height 3ft. 8ins.
Price £50 0 0
NOTE.—This seat can be supplied without ornament on back rail.

No. 406
ROMAN SEAT
Length 5ft. 9ins.
Height 2ft.
Price £20 0 0

No. 437
WALL FOUNTAIN
Height of centre from water level
6ft. 6ins.
Extreme width across basin
6ft.
Price as shown £53 0 0
upper portion with dolphin
£18 0 0
lower portion with tazza
£28 0 0
Ground basin, 7 0 0
Ground basin can be
omitted or made to any
desired diameter at pro-
portionate charge.

No. 444
SUNDERLAND FOUNTAIN
Diameter of water basin 12ft.
Diameter of tazza 2ft. 8ins.
Height of centre 5ft. 6ins.
Price £195 0 0
If without outer planting beds
£170 0 0

No. 444

No. 446
SHEFFIELD FOUNTAIN
Diameter of basin 7ft. 6ins.
Diameter of tazza 1ft. 10ins.
Height of centre 3ft. 9ins.
Price £35 15 0
Price centre only 15 15 0
Price basin only 20 0 0
A suitable playing figure can be
substituted for the floral centre.

No. 446

Illustrations from Pulham's Garden Ornament — Vases: Terminals: Pedestals: Sundials:
Seats: Fountains: Balustrades: Figures: Etc, *undated but probably circa 1925*
Royal Horticultural Society Library

363

CHIURAZZI S A ◦ FONDERIE · CERAMICA · MARMERIA ◦ NAPOLI

N.º 78. — Discobolo

N.º Ufficiale Museo di Napoli

5626

Bronzo da Ercolano 1754

Col corpo inclinato è in atto di lanciare il disco. Gli occhi sono di pietra. L'interpetrazione moderna lo danno per un Efebo sul punto di impegnarsi ad una lotta. — Copia di arte greca del IV secolo. Tra i capolavori rinvenuti negli scavi di Ercolano (villa dei Pisani).

78. - Chiurazzi - Napoli

N.º 79. — Discobolo.

N.º Ufficiale Museo di Napoli

5627

Bronzo da Ercolano 1754

Fa riscontro all'altro ed è nell'atto di seguire attentamente il disco ch'egli ha lanciato. - Opera indiscutibilmente dell'istesso autore.

79. - Chiurazzi - Napoli

CHIURAZZI S A ◦ FONDERIE · CERAMICA · MARMERIA ◦ NAPOLI

86. - Chiurazzi - Napoli

N.º 86. - Fauno dormente

N.º Ufficiale Museo di Napoli

5624

Bronzo da Ercolano 1753

La tranquillità del sonno è meravigliosamente rappresentata. Ha coda, cornia nascente e gorgie caprine. Fusione avvenuta nel III. Secolo a. C.

N.º 87. - Fauno ebbro

N.º Ufficiale Museo di Napoli

5628

Bronzo da Ercolano 1754

Scultura realistica di gran merito. III. Secolo a. C.

Il fauno, sdraiato su una pelle di leone e appoggiato su un otre, è sul colmo dell'ubbriachezza. Solleva il braccio destro facendo scoppiettare le dita in segno di disprezzo di tutte le cose.

87. - Chiurazzi - Napoli

CHIURAZZI S A ◦ FONDERIE · CERAMICA · MARMERIA ◦ NAPOLI

91. - Chiurazzi - Napoli

N.º 91. - Narciso o Dionisio

N.º Ufficiale Museo di Napoli

5003

Bronzo da Pompei 1862

Di straordinaria bellezza questa statuetta, per le forme esageratamente slanciate, è della scuola caratteristica di Prassitele. Coronato d'edera, munito di nebride e di alti calzari rappresenta Dionisio. Cosa faccia il dio non è chiaro. Probabilmente scherzava con la pantera che doveva trovarsi accanto. — Si pretendeva che questa statuetta rappresentasse Narciso, immobile, attento ad ascoltare la ninfa Eco che si consuma d'amore per lui, e che riempie la montagna e le valli dei suoi lamenti.

N.º 92. - Fauno danzante.

N.º Ufficiale Museo di Napoli

5002

Bronzo da Pompei 1830

Eccellente statuetta di schietta ispirazione d'arte ellenica.

L'artista nel rendere l'audace movimento di slancio per la danza e la esaltazione orgiastica, ha creato uno dei più superbi capolavori di arte.

92. - Chiurazzi - Napoli

97. - Chiurazzi - Napoli

N.º 97. — Apollo.

N.º Ufficiale Museo di Napoli

5613

Bronzo da Pompei

Di arte ellenistica. — Apollo ha interrotto il suono della lira, e sembra ascoltare la preghiera dell'orante. Sta in riposo sulla gamba destra e col braccio sinistro si appoggia ad una colonna.

N.º 98. — Bacco stante.

N.º Ufficiale Museo di Napoli

5009

Bronzo da Ercolano.

Potrebbe essere identificato per un Apollo, ma il tirso nella destra e il *kautharos*, che ora manca, sono i segni di Bacco.

98. - Chiurazzi - Napoli

N.° 168. — Heracle.

N.° Ufficiale Museo di Napoli

6001

Marmo - Collezione Farnese

Copia di Glicone Ateniese, come si è firmato sul masso. L'originale di Lisippo, l'infaticabile artista greco, aveva ideato, probabilmente, il dio in riposo dopo le sue dodici fatiche. Glicone ha esagerato la struttura muscolare, ma una copia, che è in palazzo Pitti, ha rivelato la scultura di Lisippo.

Nelle sue forme straordinarie le proporzioni sono assai svelte.

168. - Chiurazzi - Napoli

N.° 169. — Flora o Afrodite

N.° Ufficiale Museo di Napoli

6409

Marmo - Collezione Farnese

La colossale statua fu rinvenuta nelle terme di Caracalla nel 1540 insieme a quella di Heracle di Lisippo.

Fu supposta Flora per erronea interpetrazione del restauratore che le pose un mazzo di fiori nella sinistra. Ma per la sua eleganza e spigliatezza i critici vi riscontrano i caratteri di Afrodite, facendone risalire la scultura al IV secolo a. C.

169. - Chiurazzi - Napoli

N.° 710. — Vaso Medici

Galleria degli Uffizii - Firenze

Scultura ellenistica. Lavoro di mirabile esecuzione.

Il rilievo rappresenta il sacrifizio di Ifigienia.

710. - Chiurazzi - Napoli

711. - Chiurazzi - Napoli

N.° 711. — Chimera di Arezzo

Museo Archeologico - Firenze

Bronzo

Scultura jonica - etrusca del V Secolo a. C. Il mostro è in atto di slanciarsi su Bellerofonte prima di essere da questi ucciso.

712. - Chiurazzi - Napoli

N.° 712. — Giunone

Museo Nazionale - Firenze

Bronzo

Graziosissima statuetta di Giunone opera di Giambologna.

720. - Chiurazzi - Napoli

N.° 720. — Hermes

Collezione Lord Landdowne - Londra

Items from the Chiurazzi catalogue of 1929
Gennaro Chiurazzi, Naples

NO. 14A.   NO. 14B.

DANCING GIRLS. No. 14
3 FT 6INS.

LEAD GARDEN ORNAMENTS

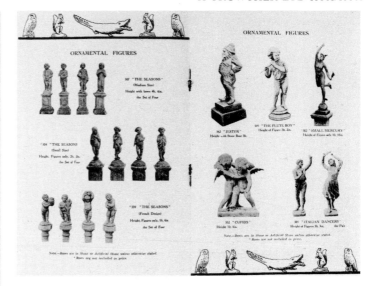

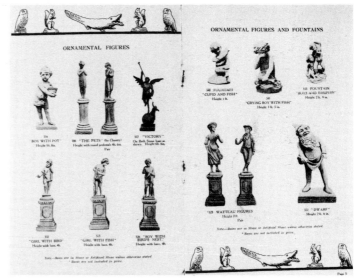

Four photographs of H Crowther Ltd stock items of the 1930s (left); and five items from a mid-twentieth century illustrated catalogue (above)

H Crowther Ltd

Lead vases and musician figures from J P White's 1935 catalogue Bird Baths, Garden Figures, Vases and Ornaments
H Crowther Ltd

FOOTNOTES

CHAPTER ONE: LEAD

1 T Friedman and T Clifford, *The Man at Hyde Park Corner, Sculpture by John Cheere 1709-1787*, exhibition catalogue, Temple Newsam House, 1974. This is the authoritative publication on John Cheere.

2 Information kindly supplied by Mr P I King MA, at the Northamptonshire Record Office. A letter from John Van Nost at Highpark [sic] in 1713 relates: 'For the amount of y Bill is £65 05s 0d when the gladiator is gilt. Dryden (Cannons Ashby) D (CA) 938.

3 M R Apted, 'Arnold Quellin's Statues at Glamis Castle', *The Antiquaries' Journal*, 1984, vol LXIV, part 1. The four statues were 'coloured over in the manner of brass'. I am most grateful for Mr Apted's help.

4 C Cruft, 'James, 2nd Duke of Atholl and John Cheere', *Studies in Scottish Antiquity*, Edinburgh, 1984.

5 J Ralph, *A Critical Review of the Publick Buildings, Statues and Ornaments in and about London and Westminster*, 1734, pp34-36.

6 L Weaver, *English Leadwork: Its Art and History*, Batsford, 1909, p172.

7 See note 5 above.

8 Rupert Gunnis, *Dictionary of British Sculptors 1660-1851*, 1951, 2nd edn, 1969, p279.

9 Apted, op cit.

10 The elder Van Nost's 1712 Sale Catalogue (see note 12 below) lists two of Quellin's statues: 'King James big as the life, in Stone, of Mr Quellin' and 'Neptune in Stone, large life, of Mr Quellin'.

11 Greater London Record Office, Archdeaconry of Middlesex, AM/PW/1710/89.

12 A Catalogue of Mr Van Nost's Collection of Marble and Leaden Figures, Bufto's and Noble Vafes, Marble Chimney Pieces, and Curious Marble Tables, to be sold by AUCTION, at his late Dwelling Houfe in Hyde-Park-Road (near the Queen's Mead-houfe) on Thursday the 17th of this Inftant, April, 1712.

13 The younger John Van Nost's name appears in the rate book for the family yard at Stone Bridge in September 1710, Westminster Archives F3511.

14 M I Webb, 'Henry Cheere, Henry Scheemakers and the Apprenticeship Lists', *The Burlington Magazine*, 1957, vol 90.

15 Gunnis, op cit, p282.

16 Friedman and Clifford, op cit. The *London Evening Post*, 10-12 December 1751, mentions that amongst others John Cheere, his foreman, James Hoskins, and apprentices Mr John Fulford, Mr Richard Breach, Mr John Candy and Mr Benjamin Grant witnessed a cure for William Collins' leg.

17 According to Cheere's will, the leases to his house and grounds in Piccadilly were 'Granted to my said Brother and Me'. Public Record Office, PROB 11/1155.

18 There is no definite information to confirm this, but the brothers are known to have supplied ornaments to the same estates, such as West Wycombe, Newhailes, and perhaps also Langley Park. Further to this Friedman and Clifford, op cit, suggest that Henry may have been instrumental in Cheere's commission to supply a huge collection of lead work to Queluz in Portugal.

19 Gunnis, op cit, p99. This manuscript is dated 1772.

20 Ibid.

21 S Y Legouix, 'John Cheere's Statue of George II', *The Connoisseur*, April 1975. However, in Hogarth's illustration the figure's cloak extends from his neck to his feet, and this is not the case on the statue at Jersey.

22 Information kindly supplied by the Reverend F J Turner at Stonyhurst College. *The Stonyhurst Magazine* January 1964, vol 34, includes details of the elder Van Nost's work: 'Ap 5th 1700. By Bill payable to Mr John Nost in part of payment of £150 for ye figures of Mettle viz pegasus & fame for ye fountain in ye high parterre £25 0s 0d'.

23 Castle Howard Archives G2/2/51. By kind permission of the Hon Simon Howard.

24 Information kindly supplied by J P Haworth, discovered by M Farr at the Warwick Record Office, and reproduced by kind permission of Lady Alice Fairfax-Lucy. Lucy Mss L6/1099: 'A bill of Work done for ye Hon ble George Lucy Esq pr Edwd Hurst Sept 16 1718 for a Large Diana with A Buck £21-00-0 for a shepard and shepardis — £20-00-0'.

25 Weaver, op cit, p194.

26 Information kindly supplied by L Baden, and taken from K Woodbridge's papers.

27 W R Lethaby, *Leadwork Old and Ornamental and for the most part English*, Macmillan, 1893, p103.

28 Gunnis, op cit, pp284-285.

29 Information kindly supplied by N Stockton and D Harris. Dated 8 September 1703.

30 Melbourne Muniment Room.

31 Ibid.

32 See note 12 above.

33 Van Nost frequently supplied pedestals to support his works; however in this case the pedestal was carved by Devigne, whose drawing survives in the Melbourne Muniment Room.

34 H Faber, *Caius Gabriel Cibber 1630-1700*, Oxford, 1926.

35 Melbourne Muniment Room, Box 219, 7 August 1706.

36 Information kindly supplied by Mrs Collier, Archivist for the Painshill Park Trust.

37 Information supplied by Christopher Rowell.

38 Victoria and Albert Museum, *Masterpieces*, sheet 18 'Giambologna's Samson and a Philistine, HMSO, 1978; information also kindly supplied by Malcolm Baker.

39 Francis Thompson, *A History of Chatsworth*, London, 1949.

40 John Harris, *The Building of Denham Palace*, Records of Buckinghamshire, 1957-8, vol XVI, part III, p194.

41 Gunnis, op cit.

42 Ibid.

43 Castle Howard Archives, G2/2/51.

44 *Country Life*, 17 October, 1974, p1088.

45 See note 12 above.

46 Information kindly supplied by Peter Day.

47 Graham and Collier's account book, Chatsworth.

48 Castle Howard Archives J14/28/2.

49 The original marble figure is now in the Uffizi, Florence. This was a popular Cheere model, and he is known to have supplied a plaster copy to Croome Court, whilst lead statues (undocumented) but possibly by Cheere, survive at Wilton, Rousham and Castle Hill.

50 Castle Howard Archives G2/2/52.

51 Francis Haskell and Nicholas Penny, *Taste and the Antique: The Lure of Classical Sculpture 1500-1900*, Yale University Press, 1982, p211, fig 109.

52 This is almost certainly ex-Chiswick, and was removed to Chatsworth at the turn of the century. Unfortunately no record concerning the figure maker responsible has come to light, but if it was supplied around the same time as Samson slaying the Philistine (see p43 and Colour Plate 8), this would coincide with Carpentiere's period of production.

53 Information kindly supplied by Jimmy Crowther of H Crowther.

54 Haskell and Penny, op cit, pp229-232.

55 J Addison, *Remarks on several Parts of Italy, &c, in the years 1701, 1702, 1703*, London, 1705, p349.

56 Castle Howard Archives G2/2/51.

57 Castle Howard Archives G2/2/52.

58 C Hussey, *English Gardens and Landscapes*, London, 1967, p127, note 1.

59 See note 12 above.

60 Cruft, op cit, p292, fig 132.

61 R A Preston, of the Shropshire Library, kindly informed me that this figure was originally at Condover Hall. By 1767 it was *in situ*, for it is illustrated within a view entitled 'West View', (in fact the northeast front), in the survey of Condover of that date. Shropshire Record Office 2789.

62 Information kindly supplied by J M Marsden.

63 Ibid. The Hercules at Chirk was probably supplied

between 1720 and 1735, for it is not illustrated in Tillemans' landscape of 1720, but is in two views by Badeslade fifteen years later.

64 Several photographs by Rupert Gunnis of the gardens at Elvaston Castle are now in the Courtauld Institute. One of these illustrates a similar Hercules to that of Cheere and Carpentiere, but unfortunately it has disappeared. No traces can be found of who supplied this or the other lead statuary that was at the estate.

65 Faber, op cit.

66 Public Records Office, Works 5/51.

67 Weaver, op cit, p202, fig 332.

68 Bailey S Murphy, *English and Scottish Wrought Ironwork*, London, 1904.

69 In the North Sub Corridor and the Painted Hall. Cibber supplied a number of statues to the estate, but no record of their purchase has come to light. Information kindly supplied by Peter Day.

70 In the Formal Garden.

71 Ibid.

72 H I Triggs, *Formal Gardens in England and Scotland*, London, 1902, 2nd edn, Woodbridge, 1988, plate 30.

73 Bedfordshire Record Office, Bills for Wrest Park 1727-1728, L31/199, record a payment to 'Nost the figure Maker £12 17s' on 18 December 1727.

74 Gunnis, op cit.

75 Northamptonshire Record Office, Dryden (Cannons Ashby) D (CA) 938.

76 *Country Life*, 6 November 1980.

77 Public Record Office, Works 5/51.

78 Ibid.

79 Melbourne Muniment Room, Box 219.

80 Hussey, op cit.

81 Public Record Office, Works 5/51. In October 1701, Thomas Highmoore was paid 'For Brunsing the Blackamoor that supports the dyall'.

82 *Country Life*, 23 January 1964, p175. It cost £8.

83 Information kindly supplied by Charles Foster. The sundial supports a bronze plate made by Henry Wing, London, a late seventeenth/early eighteenth century clockmaker. This could, of course, be a later addition, but I am inclined to think it is not, and therefore probably dates the figure to the early eighteenth century, perhaps by the elder John Van Nost.

84 Blair Castle Charter Room, Bundle 55.

85 F Souchal, *French Sculptors of the 17th and 18th Centuries*, vol III, Cassirer, 1987.

86 Information kindly supplied by Phillip Heath.

87 Both these figures correspond to models now at Anglesey Abbey, which originally adorned the gardens at Stowe and, no doubt, formed part of Apollo and the Muses, supplied by Van Nost.

88 Purchased from Cheere's old stock in 1812.

89 Almost certainly supplied by Cheere, who provided numerous leads for the estate.

90 Information discovered by Kenneth Woodbridge, and supplied by Laura Baseden, via Mr Mitchell at the Wessex Regional Office of the National Trust.

91 Kenneth Woodbridge, *The Stourhead Landscape*, The National Trust, 1982, pp49-50.

92 Gunnis, op cit, p99.

93 Rysbrack supplied figures of Hercules, Flora and Bacchus, as well as busts of Milton Blind and as a Young Man.

94 'Biel' by TNDL, *Country Life*, 30 August 1902, p276.

95 R Strong, M Binney, J Harris, *The Destruction of the English Country House*, 1974, p191.

96 Gunnis, op cit.

97 Cruft, op cit.

98 Ibid.

99 *Country Life*, 15 July 1899, pp41-42.

100 This may be the Fox and Gamekeeper at Weald Hall referred to by Weaver, op cit, p180.

101 An almost exact model of the Diana and Endymion is illustrated in Plate 1:20.

102 Information kindly supplied by Mr Alan Hunter of the NIAE at Wrest Park, and taken from the 'History of Wrest House', *Bedfordshire Historical Record Society*, 1980, vol 59, pp65-87.

103 Information from Alan Hunter.

104 Models of both Venus and Adonis, and Diana and Endymion were supplied by Cheere to Queluz in 1756.

105 Private archive.

106 Victor Gray kindly informed me that no reference to these figures survives in the Copped Hall Archives deposited in the Essex Record Office.

107 No documentary evidence survives to confirm Cheere as

the supplier of the lead figures to Queluz. However, bearing in mind the fact that many are duplicates of Cheere's models, it seems more than likely that they are by him. Friedman and Clifford cited this in their 1974 exhibition catalogue (see note 1 above), and kindly informed me that the commission is recorded in a letter dated 1756 in the Lisbon Archives, signed by the Portuguese Minister in London, recording the purchase of ninety-eight lead figures for a total of £871 17s 1d.

108 *Country Life*, 5 November 1910, pp646, 653.

109 Cruft, op cit, p292.

110 Information kindly supplied by Lady Dalrymple.

111 This fact was kindly brought to my attention by Paul Duncan, and I am most grateful to Dr I Brown at the National Library of Scotland for sifting through the Newhailes Archives to trace the document. It reads: 'Novbr ye 19th 1740. Recd of ye Honble James Dalrymple by ye Hands of Mr George Honeymoon ye sum of forty five Pounds three shillings in full for two Statues of Gladiators & two Sphynxs & in full of all demands — me John Cheere'.

112 Information kindly supplied by Hoare's Bank with the consent of the Duke of Northumberland.

113 Information kindly supplied by Sir Francis Dashwood, Bt.

114 This set was removed from the bridge many years ago. It was put up for sale by Phillips of Knowle on 19 March 1986, but, due to an injunction, withdrawn.

115 Weaver, op cit.

116 J Kenworthy-Browne, 'Mathew Brettingham's Rome Account Book 1747-1754', *Walpole Society Annual Report*, 1983, XLIX. I am most grateful to Mr Kenworthy-Browne for informing me of this aspect of Cheere's production.

117 A Michaelis, *Ancient Marbles in Great Britain*, Cambridge University Press, 1882, p304.

118 *Petworth House*, The National Trust Guide, 1985.

119 Cited by Aileen Ribeiro in 'Fashionable Rural Masquerades', *The Antique Collector*, September 1983, p78.

120 See note 24 above.

121 Gunnis, op cit.

CHAPTER TWO: STONE

1 R Pococke, *The Travels Through England of Dr Richard Pococke*, London, 1888-89, vol 2, p93.

2 John Kenworthy-Browne, 'Rysbrack's Saxon Deities', *Apollo*, September 1985, pp220-227. I am indebted to Mr Kenworthy-Browne both for his help and for lending me a photograph of Friga. I would strongly recommend his eight-page article which provides fascinating reading.

3 Gilbert West, *Stowe*, 1732.

4 'The faire majestic paradise of Stowe', *Apollo*, June 1973.

5 George Clarke, 'Grecian Taste and Gothic Virtue: Lord Cobham's gardening programme and its iconography', *Apollo*, June 1973. This article fully explores the Whiggish ideology around which the gardens were conceived.

6 Information supplied by Mary L Robertson, Curator of Manuscripts at the Huntington Library, California, where the Stowe papers are now housed. This entry is taken from Cobham's account book for 1736-1741, ST 161.

7 Clarke, op cit.

8 *A Catalogue of the Genuine and Curious Collection of Models, and Marbles... of Mr Peter Scheemakers*, Langford, 10 and 11 March 1756.

9 *A Collection of Models and Casts, of Mr Peter Scheemakers*, (Langford, 6 and 7 June 1771).

10 Daniel Defoe, *A Tour Through the Whole Island of Great Britain*, 1742.

11 Cited by Margaret Jourdain in *The Works of William Kent*, 1948, and taken from a letter in the Althorp Library, Northamptonshire.

12 Defoe, op cit.

13 Daniel Lysons, *The Environs of London*, 1796.

14 Supplied in 1743.

15 Information supplied by Pamela Kingsbury. Burlington's account book records payment on 'May 24, 1749, Mr Michael Rysbrack, statuary for the figure of a goat in Portland stone & a box to send it to Chiswick £37 16s 0d'. The goat was still *in situ* in 1909 when Lawrence Weaver in his *English Leadwork, its Art and History* refers to it, but was removed to Chatsworth (presumably when Chiswick was sold in 1928) where it remains

today. Rysbrack's terracotta model is now at Anglesey Abbey.

16 Cited by M I Webb in her article entitled 'Giovanni Battista Guelfi: an Italian Sculptor working in England', *The Burlington Magazine*, 1955, vol XCVII, pp139-145, and taken from *The Walpole Society*, XXII, Vertue III, pp73-74.

17 Information supplied by the Squire de Lisle. Quenby Hall was purchased in 1759 by Shukburgh Ashby (1724-1792) and refurbished in the following years. Unfortunately the estate records were burnt during the Second World War but it is probable the Lions are by John Cheere. They first appear in a print of circa 1790.

18 The exact date this pair of lions was supplied is not certain. They do not feature in John Wotton's painting of circa 1735-40 (Robin Fausset 'The Creation of the Gardens at Castle Hill' *Garden History Society*, vol 13, no 2) and so were presumably purchased at a later date, probably in the 1770s during the 2nd Lord Fortescue's alterations. This perhaps can be substantiated by the fact that the Holwell Temple was completed in 1772 and was adorned by three lead figures.

19 Information supplied by Sir Francis Dashwood, Bt. The lions were supplied between 1750 and 1781, for they are conspicuous by their absence from Hannan's painting of the earlier date, and feature in Daniell's of the later date. Both John and Henry Cheere are known to have been paid for work at West Wycombe around 1770.

20 Information supplied by Ruth Shrigley, Sir Thomas Egerton's account book records a payment to Cheere in 1774 of £56 10s 0d, and this no doubt refers to the lions.

21 T Friedman and T Clifford, *The Man at Hyde Park Corner, Sculpture by John Cheere 1709-1787*, exhibition catalogue, Temple Newsam House, 1974, Appendix A, no 92.

22 I Hall, *William Constable as Patron (1721-1791)*, exhibition catalogue, Ferens Art Gallery, 1970, nos 114 a & b.

23 Unfortunately I have not been able to confirm Cheere's hand in this pair, but in the light of the comparative size, I have assumed so.

24 See note 21 above.

25 Thomas Faulkner, *The History and Antiquities of Brentford, Ealing and Chiswick*, London, 1845, p430.

26 L Weaver, *English Leadwork, its Art and History*, Batsford, 1909, p180.

27 François Souchal, *French Sculptors of the 17th and 18th Centuries*, 3 vols, Cassirer, 1977, 1981, 1987, vol II, pp130-131.

28 A Michaelis, *Ancient Marbles in Great Britain*, Cambridge, 1882, Chapter 1.

29 Information supplied by Dr Helen Whitehouse, Keeper of the Egyptian Department at the Ashmolean Museum. I am indebted to Dr Whitehouse for her help in my researches on the two marble sphinxes.

30 Sarah Markham, *John Loverday of Caversham 1711-1789*, Michael Russel, 1984.

31 Two prominent artists are recorded to have worked for Lord Arundel, Hubert Le Sueur and Francesco Fanelli.

32 *Walpole Society*, XXII, Vertue III, pp73-74.

33 Michaelis, op cit, p39.

34 After the death of Lord Burlington, Chiswick House passed to the Dukes of Devonshire, and this gateway was removed to their London home, Devonshire House. After its demolition, the gate piers were retained as an entrance to Green Park.

35 Information supplied by Pamela Kingsbury. Burlington's account book is now in the Library at Chatsworth.

36 Francis Haskell and Nicholas Penny, *Taste and the Antique: the Lure of Classical Sculpture 1500-1900*, Yale University Press, 1982. Ninety-five antique subjects catalogued; I highly recommend this book for its wealth of information.

37 Information kindly supplied by Leslie Harris, Honorary Archivist at Kedleston.

38 G Jackson-Stops (ed), *The Treasure Houses of Britain*, exhibition catalogue, Yale University Press, 1985, p318.

39 Ibid.

40 Michaelis, op cit, pp294-295.

41 Ibid, p63.

42 Ibid, note 159.

43 Christopher Hussey, *English Country Houses: Mid-Georgian (1760-1800)*, 3 vols, London, 1955, Woodbridge, 1984, p141.

44 A T Bolton, *The Architecture of Robert and James Adam*, 2 vols, London, 1922, Woodbridge, 1984.

45 'The History of Wrest House, the Earl de Grey's letter to his daughter Anne', *Bedfordshire Historical Record Society*, 1980, vol 59, p83.

46 Isaac Ware, *A Complete Body of Architecture*, London, 1767, Book II, p250, plate 28.

47 Gertrude Jekyll, *Garden Ornament*, 1918, Woodbridge, 1982.

48 James Gibbs, *A Book of Architecture*, London, 1728.

49 T Friedman, *James Gibbs*, Yale University Press, 1984.

50 *Country Life*, 6 September 1979, kindly brought to my attention by J M Farr, Cambridge County Archivist.

51 Information kindly supplied by Mr Gibbons.

52 Christopher Hussey, *English Gardens and Landscapes 1700-1750*, London, 1967.

53 Information supplied by Eeyan Hartley, Keeper of Archives at Castle Howard, to whom I am most grateful.

54 *The Official Descriptive and Illustrated Catalogue of the Works of Industry of all Nations*, London, 1851.

55 Castle Howard Archives, F5/73.

56 J B Papworth, *Hints on Ornamental Gardening*, London, 1823.

57 Defoe, op cit.

58 John Wood, *An Essay Towards a Description of Bath*, 1765, Redwood Press Reprint, 1969, p426.

59 R Gunnis, *Dictionary of British Sculptors 1660-1851*, 1951, 2nd edn, 1969, p22.

60 Wood, op cit, p424.

61 Op cit.

62 John Vardy, *Some Designs of Mr Inigo Jones and Mr Wm Kent*, 1744, reprint 1967. It seems reasonable to assume that William Kent designed these specifically for Pope's garden at Twickenham. As Pope was friendly with both Kent and Ralph Allen, perhaps these were carved from Bath stone.

63 Information supplied by K J Birch, to whom I am most grateful for his help on the Bath mason-carvers and, in particular, the Parsons family.

64 Thomas Parsons, *A Collection of Vases, Terms . . .* nd, now in Bath Reference Library, 38:18.

65 Longford Castle Muniment Room.

66 Gunnis, op cit, p292.

67 Information supplied by Leslie Harris.

68 Information supplied by the Earl of Egremont. As Parsons mentions the vases were for the 'late Earl', they were presumably supplied to the 2nd Earl, who died in 1763.

69 These are clearly visible in George Lambert's 1742 painting of Chiswick House from the West.

70 Gunnis, op cit, p292.

71 Correspondence and articles in *Geological Curator*, 1983, vol 3, nos 6 and 7.

72 22 September 1813. Information kindly supplied by K J Birch.

73 Gunnis, op cit, p102.

74 Lady Victoria Manners, 'Garden Sculpture by Caius Cibber', *Country Life*, 27 September 1930.

75 Gunnis, op cit, pp141, 360.

76 Ibid, p82.

77 Ibid, pp351, 353.

78 Castle Howard Archives, G2/2/50.

79 Souchal, op cit; also Terence Hodgkinson's article 'Companions of Diana at Cliveden', *National Trust Studies*, Sotheby Parke Bernet, 1979.

80 Ibid, vol I, p309. This statue is now in the Arras Museum.

81 Information supplied by François Souchal.

82 Information from Lord Hastings.

83 *Country Life*, 15 September 1928.

CHAPTER THREE: BRONZE

1 *Walpole Society*, Vertue III, p72.

2 Information kindly supplied by Professor H A D Miles, Barber Institute of Fine Arts, Birmingham.

3 Information kindly supplied by George Clarke. Viscount Cobham's account book in the Huntingdon Library for 1723/4 (ST 132), records a payment to Van Nost on 10 February: 'To Mr Nost a statuary in full £150 0s 0d'.

4 François Souchal, *French Sculptors of the 17th and 18th Centuries*, 3 vols, Cassirer, 1977, 1981, 1987. Vol II, p233, relates that Ballin's designs were modelled by Legendre, Magnier, Tuby and Duval and cast by Duval.

5 These forty-six vases had been buried in the grounds of the Chateau at the time of the Franco-Prussian war.

6 A photograph of Bagatelle circa 1890 illustrates fourteen vases on the Cour d'Honneur.

7 A letter dated 22 June 1855 (reproduced in *The Hertford-Mawson Letters*, Wallace Collection, 1981) from the Marquis to Mawson refers to his return to Paris, 'to attend to my duties as juror'.

8 Information kindly supplied by John McKee, Librarian, Wallace Collection.

9 A Darcel 'La Fonte', *Gazette des Beaux-Arts*, 1867, no 2, pp438-441.

10 *La Revue de Paris*, vol 5, 1903, relates that, through the Marquis' personal relationship with the Emperor, he was able to make casts of the vases at Versailles of various forms and in bronze.

11 7th Viscount Powerscourt, *Description and History of Powerscourt*, published privately, nd, p86.

12 *Country Life*, 29 June 1912, p977.

13 Information kindly supplied by John McKee.

14 The pairs of Naiad and Harpy adorned a flight of steps leading to the Terrace, whilst the pair of Satyr and Satyr Mask were on the steps leading to the lake. All four pairs are clearly visible in *Country Life*, 23 February 1901, pp240 and 241.

15 26 November 1910, pp754-760.

16 29 June 1912, pp976-977.

17 The pairs of Satyr Mask and Lion are clearly visible in the *Country Life* article on Knole, of 25 May 1912, whilst one of Janus design (assumed to be part of a pair) is also illustrated.

18 *Country Life*, June 1, 1912, p837.

19 Victoria Glendinning, *Vita: The Life of V Sackville-West*, London, 1983, relates that in 1932 Victoria Sackville-West sent to her daughter at Sissinghurst 'eight bronze garden urns from Bagatelle' (p247). However, five pairs of Bagatelle urns are known to have been at Sissinghurst.

20 By Wilson & Co, June 1923. Respectively these were lots 561, 562, 563, 570 and 564. Whether these were prior to 1923 is unclear; a painting of the south front of Knole in 1901 (kindly shown to me by Nigel Nicolson) illustrates ten indistinct vases raised on short stone plinths; by 1912 they had disappeared.

21 Information kindly supplied by John McKee.

22 Ibid.

23 Ibid. Whether Birch was a dealer or connected in some way with the Scott family is unclear.

24 12 September 1936, p276. The Comte d'Artois had built the chateau in the eighteenth century.

25 Sotheby's Billinghurst, 28 May 1986, lot 199.

26 *Country Life*, 29 November 1984, Supplement 84.

27 7th Viscount Powerscourt, op cit, p86.

28 Illustrated surmounting the balustrading on the East Terrace in *Country Life*, 28 November 1903, p765.

29 Information kindly supplied by John McKee.

30 Antoine Durenne, *Fonte de Fer. A. Durenne, Maître de Forges*, Paris, 1877, Série F. Copies of Janus, Naiad, Sphinx, Wolf and Harpy are illustrated on p398. These five and the Cupid design were available in the same size as the Bagatelle copies, as well as in two smaller sizes.

31 Information kindly supplied by John McKee. A vase illustrated in *Country Life*, 10 April 1986, bears a Dugel founder's mark.

32 R Marks and B J R Blench, *The Warwick Vase*, Burrell Collection, 1979, p6.

33 Ibid.

34 N M Penzer in *Apollo*, LXII, no 370, December 1955, pp183-188; LXIII, no 371, January 1956, pp18-22; LXIII, no 372, February 1956, pp71-75. These articles are the most authoritative on the vase.

35 Walter G Strickland, *Dictionary of Irish Artists*, Dublin and London, 1913, p478.

36 See note 3 above.

37 Rupert Gunnis, *Dictionary of British Sculptors 1660-1851*, 1951, 2nd edn 1969, p70. Gunnis suggests that Burchard may have been a pupil or assistant of Van Nost.

38 *The Survey of London*, vol XXXIV, London, 1966, illustrates in plate 50c the south-east corner of Leicester Square (Leicester Fields) with the statue of George I. The illustration is dated 1801.

39 Among the works executed by Francis for the royal family may be mentioned, a statue of the Prince Consort and busts of the Duke and Duchess of Saxe-Coburg (Gunnis, op cit).

40 Information supplied by Mrs Julian Harland, taken from Queen Victoria's diary and reproduced by gracious permission of Her Majesty The Queen.

41 Information kindly supplied by Edward A Sibbick, Archivist at Osborne House.

42 Francis Haskell and Nicholas Penny, *Taste and the Antique: the Lure of Classical Sculpture*, Yale University Press, 1982, pp271-272.

43 Chiurazzi S/A, *Fonderie-Ceramica-Marmeria*, catalogue, Naples, 1929, p38.

44 *Coade's Gallery or Exhibition of Artificial Stone*, Lambeth, 1799, p35.

45 *A Catalogue of Five Hundred Articles made of Patent Terra Cotta*, by J M Blashfield, 1855, no 289.

46 *Ornamental Castings Manufactured by the Coalbrookdale Company*, July 1877, no 107. The fact that the figure was priced at £2 2s suggests that it was a statuette.

47 An extant model is at Osborne house, and a line drawing featured in the firm's 1863 catalogue.

48 In the sale of the elder Van Nost's collection on 17 April 1712, Lots, 19, 46 and 66 were respectively, 'The Grecian Venus, lead...; The Grecian Venus, big as the life, Lead...; The Grecian Venus, small life, lead...' These were no doubt copies of the Venus de Medici. In Carpentiere's list of figures sent to Castle Howard (Castle Howard Archives G2/2/51), a Venus de Medici is listed, whilst John Cheere is known to have supplied in 1762 a statue of Venus de Medici to Bowood. A T Bolton, *The Architecture of Robert and James Adam*, London, 1922, Woodbridge, 1984, vol 1, p214.

49 Haskell and Penny, op cit, pp325-328.

50 G Jackson-Stops (ed), *The Treasure Houses of Britain*, exhibition catalogue, Yale University Press, 1985, pp292-293.

51 Op cit, note 7.

52 Information kindly supplied by Dr Helmut Börsch-Supan of the Verwaltung der Staatlichen Schlösser und Garten, Berlin.

53 *The Art-Journal Illustrated Catalogue of the Great Exhibition*, London, 1851, p235.

54 *The Official Descriptive and Illustrated Catalogue of the Works of Industry of all Nations*, London, 1851, pp1063-4. The firm's copy of 'The Boy with the Swan' is illustrated on p1064.

55 *The Art-Journal...*, op cit, p37.

56 Information kindly supplied by Edward A Sibbick.

CHAPTER FOUR: ARTIFICIAL STONE

1 Richard Holt, *A Short Treatise on Artificial Stone*, London, 1730.

2 One for producing artificial stone (AD 1722, No 447), the other for making earthenware (AD 1722, No 448).

3 Daniel Pincot, *An Essay on the Origins, Nature, Uses and Properties of Artificial Stone*, London, 1770.

4 Information supplied by Jeremy Rex Parker of Christie, Manson and Woods Ltd.

5 The Society of Artists, *The Society of Artists' Catalogue of Exhibitions, 1762-1783*, 26 April 1771.

6 See note 4 above.

7 Ibid.

8 Pincot, op cit.

9 Information from Kenneth Woodbridge's papers, supplied by Laura Baseden.

10 Information discovered by Timothy Connor, supplied by Alison Kelly.

11 Information supplied by Alison Kelly.

12 *A Descriptive Catalogue of Coade's Artificial Stone Manufactory*, London, 1784.

13 *The Somerset House Gazette*, London, 13 March 1824, p381.

14 Grog: a form of crushed stoneware, perhaps consisting, in this case, of fired reground Coade stone.

15 I C Freestone, M Bimson, and M S Tite, 'The Constitution of Coade Stone', *Ceramics and Civilization, Volume I: Ancient Technology to Modern Science*, W D Kingery (ed), American Ceramic Society, Columbus, Ohio, 1985.

16 A number of these models, which are made of plaster, were excavated during building work for the Royal Festival Hall; some are now on display at the Museum of London.

17 Llewellynn Jewitt, *The Ceramic Art of Great Britain*, 2 vols, 1st edn, London, 1878, p140.

18 *A Descriptive Catalogue...*, op cit.

19 Lithodipyra: stone twice fired.

20 Eleanor Coade, *Etchings of Coade's Artificial Stone Manufactory*, ?1777, 1778, 1779. There is some uncertainty as to the date of publication; the British Museum copy is dated 1777, 1778, 1779, whilst the Sir John Soane's Museum copy has some pages marked with various dates in 1778.

21 *A Descriptive Catalogue...,* op cit.

22 *The Survey of London,* vol XXIII, part 1, London, 1951, states that John Sealy was the son of James Sealy, and his wife Mary, a daughter of Thomas Enchmarch, a merchant of Tiverton. Mary was the sister of Eleanor Coade senior.

Sealy appears by 1792 to have had some considerable responsibility for running the manufactory as a letter published in Jewitt, op cit, implies that Sealy was in control of the business in Mrs Coade's absence.

23 Eleanor Coade and John Sealy, *Description of Ornamental Stone in the Gallery of Coade & Sealy,* London, 1799.

24 James Stuart, and Nicholas Revett, *The Antiquities of Athens,* 4 vols, London, 1762-1816.

25 Rupert Gunnis, *Dictionary of British Sculptors 1660-1851,* 1951, 2nd edn 1969, states that Croggon received £5,290 between 1826 and 1828 for decorative work at Buckingham Palace.

26 Alison Kelly, 'Mrs Coade's Stone', *The Connoisseur,* vol CXCVII, January 1978, pp14-25.

27 Advertisement in *The Builder,* 21 August 1847.

28 Advertisement in *The Builder,* 8 July 1854.

29 Kelly, op cit 1978.

30 Information from Alison Kelly; examples of these vases, individually or in pairs, occur at Castle Howard, Blaise Castle, Chiswick House, Coleorton, Kedleston, Uppark, Cobham Hall, Broadlands, Brocklesby, Temple Newsam and Kew.

31 The Society of Artists, op cit.

32 See note 9 above.

33 Royal Archives 26736, supplied by Pamela Clark, and reproduced by gracious permission of Her Majesty The Queen.

34 *A Descriptive Catalogue...,* op cit.

35 Coade, *Etchings...,* op cit.

36 See note 33 above.

37 C H Tatham, *Etchings of Ancient Ornamental Architecture drawn from the originals in Rome*

and other parts of Italy, London, 1799-1800.

38 Thomas Hope, *Household Furniture and Interior Decoration...,* London, 1807, reprinted 1970 with a preface by Clifford Musgrave.

39 Humbert & Flint sale, 17 September 1917.

40 Alison Kelly, 'Coade Stone at National Trust Houses', *National Trust Studies,* London, 1980.

41 Jewitt, op cit.

42 Bacon used a similar figure in reverse for his monument to William Pitt in Westminster Abbey: M Whinney, *Sculpture in Britain 1530-1830,* London, 1964.

43 Alison Kelly, op cit 1980.

44 Freestone, et al, op cit.

45 Tatham, op cit.

46 *A Descriptive Catalogue...,* op cit.

47 J M Blashfield, *An Account of the History and Manufacture of Ancient and Modern Terra Cotta...,* London, 1855, p16.

48 Ibid, pp25-27.

49 B H Cowper, *A Descriptive, Historical and Statistical Account of Millwall,* London, 1853, p68.

50 'Discussion of Barry's Paper on Blashfield's Terra Cotta Work at Dulwich College', *RIBA Transactions,* 1868/9, p18.

51 Cowper, op cit, p69.

52 'Discussion...', op cit, p19.

53 Charles Barry, 'Terra-Cotta Work at the New Dulwich College by Mr Blashfield of Stamford', *RIBA Transactions,* 1868.

54 Blashfield, *An Account...,* op cit, p27.

55 Barry, op cit, p7.

56 Ibid. Barry goes on to reveal that 'To thoroughly burn a kiln containing some 25 tons of hollow terra cotta ware 1½in to 2in thick, will consume 20 tons of coal'.

57 A J Francis, *The Cement Industry 1796-1914: A History,* London, 1977, pp26-42.

58 Ibid, p39.

59 Jewitt, op cit, p433.

60 Rita J Ensing, *Kensington Society Annual Report, 1976-77,* pp26-40.

61 *The Builder,* 23 December 1848.

62 Alison Kelly, 'Imitating Mrs Coade', *Country Life,* 10 November 1977.

63 Barry, op cit, p4.

64 N C Birch, *Stamford: an Industrial History,* Lincolnshire Industrial Archaeology Group, 1972. No exact evidence exists

to support this; however, bearing in mind Blashfield's interest in terracotta, and the confusion as to the exact date the manufactory was established, it would seem probable that this was the case.

65 Barry, op cit, p5. It seems probable that the moulds for these vases were supplied to Minton by Blashfield from the existing stock of Wyatt, Parker & Co, since they are illustrated in the Wyatt, Parker & Co catalogue of *Figures, Vases, Fountains &c...,* model numbers 35a and 36a, modified copies of the Borghese and Medici Vases (approx 1 foot 9ins. high).

66 A D 1854, No1369, sealed 22 August 1854.

67 Model nos 101 Tracery for parapet; 162 Vase; 340 Pedestal for a statue.

68 Model nos 211 Small Greek console; 244 Small Greek truss.

69 Model nos 170 Australia; 171 Triton; 179 Erin; 337 Mignonette box; 338 The Boy's Own Book; 339 The First Letter.

70 Model nos 180 Gothic vase; perhaps 273 Pedestal for a Gothic vase.

71 Model nos 204 Group of Cupids; 323 'A vase, similar to No 153 but decorated with bassi relievi, from FIAMINGO'.

72 Model nos 232 Bust of Queen Victoria; 249 Bust of the Duke of Wellington.

73 Model no 233 Statue of a Sleeping Cupid.

74 Model no 239 Statue of a Boy with a Bird.

75 Model nos 274 Bust of Washington; 388 Statuette of William Pitt.

76 Model nos 293 Cup; 294 Cup; 423 Vase.

77 See Plate 4:19.

78 Model nos 344 The Tempest Vase (designed by Blashfield); 350, Statuette of a Boy with a Shell; 368 Angle bracket; 446 The Midsummer Night's Dream Vase.

79 Model nos 348 Statuette of Victory; 349 Statuette of History (both reduced from the originals).

80 Model nos 345 Pair of Greyhounds; 444 Statue of Girl at the Spring.

81 *A Selection of Vases, Statues, Busts &c From Terra Cottas by J M Blashfield,* London, 1857, p4.

82 *A Catalogue of Five Hundred Articles, made of Patent Terra Cotta, by J M Blashfield,*

London, 1855.

83 Barry, op cit, p10.

84 *Art-Journal,* 1856, p374.

85 Cowper, op cit.

86 *The Builder,* 26 June 1858, p448.

87 Birch, op cit.

88 Ibid.

89 'Discussion...', art cit, p25.

90 *John Marriot Blashfield, Wharf Road, Stamford, Lincolnshire, Manufacturer of Terra Cotta and Architectural Pottery,* illustrated catalogue, London, 1870.

91 Information from John F Smith.

92 Information from John F Smith. The first sale was held on 25 August, but nothing was sold, the second on 2-5 November failed to achieve any reasonable prices.

93 Barry, op cit, p8.

94 Blashfield, illustrated catalogue 1870, op cit, plate 14.

95 Ibid, no plate number.

96 Ibid, plate 37.

97 A Michaelis, *Ancient Marbles in Great Britain,* Cambridge University Press, 1882, pp663-664.

98 Birch, op cit, p11.

99 *Figures, Vases, Fountains &c. Executed in Marble and Artificial Stone, by Wyatt, Parker & Co., Holland Street, Blackfriars Bridge, Surrey,* London. 1841.

100 Information from John F Smith.

101 *A Catalogue...,* op cit.

102 Blashfield, illustrated catalogue 1870, plate 70.

103 Information from Dr Susan Walker; see also B F Cook, *The Townley Marbles,* British Museum Publications, 1983. Hamilton discovered this vase whilst excavating at Monte Cagnolo the supposed site of the Emperor Antoninus Pius' Villa.

104 *A Selection...,* op cit, plate 73.

105 *The Builder,* 24 October 1857, p613.

106 *The Oxfored Chronicle, Berks and Bucks Gazette,* 24 October 1857 wrote: 'The cost of the fountain will be defrayed by private subscriptions...'

107 Francis, op cit.

108 W Branch Johnson, *Industrial Archaeology of Hertfordshire,* David and Charles, 1970.

109 *The Builder,* 1845, p160.

110 Sally Festing, 'Cliffs, Glades and Grotto at Merrow Grange' *Garden History,* 1983, vol 11 no 2; 'Pulham has done

his work well', *Garden History*, 1984, vol 12, no 2.
111 *The Art-Journal Illustrated Catalogue of the Great Exhibition, 1851,* London, 1851, p303.
112 *Art-Journal,* 1859, pp27-28.
113 J B Waring, *Masterpieces of Industrial Art and Sculpture in the International Exhibition,* London, 1862, plate 186.
114 Jewitt, op cit, pp428-429.
115 *Garden Ornament, Vases: Terminals: Pedestals...,* illustrated catalogue, circa 1925.
116 *The Art-Journal Illustrated Catalogue of the International Exhibition, 1862,* London, 1862, p162.
117 *Garden Ornament...,* op cit, p76.
118 Gertrude Jekyll, *Garden Ornament,* London, 1918, reprinted Woodbridge 1982, p393.
119 Jewitt, op cit, p429.
120 Barry, op cit, p4.
121 *The Builder,* 21 July 1843, p12.
122 *The Builder,* 26 July 1851, p474.
123 According to Gunnis, op cit, p23, Austin signed a number of commemorative tablets.
124 Barry, op cit.
125 *The Builder,* 7 March 1857, p144.
126 Information supplied by Lesley Marshall of the Camden Local History Library, from research carried out by Westminster City Libraries, using the London Post Office directories.
127 *The Builder,* 1843.
128 *The Builder,* 7 March 1857, p144.
129 Unfortunately very little is known about this firm which was operating from the early years of the nineteenth century. According to Rupert Gunnis, op cit, the business was started by a Dutchman, Van Spangen, and manufactured a form of terracotta. Gunnis goes on to relate (p408) that the firm produced in 1801 'Statues of "Faith", "Hope" and "Charity" for the Freemasons' Charity School in St. George's Field's, Southwark'. The author has not come across any of the firm's models.
130 Barry, op cit, p4.
131 *The Architectural Magazine,* 1834, p295.
132 Ibid, p300.
133 *The Builder,* 1843, p12.
134 *The Official Descriptive and Illustrated Catalogue of the Works of Industry of All Nations,* London, 1851, p852.

135 M Hadfield, R Harling and L Highton, *British Gardeners: a Biographical Dictionary,* Zwemmer/Condé Nast, 1980.
136 J C Loudon, article on Austin's fountains, *The Architectural Magazine,* 1834. A variation of the fountain is illustrated on p299. The three entwined dolphins and the base are the same, but instead of the tazza bowl a clam shell has been used in which a water creature or Naiad is seated blowing a conch.
137 *The Builder,* 26 July 1851, p474.
138 Loudon, art cit; *The Builder,* 1843, p12.
139 *The Builder,* 26 July 1851, p474.
140 *The Architectural Magazine,* 1834, p216.
141 *The Builder,* 26 July, 1851, p474.
142 Kelly, op cit 1980, pp26, 104-106.
143 Illustrated in *The Doulton Story,* exhibition catalogue, Victoria and Albert Museum, 1979.
144 Information supplied by Miss Valerie Baynton, MA, Curator of the Sir Henry Doulton Gallery.
145 Jewitt, op cit, 2nd edn, London, 1883, reprinted 1985, pp97-98.
146 Melpomene bears striking similarities in pose and dress to an antique statue illustrated in Salomon Reinach *Repertoire de la Statuaire Grecque et Romaine,* 3 vols, Paris, 1898, vol II, p666. This is described as: '8. Panticapée. Ermitage'.
147 It is apparent from Doulton catalogues dating after 1875, that many of the vases and statues were facsimiles of those in Blashfield catalogues. Examples of these are the Townley Vase, the tazza-shaped vase with a relief of putti, and the figures entitled The Wounded Bird and The Pet in Doulton's 1880s catalogues.

CHAPTER FIVE: MARBLE

1 Cited in A Michaelis, *Ancient Marbles in Great Britain,* Cambridge, 1882, p35.
2 Luciana and Tizano Mannoni, *Marble, the History of a Culture,* Facts on File Inc, 1985, p277.
3 Information supplied by Nigel Bartlett.
4 T Matthews, *The Biography of John Gibson, RA,* London, 1911, pp45-46.
5 Included in *Opuscoli Morali di L B Alberti,* Venice, 1568.
6 Mannoni, op cit, p145.
7 B Read, *Victorian Sculpture,* Yale University Press, 1982, p62.
8 Cited in T Friedman and T Stevens, *Joseph Gott 1786-1860, Sculptor,* exhibition catalogue, Temple Newsam House, 1972, p7.
9 6th Duke of Devonshire, *Handbook to Chatsworth and Hardwick,* 1844.
10 John Kenworthy-Browne, 'A Ducal Patron of Sculptors', *Apollo,* October 1972, pp322-331.
11 Mrs Jameson, *A Hand-Book to the Courts of Modern Sculpture,* London, 1854.
12 John Tallis, *Tallis's History and Description of the Crystal Palace and the Exhibition of the World's Industry in 1851,* London, 1852.
13 Sotheby's, Sussex, Wilsford Manor, 14 October 1987, lot 496.
14 Cornelius C Vermeule, *Greek and Roman Sculpture in America,* University of California Press, 1981, plate 302.
15 Francis Haskell and Nicholas Penny, *Taste and the Antique: The Lure of Classical Sculpture,* Yale University Press, 1982, pp172-173.
16 Rupert Gunnis, *Dictionary of British Sculptors 1660-1851,* 1951, 2nd edn 1969.
17 Ibid.
18 Joyce McGown, *The Searching Eye in Venice,* London, p36.
19 Paul Hetherington, 'The Venetian Well-Heads of Hever Castle, Kent', *Apollo,* March 1985, pp162-167. Mr Hetherington's is the foremost article on the well-heads at Hever, and I would highly recommend anyone further researching this field to consult both this and his earlier article 'Two Medieval Venetian Well-Heads in England', *Arte Veneta,* 1980, XXXIV, pp9-17.
20 Ibid.

CHAPTER 6: CAST- AND WROUGHT-IRON

1 Erected in the early 1710s.
2 Isaac Ware, *A Complete Body of Architecture,* 1767 edn, chapter XXVII, p89.
3 Published 1824.
4 The preface is signed 'L.N.C. 66, Great Queen Street, Lincoln's Inn Fields, October 10th, 1823'. It had been published in a slightly reduced form a year earlier, entitled *The Ornamental Metal Workers' Director.*
5 Digby Wyatt, *The Industrial Arts of the XIX Century,* vol I, 1851, plate XIX, second page.
6 *The Art-Journal Illustrated Catalogue of the International Exhibition, 1862,* London, 1862, p75.
7 *Art-Union,* August 1846, p219.
8 *Art-Journal,* 1850, p282.
9 Information supplied by Mark Higginson.
10 Frank Rodgers, 'Andrew Handyside — Engineer Extraordinary', *Derbyshire Life & Countryside,* September 1975, pp60-61.
11 *Art-Journal,* 1850, p282.
12 *The Art-Journal Illustrated Catalogue of the Great Exhibition, 1851,* London, 1851.
13 Information supplied by D W Hopkin, Erewash Museum, Ilkeston.
14 Class XXII.
15 *The Art-Journal Illustrated Catalogue... 1862, op cit,* p20.
16 Classes VII and XXXI.
17 *Works in Iron,* London, 1868.
18 Ibid, p96.
19 The company had also been awarded a 'Gold Medal for ornamental Fountains and Vases... at the Birmingham Meeting of the Royal Horticultural Society, 1872; and 'the Gold Medal in the Cordova Exhibition of the Argentine Republic in 1871'.
20 *Handyside's Ironwork (Catalogues B & C). Ornamental Ironwork Manufactured by Andrew Handyside & Co Ltd,* London, 1874.
21 Rodgers, op cit.
22 Ewing Matheson (of the firm of Andw. Handyside & Co.), *Works in Iron — Bridge and Roof Structures,* London, 1873, p283.
23 *Works in Iron,* op cit, p96.
24 Ibid.
25 Ibid.
26 *Art-Journal,* 1852, p21.
27 *Handyside's Ironwork,* op cit, Catalogue B, p531 (Sundries).
28 *Works in Iron,* op cit, p96.
29 Ibid.
30 Illustrated in the *Art-Journal,* 1850, p282.
31 Lewis N Cottingham, *The Smith and Founder's Director,* 2nd edn, London, 1824, preface.
32 *Handyside's Ironwork,* op cit.
33 Information supplied by Mark Higginson.
34 Information supplied by Mrs Middlemass and Mr Hunt.

35 These are copies of the Warwick Vase, larger copies of model number 8 (illustrated top centre Plate 6:5). They bear oval plaques inscribed 'BRITANNIA FOUNDRY DERBY'.

36 It is described as 'a large FOUNTAIN for garden or conservatory', p20.

37 The information on the history of the company is taken from Arthur Raistrick's authoritative publication, *Dynasty of Iron Founders: The Darbys and Coalbrookdale*, Longmans, Green & Co, 1953.

38 Cited by Ian Lawley in *Art and Ornament in Iron: Design and the Coalbrookdale Company*, Design Council, 1980.

39 Wyatt, op cit, plate XIX, 'Fountain and Ornamental Gates in Cast Iron, by The Coalbrookdale Company'.

40 *Art-Union*, August 1846, pp219-226.

41 Ibid.

42 Ibid.

43 Ibid.

44 Report of the Jury of the International Exhibition, 1851, Class 22, Chairman Hon Horace Greely.

45 Wyatt, op cit.

46 *Eddowes's Shrewsbury Journal* (second sheet), Wednesday 2 May 1855, Coalbrookdale; contributions of Miss Mary Darby and the Company to the Paris Exhibition; information supplied by R A Preston.

47 J B Waring, *Masterpieces of Industrial Art and Sculpture in the International Exhibition, 1862*, London, 1862, plate 140, 'Park Entrance-Gates, by the Coalbrookdale Company, Shropshire'.

48 Ibid.

49 This incorporated several of Bell's statues of Fame.

50 Waring, op cit.

51 Ibid.

52 Ibid.

53 *The Art-Journal Illustrated Catalogue. . ., 1862*, op cit, p73.

54 Information supplied by John Powell of the Ironbridge Gorge Museum. The figures raised on stone piers in Cambridge Gardens, Regent's Park, represent female figures.

55 Precisely what this 'Painted Oak' finish looked like is unclear, possibly like simulated oak. If this was the case, which seems likely, then the company may have been using a similar process to that described in detail by J C Loudon in his *Encyclopaedia*, 3rd edn, London, 1857.

56 This was particularly uncommon, and was used mainly for pedestals, such as that supporting vase number 37 in Plate 6:22.

57 According to the *Art-Union*, August 1846, p233: 'The method by which the effect of bronzing is produced is comparatively simple, viz. the application, by means of a brush, of a green pigment, which dries without any glaze on its surface; and it is subsequently touched up in the prominent parts with a dust bronze'.

58 According to Raistrick, op cit, the company was using a modified process to that patented by Elkington, Mason & Co. The finish seems to have been restricted only to smaller items.

59 Information supplied by Mrs Middlemass.

60 Information supplied by Ian Lawley.

61 *The Coalbrookdale Illustrated Catalogue*, Section III, *Garden and Park Embellishments*, 1875, p262.

62 Ibid.

63 Ibid.

64 Ibid.

65 Bell's life-size statue of Andromeda: Wyatt, op cit, plate LIII; a statuette by B W Hawkins of Death of a Stag: Raistrick, op cit.

66 *Eddowes's Shrewsbury Journal*, 2 May 1855: 'A group of ornamental bronze vases, intended for hall or gardens. . . These are 3 feet high, presenting subjects in bas-relief'. It seems reasonable to assume that these may be the pair illustrated in the *Art-Journal* at the Paris Exhibition; information supplied by R A Preston.

67 According to the explanation of the manufactory, subjoined to the *Art-Union's* article of 1 August 1846, 'Several of the patterns in use are of brass'. Furthermore the company was also producing brass jets for its fountains.

68 *The Coalbrookdale Company's Illustrated Catalogue, Spring 1893*, 1893, includes a single armchair model of the design.

69 *The Coalbrookdale Illustrated Catalogue. . .*, op cit, 1875.

70 See note 55 above.

71 A copy of this is in the Coalbrookdale Museum Library, and is believed to date from 1929.

72 *The Art-Journal Illustrated Catalogue. . ., 1862*, op cit, p19.

73 Ibid.

74 *The Coalbrookdale Illustrated Catalogue. . .*, op cit, 1875, introduction.

75 Ibid, p326.

76 *Eddowes's Shrewsbury Journal*, 2 May 1855, op cit.

77 *The Coalbrookdale Illustrated Catalogue. . .*, op cit, 1875, p353.

78 Cited by Lawley, op cit.

79 Information supplied by Andrew Barber; the dogs are featured in *Country Life*, 6 and 13 August 1921.

80 Information supplied by Geoffrey Starmer.

81 Ibid.

82 Wyatt, op cit, plate XXXIX.

83 Alfred Darcel, 'La Fonte', *Gazette des Beaux-Arts*, Paris 1867, p439.

84 Information supplied by Laure de Margerie.

85 Ibid.

86 *The Art-Journal Illustrated Catalogue. . ., 1862*, op cit.

87 Christopher Payne, *Animals in Bronze: Reference and Price Guide*, Woodbridge, 1986.

88 Barnard, Bishop & Barnard Ltd, *Norfolk Iron Works, Norwich*, 1930.

CHAPTER 7: TWENTIETH CENTURY GARDEN ORNAMENTS

1 Information supplied by J F J Collet-White from the Bedfordshire Record Office, CRT 180/352 (J P White's obituary, 1917).

2 *Country Life* advertisements, for example 21 July 1900.

3 See note 1 above.

4 *A Complete Catalogue of Garden Furniture and Garden Ornament*, London, 1906.

5 See note 1 above.

6 Information supplied by P R Mardlin, former employee at the Pyghtle Works.

7 Ibid.

8 *A Complete Catalogue. . .*, op cit, p113.

9 Ibid, p114.

10 *Bird Baths, Garden Figures, Vases and Ornaments*, catalogue, Bedford, June 1935, p50.

11 Ibid.

12 Ibid, p2.

13 *A Complete Catalogue*, op cit, p134.

14 Cited by Lawrence Weaver, *English Leadwork, its Art and History*, London, 1909, p222.

15 Ibid, pp242-243.

16 Information supplied by H Crowther Ltd.

17 Weaver, op cit, p239.

18 *The Bromsgrove Guild*, The Norton Museum, pamphlet WQ706.

19 Bromsgrove Guild, *Garden Ornaments*, September 1908, pp18 and 19; also Weaver, op cit, p245.

20 Weaver, op cit, p247.

21 *The Bromsgrove Guild*, op cit.

22 I am indebted to Jim, Paul and David Crowther of H Crowther Ltd for information on the history of the firm and other twentieth century leadwork manufacturers.

23 Information supplied by Robert Bowman.

24 Information supplied by Richard Crowther.

25 28 November 1903.

26 Yves Devaux, *L'Univers des Bronzes*, Pygmalion, 1978, p295.

27 Information supplied by Yves Delachaux, export manager of GHM.

28 G W Yapp, *Art, Industry, Metalwork*, London, 1876.

SELECT BIBLIOGRAPHY

Addison, J, *Remarks on Several Parts of Italy, &c in the years 1701, 1702, 1703,* London, 1705.

Alfonso, Simonetta Luz, *Queluz Palace,* illustrated guide, Portugal, 1986.

Alberti, L B, *Opuscoli Morali di L B Alberti,* C Bartoli, Venice, 1568.

Alcock, Sheila (ed), *Historic Houses, Castles and Gardens,* British Leisure Publications, 1985 edn.

Apted, M R, 'Arnold Quellin's Statues at Glamis Castle', *The Antiquaries' Journal,* 1984, vol LXIV, part 1.

Argenville, Dezalier, D', *The Theory and Practice of Gardening,* 1709, translated into English by John James 1712.

Art-Journal, *The Art-Journal Illustrated Catalogue of the Great Exhibition, 1851,* London, 1851.

The Art-Journal Illustrated Catalogue of the International Exhibition, 1862, J S Virtue, London, 1862.

Avery, Charles, *Giambologna — The Complete Sculpture,* Phaidon-Christie's, 1987.

Barbedienne, Ferdinand, *A Catalogue of Artistical Bronzes by F Barbedienne,* Paris, 1862.

Bronzes D'Art F Barbedienne, Paris, 1884.

Barbezat, *Barbezat & Cie Ancienne Maison André, Hauts Fourneaux &c Fonderies du Val d'Osne,* illustrated catalogue, Paris, 1858.

Barnard, Bishop & Barnard Ltd, *Norfolk Iron Works, Norwich,* illustrated catalogue, 1930.

Barre, D C, and Chaplin, R A, *William Winde: Advice on Fashionable Interior Decoration,* Winde-Bridgeman correspondance for Castle Bromwich Hall 1685-1703, Staffordshire, 1983.

Barry, Charles, 'Terra Cotta Work at the New Dulwich College by Mr Blashfield of Stamford', *RIBA Transactions,* London, 1868.

'Discussion of Barry's Paper on Blashfield's Terra Cotta Work at Dulwich College', *RIBA Transactions,* London, 1868/69.

Batey, Mavis, 'The Way to View Rousham by Kent's Gardener', *Garden History,* Autumn 1983, vol 11, no 2.

Beard, Geoffrey, *Craftsmen and Interior Decoration in England 1660-1820,* Bloomsbury Books, *1981.*

Berrall, Julia S, *The Garden: Illustrated History,* Penguin, 1966.

Binney, Marcus, 'Nun Monkton Priory, Yorkshire', *Country Life,* 6 November 1980.

Birch, N C, *Stamford: an Industrial History,* Lincolnshire Industrial Archaeology Group, 1972.

Blashfield, John M, *An Account of the History and Manufacture of Ancient and Modern Terra Cotta. . . ,* London, 1855.

A Catalogue of Five Hundred Articles, made of Patent Terra Cotta, by J M Blashfield, London, 1855.

A Selection of Vases, Statues, Busts &c From Terra Cottas by J M Blashfield, illustrated catalogue, London, 1857.

John Marriot Blashfield, Wharf Road, Stamford, Lincolnshire, Manufacturer of Terra Cotta and Architectural Pottery, illustrated catalogue, London, 1870.

Bolton, Arthur T, *The Architecture of Robert and James Adam,* 2 vols, London, 1922, Woodbridge, 1984.

Bowder, Diana, *Who Was Who in the Roman World 753BC-AD476,* Phaidon, 1980.

Bradshaw, Peter, *18th Century English Porcelain Figures 1745-1795,* Woodbridge, 1981.

Branch Johnson W, *Industrial Archaeology of Hertfordshire,* David & Charles, 1970.

Bridgeman, Sarah, *General Plan of the Woods, Park and Gardens of Stowe,* London, 1739.

Bromsgrove Guild, *Garden Ornaments,* illustrated catalogue, September 1908.
The Bromsgrove Guild, pamphlet WQ706, The Norton Museum.

Brooke, E Advino, *The Gardens of England,* London, 1858.

Bulfinch, Thomas, *Myths of Greece and Rome,* Penguin, 1981.

Charles, R, *The Compiler,* London, 1879.

Charlton, John, *A History and Description of Chiswick House and Gardens,* HMSO, 1984.

Chiurazzi: *Chiurazzi Societe Anonima Fonderie-Ceramica-Marmeria, Napoli, 1929,* Naples, privately, 1929.

Clarke, George, 'Grecian Taste and Gothic Virtue: Lord Cobham's Gardening Programme and its Iconography', *Apollo Magazine,* June 1973.

Coade, Eleanor, *Etchings of Coade's Artificial Stone Manufactory,* London, ?1777/8/9.
A Descriptive Catalogue of Coade's Artificial Stone Manufactory, London, 1794.

Coade, Eleanor, and Sealy, John, *Description of Ornamental Stone in the Gallery of Coade & Sealy,* London, 1799.

Coalbrookdale, *The Coalbrookdale Illustrated Catalogue (Section III): Garden and Park Embellishments,* 1875.
Ornamental Castings Manufactured by the Coalbrookdale Company, illustrated catalogue including price list, July 1877.
The Coalbrookdale Company's Illustrated Catalogue, Spring 1893.
The Coalbrookdale Illustrated Catalogue of Garden and Park Furniture, 1907.
Allied Ironfounders' Export Catalogue, circa 1929.

Cook, B F, *The Townley Marbles,* British Museum, 1985.

Cook, Olive, *The English Country House — An Art and Way of Life,* Thames & Hudson, 1974.

Cottingham, Lewis N, *The Smith & Founder's Director,* London, 1824.

Cowper, B H, *A Descriptive, Historical and Statistical Account of Millwall,* London, 1853.

Crowther, H, *Lead Garden Ornaments,* London, privately, 1920.

Crowther Ltd, H, *English Lead Garden Ornaments,* London, privately, 1987.

Cruft, C, 'James, 2nd Duke of Atholl and John Cheere', *Studies in Scottish Antiquity,* Edinburgh, 1984.

Defoe, Daniel, *A Tour Through the Whole Island of Great Britain,* 1742 edn.

Devaux, Yves, *L'Univers des Bronzes,* Pygmalion, 1978.

Devonshire, William Spencer, 6th Duke of, *Handbook to Chatsworth and Hardwick,* 1844.

Dossie, Robert, *A Hand Maid to the Arts,* 2 vols, London, 1758.

Doulton and Co, *Architectural Terra Cotta for Construction and Decoration,* illustrated catalogue, London, 1893.

Terra Cotta Garden Vases, Pedestals, Flower Pots and Every Other Description of Horticultural Terra Cotta, illustrated catalogue, London, 1893.

The Doulton Story, exhibition catalogue, Victoria and Albert Museum, 1979.

Durenne, Antoine, *Fonte de Fer. A Durenne, Maitre de Forges: Edition de 1877 (Série F),* illustrated catalogue, Paris, 1877.

Fonte de Fer. A Durenne, Maitre de Forges: Edition de 1889 (Série R), illustrated catalogue, Paris, 1889.

Ensing, Rita J, *Kensington Society Annual Report, 1976-1977,* Kensington Society.

Esdaile, K A, 'Signor Guelfi, an Italian', *Burlington Magazine,* 1948, vol XC.

Faber, H, *Caius Gabriel Cibber,* Oxford, 1926.

Faulkner, Thomas, *The History and Antiquities of Brentford, Ealing and Chiswick,* London, 1845.

Fausset, Robin, 'The Creation of the Gardens at Castle Hill, South Molton, Devon', *Garden History,* 1985, vol 13, no 2.

Festing, Sally, 'Cliffs, Glades and Grotto at Merrow Grange', *Garden History,* 1983, vol 11, no 2.

'Pulham has done his work well', *Garden History,* 1984, vol 12, no 2.

Fleming, Laurence, and Gore, Alan, *The English Garden,* Michael Joseph, 1979.

Flemming, John, Honour, Hugh and Pevsner, Nikolaus, *The Penguin Dictionary of Architecture,* Penguin, 1976.

Francis, A J, *The Cement Industry 1769-1914: A History,* London, 1977.

Freestone, I C, Bimson, M, and Tite, M S, 'The Constitution of Coade Stone', *Ceramics and Civilization, Volume I: Ancient Technology to Modern Science,* W D Kingery (ed), American Ceramic Society, Columbus, Ohio, 1985.

Friedman, T, *James Gibbs,* Yale University Press, 1984.

Friedman, T, and Clifford, T, *The Man at Hyde Park Corner, Sculpture by John Cheere 1709-1787,* exhibition catalogue, Temple Newsam House, 1974.

Friedman, T, and Stevens, T, *Joseph Gott 1786-1860: Sculptor,* exhibition catalogue, Temple Newsam House, 1972.

Gardner, John Starkie, *English Ironwork of the 17th and 18th Centuries: an Historical and Analytical Account of the Development of the Exterior Smith Craft,* Batsford, 1911.

Geiss, Morris, *Zinkguss — Ornamente, Statuen und Sculpturen,* illustrated catalogue, Berlin, 1863.

Giambologna, 'Giambologna's Samson and a Philistine', Masterpeice sheet 18, Victoria and Albert Museum, 1978.

Gibbon, Michael, 'The History of Stowe — XV (Garden Ornaments), *The Stoic,* March 1972, vol XXV, no 2.

Gibbs, James, *A Book of Architecture,* London, 1728.

Girard, Jacques, *Versailles Gardens: Sculpture and Mythology,* Versailles, 1985.

Girouard, Mark, *Life in the English Country House,* Penguin, 1980.

Glendinning, Victoria, *Vita: The Life of Vita Sackville-West,* 1983.

Gowing, C N, and Clarke, G B, *Drawings of Stowe by John Claude Nattes in the*

Buckinghamshire County Museum, Buckinghamshire County Museum and Stowe School, 1983.

Graves, Algernon, *A Dictionary of Artists who have exhibited works in the principal London exhibitions from 1760-1893,* Henry Graves & Co, 2nd edn, 1895.

Graves, Robert, *The Greek Myths,* 2 vols, 1960, reprint 1985.

Great Exhibition, *The Official Descriptive and Illustrated Catalogue of the Works of Industry of All Nations,* London, 1851.

Green, David, *Grinling Gibbons — His Work as Carver and Statuary,* Country Life, 1964.

Grey, Earl de, 'History of Wrest House', *Bedfordshire Historical Record Society,* 1980, vol 59.

Gunnis, Rupert, *Dictionary of British Sculptors 1660-1851,* 1951, 2nd edn, Abbey Library, 1969.

Hadfield, Miles, Harling, Robert, and Highton, Leonie, *British Gardeners: A Biographical Dictionary,* Zwemmer/Condé Nast, 1980.

Hall, I, *William Constable as Patron,* exhibition catalogue, Ferens Art Gallery, 1970.

Hall, James, *Hall's Dictionary of Subjects and Symbols in Art,* John Murray, 1974.

Handyside & Co, Andrew, *Works in Iron,* London, 1868.

Handyside's Ironwork (Catalogues B & C): Ornamental Ironwork Manufactured by Andw Handyside & Co Ltd, illustrated catalogue, London, 1874.

Harris, John, 'The Building of Denham Place', *Records of Buckinghamshire,* 1957-1958, vol XVI, part III.

Haskell, Francis, and Penny, Nicholas, *Taste and the Antique: The Lure of Classical Sculpture 1500-1900,* Yale University Press, 1982.

The Most Beautiful Statues — The Taste for Antique Sculpture 1500-1900, Ashmolean Museum, Oxford, 1981.

Hawks le Grice, Count, *Walks Through the Studii of the Sculptors at Rome,* 1841.

Hetherington, Paul, 'The Venetian Well-Heads of Hever Castle, Kent', *Apollo,* March 1985.

Hinks, Roger P, *Greek and Roman Portrait Sculpture,* British Museum, 1976.

Holt, Richard, *A Short Treatise on Artificial Stone,* London, 1730.

Hope, Henry, *Hope's Leadwork for the Garden,* illustrated catalogue, New York, 1932.

Hope, Thomas, *Household Furniture and Interior Decoration, executed from Designs by Thomas Hope,* London, 1807, reprinted 1970 with a preface by Clifford Musgrave.

Howarth, David, *Lord Arundel and His Circle,* Yale University Press, 1985.

Hussey, Christopher, 'A Georgian Arcady', (I & II), *Country Life,* June 1946.

English Country Houses: Early, Mid- and Late Georgian, 3 vols, London, 1955, Woodbridge, 1984.

English Gardens and Landscapes 1700-1750, London, 1967.

Jackson Stops, Messrs, *Particulars of Stowe House near Buckingham and the Remaining Portions of the Estate... October 11 1922,* illustrated catalogue, 1922.

Jackson Stops, Gervaise (ed), *The Treasure Houses of Britain,* Yale University Press, 1985.

James, John, see Argenville, Dezalier, D'

Jameson, Mrs, *A Hand-Book to the Courts of Modern Sculpture,* London, 1854.

Jekyll, Gertrude, *Garden Ornament,* London, 1918, Woodbridge, 1982.

Jewitt, Llewellynn, *The Ceramic Art of Great Britain,* 1st edn London, 1878, 2nd edn London, 1883, reprinted 1985.

Jones, Owen, *The Grammar of Ornament,* Day & Son, 1856.

Jourdain, Margaret, *The Works of William Kent,* London, 1948.

Kelly, Alison, 'Mrs Coade's Stone', *The Connoisseur,* vol CXCVII, 19 January, 1978.

'Coade Stone in National Trust Houses', *National Trust Studies,* London, 1980.

Kenworthy-Browne, John, 'A Ducal Patron of Sculptors', *Apollo,* October 1972.

'Mathew Brettingham's Rome Account Book 1747-1754', *Walpole Society,* 1983, XLIX.

'Rysbrack's Saxon Deities', *Apollo,* September, 1985.

Kenworthy-Browne, J, and Vermule, C, *The Sculpture Collection at Petworth,* National Trust, nd.

Law, Ernest, *A Short History of Hampton Court,* London, 1897.

Lawley, Ian, *Art and Ornament in Iron: Design and the Coalbrookdale Company,* Design Council, 1980.

Legouix, S Y, 'John Cheere's Statue of George II', *The Connoisseur,* April 1975.

Lethaby, W R, *Leadwork Old and Ornamental and for the most part English,* London, 1893.

London County Council, *The Survey of London,* vol XXIII, 1951, vol XXIV, 1966.

Loudon, J C, *The Architectural Magazine,* London, 1834.

Encyclopaedia, 3rd edn, London, 1857.

McGown, Joyce, *The Searching Eye in Venice,* London, 1983.

Mann, J G, *Sculpture,* Wallace Collection catalogue, London, 1981.

Manners, Lady Victoria, 'Garden Sculpture by Caius Cibber', *Country Life,* September, 1930.

Mannoni, Luciana and Tiziano, *Marble: the History of a Culture,* Facts on File Inc, 1985.

Markham, Sarah, *John Loverday of Caversham 1711-1789,* Michael Russel, 1984.

Marks, R, and Blench, B J R, *The Warwick Vase,* The Burrell Collection, 1979.

Matheson, Ewing (of the firm of Andw Handyside & Co), *Works in Iron: Bridge and Roof Structures,* London, 1873.

Matthews, T, *The Biography of John Gibson, R A, Sculptor, Rome,* London, 1911.

Meyer, Franz Sales, *Handbook of Ornament,* 1892, reprinted Dover, 1957.

Michaelis, A, *Ancient Marbles in Great Britain,* Cambridge University Press, 1882.

Montfaucon, Bernard de, *L'Antiquité Expliquée et Representée en Figures,* 10 vols, Paris, 1719, translated into English 1721.

Moore, Andrew, W, *Norfolk and the Grand Tour,* exhibition catalogue, Norfolk Museum Services, 1985.

Moore, Susan, 'Hail! Gods of our Fore-Fathers: Rysbrack's "Lost", Saxon Deities at Stowe', *Country Life,* 31 January 1985.

Murphy, Bailey S, *English and Scottish Wrought Ironwork*, Batsford, 1904.

Nost, John Van (the elder), *A Catalogue of Mr Van Nost's Collection of Marble and Leaden Figures... This 17th... April 1712*, London, 1712.

Papworth, John Buonarotti, *Hints on Ornamental Gardening*, London, 1823.

Parker, Jean, 'The Pyghtle Works', *Bedfordshire Magazine*, Winter 1986, vol 20, no 159.

Parsons, Thomas, *A Collection of Vases, Terms...*, ?Bath, privately, circa late eighteenth century.

Paulson, Ronald, *Meaning in English Art of the 18th century*, Harvard University Press, 1975.

Payne, Christopher, *Animals in Bronze*, Woodbridge, 1986.

Peach, R E M, *The Life and Times of Ralph Allen of Prior Park*, D Nutt, 1895.

Penzer, N M, 'The Warwick Vase', *Apollo*, 1955-1956, nos 370, 371 and 372.

Physick, John, *Designs for English Sculpture 1680-1860*, London, 1969.

Picon, Carlos A, *Bartolomeo Cavaceppi: Eighteenth Century Restorations of Ancient Marble Sculptures from English Private Collections*, exhibition catalogue, Clarendon Gallery, privately, 1983.

Pincot, Daniel, *An Essay on the Origins, Uses and Properties of Artificial Stone*, London, 1770.

Plumb, J H, *England in the Eighteenth Century*, London, 1963.

Pococke, R, *The Travels Through England of Dr Richard Pococke*, 2 vols, London, 1888, 1889.

Pope, Alexander, Epistle IV, 'Of the Use of Riches', 1731.

Powerscourt, 7th Viscount, *Description and History of Powerscourt*, privately, nd.

Pulham & Son, Garden Craftsmen, *Garden Ornament — Vases: Terminals: Pedestals: Sundials: Seats: Fountains: Balustrades: Figures: Etc.* nd, circa 1925.

Radice, Betty, *Who was Who in the Ancient World*, Penguin, 1973.

Raistrick, Arthur, *Dynasty of Iron Founders: The Darbys and Coalbrookdale*, Longmans, Green & Co, 1953.

Ralph, James, *A Critical Review of the Publick Buildings, Statues and Ornaments in and about London and Westminster*, London, 1734.

Read, B, *Victorian Sculpture*, Yale University Press, 1982.

Reinach, Salomon, *Repertoire de la Statuaire Grecque et Romaine*, 3 vols, Paris, 1898.

Ribeiro, Aileen, 'Fashionable Rural Masquerades', *The Antique Collector*, September, 1983.

Richter, G M A, *The Portraits of the Greeks*, Phaidon, 1984.

Rodgers, Frank, 'Andrew Handyside — Engineer Extraordinary', *Derbyshire Life & Countryside*, September, 1975.

Roper, Lanning, *The Gardens of Anglesey Abbey, Cambridgeshire*, Faber & Faber, 1964.

Scheemakers, Peter, *A Catalogue of the Genuine and Curious Collection of Models and Marbles*, sale catalogue, Langford, London, 10 and 11 March 1756.
A Collection of Models and Casts, of Mr Peter Scheemakers, sale catalogue, Langford, London, 6 and 7 June 1771.

Seeley, J, *Stowe — A Description of the House and Gardens,* London, 1817.

Shenstone, William, *Unconnected Thoughts on Gardening,* nd.

Sicca, Cinzia Maria, 'Lord Burlington at Chiswick: Architecture and Landscape', *Garden History,* Spring 1982, vol 10, no 1.

Smith, John T, *Nollekens and His Times,* 1828, reprinted Century Hutchinson, 1986.

The Streets of London, London, 1854.

Snodin, Michael (ed), *Rococo - Art and Design in Hogarth's England,* exhibition catalogue, Victoria and Albert Museum, 1984.

Society of Artists, *The Society of Artists' Catalogue of Exhibitions, 1762-1783,* London, nd.

Souchal, François, *French Sculptors of the 17th and 18th Centuries,* 3 vols, Cassirer, 1977, 1981, 1987.

Strickland, Walter G, *A Dictionary of Irish Artists,* Maunsel & Co, Dublin and London, 1913.

Strong, Roy, *The Renaissance Garden in England,* Thames & Hudson, 1979.

Strong, R, Binney, M, and Harris, J, *The Destruction of the English Country House,* Thames & Hudson, 1974.

Stuart, James, and Revett, Nicholas, *The Antiquities of Athens,* 4 vols, London, 1762-1816.

Summerson, John, *A New Description of Sir John Soane's Museum,* 5th revised edn, Sir John Soane's Museum, 1981.

Sutton, Denys, 'The Faire Majestic Paradise of Stowe', *Apollo,* June 1973.

Tallis, John, *Tallis's History and Description of the Crystal Palace and the Exhibition of the World's Industry in 1851,* London, 1852.

Tatham, C H, *Etchings of Ancient Ornamental Architecture drawn from the Originals in Rome and other parts of Italy...,* London, 1799-1800.

Thomassin, Simon, *Recueil des Figures, Groupes, Thermes, Fontaines et Vases...dans le Château et Parc de Versailles,* 1694.

Thompson, Francis, *A History of Chatsworth,* London, 1949.

Triggs, H I, *Formal Gardens in England and Scotland,* London, 1902, Woodbridge, 1988.

Vardy, John, *Some Designs of Mr Inigo Jones and Mr Wm Kent,* 1744, reprinted Gregg Press, 1967.

Vermeule, Cornelius, C, *Greek and Roman Sculpture in America,* University of California Press, 1981.

Ware, Isaac, *A Complete Body of Architecture,* London, 1767 edn.

Waring, J B, *Masterpieces of Industrial Art and Sculpture in the International Exhibition, 1862,* London, 1862.

Waters, W G, *Italian Sculptors,* London, 1926.

Weaver, Lawrence, *English Leadwork, its Art and History,* London, 1909.

Webb, M I, *Southill — A Regency House,* Faber & Faber, 1951.

'Giovanni Battista Guelfi: an Italian Sculptor Working in England', *Burlington*

Magazine, vol XC, 1957.

West, Gilbert, *Stowe,* Lodon, 1732.

Whinney, Margaret, *Sculpture in Britain 1530-1830,* Harmondsworth, 1964.

English Sculpture 1720-1830, London, 1971.

Whistler, L, Gibbon, M, and Clarke, G, *Stowe — A Guide to the Gardens,* 3rd edn, Stowe School, 1974.

White, John P, & Sons, *A Complete Catalogue of Garden Furniture and Garden Ornament,* London, 1906.

Bird Baths, Garden Figures, Vases and Ornaments, Bedford, June 1935.

Wilson, Michael I, *William Kent, Architect, Designer, Painter, Gardener 1685-1748,* London, 1984.

Wood, John, *An Essay Towards a Description of Bath,* 1765, reprinted Redwood Press, 1969.

Woodbridge, Kenneth, 'William Kent's Gardening: The Rousham Letters', *Apollo,* 1974.

The Stourhead Landscape, The National Trust, 1982.

Worlidge, John, *Systema Horticulturae: or, The Art of Gardening,* 1677, reprinted Garland Publishing, 1982.

Wyatt, Digby, *The Industrial Arts of the XIX Century,* 1851, vol I, plate XIX, second page.

Wyatt, Parker & Co, *Figures, Vases, Fountains &c executed in Marble and Artificial Stone,* London, 1841.

Yapp, G W, *Art, Industry, Metalwork,* London, 1878.

INDEX

386

NICHOLAS GIFFORD-MEAD

68 Pimlico Road, London SW1W 8LS
Tel: 0171 730 6233 Fax: 0171 730 6239

PERIOD GARDEN ORNAMENTS, SCULPTURE AND CHIMNEY-PIECES

NICHOLAS GIFFORD-MEAD

CONSULTANT: JOHN P.S. DAVIS

Life-size group of the *Valet de Limiers* by Alfred Jacquemart.
One example from our outstanding collection of park and garden statuary.

SEAGO

FINE 17TH, 18TH AND 19TH CENTURY ANTIQUE GARDEN SCULPTURE

22 PIMLICO ROAD, LONDON SW1W 8LJ. TEL: 0171-730 7502. FAX: 0171-730 9179

Facing page: An important mid-18th century lead statue of *Time,* from the foundry of John Cheere (d.1787) at Hyde Park Corner. Ex Fonthill House, Wiltshire, home of Alderman William Beckford 1709-1770.

A similar statue may be seen at Blair Atholl, Perthshire, seat of the Duke of Atholl. The archive accounts in the house include John Cheere's original bill (dated 1743) for this figure.

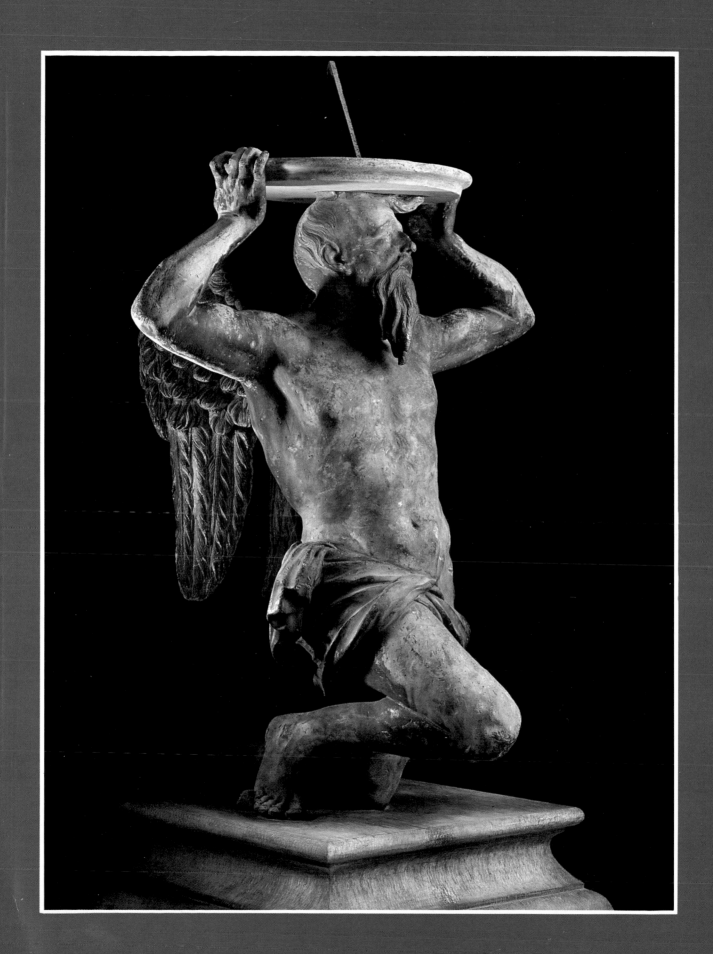